3704214233

D0336779

Tourism SMEs, Service Quality and Destination Competitiveness

Tourism SMEs, Service Quality and Destination Competitiveness

Edited by

Eleri Jones and Claire Haven-Tang

Welsh School of Hospitality,
Tourism and Leisure Management,
University of Wales Institute, Cardiff,
Cardiff, UK

OXSTALLS LEARNING CENTRE
UNIVERSITY OF GLOUCESTERSHIRE
Oxstalls Lane
Gloucester GL2 9HW
Tel: 01242 715100

CABI Publishing

CABI Publishing is a division of CAB International

CABI Publishing
CAB International
Wallingford
Oxfordshire OX10 8DE
UK

Tel: +44 (0)1491 832111
Fax: +44 (0)1491 833508
E-mail: cabi@cabi.org
Website: www.cabi-publishing.org

CABI Publishing
875 Massachusetts Avenue
7th Floor
Cambridge, MA 02139
USA

Tel: +1 617 395 4056
Fax: +1 617 354 6875
E-mail: cabi-nao@cabi.org

© CAB International 2005. All rights reserved. No part of this publication may be reproduced in any form or by any means, electronically, mechanically, by photocopying, recording or otherwise, without the prior permission of the copyright owners.

A catalogue record for this book is available from the British Library, London, UK.

Library of Congress Cataloging-in-Publication Data
Tourism SMEs, service quality, and destination competitiveness / edited by Eleri Jones and Claire Haven-Tang.
    p. cm.
  Includes bibliographical references and index.
  ISBN 0-85199-011-8 (alk. paper)
  1. Tourism--Economic aspects. 2. Small business. I. Jones, Eleri Ellis. II. Haven-Tang, Claire. III. Title.

  G155.A1T589573 2005
  338.4′791--dc22

2004018806

Typeset in Souvenir by AMA DataSet Ltd, UK.
Printed and bound in the UK by Cromwell Press, Trowbridge.

Contents

About the Authors

Wolfgang Georg Arlt, PhD, is a Professor of Tourism Business at the University of Applied Sciences in Stralsund, Germany. He graduated from FU Berlin with Sinology (MA 1985) and Political Sciences (PhD 2001). He acts as a consultant for the Asian–European Business and Cultural Cooperation, especially on transportation and tourism issues. He has taught at Chinese and German universities since 1997 and is responsible for the China Outbound Tourism Research Project.

Marcjanna M. Augustyn, PhD, is a Principal Lecturer in Leisure, Tourism and Hospitality and the Head of the Department of Leisure, Tourism and Hospitality at the University of Wolverhampton. Her research interests are wide-ranging and include: strategy and quality issues in tourism SMEs, tourism policy formulation in public-sector organizations and development and management of tourism destinations and she has published extensively in these areas. She also acts as the Book Review Editor for *Tourism Analysis. An Interdisciplinary Journal*. She is a member of AIEST (International Association of Scientific Experts in Tourism).

Zsuzsanna Behringer, PhD, is the Director of the Hungarian National Tourist Office (HNTO) Directorate for Marketing Research. In addition to preparing analyses and reports she is responsible for HNTO's research plan, participates in strategy development, coordinates the research activity of the Directorate for Marketing Research, the regional marketing directorates and foreign representative offices of HNTO and edits *Tourism Bulletin*, the quarterly scientific periodical of HNTO. Her PhD research at the University of Economic Sciences and Public Administration (Budapest) was on the effect of the economic regulatory system on organized tourism in the 1980s. She regularly lectures at the University of Economic Sciences and Public Administration (Budapest).

David Botterill, PhD, is a Professor and the Director of Research and Graduate Studies for the Welsh School of Hospitality, Tourism and Leisure Management at the University of Wales Institute, Cardiff (UWIC). His research interests are in the application of the philosophies, concepts and methods of the social sciences to the study of tourism. His most recent publications deal with the epistemologies of tourism studies and the establishment of a critical realist tourism research agenda.

Jack Carlsen, PhD, is a Professor and MUI (Malayan United Industries) Chair in Tourism and Hospitality Studies within the Curtin Business School, Curtin University of Technology, Western Australia. He received his first grant for family business research in 1998 and has since published papers in the *Journal of Sustainable Tourism*, *Tourism Management* and *Family Business Review* and presented papers at the International Congress of Small Business, Asia Pacific Tourism Association and the Council of Australian University Tourism and Hospitality Education conferences. He has a Bachelor of Economics and a PhD from the University of Western Australia.

Eric Chan is a Lecturer in the School of Hotel and Tourism Management at the Hong Kong Polytechnic University. His teaching responsibilities include courses in hotel and catering property and facilities management, hotel environmental management, reservation and information management and leisure behaviour. He has delivered a range of tailor-made training programmes and teaching materials for the hospitality industry, including front office operations for leading Hong Kong hotels. He has assisted the Hong Kong Quality Assurance Agency audit team in their assessment of the ISO 9000 quality management system in hotels. He has a Masters degree from Macquarie University, Australia, and is currently a PhD candidate in the Business School at Oxford Brookes University, UK.

MariaLaura Di Domenico, PhD, is a Research Associate in social and community enterprise at the Judge Institute of Management, University of Cambridge. Previously she was Senior Lecturer in Tourism at the University of Westminster. She completed her PhD at the University of Strathclyde, Business School in Glasgow, where she researched the role definitions and orientations of owners of small-scale tourism firms in Scotland. Her current research interests involve small businesses, entrepreneurship, social enterprises, lifestyle choices, definitions of identities and heritage tourism. She has published her research as journal articles, book chapters, research reports and monographs, and has presented her work at international and national conferences.

Donald Getz, PhD, is a Professor of Tourism and Hospitality Management in the Haskayne School of Business, University of Calgary, Canada. His research interest in family business began with doctoral research in the Highlands of Scotland, as many of the tourism and hospitality businesses studied were operated by individuals or families. He has conducted specific family-business research in Canada, Denmark, Sweden, New Zealand and Australia, involving a number of individual and institutional collaborators. This work has been financially supported in part by the Family Business Research Endowment at the University of Calgary.

C. Michael Hall, PhD, was a Professor in the Department of Tourism, University of Otago, Dunedin, New Zealand and Honorary Professor, Stirling University, Scotland at the time of writing this contribution. He has wide-ranging interests in tourism, leisure and regional development and is co-editor of *Current Issues in Tourism*.

Claire Haven-Tang, PhD, was a Senior Research Associate in the Welsh School of Hospitality, Tourism and Leisure Management at the University of Wales Institute, Cardiff (UWIC), where she was involved in the organization of the Tourism Research 2002 Conference and a number of pedagogic research studies for the Learning and Teaching Support Network for Hospitality, Leisure, Sport and Tourism. Her doctoral thesis investigated attitudes in Wales towards tourism and hospitality careers and her main research interests are tourism and hospitality employment issues. She has also worked on value for money studies involving the Department for Culture, Media and Sport at the National Audit Office. She is now an independent tourism consultant, although she retains strong links with UWIC.

Anne-Mette Hjalager, PhD, is an independent consultant and contract researcher based in the Science Park in Aarhus, Denmark. Over the past 10 years she has worked intensively with labour market, industrial policy and innovation issues. She is involved in research with the Copenhagen Business School, assists regional and national authorities with analysis and evaluations and is supporting the Danish government and the European Union in policy planning for the tourism sector.

Diana James has been the Executive Director of the Tourism Training Forum for Wales since its incorporation in November 2001. Formerly she worked for 9 years for the Wales Tourist Board, heading its training and business support department. Prior to this she spent 3 years as the Staff Development Officer for Wales for the government's Professional, Industrial and Commercial Updating (PICKUP) programme, which supported colleges and universities in developing their income-generating activities. Previously she was a lecturer in the further education sector and her early career was in human resource management in the retail sector.

Tim Jenkins, PhD, is a Senior Research Associate in the Institute of Rural Sciences at the University of Wales, Aberystwyth. His research interests lie mainly in the fields of rural development (in both high-income and low-income countries) and ecological economics.

Eleri Jones, PhD, is a Professor and Head of the Welsh School of Hospitality, Tourism and Leisure Management at the University of Wales Institute, Cardiff. She manages an extensive portfolio of European projects designed to promote interaction between the university and the tourism industry across Wales. NEAT (Network of Excellence for Action in Tourism) established clusters of tourism-sector businesses in unitary authorities across south-east Wales; DISC (Developing Innovation in Small Companies) developed a toolkit to promote innovation and facilitate structured conversations in tourism SMEs; SPICE (Strategic Project for In-Company Education) provided training in response to SME needs. Eleri has supervised knowledge transfer partnerships with Welsh tourism SMEs, as well as a number of international PhD students undertaking tourism SME research.

Mokhtar Jwaili is a Doctoral Researcher in the Welsh Enterprise Institute at the University of Glamorgan Business School. His PhD focuses on the marketing interface and small Libyan tourism firms. Previously he was a member of the teaching staff at the Al-Fateh University and the National Institute of Management in Tripoli and at the Higher Institute for Administrative and Financial Professions. His professional experience includes Chairmanship and Vice Chairmanship of the Nozha Voyages Tourism Services Company in Libya and he is currently the company's UK representative.

Conrad Lashley, PhD, is Professor and Head of the Centre for Leisure Retailing at Nottingham Business School. He is also series editor for Butterworth-Heinemann's Hospitality, Leisure and Tourism series. He has authored, co-authored or edited 16 books, including *Empowerment: HR Strategies for Service Excellence*. He has extensive experience of research on management development and business performance in hospitality firms and in evaluating the benefits of training interventions within the sector. Recent research team leadership includes projects for the North West Tourism Network and the Hospitality Training Foundation.

Marsaili MacLeod was a member of the Rural Economy Team at the Scottish Agricultural College (SAC) and is now based at the University of Aberdeen. Her research interests lie broadly in the differential socio-economic development of rural areas and the manifestations of rural policy at the local and regional level. She is actively involved in rural development research in issues connected to rural public policy, business and institutional development, rural labour market analysis and farm pluriactivity. Before joining SAC, Marsaili was Manager of Sutherland Partnership, a strategic rural development organization in north-west Scotland.

Geoffrey Manyara is a researcher in the Welsh School of Hospitality, Tourism and Leisure Management at the University of Wales Institute, Cardiff (UWIC). His main area of interest is the development of appropriate models for tourism development that seek to alleviate poverty in developing countries. He gained a Bachelor of Science in tourism in 1997 from Moi University, Kenya, and in 2001 graduated from Wageningen University, The Netherlands, with a Master of Science in Leisure and Environment.

Tünde Mester is Chief Researcher at the Hungarian National Tourist Office's Directorate for Marketing Research and is involved in: tourism statistics, analysis of the environment of tourism, trends in tourism, tourism in the European Union (EU), city tourism, different national and international research projects and evaluation of marketing activity. She obtained a Masters degree from the University of Economic Sciences and Public Administration (Budapest) in 2000.

Stephen Moore is a Senior Lecturer in the Welsh School of Hospitality, Tourism and Leisure Management at the University of Wales Institute, Cardiff (UWIC). His key subjects are strategic management and marketing focused towards service sector industries. He is Chief Examiner for Hospitality and Catering for the Awarding Body, Edexcel. His research interests include the types of training undertaken in the hospitality industry and the effectiveness of the different training models employed. He has a particular interest in the suitability of vocational qualifications used in the hospitality industry, including national vocational qualifications (NVQs). His PhD research is concerned with assessing the attitudes of education/training providers towards the NVQ system, and whether an alternative training paradigm may be more appropriate.

Alison Morrison, PhD, is a Professor and Head of the Scottish Hotel School. Her first degree is in Hotel and Catering Management from the University of Strathclyde. Alison also has an MSc in Entrepreneurship from Stirling University and a PhD from the University of Strathclyde entitled 'Small firm strategic alliances: the UK hotel industry'. Alison has edited and authored five textbooks in the areas of marketing, hospitality, entrepreneurship and franchising and has published widely in generic business and specialist hospitality and tourism academic journals. She regularly undertakes international assignments teaching and consulting on entrepreneurship within the hospitality and tourism sectors.

Hilary C. Murphy, PhD, is a Senior Lecturer at Swansea Institute specializing in marketing information systems and web-based marketing. Her key research areas are in the use of marketing and information technology (IT) in the hospitality and tourism sectors and she has published in several international journals and delivered key papers at international conferences in these areas. She is also a business consultant for the Xansa group for their business travel and leisure sector. Her PhD is on the diffusion of information and communications technology in the hospitality sector.

Tove Oliver, PhD, is a Research Associate in the Institute of Rural Sciences at the University of Wales Aberystwyth, having received her PhD from the Nottingham Business School, Nottingham Trent University. Her current research interests are in tourism's role in rural development, cultural tourism and the consumer psychology of tourism. Tove is now based at the Higher Education Funding Council, Wales.

John Pheby, PhD, is Professor of Entrepreneurship at the University of Luton. His research interests include new venture creation, strategies for SME growth and social enterprise. He is a Fellow of the Institute of Business Advisers and is currently engaged in a major project to assist members within a disadvantaged community to start their own businesses. He is the founder of the *Review of Political Economy* and the *International Journal of Entrepreneurial Behaviour and Research*.

Abraham Pizam, PhD, is Dean and Professor of Tourism Management in the Rosen School of Hospitality Management, at the University of Central Florida, Orlando, Florida, USA. He has conducted research projects, lectured and served as a consultant in more than 30 countries. Professor Pizam is the author of 143 scientific publications and five books, and is on the editorial staff of 14 academic journals in the field of tourism/hospitality management.

Kristy Rusher has a law degree and an MBA from the University of Otago, New Zealand. Kristy is currently the Executive Director of a regional tourism organization in the South Island of New Zealand, having previously undertaken research while working in the Department of Tourism at the University of Otago.

Hugh Smith has worked at the Moffat Centre for Travel and Tourism Business Development at Glasgow Caledonian University since 2001, in both the research and business consultancy fields. He has a background in finance and tourism and is currently studying for a PhD in tourism which relates to the management issues involved in the operation of dark tourism attractions.

Dana V. Tesone, PhD, is an Assistant Professor with the Rosen School of Hospitality Management at the University of Central Florida, where he teaches management and technology courses. His background includes administrative and executive positions with academic institutions and corporate organizations, including Vice-President of Human Resources at a leading resort property in south Florida. He is currently conducting research in the areas of leadership, organizational theory and technology.

Brychan Thomas, PhD, is a Research Fellow and Project Director in Small Business and Innovation in the Welsh Enterprise Institute at the University of Glamorgan Business School. He has been a senior consultant for a Welsh Development Agency project on higher education and small firms in Wales and is currently Project Manager for a Learning Chamber project with Cardiff Chamber of Commerce. Other projects include: examining Science Communication and Education; South Wales E-Commerce and SMEs (E-CoSME); and Memoria (technology transfer into small museums) European Framework V project. He has over 150 publications in the areas of science communication, innovation and small business policy.

Stephen Wanhill, PhD, is a Professor of Tourism Research in the School of Service Management at Bournemouth University. He has recently completed a programme as Director of the Unit for Tourism Research, Centre for Regional and Tourism Research, Bornholm, Denmark. His principal research interests are in the field of tourism destination development and to this extent he has undertaken a wide range of tourism development strategies, tourism impact assessments, project studies and lecture programmes, both in the UK and worldwide. He has acted as tourism policy adviser to the Select Committee on Welsh Affairs, House of Commons, and has been a Board Member of the Wales Tourist Board with responsibilities for the development and research divisions. He is the editor of the journal *Tourism Economics*.

Fiona Williams is a researcher in the Rural Economy Team at the Scottish Agricultural College (SAC). Her research remit to date is in rural development and policy, with a specialist responsibility for tourism. She is a key researcher on the EU Framework V project (coordinated by SAC), Aspatial Peripherality, Innovation and the Rural Economy, and is leading the tourism thematic study of this work. Recent research and consultancy work include: Success Factors in Dynamic Rural Areas (SEERAD), the Role of Regional Milieux in Rural

Economic Development (Northern Periphery Programme) and Grampian leisure and tourism market profile information for Scottish Enterprise Grampian. She previously completed her MPhil at the University of Wales Institute, Cardiff.

Simon Wong, PhD, is a Senior Lecturer at the School of Hotel and Tourism Management at the Hong Kong Polytechnic University. Having gained over 10 years' industry experience in HRM, his subjects include: strategic human resources management, training and development and employee relations. Before entering the teaching arena he worked with many leading Hong Kong hotels and was the Personnel Manager for Adidas Asia/Pacific Limited. His expertise on training focuses on the use of experiential training methods to conduct interactive seminars such as team building, leadership, motivation and organizational behaviour. He is completing his PhD from Bournemouth University, UK, which investigates the relationship between creativity and job-related motivators in the hotel industry.

Preface

A successful tourism destination must embrace an integrated approach towards the many components of the tourism system. The role of destination management organizations (DMOs) is vital to providing leadership and coordination for destination stakeholders (Ritchie and Crouch, 2003). Tourism small and medium-sized enterprises (SMEs) have very different approaches to the setting and maintenance of quality standards that are critical to competitiveness at an individual business and destination level. Coupled with this, the tourism industry experiences significant staffing problems due to its poor image. The recruitment and retention of staff of an appropriate calibre is a major issue for many businesses. High staff turnover militates against investment in employee development. Public-sector interventions, e.g. by DMOs and related business support services, seek to promote regional integration and quality standards through the development of regional approaches to benchmarking, training and marketing to enhance destination image and its appropriate projection, maximizing the potential of tourism as a vehicle for economic development. Orthodox approaches to considerations of service quality management do not map well onto the heterodoxy of tourism SMEs and microbusinesses, due to the inherent characteristics of tourism SMEs and the problems associated with their understanding of service quality and how to achieve it.

Furthermore, many tourism SMEs have difficulties in asserting their own identity, in terms of the role they play in the bigger picture of destination development. Ritchie and Crouch (2003) assert that growth in tourism has resulted in changes to the way destinations are managed. As competition for a share of the tourism market has increased, destinations have had to adopt a more proactive approach to tourism marketing. As a result, many destinations are working to identify how they can become competitive or how they can retain their competitive advantage over other tourism destinations. Competitive advantage refers to a destination's ability to use its resources (regardless of whether these resources are in abundance or short supply) effectively over the long term and is determined by the extent to which a destination 'has a tourism vision, shares this vision among stakeholders, understands its strengths as well as its weaknesses, develops an appropriate marketing strategy and implements it successfully' (Ritchie and Crouch, 2003: 23).

The book is based on an edited collection of papers drawn from academic and practitioner research presented, in most part, in Panel 1: Competitiveness and Quality in a Tourism SME Economy at Tourism Research 2002, held in Cardiff from 4 to 7 September 2002, and comments on a range of SME issues. The contributions explore various aspects of the model proposed in Chapter 1 (see Fig. 1.1) and the collection is arranged into sections to reflect the model: destination; tourism SMEs; employees; public-sector interventions and marketing/image. The chapters focus on SMEs in diverse destinations, including: Australia; Austria; Canada; central Florida; Czech Republic; Denmark; England; France; Germany; Greece; Hong Kong; Hungary; Ireland; Kenya; Libya; Mexico; New Zealand; Scotland; Spain; Switzerland; and Wales. They emphasize the critical importance of the tourism industry and its SME backbone to the economic health and well-being of developing and developed countries. They explore some of the challenges to top-down, government-driven DMO-mediated interventions to promote business growth and enhance regional integration, especially for peripheral and rural destinations. However, they also emphasize the common challenges to sustaining competitiveness, enhancement of service quality standards of tourism SMEs due to the endemic weak business models and underdeveloped management infrastructures and quality systems at a business level and the obstacles to creating a 'joined-up' destination with a coherent marketing image. The chapters highlight the issues of inputting business support to lifestyle businesses that are not interested in growth as a business strategy or in contributing to destination development. The implications of this, not only for the individual SME but also for the image of the destination, are profound.

Chapter 1: Jones and Haven-Tang: Tourism SMEs, Service Quality and Destination Competitiveness

This chapter explores SME issues in defining service quality and the link between service quality and destination competitiveness. The chapter develops a model of a destination, linking the public and private sectors through the strategies for raising quality standards and achieving coherence of destination image through marketing to potential customers, and sets the scene for the other contributions in the book as these issues are not confined to any one destination – individual tourism SMEs and destinations face similar issues around the globe.

Destination

This section explores destination characteristics that contribute to destination competitiveness. Some destination characteristics, e.g. geography, are immutable;

however, skilful destination policy and planning coupled with appropriate management of individual resources can enhance destination competitiveness. Empowerment of individuals is fundamental to the healthy interaction of destination stakeholders, leading to consensus on purpose and development of a sense of place.

Chapter 2: Oliver and Jenkins: Integrated Tourism in Europe's Rural Destinations: Competition or Cooperation?

Oliver and Jenkins explore the issue of integrated tourism in rural regions of Europe, identifying and discussing seven characteristics of integrated tourism: networks; scale; endogeneity; embeddedness; sustainability; complementarity; empowerment.

Chapter 3: Williams and Macleod: The Peripherality, Tourism and Competitiveness Mix: Contradictory or Confirmed?

Williams and Macleod discuss the role of tourism as a tool for rural economic development through a transnational study of peripheral disadvantage through five themes: governance; business networks; social capital; information technology; tourism.

Chapter 4: Manyara and Jones: Policy Options for the Development of an Indigenous Tourism SME Sector in Kenya

Manyara and Jones explore the application of the sustainable livelihoods concept to the diversification of tourism development in Kenya in achieving the World Tourism Organization's criteria for poverty alleviation and developing new tourism products. Empowerment of local communities and support of entrepreneurship are seen as critical to the development of tourism SMEs, enabling commodification of natural resources by local communities and linking economic development to poverty alleviation.

Tourism SMEs

This section considers competitiveness and quality from a tourism SME perspective in terms of strategies adopted for business growth and product/service enhancement. Key issues include: the exploitable resource base and entrepreneurial characteristics. A fortress mentality and issues in relation to knowledge exploitation and technology transfer characterize the idiosyncrasies of tourism SME owner-managers and the major challenges to destination development.

Chapter 5: Getz, Carlsen and Morrison: Quality Issues for the Family Business

Getz *et al.* focus on quality issues within family businesses, including business/product quality, service quality and implications for destination quality and competitiveness. Case studies illustrating quality management in family tourism businesses are taken from Australia, Canada and New Zealand, demonstrating that many family businesses place particular emphasis on the quality of their business, product and service.

Chapter 6: Augustyn and Pheby: Capability-based Growth: the Case of UK Tourism SMEs

Augustyn and Pheby consider the nature of platform capabilities for growth in the UK tourism industry, focusing on the way that SMEs convert their resource base into distinct capabilities (operational skills, privileged assets, growth-enabling skills and special relationships) to provide competitive advantage and fuel business growth.

Chapter 7: Di Domenico: Producing Hospitality, Consuming Lifestyles: Lifestyle Entrepreneurship in Urban Scotland

Di Domenico uses symbolic interactionism to explore the entrepreneurial characteristics of Scottish guest-house owner-occupiers and the rejection, by many, of growth as a business strategy. It examines lifestyle entrepreneurs who hold predominantly non-economic business values and orientations and define business success using a broad range of criteria. She argues that it is necessary to broaden our analytic approach, rather than conceptualizing tourism entrepreneurship purely in terms of economics-driven business models.

Chapter 8: Murphy: Modelling the Integration of Information and Communication Technologies in Small and Medium Hospitality Enterprises

Murphy focuses on the diffusion of information and communication technologies (ICTs) in the hospitality and tourism sector, with particular reference to small and medium-sized hospitality enterprises (SMHEs). She specifically evaluates the critical internal and external factors that influence the diffusion of ICTs in this sector from a baseline of Gamble's 1984 model of diffusion and builds towards populating a new model that takes into account the emerging internal and external factors that have an impact on this sector.

Chapter 9: Hall and Rusher: Business Goals in the Small-scale Accommodation Sector in New Zealand

Hall and Rusher profile the bed and breakfast sector in New Zealand, describing a national survey of owners' management attitudes and operational decision making. They focus on issues associated with lifestyle entrepreneurship and question the degree to which lifestyle entrepreneurs engage in behaviour that may promote destination competitiveness.

Employees

Employees are a critical asset within the tourism and hospitality industry for sustaining and enhancing competitiveness and quality. The theme of this section is the recruitment of potential employees, the retention of current employees within the sector and attitudes towards training. The key issues considered are industry image and economic performance.

Chapter 10: Haven-Tang and Botterill: The Future of the Tourism and Hospitality Workforce Begins at Home

Haven-Tang and Botterill report on an investigation of parental attitudes in Wales towards careers in tourism and hospitality. The findings illustrate that a career in tourism and hospitality would incorporate the majority of the important career factors, and yet few parents selected tourism or hospitality as career choices for their child. This demonstrates that, although attitudes represent a pre-disposition to behaviour, how individuals actually act in a particular situation will be dependent upon the immediate consequences of that behaviour. They conclude that the future of the tourism and hospitality workforce begins at home and employers must appreciate this factor in order to sustain a skilled workforce.

Chapter 11: Hjalager: HRM Behaviour and Economic Performance: Small versus Large Tourism Enterprises

Focusing on the Danish labour market, Hjalager compares human resource management (HRM) policies and practices between small and large enterprises, contributing to the discussion of the basic rationales governing HRM policies in the tourism industry. Key findings include: tourism enterprises with low value added have a systematically higher labour turnover than those with a better economic performance; high performance does not correspond to high educational levels in tourism; retention rates are significantly higher in large tourism enterprises, as are salary levels; employees who change jobs will earn more, especially if they leave the tourism sector altogether; and career shifts to larger enterprises result in significant increases in salary.

Chapter 12: Lashley: Insights into Skill Shortages and Skill Gaps in Tourism: a Study in Greater Manchester

Reporting the findings of commissioned research into potential skill shortages and gaps that might present barriers to future tourism development, Lashley suggests that recruitment difficulties due to skill shortages mask fundamental deficits in management skills and training. The chapter enhances understanding of current tourism employment and trends and identifies current skill shortages and gaps.

Chapter 13: Moore: A Typology of Approaches towards Training in the South-east Wales Hospitality Industry

Moore considers factors that influence attitudes to training in the hospitality industry in south-east Wales and highlights differences between SMEs and larger companies from the different sectors within the hospitality industry. A model of the key factors influencing training approaches is presented, which, it is hoped, will raise SME awareness of strategies to enhance staff retention, maintain a skilled workforce and ensure service quality.

Chapter 14: Pizam and Tesone: The Utilization of Human Resources in Tourism SMEs: a Comparison between Mexico and Central Florida

Pizam and Tesone describe and compare the results of two separate studies on the utilization of human resources in tourism SMEs, with a special emphasis on training and educational activities. The studies were conducted in Mexico and central Florida and the authors propose a series of recommendations for each location, in order to address some of the critical issues identified by the studies.

Public-sector Interventions

Government investment support interventions at a destination level are aimed at business development to coordinate business support, business-to-business networking and collaboration to sustain competitive advantage and enhance service quality at the destination level.

Chapter 15: Wanhill: Investment Support for Tourism SMEs: a Review of Theory and Practice

Wanhill explores investment support at a destination level for tourism SMEs and illustrates some of the pitfalls and challenges to practice through a range of case studies. He discusses how, in many parts of the world, governments have intervened in tourism development because of the complexity of the tourism product and the need to ensure that tourism development corresponds with national tourism policy objectives.

Chapter 16: Smith: Business Confidence in Wales: the *Wales Tourism Business Monitor*

Smith describes the objectives of the *Wales Tourism Business Monitor*, which provides a monthly analysis and interpretation of sector-specific data on business confidence in the Welsh tourism sector in support of the Wales Tourist Board's intention of providing market intelligence, setting standards and developing a proactive partnership with industry. The results for 2001 to 2002 are presented, together with consideration of the wider economic factors affecting the Welsh tourism sector.

Chapter 17: Behringer and Mester: The Role of a National Tourism Organization in Developing a National Tourism Quality Scheme: the Case of Hungary

Behringer and Mester look at the role of the Hungarian National Tourist Office in developing the Hungarian Tourism Quality Award (HTQA). Privatization has led to a significant increase in the number of tourism SMEs in Hungary and consumers are demanding higher-quality products. Therefore, they focus on the need for tourism SMEs to address issues of standardization and quality control.

Chapter 18: James: Leadership and Coordination: a Strategy to Achieve Professionalism in the Welsh Tourism Industry

James describes the evolution of the Tourism Training Forum for Wales (TTFW) alongside the changing political scene in Wales. TTFW was established to enhance the competitiveness of tourism-sector businesses through high-quality education and training interventions at a national level and she outlines the strategic approach taken to provide leadership and coordinate stakeholders in achieving professionalism in the industry in Wales.

Marketing/Image

Healthy destinations are able to develop coherent marketing images that enhance perception of quality and destination competitiveness. This section explores how tourism SMEs can enhance their performance through enhanced understanding of customers and their behaviour and appropriate exploitation of enabling technologies.

Chapter 19: Chan and Wong: Identifying and Exploiting Potentially Lucrative Niche Markets: the Case of Planned Impulse Travellers in Hong Kong

Chan and Wong consider issues associated with guests who arrive at tourism destinations without booking and the factors influencing their hotel selection. A study of international tourists to Hong Kong revealed that two major factors, 'hotel product attribute' and 'airport information', dominated their selection criteria. The results also show that 'convenient hotel location' and 'good hotel service' are still the key influential factors for planned impulse travellers (PITs) in selecting hotels. Chan and Wong also propose strategies for small hoteliers to support such travellers, including co-branding partnerships and sharing of airport transportation.

Chapter 20: Jwaili, Thomas and Jones: Small and Medium-sized Libyan Tourism Enterprises and the National Tourism Development Plan for Libya

The tourism industry is becoming increasingly important for Libya in terms of investment, job creation, competitiveness and quality and is perceived as the best long-term alternative to the oil industry. Jwaili *et al.* consider the role of tourism SMEs in destination development in Libya and their reaction to the implementation of the National Tourism Development Plan (1998–2018), which identifies a number of initiatives to develop the Libyan tourism industry – specifically the role of the public sector in destination development through short- and long-term planning, marketing, infrastructure and human resource development. They propose a series of recommendations for public-sector interventions appropriate to SME development within the Libyan tourism sector.

Chapter 21: Arlt: 'A Virtual Huanying, Selamat Datang and Herzlich Willkommen!' The Internet as a Cross-cultural Promotional Tool for Tourism

Arlt explores the role of the Internet as a cross-cultural incoming tourism communication tool. He emphasizes the opportunities for SMEs to 'stand out from the Internet crowd'. Visitor images of destinations are important drivers of consumer choice and therefore how destinations provide information to visitors through the Internet and other communication channels is critically important to image formation.

Conclusion

Chapter 22: Haven-Tang and Jones: The Heterodoxy of Tourism SMEs

Haven-Tang and Jones reflect on the various contributions and draw the book to its conclusion. The case studies draw on a range of destinations and thus the book provides a wide overview of tourism SMEs and destination competitiveness and the implications for service quality. The authors reflect on the lessons learnt from the international case studies and refine the model to reflect the heterodoxy of SME business approaches and the challenges for destination competitiveness.

References

Gamble, P. (1984) *Small Computers and Hospitality Management*. Hutchinson, London, 185 pp.

Ritchie, J.R.B. and Crouch, G.I. (2003) *The Competitive Destination: a Sustainable Tourism Perspective*, CAB International, Wallingford, UK, 272 pp.

1

Tourism SMEs, Service Quality and Destination Competitiveness

ELERI JONES AND CLAIRE HAVEN-TANG

Welsh School of Hospitality, Tourism and Leisure Management, University of Wales Institute, Cardiff, UK

1.1 Tourism: a Key Driver for Economic Development

Tourism is the world's largest industry and makes a major contribution to the economies of most developed and developing countries. Tourism is being used as 'a ubiquitous vehicle for economic development and diversification and ... an integral element of economic development policy' (Sharpley, 2002: 221) at a local, regional and national level. In the UK, for example, 'a growing number of local authorities have sought to capture the potential economic benefits afforded by tourism ... not only in locations traditionally associated with the activity (such as seaside resorts) but also elsewhere (e.g. in areas of industrial decline)' (Thomas and Long, 2001: 229). Globally, the World Travel and Tourism Council (WTTC) estimates tourism employment at 214,697,000 jobs or 8.1% of total employment, contributing US$4217.7 billion or 10.4% of gross domestic product (GDP) in 2004 (WTTC, 2004), and predicts that tourism employment will grow to be a quarter of a billion jobs by 2014 (WTTC, 2003). However, the global impact of events such as the terrorist attacks of 11 September 2001 and the war in Iraq on tourism activity and therefore on national economies is difficult to predict but cannot be underestimated.

Sustaining tourism as a vehicle for economic development in any destination depends on maintaining destination competitiveness. Kozak (2004: 72, citing the President's Commission on Industrial Competitiveness in the USA) defines competitiveness as 'the degree to which a nation can, under free market conditions, produce goods and services that meet the test of international markets, while simultaneously maintaining and expanding the real income of its citizens'. Ritchie and Crouch (2003) identify six dimensions of destination competitiveness (economic, political, social, cultural, technological and environmental) and suggest that:

> what makes a tourism destination truly competitive is its ability to increase tourism expenditure, to increasingly attract visitors while providing them with satisfying memorable experiences, and to do so in a profitable way, while enhancing the

©CAB International 2005. *Tourism SMEs, Service Quality and Destination Competitiveness* (eds E. Jones and C. Haven-Tang)

> well-being of destination residents and preserving the natural capital of the destination for future generations.
>
> (Ritchie and Crouch, 2003: 2)

However, competitiveness is a dynamic issue and is not destination-specific – the goalposts are continually shifting and therefore a destination proposition needs to be constantly reappraised against competitor destinations. As Ritchie and Crouch (2003: 1) emphasize:

> those who are responsible for destination management are operating according to a constantly evolving set of rules that continually redefine the exact nature of competition. Even though the factors that determine the attractiveness of a destination may remain constant, the changing nature of the competition requires ongoing assessment of the ability of a destination to compete.

Poon (1993: 24) states that destinations should follow some key principles in order to be competitive and ensure that a new and more sustainable tourism industry is developed – 'put the environment first; make tourism a lead sector; strengthen the distribution channels in the marketplace; and build a dynamic private sector'. The private sector often controls the businesses that deliver the tourism product and is supported by the public sector. As Poon (1993: 334) emphasizes: 'Private and public-sector cooperation is key to the success of any tourism destination.'

Across destinations the presence and influence of large international chains vary, and yet the backbone of the tourism industry comprises a plethora of private-sector small and medium-sized enterprises (SMEs) dominated by microbusinesses, often employing fewer than ten people. While the significance of small firms in delivering a substantial part of the total tourism output is an established feature of the tourism industry, small firms present particular challenges to destination managers for a variety of reasons, which will be explored in this chapter. The chapter proposes a model (section 1.2) of how a destination can be considered at different levels: employee; tourism businesses including SMEs; destination. It goes on (section 1.3) to examine the challenges for managing service quality and destination competitiveness. The nature of tourism employment and the special characteristics of tourism SMEs are considered in sections 1.4 and 1.5. The alternative perspectives of employee, tourism SME and destination on the enhancement of destination competitiveness are explored in section 1.6. The chapter concludes (section 1.7) by emphasizing the importance of recognizing the heterogeneity of tourism SME motivations and business approaches and the need for a new heterodoxy (rather than an unorthodoxy) appropriate to business management in tourism SMEs.

1.2 Entities in Destination Competitiveness

A destination can be considered as a hierarchy of entities – 'destination', 'tourism businesses including SMEs' and 'employee' – together with the public-sector interventions that support and coordinate the strategic development of the destination to project a coherent image to potential customers (see Fig. 1.1).

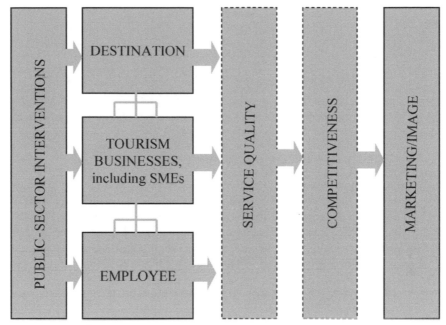

Fig. 1.1. Modelling the role of SMEs in service quality and destination competitiveness.

1.3 The Challenges for Managing Service Quality and Destination Competitiveness

1.3.1 The unique characteristics of tourism products

Tourism products have unique characteristics differentiating them from manufactured products: intangibility (Shostack, 1977); perishability (Zeithaml *et al.*, 1985; Onkvisit and Shaw, 1991; Hartman and Lindgren, 1993); inseparability of production and consumption (Grönroos, 1978; Bowen, 1990; Onkvisit and Shaw, 1991); heterogeneity (Zeithaml *et al.*, 1985; Onkvisit and Shaw, 1991); and – perhaps most importantly in the context of destination brand-building – interdependence (O'Connor, 1999). Interdependence is particularly important because tourism products are generally bought in combination and from different suppliers, rather than as a package or individually – tourists usually want to buy somewhere to stay and things to do as well as food, transport and a diverse range of other products.

1.3.2 A fragmented sector

Fragmentation derives from the interdependent products typically comprising a holiday or business trip straddling several different standard industrial classifications. In the UK, for example, the sector footprint was redefined during 2003 in the wake of the emerging Sector Skills Councils (the new Sector Skills Council for Hospitality, Leisure, Travel and Tourism is to be known as People 1st) in terms of Standard Industrial Classification (SIC) codes as summarized by Haven and Jones (2004: 13; see Table 1.1).

People 1st (2003: 1.1) assert the cohesion of the sector:

> The purpose of the sector is the provision of accommodation, food, drink and leisure activities. The sector is closely bound to ensure a high standard of customer service and a quality 'visitor' experience. The visitor is at the heart of the sector and further synergy is found in common vertical and horizontal ownership, which means that many operators can be found in more than one industry.

However, this assertion is not always echoed by the sector and some businesses, e.g. pubs, some (notably ethnic) restaurants, shops co-located with visitor attractions and some golf clubs, do not see themselves as part of the tourism industry. Despite this, however fragmented the individual businesses in a particular destination are on the supply side, they are seen collectively by potential customers on the demand side as a coordinated set of 'places to stay and things to do' and herein lies the dilemma, i.e. that 'destinations may be much less coordinated than desirable' (Jones et al., 2004: 73).

1.3.3 A mix of large and small companies

The tourism industry comprises a mix of small numbers of large, often multinational, businesses and large numbers of often family-run SMEs and microbusinesses. The ratio of large tourism organizations to tourism SMEs, especially microbusinesses, has implications for destination

Table 1.1. Standard Industrial Classification (SIC) codes and the sector footprint for People 1st in the UK (from Haven and Jones, 2004: 13).

Industry	Official SIC used
1. Hotels	55.1
2. Restaurants	55.3
3. Pubs, bars and nightclubs	55.4, 92.34
4. Contract food service providers	55.5
5. Membership clubs	92.34
6. Events	–
7. Gambling	92.71
8. Travel services	63.3
9. Tourist services	63.3
10. Visitor attractions	92.33, 92.53
11. Youth hostels	55.21
12. Holiday parks	55.23
13. Self-catering accommodation	55.23
14. Hospitality services	–

competitiveness. In destinations where the presence of large and chain businesses outweighs tourism SMEs, there will be far more direct competition between large organizations in terms of capacity, product and possibly brand names. As a result, large tourism organizations may seek competitive advantage through carefully scripted approaches to service quality management to enhance the visitor experience and contribute to improved perceptions of the destination. Despite the ability of SMEs to create unique selling propositions (USPs) through product customization and individualized service quality, the reality of the situation is that some large organizations face little or no competition from SMEs and, with their global brands maintained through strategic resource management (coherent property management, systematic approaches to quality management, well-developed training programmes and carefully coordinated marketing), become insular and detached from the destination. They look to their parent company rather than the destination for leadership, particularly in peripheral destinations. Therefore, their enthusiasm for destination partnerships to promote destination competitiveness may be less than that of SMEs, who must work collaboratively to ensure that destination service quality standards are maintained, despite fragmentation and diversity. Thus, large and small businesses enjoy different relationships with the destination and often operate as a two-tier system posing different challenges for destination managers.

1.3.4 Service quality

Service quality in the tourism industry has received considerable attention for decades. An emphasis on service quality has made customers more sophisticated and demanding and the relationship between service quality and variables such as investment return, costs, productivity, sales growth, prices, customer satisfaction and loyalty has been the basis for much current research (Anderson and Fornell, 2000, cited in Skalpe and Sandvik, 2002).

Simultaneous production and consumption make people the key to successful service delivery. The customer experience comprises a series of server interactions at the point of service (Hoque, 1999; Svensson, 2003). Each party has different expectations of the interaction, which is coloured by diverse issues, including perceptions of value for money and service context (Svensson, 2003), and dissatisfied customers are likely to become ex-customers. Expectations of service quality by staff and customers are generated by culture and prior socialization (Weiermair, 2000) and attempts to enhance service quality may be compounded by cross-cultural service encounters. Tsang and Qu (2000) identify that the less than international standard of service quality in many hotels in China results from difficulties in finding qualified employees to provide a service to meet the expectations of foreign tourists, coupled with the service attitude problems of employees. Pizam and Ellis (1999) state that customer satisfaction is the major performance indicator of service quality and emphasize its cost-effectiveness as a promotional tool resulting in return visits and word of mouth publicity (Heung, 2000).

In analysing service quality, both employee and customer perceptions must be examined (Randall and Senior, 1996). If employees and customers share the same values, then service quality expectations should be met. Where gaps exist, for cultural and other reasons, procedures need to be in place for employee development and training. Randall and Senior (1996) assert that the concept of satisfaction relates to specific transactions, whereas service quality is a more holistic evaluation by customers of their complete experience and overall service quality may be perceived as acceptable, even if one particular transaction was unsatisfactory: 'The important aspect to consider is the holistic character of the consumer act. The consumer [tourist] judges the total holiday experience, even though tourists experience a multitude of individual service encounters and can also evaluate their inherent qualities' (Weiermair, 2000: 398). Douglas and Connor (2003: 172) emphasize that the key factor in providing quality is to focus on the customer in delivering the expected service and to ensure that the customer understands that they are empowered to influence service quality – 'the focus should be not so much provider and recipient as a "partnership" in the overall service experience'.

There is a temptation in the tourism industry to assume that, because the service encounter is rooted in personal experience, any assessment of quality is going to be intangible. This temptation should be resisted and every effort should be made to establish standards and performance measures. Increasing competition in the tourism market means that tourism SMEs need to focus on quality improvement to achieve competitive advantage. Ribeiro (2003: 185) asserts that 'restaurant enterprises concerned with quality need to be able to combine, balance and juggle the tangible and intangible product'.

1.3.5 Service quality and competitive advantage

Service quality is the key to competitive advantage. Kandampully (2000) asserts that competition within the tourism industry is fuelled by a preoccupation with service quality to add value and enhance the complete tourism experience. A study by Skalpe and Sandvik (2002) confirmed the economic importance of service quality to hotels, supporting Bernhardt *et al.* (2000), who found that overall customer satisfaction was related to sales growth and profitability in restaurants. Both studies found evidence to support the fact that the long-term effects of service quality are more important than short-term ones. In contemplating quality issues in the Spanish restaurant sector, Ribeiro (2003: 184) comments that 'it is those restaurants that are best prepared – by anticipating the expectations of consumers and establishing services that offer differentiated quality – that are most likely to survive and to emerge as profitable in the future'.

Augustyn (1998: 147) asserts that, while the majority of tourism SMEs accept the importance of service quality in order to maintain competitive advantage, they are primarily concerned with their facilities or products:

> Private tourism companies have widely accepted that quality is one of the most important factors of their competitiveness in the global tourism market. To this end,

a number of big tourism companies spend vast sums of money on developing quality systems, whereas small tourism enterprises at least aim at upgrading their facilities.

Similarly, Church and Lincoln (1998) found that, while tourism SMEs require quality products in order to retain existing customers, tourism SMEs also recognize that quality products can be used to establish competitive advantage, in order to attract new customers. However, Church and Lincoln (1998: 139) argue that in order to provide tourism SMEs with competitive advantage, the product and/or service is required to progress from 'quality' to 'excellence':

> excellence can be said to be exceeding the expectations of customers. The flexibility and innovative nature of small firms makes this strategy a real possibility. However, the sustainability of this advantage is more debatable, as other firms can see the success of any initiative and copy it with relative ease.

Kozak and Rimmington (1998) report that tourism SMEs are neither a uniform group nor able to give a consistently high service delivery. Customer satisfaction depends on the total customer experience and thus poses specific challenges for the tourism industry in the management of service delivery interaction and service quality, due to the fragmentation of the experience for many customers, as a result of potential contact with a plethora of tourism intermediaries (Baum, 1995).

1.3.6 Managing service quality

Managing customer–server interactions is one of the most difficult but crucial tasks for tourism managers (Baum, 1997). Employers must define service quality goals and achieve employee commitment to them, as well as ensuring employees have the appropriate skills, knowledge, attitude, authority and access to information necessary for providing high-quality customer service (Hoque, 1999; Evans *et al.*, 2003). Ultimately, responsibility for high-quality service provision rests with front-line staff (Schaffer, 1984; Mattsson, 1994). Tourism SMEs must promote a customer focus among staff to ensure that their product meets and exceeds customer expectations rather than founding their quality management system on physical inspection of the facilities against national quality standards schemes.

> Despite the fact that the quality of the physical part of the tourism product is important, the quality of the human part of the service offered constitutes a critical success factor. A room of top quality standard is not in a position to compensate for the unfriendly and inhospitable behaviour of staff.
>
> (Augustyn, 1998: 149)

Church and Lincoln (1998) recognize that, while informal approaches to service quality can be effective in some tourism SMEs, they are often inadequate. However, mechanistic approaches to quality can hamper creativity and innovation and have a negative effect on the performance of tourism SMEs (Church and Lincoln, 1998). They suggest zero defects approaches to preventive quality control systems, such as hazard analysis and critical control points, failure modes and effects analysis, utilized with a quality management strategy, such as Investors in People (IiP), benchmarking, BS EN ISO 9000, total quality management or quality costing, to achieve a holistic approach to service quality management.

Kandampully (2000: 16) proposes 'service packaging' as a strategy for allowing tourism managers the flexibility to manage service quality and demand simultaneously:

> A service packaging strategy will enable tourism firms to effectively manage their resources and utilise their full market potential . . . firms will be able to modify products and services according to the varying needs of the customer . . . thus projecting a clear message to their present and prospective customers of their superior service . . . Moreover, customer perceived superiority of an organisation will render it less vulnerable to price sensitive competition. The ability to distance itself from the competition will undoubtedly engender a tourism firm with a competitive advantage, a predictable demand pattern, and the subsequent ability to effectively manage its all important human resources.

Fletcher (1999: 150) warns that the implementation of a service quality strategy is multidimensional. An organization has to prepare for change by identifying and prioritizing the required alterations and developing skills, such as listening, communication and leadership, to support the service quality strategy and develop an effective team across the entire operation.

1.4 The Nature of Tourism Employment

Baum (1997) summarizes some international human resource issues facing all tourism employers, including: demographic trends; the shrinking labour market and skills shortages; the image and perceptions of tourism employment; remuneration; labour turnover; attitudes towards education and training; reactive human resource policies and practices. Baum (1997) asserts that, while there are areas of commonality, e.g. global skills shortages for key front-line operational, technical and managerial areas, human resource issues are not internationally generic and the factors leading to skills shortages vary between developed and developing countries. In developed countries, skills shortages reflect demographic shifts with fewer young people entering the industry, a more educated population, low image and status of the industry, which combine to create recruitment difficulties, whereas, in developing countries, educational, technical, cultural and language barriers may raise entry thresholds and make tourism employment inaccessible (Baum, 1997). Thus, jobs deemed to be unskilled or semi-skilled in developed countries are not perceived as such in developing countries.

1.4.1 Labour market issues and warm body syndrome

Employment in tourism businesses is characterized by low pay, long working hours, lack of training and high labour turnover. High labour turnover allows numerical flexibility to match demand but exacerbates operational difficulties and militates against investment in training (Lashley and Chaplain, 1999). The tourism labour force has become increasingly flexible and casualized, affecting consideration of the industry as a viable career choice with 'knock-on' effects for labour supply (Haven, 2002). Labour supply issues have an impact on labour demand, and many operators are recruiting from overseas with concomitant implications for delivering what the Wales Tourist Board (WTB) term a 'sense of place'. Recent research (Haven and Jones, 2004) found widespread skill gaps among existing employees, particularly in relation to customer service skills. Some operators are moving away from the traditional benefits of recruiting people with craft skills to training individuals with the right attitude, enthusiasm and interest post-recruitment.

1.4.2 Images of tourism employment

Although the development of the tourism industry creates new employment opportunities, critics contend that tourism employment provides predominantly low-paid, low-skilled jobs that are demeaning (Choy, 1995). Negative aspects of tourism employment focus on physical demands and poor conditions of work resulting in unskilled labour, the transferability of skills between a broad range of establishments and high levels of absenteeism (Biswas and Cassell, 1996) and casual/part-time employment. Casual and part-time tourism employees may not be inclined to view tourism employment as a long-term career option and as a result may be unwilling to invest in developing tourism-related skills and achieving tourism-related qualifications. Additionally, reports of poor pay, attempts to circumvent the national minimum wage and exploitation of asylum seekers do little to promote the image of tourism employment as a worthwhile career choice (Hayter, 2001). There has been little progress in terms of improving the image of the tourism industry, in particular the hospitality sector, as a worthwhile career choice. Successive studies (Hotel and Catering Industry Training Board, 1981; Hotel and Catering Training Company, 1993, 1994; Haven, 2000) show UK employers need to address negative issues regarding career opportunities.

1.4.3 High labour turnover

Poor image is compounded by the high incidence of labour turnover within the industry. While labour turnover is often accepted as being an inevitable part of the tourism industry, some perceive it to be beneficial, enabling manipulation of workforce size to match demand and control labour costs (Lashley and Chaplain 1999; Torrington et al., 2002). Torrington et al. (2002) assert that organizations need rejuvenation through new recruits bringing new ideas and experiences to make organizations more dynamic. Bowey (1976, cited in Deery and Shaw, 1997) and Riley (1980) argue that the value of labour turnover lies in the mobility for staff, which facilitates employee skills acquisition. However, people who leave represent a lost resource and labour turnover is a cost to tourism businesses, creating severe operational difficulties and reducing profitability (Johnson, 1981). High labour turnover is symptomatic of poorly managed organizations (Torrington et al., 2002), affects organizational morale (Deery and Iverson, 1996), creates poor images in the labour market and makes it harder to recruit good performers in the future (Torrington et al., 2002). Research (e.g. HtF, 2001) has shown that high staff turnover militates against investment in employee development and training. Many employers are unwilling to invest money in training beyond induction, unless they have to do so to meet legal requirements, as they are unlikely to recoup the advantages of employee development and training.

1.4.4 Part-time and casual employment

Part-time employment characterizes the tourism industry, particularly in the UK, where it accounts for 49% compared with Austria 16.5%, France 23%, Greece 0.5% and Italy 11.5% (Keep and Mayhew, 1999). It is a common antidote to uneven work distribution and enables numerical flexibility of staff. However, it is essential that these temporal fluctuations are predictable and that regular and dependable part-time jobs can be provided. Isolated peaks of demand pose major issues in a labour-intensive industry. The dominance of self-employment and small family businesses within the tourism industries in the UK provides an alternative response to fluctuations in demand, in the form of self-exploitation – 'rhythmic fluctuation in demand will be met by a willingness to work very long hours' (Shaw and Williams, 1994: 148).

1.5 Special Characteristics of Tourism SMEs

Both large and small tourism businesses suffer the issues outlined in section 1.4, however, there are some characteristics that relate specifically to tourism SMEs, some of which present particular challenges to the competitiveness of destinations dominated by SMEs.

1.5.1 SMEs generate more interesting employment opportunities

Armstrong and Taylor (1993, cited in Wanhill, 2000) proclaim the ability of SMEs to: create new jobs at a time when major corporations are downsizing; improve industrial relations; create diversified and flexible industrial bases; stimulate competition and innovation; and generate energetic enterprising cultures. Wanhill

(2000: 135) notes that 'the significance of new firms in job generation, innovation and economic change is widely accepted . . . and tourism-SMEs are assigned an important role by the EU as an aid to regional convergence'. Apparently people enjoy working for smaller organizations – they offer challenges; decision making is more instant; communications are better; employees are more involved in setting business goals; they provide superb development opportunities; and they are not as tied by regulations (Stredwick, 2002).

1.5.2 Business failure rates

However, Wanhill (2000) warns of the controversial evidence about SMEs, especially when business start-up and failure rates are examined. According to the Best Practice Forum, for example, one in eight UK hospitality businesses fails every year making hospitality an extremely vulnerable business area (Deakin, 2004). In its 1996 publication *Tourism – Competing with the Best*, the Department of National Heritage (1996) stated that small firms are more vulnerable than larger firms to market pressures and so are less likely to invest in long-term human resource strategies, which may cause financial difficulties in the short term. This is illustrated by Shaw and Williams (1990, cited in Wanhill, 2000), who identified many family enterprises with little market stability, low levels of capital investment, weak management skills and resistance to change, which created barriers to successful tourism development.

1.5.3 Flexibility and innovation

Peacock (1993) argues that standardization, which is inherent to large organizations, enhances quality but restricts flexibility. SMEs can exploit their flexibility and their market proximity and personal contact with customers provides significant advantages for SMEs in terms of potential responsiveness to customer needs (Beaver *et al.*, 1998). SMEs are notoriously reluctant to adopt new technologies as evidenced by their resistance to the adoption of information and communication technology, e.g. the Internet, which has implications for web marketing and their individual participation in the global marketplace, with impacts on destination competitiveness (Buhalis and Main, 1998), and challenges the introduction of destination management systems.

1.5.4 Entrepreneurial motivations

Beaver *et al.* (1998) offer a taxonomy of entrepreneurial types including: the 'entrepreneurial venture', describing firms dedicated to growth and grasping of opportunities as they emerge; 'lifestyle enterprise', providing economic survival and a desired lifestyle for the owner-manager; the 'family enterprise', providing family members with homes and jobs; the 'female enterprise', for women entrepreneurs; and the 'ethnic enterprise'. However: 'The entrepreneurial metaphor can suggest more homogeneity than is the case' (Beaver *et al.*, 1998: 165). Certainly these labels do little to facilitate destination management, which benefits from enhanced understanding of individual business motivations and objectives. Beaver *et al.* (1998) identify self-employment and control as important motives for entrepreneurs and disparities among tourism SMEs in relation to the aims and objectives of the individual business, which are not always consistent with commercial objectives, such as business growth and profit maximization. As noted by WTB: 'The decision to enter the industry is often motivated by non-commercial reasons, quality of life and a desire to be one's own boss are more important considerations' (WTB, 2000: 40).

1.5.5 Business strategies

Individually tourism SMEs have very different business strategies and, although some are well managed and effectively exploit their resources for business growth, others may be seriously deficient in business and management skills. In particular, strategies in relation to the setting and maintenance of quality standards are critical to business and destination competitiveness. Haven and Jones (2004) report that employees and red tape cause problems for lifestyle businesses and obstruct expansion – indeed, some operators are deliberately selecting downsizing as a business strategy to run employee-free businesses, which runs counter to the European vision of SMEs as key to economic development. There are undeniable challenges related to inputting business support to lifestyle businesses that are not interested in growth as a business strategy or in contributing to destination development (Tinsley and Lynch, 2001). A more sophisticated understanding of SME heterogeneity must be reflected in public policy designed to influence tourism SMEs to promote destination development.

1.5.6 Ease of entry leads to weak endemic business models

There are 'few handicaps to entering the industry but some operators are poorly prepared and therefore businesses are underperforming' (WTB, 2000: 40). The ease of entry to the tourism industry for new operators often results in weak endemic business models, perpetuated by an 'anyone can do it' mentality. Skill gaps exist among some owner-managers, who often lack the abilities to manage their business and/or their staff. This has major implications for an SME's human resource function, where 'poor retention rates are often the result of poor management abilities' (Haven and Jones, 2004: 25). Operators often do not recognize the extra pressures that labour turnover and recruitment difficulties create for existing staff and the impact of not being able to operate at full capacity on product development, business performance and investment in training and development (Haven and Jones, 2004). The WTB strategy (WTB, 2000: 64) reports the tendency for some operators to 'compete on price rather than on value', ignoring other aspects of customer perceptions of quality. Ultimately, this reduces competitiveness, restricts profitability and limits the opportunity for reinvestment at an individual business level with impacts upon the destination. Beaver *et al.* (1998: 157) describe the inherent role of personalized preferences, prejudices and attitudes of owner-managers and the uniqueness of SME management, which they termed:

> an adaptive process, concerned with adjusting a usually limited amount of resources in order to gain the maximum immediate and short-term advantage. In the small firm, efforts are concentrated not on predicting but on controlling the operating environment, adapting as quickly as possible to the changing demands of that environment and devising suitable tactics for mitigating the consequences of any changes which occur.

1.5.7 Fortress mentality and resistance to participation in the development of destination propositions

Lynch (2000) comments on the 'fortress mentality' of SMEs and their resistance to external interventions. Tourism SMEs may not access formal sources of business support in the early stage of their life cycle (Birley, 1985) and may be heavily influenced by social networks of friends and acquaintances (Dodd, 1997). Cultures of self-reliance are barriers to accessing support and sharing good practice with other businesses (WTB, 2000). Tinsley and Lynch (2001) emphasize the importance of SME networks and their dynamic nature in destination development, but recognize that destination development is usually expressed in terms of physical, infrastructural, developments rather than the behaviour of individual businesses or destination networks. The assertion by Gunn (1993: 68) that 'service businesses gain from clustering' is not always appreciated by the businesses themselves and many neither communicate nor cooperate with each other or with the public-sector support agencies.

1.5.8 Lack of management skills and attitudes towards training

Dewhurst and Burns (1993) report that SMEs operate in a very distinct manner due to the lack of specialist managers to oversee their various activities. Financial constraints exacerbate lack of management skills and militate against training, future investment and knowledge management, with serious implications for the future of an individual tourism SME and, ultimately, the destination. Despite the fact that tourism SMEs are 'commercially satisficing', the fact that the business meets immediate survival needs, pays the bills and delivers an appropriate level of security deters some owner-managers from investing in training. Owner-managers may only train when the venture is under particular threat or has to meet legislative requirements, e.g. food hygiene training (Thomas *et al.*, 2000). Tourism SMEs challenge public-sector training interventions since 'traditionally, acceptance of the need for training is low', which WTB (2000: 71) argues highlights the need for a 'more flexible approach for training delivery. This could involve . . . innovative approaches . . . to foster improved networking between businesses and the sharing of good practice from experienced operators.' Tourism SMEs often face conflict between staff skills development needs and customer pressure (Haven and Jones, 2004). It is important to encourage employers to see the bigger picture – i.e. the industry needs to invest in its staff to achieve a good reputation and deliver a quality product.

1.5.9 Poor market intelligence

Poor market research and knowledge management about customers means that tourism SMEs can be introspective and fail to achieve their full potential. Tourism businesses must understand their market and build this knowledge into their organizational goals. Despite this, many tourism destinations are dominated by tourism SMEs with:

> little global know-how and global reach. In order to create and market internationally appealing tourism products, to achieve competitive advantages and to sustain competitiveness against global or trans-national tourism firms, a number of tourism and hospitality management know-how gaps have to be specified and corrective management measures undertaken, including: intercultural management skills; proper choice and implementation of market entry strategies in foreign markets; and know-how concerning regionally/culturally differentiated travel motivations and tourism behaviour of customers.
>
> (Weiermair, 2000: 407)

1.5.10 Lack of an integrated approach to business planning and functionality

Many tourism SMEs do not adopt an integrated approach to business planning. Indeed, many tourism microbusinesses do not develop a written business plan against which to monitor business performance except in response to external pressure, e.g. when applying for a loan from a bank or a grant from the public sector. One example of poor integration relates to the ineffective way that some SMEs exploit information and communications technology, specifically the Internet and Internet marketing. Despite the phenomenal growth in the number of tourism SME websites, the integration of their websites into wider business strategies and business cultures is a cause for concern (Morrison, 2002). Many tourism SME owner-managers opt for tourism entrepreneurship to achieve personal autonomy and perceive that representation on availability databases challenges that autonomy, posing issues for destination management organizations (DMOs).

1.6 Enhancing Destination Competitiveness

This section will consider public-sector interventions that can be used to enhance destination competitiveness. The range of interventions is not exhaustive and is arranged to reflect the destination hierarchy: employee-oriented interventions, tourism SME-oriented interventions and destination-oriented interventions.

1.6.1 Enhancing service quality and destination competitiveness through employee-oriented interventions

1.6.1.1 Training

Skills shortages encourage employers to recruit people without the necessary qualifications and to train post-recruitment. Public-sector interventions should be designed to 'increase the demand for skills among employers' (Thomas and Long, 2001: 238). Training potential employees to create a pool of appropriately skilled employees is one way to address skills shortages and encourage employers to recruit qualified staff. Raising entry thresholds will raise levels of professionalism in the industry and enhance the image of tourism employment and the perceived status of tourism as a career option. Links between employee performance and service quality are well documented, Hickman and Mayer's (2003) study of the Florida Theme Park, for example, evidences the benefits of motivated and loyal employees, predominantly higher levels of customer satisfaction and greater customer loyalty. Thus, raising employee skills levels should contribute to the raising of service quality standards at a business level and will in turn contribute to destination competitiveness.

Baum (1995) argues that, in other European countries, hotel employment in particular has a stronger tradition of perceived professionalism than within the UK. Baum (1995) cites Switzerland as an example of a destination where specific qualifications are required in order to work in particular management and skill areas. The traditions of tourism management education and training in other European countries serve to illustrate the importance awarded to the development of practical skills. Weak internal labour markets are often characterized by an absence of professionalism together with a demand for seamlessness between operational and managerial functions. Sheldon (1989, cited in Baum, 1995) identifies that the defining characteristics of professionalism include: substantial profession-specific knowledge and competences requiring an extended period of education and training; a code of ethics promoted through a professional body which also licenses practice; occupational complexity; high status and income.

1.6.1.2 Remuneration

Remuneration is also associated with extant levels of professionalism in an industry. Levels of pay are dependent upon the market demand for particular skills. Industries that have weak internal labour markets, such as the tourism industry, often demand fairly generic skills, which are accessible at a low cost within the marketplace. With probably more discussion around it than for any other sector in relation to the national minimum wage in the UK, the tourism industry does little to counteract the perception of low pay and low-skilled employment. The situation within the tourism industry in the UK with regard to a lack of professionalism is hindered by the trend towards deskilling, fuelled by the need to minimize costs and address labour shortages. Consequently, qualified individuals may not consider the tourism industry to provide viable career opportunities. Baum (1995) asserts that increasing flexibility within the tourism workforce could be detrimental, as it will only serve to weaken the labour market, as deskilling and flexible working practices are deemed to be contradictory to the features of a strong labour market. Nevertheless, deskilling and flexibility are compatible in the tourism industry, as the simplification of various tasks places them within the skill capabilities of a much wider range of employees.

1.6.2 Enhancing service quality and destination competitiveness through tourism SME-oriented interventions

1.6.2.1 Grading schemes and other approaches to benchmarking best practice

Kozak and Rimmington (1998) argue that there are considerable advantages for tourism SMEs and tourism destinations in using benchmarking as a means of improving service quality, although they concede that the volatility of the sector means that tourism SMEs often lack the resources to carry out benchmarking exercises. Accommodation grading schemes and other external awards, such as IiP, are important destination level vehicles for influencing the performance level of an organization. As benchmarks, grading and award schemes indicate how tourism SMEs perform against a range of standards and schemes and:

> can act as stimuli to the improvement of facilities and services. Improvements gained through awards can include more professional business processes that will affect long-term business performance . . . likely to have a positive effect on the performance of the overall destination.
>
> (Kozak and Rimmington, 1998: 187)

However, tourism SMEs need to be motivated to engage in such schemes, which can also create benefits for tourism destinations – most notably that the destination can measure the quality of tourism SMEs within the area and plan destination developments accordingly. Unfortunately, the objectives of participating in various quality schemes for tourism SMEs may differ. At the destination level, tourism quality schemes are often introduced as an attempt to increase the competitiveness of a destination in the worldwide tourism market. However, at the individual business level, while tourism SMEs often participate in quality systems, such as accommodation quality grading schemes, their objectives are generally to enhance their promotional strengths rather than to increase customer satisfaction and add to the competitiveness of the destination (Augustyn, 1998).

1.6.2.2 Management development for tourism SME owner-managers

Deficiency of management skills in a small firm is a systemic problem resulting in a weak endemic business model and a knock-on effect that potentially can manifest itself in all functional areas: financial management, property management, quality management, human resource management, health and safety management, risk management, knowledge management. Small organizations are often unimaginative in how they manage staff and would derive business benefit from innovatively adapting orthodox human resource management approaches to meet their needs (Stredwick, 2002); this contrasts strongly with larger organizations which recognize the need for innovative human resource management and by nature of their size and prominence are able to influence industry standards (Hoque, 1999). Collaboration between larger organizations and SMEs can bring benefits to both. Thus, addressing management deficiencies as a specific aspect of public-sector training provision within a destination can bring major business benefits.

1.6.2.3 Promoting best practice approaches to human resource management

Tourism is a human resource-dependent industry, which must compete for scarce resources to ensure its survival. The success of individual businesses and ultimately the destination depends on the quality of the people it employs. Tourism SMEs need to take ownership of human resource issues, break the cycle of service failure and revisit employment and management practices rather than rely on image manipulation to attract more employees into the industry. Finding employees, especially temporary employees, may often not be a problem for some tourism SMEs. However, the real challenge for tourism SMEs in relation to human resource management is finding employees with the right skills, knowledge and attitudes to their work, who can be retained by organizations in order to achieve their goals (Finegan, 2000; Davidson, 2003).

The human resource strategy wheel, devised by Zeithaml and Bitner (2000), summarizes key steps in attracting and retaining employees – hiring the right people; developing people to deliver service quality; providing needed support systems; retaining the best people – and provides a useful framework against which efforts in the area of employee development can be measured. It enables organizations to benchmark employee training and development, as was illustrated in the Florida Theme Park case study (Mayer, 2002). Despite the challenge to resources, tourism SME managers must strive to create a training culture, i.e. a culture that sees training as an investment rather than a cost (Baum, 1997).

Successful service comes from staff who are committed to doing whatever it takes to ensure customer satisfaction, and employee empowerment is one mechanism for encouraging the level of commitment necessary to achieve organizational goals (Lashley, 1995). The creation of an internal labour market, through developing appropriate training, promotional opportunities, enhanced job security and consideration of job design and job roles, including job enlargement, job rotation, job enrichment and job sharing, can also be used as a strategic management tool to enhance employee retention and to develop a stable and satisfied workforce (Evans et al., 2003; Jago and Deery, 2004). Adoption of family-friendly employment policies and practices that enable employees to balance home and work life are another way of deriving business benefits through: reduced casual sickness absence; improved retention; improved productivity; improved recruitment; and improved morale and commitment (Bevan et al., 1999). Basically employers need to recognize that the best way to retain staff is to provide them with a better deal than they perceive they could get by working for alternative employers through five key factors: pay; managing expectations; induction; family-friendly human resource practices; training and development (Torrington *et al.*, 2002).

1.6.2.4 Business development support

Public-sector interventions can focus on specific aspects to encourage business development. Typical areas include helping small firms to identify and develop new markets, to understand and meet legislative requirements, e.g. health and safety legislation, food hygiene legislation, employment legislation, and to more effectively exploit new technologies, e.g. exploitation of the Internet through supporting website development. In the UK, for example, there is a plethora of generic business support available for tourism SMEs through unitary authorities and regional development agencies, as well as specific support from tourism-specific agencies aligned with national and regional DMOs. Destination networking strategies are one way of encouraging interaction between businesses and with support agencies.

1.6.2.5 Capital investment support

The public sector can use capital investment support through grants and loan schemes to orchestrate business development, particularly in relation to development of the physical infrastructure of individual businesses, in response to market intelligence. In Wales, for example, the WTB has coordinated the distribution of Section 4 grant aid to enhance the quality of the physical infrastructure of tourism businesses. Provision of grant aid can be accompanied by requirements on SME owner-managers to undertake particular activities, e.g. participation in destination management strategies and training initiatives, committing to better environmental management, exploiting new technologies more effectively.

1.6.3 Enhancing service quality and destination competitiveness through destination-oriented interventions

1.6.3.1 Marketing and market intelligence

Market intelligence at a destination level can look externally at trends in consumer behaviour and monitor competitor destinations as well as measuring destination performance. Market intelligence will facilitate the constant evolution of the rules on which a destination is predicated and enable them to be reflected in tourism policy, planning and infrastructure development through a destination's management strategy to ensure that it remains competitive (Ritchie and Crouch, 2003).

1.6.3.2 Tourism policy, planning and infrastructure development

A destination's tourism policy must allow it to 'take maximum advantage of the degree to which a destination's core resources and attractors are first capable of attracting visitors and then providing them with a memorable visitation experience' (Ritchie and Crouch, 2003: 183). Tourism planning will take account of enhancing a destination's access routes, transport networks and communications infrastructure to facilitate the visitation experience.

1.6.3.3 Marketing

Strategic marketing management or branding can be used to promote a 'country's image, attractiveness and products . . . creating product differentiation' (Kotler and Gertner, 2004: 40). DMOs are strategically placed to develop a destination brand and have 'the task of being the primary front-line promoter for any destination' (Morgan *et al.*, 2004: 13) and must take 'command of both branding and product development, in a changing and confused stakeholder market, [or else] large operators will simply take to the market what they believe is the most appealing product . . . at the expense of . . . small players' (Morgan *et al.*, 2004: 14). Kotler and Gertner (2004) identify five stages in branding: first, undertaking a SWOT analysis to determine the chief strengths, weaknesses, opportunities and threats; secondly, selecting features that provide a basis for story telling; thirdly, developing an umbrella concept for separate activities; fourthly, allocating sufficient funding to make a large impact; and, fifthly, creating controls to ensure that all products meet the brand promise. It is this fifth stage that is the most difficult to get SMEs to buy into, and SMEs must have ownership of a destination's brand propositions to ensure that individual tourism products 'chime' with the destination and 'that some kind of logic links the two' (Anholt, 2004: 27). This mandates that DMOs work 'on a collaborative and integrative basis' (Morgan *et al.*, 2004: 14).

1.7 Conclusions

This chapter has presented a hierarchical model of a destination comprising three entities – destination; tourism business; employee – to act as a framework for understanding the impact service quality has on destination competitiveness and the implications of SMEs for public-sector interventions designed to promote destination development. Throughout the chapter the significance of employees in determining service quality has been emphasized. Labour market issues have an impact on employment in large and small tourism organizations alike but have severe implications on some SMEs due to the special characteristics of tourism SMEs. A more sophisticated understanding of SME heterogeneity and individual business motivations must be reflected in public policy designed to influence tourism SMEs to promote destination development.

Financial constraints and issues of economies of scale can have major implications for tourism SME operations. What is clear is that orthodox approaches to considerations of service quality and destination competitiveness do not map well on to the heterodoxy of tourism SMEs. SMEs tend not to adopt systematic, integrated and holistic approaches to their management, to defining and managing service quality, investing in training, business planning, gathering market intelligence or approaching innovation. SMEs are unlikely to invest in research because of their small size and flexibility. They are more likely to respond to niche markets. Many SMEs do not understand the link between service quality and destination competitiveness and many fail to identify the role they play in destination competitiveness or the significance of destination competitiveness for the sustainability of their individual business. However, while SMEs may face uncertainty in terms of their market, they have the ability to demonstrate more internal consistency in terms of their actions and motivations, as SMEs determine their own objectives. Hence, although resources are limited, their small size can be advantageous, in terms of adaptability, flexibility and responsiveness to change.

Melding the diverse interests of different businesses in the tourism industry into an internationally competitive, cohesive sector with a coherent destination 'brand' proposition is the major challenge for destination management organizations and the plethora of support agencies. There are a number of issues in relation to service quality and destination competitiveness which, if addressed through training, investment and knowledge management, will have positive benefits at employee and tourism SME levels, ultimately benefiting the destination by providing competitive advantage.

References

Anholt, S. (2004) Nation-brands and the value of provenance. In: Morgan, N., Pritchard, A. and Pride, R. (eds) *Destination Branding: Creating the Unique Destination Proposition*, 2nd edn. Elsevier Butterworth-Heinemann, Oxford, UK, pp. 26–39.

Augustyn, M. (1998) The road to quality enhancement in tourism. *International Journal of Contemporary Hospitality Management* 10(4), 145–158.

Baum, T. (1995) *Managing Human Resources in the European Tourism and Hospitality Industry: a Strategic Approach*. Chapman & Hall, London, 281 pp.

Baum, T. (1997) Managing people at the periphery: implications for the tourism and hospitality industry. In: Hemmington, N. (ed.) *Proceedings of 6th Annual CHME Hospitality Research Conference*. Oxford Brookes University, Oxford, UK, pp. 86–97.

Beaver, G., Lashley, C. and Stewart, J. (1998) Management development. In: Thomas, R. (ed.) *The Management of Small Tourism and Hospitality Firms*. Cassell, London, pp. 156–173.

Bernhardt, K.L., Donthu, N. and Kennett, P.A. (2000) A longitudinal analysis of satisfaction and profitability. *Journal of Business Research* 47(2), 161–171.

Bevan, S., Dench, S., Tamkin, P. and Cummings, J. (1999) *Family-friendly Employment: the Business Case*. DfEE Research Report 136, DfEE, London.

Birley, S. (1985) The role of networks in the entrepreneurial process. *Journal of Business Venturing* 1, 107–117.

Biswas, R. and Cassell, C. (1996) Strategic HRM and the gendered division of labour in the hotel industry: a case study. *Personnel Review* 25(2), 19–34.

Bowen, J. (1990) Development of a taxonomy of services to gain strategic marketing insights. *Journal of the Academy of Marketing Science* 18(1), 43–49.

Buhalis, D. and Main, H. (1998) Information technology in peripheral small and medium hospitality enterprises: strategic analysis and critical factors. *International Journal of Contemporary Hospitality Management* 10(5), 198–202.

Choy, D. (1995) The quality of tourism employment. *Tourism Management* 16(2), 129–137.

Church, I. and Lincoln, G. (1998) Quality management. In: Thomas, R. (ed.) *The Management of Small Tourism and Hospitality Firms*. Cassell, London, pp. 138–155.

Davidson, M.C.G. (2003) Does organizational climate add to service quality in hotels? *International Journal of Contemporary Hospitality Management* 15(4), 206–213.

Deakin, M.K. (2004) Foundations of Small Hospitality business success: review of critical success factors adopted by successful British hospitality self-made entrepreneurs. In: Jones, E. and Haven, C. (eds) *Proceedings of the First Combined CHME Hospitality Research and CHME Learning and Teaching Conference*. UWIC Press, Cardiff, pp. 27–32.

Deery, M.A. and Iverson, R.D. (1996) Enhancing productivity: intervention strategies for employee turnover. In: Johns, N. (ed.) *Productivity Management in Hospitality and Tourism*. Cassell, London, pp. 68–95.

Deery, M.A. and Shaw, R.N. (1997) Turnover culture in the hotel industry: an investigation of the concept. In: Hemmington, N. (ed.) *Proceedings of 6th Annual CHME Hospitality Research Conference*. Oxford Brookes University, Oxford, UK, pp. 98–118.

Department of National Heritage (1996) *Tourism: Competing with the Best – People Working in Tourism and Hospitality*. Department of National Heritage, London.

Dewhurst, J. and Burns, P. (1993) *Small Business Management*, 3rd edn. Macmillan, Basingstoke, UK, 418 pp.

Dodd, S. (1997) Social network membership and activity rates: some comparative data. *International Small Business Journal* 15(4), 80–87.

Douglas, L. and Connor, R. (2003) Attitudes to service quality – the expectation gap. *Nutrition and Food Science* 33(4), 165–172.

Evans, N., Campbell, D. and Stonehouse, G. (2003) *Strategic Management for Travel and Tourism*. Butterworth-Heinemann, Oxford, UK, 412 pp.

Finegan, J.E. (2000) The impact of person and organizational values on organization commitment. *Journal of Occupational and Organizational Psychology* 73(2), 149–169.

Fletcher, M. (1999) The effects of internal communication, leadership and team performance on successful service quality implementation: a South African perspective. *Team Performance Management* 5(5), 150–163.

Grönroos, C. (1978) A service oriented approach to marketing of services. *European Journal of Marketing* 12(8), 588–601.

Gunn, C.A. (1993). *Tourism Planning Basics, Concepts, Cases*. Taylor and Francis, London, 300 pp.

Hartman, D. and Lindgren, J. (1993) Consumer evaluations of goods and services – Implications for services marketing. *Journal of Services Marketing* 7(2), 4–15.

Haven, C. (2000) They know all about tourism and hospitality . . . don't they? *Hospitality Review* 2(3), 32–39.

Haven, C. (2002) Attitudes in Wales towards careers in tourism and hospitality. PhD thesis, University of Wales Institute, Cardiff, UK.

Haven, C. and Jones, E. (2004) *An Assessment of the Labour Market and Skills Needs of the Tourism and Related Sectors in Wales*. Tourism Training Forum for Wales, Cardiff, UK.

Hayter, R. (2001) The 'hospitality' branding: a question of impact on the industry's image. *Hospitality Review* 3(1), 21–25.

Heung, V.C.S. (2000) Satisfaction levels of mainland Chinese travellers with Hong Kong hotel journal services. *International of Contemporary Hospitality Management* 12(5), 308–315.

Hickman, J. and Mayer, K.J. (2003) Service quality and human resource practices: a theme park case study. *International Journal of Contemporary Hospitality Management* 15(2), 116–119.

Hoque, K. (1999) New approaches to HRM in the UK hotel industry. *Human Resource Management Journal* 9(2), 64–76.

Hotel and Catering Industry Training Board (1981) *The Image of the Hotel and Catering Industry*. HCITB, Wembley, UK.

Hotel and Catering Training Company (1993) *Tomorrow's Workforce: School Pupils' Views of a Career in Hospitality*. Hotel and Catering Training Company, London.

Hotel and Catering Training Company (1994) *Employment in the Catering and Hospitality Industry – Employee Attitudes and Career Expectations*. Hotel and Catering Training Company, London.

HtF (2001) *Labour Market Review 2001 for the Hospitality Industry*. Hospitality Training Foundation, London.

Jago, L.K. and Deery, M. (2004) An investigation of the impact of internal labour markets in the hotel industry. *Service Industries Journal* 24(2), 118–129.

Johnson, K. (1981) Towards an understanding of labour turnover. *Service Industries Review* 1, 4–17.

Jones, E., Botterill, D., Lynch, P. and Thomas, R. (2004) United Kingdom. In: Morrison, A. and Thomas, R. (eds) *SMEs in Tourism: an International Review*. ATLAS, Arnhem, pp. 73–80.

Kandampully, J. (2000) The impact of demand fluctuation on the quality of service: a tourism industry example. *Managing Service Quality* 10(1), 10–18.

Keep, E. and Mayhew, K. (1999) *The Leisure Sector. Skills Task Force Research Group – Paper 8*. ESRC Centre on Skills, Knowledge and Organizational Performance, Oxford and Warwick Universities, Warwick, UK.

Kotler, P. and Gertner, D. (2004) Country as brand, product and beyond: a place marketing and brand management perspective. In: Morgan, N., Pritchard, A. and Pride, R. (eds) *Destination Branding: Creating the Unique Destination Proposition*, 2nd edn. Elsevier Butterworth-Heinemann, Oxford, UK, pp. 40–56.

Kozak, M. (2004) *Destination Benchmarking: Concepts, Practices and Operations*. CAB International, Wallingford, UK, 216 pp.

Kozak, M. and Rimmington, M. (1998) Benchmarking: destination attractiveness and small hospitality business performance. *International Journal of Contemporary Hospitality Management* 10(5), 184–188.

Lashley, C. (1995) Towards an understanding of employee empowerment in hospitality services. *International Journal of Contemporary Hospitality Management* 7(1), 27–32.

Lashley, C. and Chaplain, A. (1999) Labour turnover: hidden problem – hidden cost. *Hospitality Review* 1(1), 49–54.

Lynch, P.A. (2000) Networking in the homestay sector. *Service Industries Journal* 20(3), 95–116.

Mattsson, J. (1994) Improving service quality in person to person encounters: integrating findings from a multidisciplinary review. *Service Industries Journal* 14(1), 45–61.

Mayer, K.J. (2002) Human resource practices and service quality in theme parks. *International Journal of Contemporary Hospitality Management* 14(4), 169–175.

Morgan, N., Pritchard, A. and Pride, R. (2004) *Destination Branding: Creating the Unique Destination Proposition* 2nd edn. Elsevier Butterworth-Heinemann, Oxford, UK, 314 pp.

Morrison, A. (2002) Small hospitality business: enduring or endangered? *Journal of Hospitality and Tourism Management* 9(1), 1–11.

O'Connor, P. (1999) *Electronic Information Distribution in Tourism and Hospitality*. CAB International, Wallingford, UK, 173 pp.

Onkvisit, S. and Shaw, J. (1991) Is services marketing really different? *Journal of Professional Services Marketing* 7(2), 3–17.

Peacock, M. (1993) A question of size. *International Journal of Contemporary Hospitality Management* 5(4), 29–32.

People 1st (2003) *Market Assessment for Hospitality, Leisure, Travel and Tourism*. Hospitality Training Foundation, London.

Pizam, A. and Ellis, T. (1999) Customer satisfaction and its measurement in hospitality enterprises. *International Journal of Contemporary Hospitality Management* 11(7), 326–339.

Poon, A. (1993) *Tourism, Technology and Competitive Strategies*. CAB International, Wallingford, UK, 370 pp.

Randall, L. and Senior, M. (1996) Training for service quality in the hospitality industry. In: Olsen, M.D., Teare, M. and Gummesson, E. (eds) *Service Quality in Hospitality Organizations*. Cassell, London, pp. 164–182.

Ribeiro, D. (2003) The Spanish restaurant sector: evaluating the perceptions of quality. *Service Industries Journal* 23(2), 183–194.

Riley, M. (1980) The role of mobility in the development of skills for the hotel and catering industry. *Hospitality* March, 52–53.

Ritchie, J.R.B. and Crouch, G.I. (2003) *The Competitive Destination: a Sustainable Tourism Perspective*, CAB International, Wallingford, UK, 272 pp.

Schaffer, J. (1984) Strategy, organization structure and success in the lodging industry. *International Journal of Hospitality Management* 3(4), 159–165.

Sharpley, R. (2002) The challenges of economic diversification through tourism: the case of Abu Dhabi. *International Journal of Tourism Research* 4, 221–235.

Shaw, G. and Williams, A. (1994) *Critical Issues in Tourism: a Geographical Perspective*. Blackwell, Oxford, UK, 280 pp.

Shostack, G. (1977) Breaking free from product marketing. *Journal of Marketing* 41, 73–80.

Skalpe, O. and Sandvik, K. (2002) The economics of quality in the hotel business. *Tourism Economics* 8(4), 361–376.

Stredwick, J. (2002) *Managing People in a Small Business*. Kogan Page, London, 280 pp.

Svensson, G. (2003) A generic conceptual framework of interactive service quality. *Managing Service Quality* 13(4), 267–275.

Thomas, R. and Long, J. (2001) Tourism and economic regeneration: the role of skills development. *International Journal of Tourism Research* 3(3), 229–240.

Thomas, R., Lashley, C., Rowson, B., Xie, G., Jameson, S., Eaglen, A., Lincoln, G. and Parsons, D. (2000) *National Survey of Small Tourism and Hospitality Firms: Skills Demand and Training Practices*. Centre for the Study of Small Tourism and Hospitality Firms, Leeds.

Tinsley, R. and Lynch, P. (2001) Small tourism business networks and destination development. *International Journal of Hospitality Management* 20(4), 367–378.

Torrington, D., Hall, L. and Taylor, S. (2002) *Human Resource Management*, 5th edn. Prentice Hall, Harlow, 668 pp.

Tsang, N. and Qu, H. (2000) Service quality in China's hotel industry: a perspective from tourists and hotel managers. *International Journal of Contemporary Hospitality Management* 12(5), 316–326.

Wanhill, S. (2000) Small and medium tourism enterprises. *Annals of Tourism Research* 27(1), 132–147.

Weiermair, K. (2000) Tourists' perceptions towards and satisfaction with service quality in the cross-cultural service encounter: implications for hospitality and tourism management. *Managing Service Quality* 10(6), 397–409.

WTB (2000) *Achieving Our Potential: a Tourism Strategy for Wales*. Wales Tourist Board, Cardiff.

WTTC (2003) *Executive Summary: Travel and Tourism A World of Opportunity – The 2003 Travel and Tourism Economic Research*. Available from http://www.wttc.org/measure/PDF/Executive%20Summary.pdf Accessed on 29 November 2003.

WTTC (2004) *Travel and Tourism Forging Ahead: the 2004 Travel and Tourism Economic Research*. World Travel and Tourism Council, London.

Zeithaml, V. and Bitner, M.J. (2000) *Services Marketing: Integrating Customer Focus across the Firm*, 2nd edn. Irwin McGraw-Hill, New York, 620 pp.

Zeithaml, V., Parasuraman, A. and Berry, L. (1985) Problems and strategies in services marketing, *Journal of Marketing* 491, 33–46.

2

Integrated Tourism in Europe's Rural Destinations: Competition or Cooperation?

TOVE OLIVER[1] AND TIM JENKINS[2]

[1]Higher Education Funding Council for Wales, Cardiff, UK; [2]Institute of Rural Sciences, University of Wales, Aberystwyth, UK

2.1 Introduction

Rural activities and resource use frequently involve competition by a wide range of stakeholders, including businesses, resource controllers, communities and institutions. In many rural destinations such competition is increasingly linked to tourism, the benefits of which are dependent on a number of variables, including: the extent to which the tourism sector is serviced by local businesses; the quality of the natural environment and of local accommodation provision; the extent and nature of tourism facilities such as visitor attractions; and the existence of features of historic and cultural interest. Such considerations, and especially the need for quality in rural tourism, have recently been promoted in European policy and strategy (Ilbery and Kneafsey, 1998; European Commission, 1999). Increasingly, reference is made to the need for an integrated approach to tourism in rural destinations, which, in having clear connections with local resources, activities, products, production and service industries, and a participatory local community, is seen as potentially important in rural development (Jenkins and Oliver, 2001; Mitchell and Eagles, 2001). However, there has been relatively little theoretical research on the concept of integrated tourism and its potential benefits (and disbenefits) to rural destinations. Consequently, a coherent conceptual framework with which to explore integrated tourism in empirical terms has been lacking.

This chapter identifies and discusses seven characteristics of integrated tourism: networks; scale; endogeneity; embeddedness; sustainability; complementarity; and empowerment. The ideas to which this conceptualization gives rise are currently being applied in an interdisciplinary European Union (EU)-funded research project (Supporting and Promoting Integrated Tourism in Europe's Lagging Rural Regions – SPRITE), which attempts to analyse and develop the potential for integrated tourism in a number of specific rural destinations in six European

©CAB International 2005. *Tourism SMEs, Service Quality and Destination Competitiveness*
(eds E. Jones and C. Haven-Tang)

countries: the Czech Republic, France, Greece, Ireland, Spain and the UK. Key preliminary findings from a comparative analysis of secondary data conducted at regional level are presented.

2.2 Rural Tourism

Rural tourism can encompass all tourism based in and making use of resources in rural areas. The differentiating features of this type of tourism include its close association with the quality of the biophysical environment, a high degree of pluriactivity among hosts (with tourism businesses often part of wider ones), the importance of local culture and traditions, and the fragility of the rural economy in which it takes place (Stabler, 1997). Accessibility (i.e. the ease with which people can reach, engage with and use a site or attraction in both locational and economic terms) is also a critical factor in the success of rural tourism.

Rurality is more than a geographical concept: in the tourism context, it reflects a lifestyle, a set of values and an environment desirable for its 'difference', relative isolation and pace of living (Long and Lane, 2000), as well as for its special aesthetic qualities and even its spirituality. 'Rural culture' is a key commodity of many rural destinations (Hopkins, 1998). Tourism in rural areas can encompass many activities focused upon different types of resource, often with cultural and natural components. The range of potential activities that may be undertaken in a rural context include: touring; water-based activities; land-based activities; aerial activities; cultural and educational activities; conservation activities; gastronomic activities; health and fitness activities; 'metaphysical' activities such as pilgrimage and retreats. Rural tourism goes beyond simply complementing traditional activities such as agriculture, and can act as a catalyst for a whole range of new entrepreneurial activities, partnerships and networks. Inevitably, however, there are contested opinions as to what is desirable in rural tourism development and, moreover, there is no universal agreement about the net benefits of rural tourism. In part, this reflects a shortage of theoretical research placing rural tourism in a conceptual framework (Butler and Clarke, 1992). As a result, tourism has only recently received serious academic attention as a mechanism for rural development, and the dynamics involved in exploiting tourism as an opportunity for the revitalization of rural communities and economies is not yet fully understood (Page and Getz, 1997).

2.3 Integrated Tourism

The concept of 'integrated tourism' is proposed here as an aid to understanding tourism's potential for contributing to rural development. A brief analysis of how the term is currently understood by tourism theorists and practitioners across the six European countries participating in the SPRITE project reveals little consensus and there is much overlap with concepts such as 'ecological tourism' (Slováckóva, 2000), 'sustainable tourism' and *'tourisme durable'* (McIntyre, 1997).

It is clear that the concept is understood in a number of different ways. These include, for example: institutional integration, as in the integration of agencies into partnerships or other formal semi-permanent structures; economic integration, as in the integration of other economic sectors with tourism, particularly retailing and local industries such as farming; policy integration, as in the integration of tourism with broader national and regional goals for economic growth, diversification and development; and personal integration, as in the integration of tourists into local communities as 'guests', such that they occupy the same physical spaces and satisfy their existential and material needs in the same manner as members of the host society.

Clearly, therefore, the term 'integration' is both fluid and evolving. Traditionally, the tourism literature has tended to define it in terms of the extent to which tourism is integrated into broader economic and social development contexts, goals and decisions (Swarbrooke, 1999; Sharpley, 2000); but, in more recent literature, the importance of local participation and control is emerging, with integration defined according to the percentage of local people employed, the type and degree of participation, decision making power and ownership of resources in the local tourism sector (Mitchell and Eagles, 2001).

Broadly, integrated tourism can be defined as tourism that is explicitly linked to the economic, social, cultural, natural and human structures of the localities in which it takes place. In practical terms, it is tourism which has clear connections with local resources, activities, products, other production and service industries, and a participatory local community. Integrated tourism derives from a complex contextual environment. This includes numerous socio-economic trends in production and consumption (for example, increasing concerns for the quality of life) and the actor-specific and sector-specific conventions that underpin such trends (for example, moves away from purely commercial conventions towards more ecological ones) (Jenkins and Oliver, 2001). Figure 2.1 is based on conventions theory and the 'four worlds of production' framework (see Salais and Storper, 1992; Storper and Salais, 1997). This suggests that a successful integrated tourism trajectory is towards the quadrant defined by the dedicated and specialized (as opposed to generic and standardized) production, where non-industrial and non-commercial conventions are paramount.

2.4 Integrated Tourism in Europe's Rural Destinations

The overall intention of the SPRITE project is to develop the potential for better integrated tourism, by working from the premise that enhancing the sustainable economic potential of rural destinations requires partnerships among rural enterprises and the sustainable and yet productive use of the rural destination itself. Two destinations in each of six European countries have been selected for study (Fig. 2.2). They comprise:

- Šumava Mountains; Novobystricko (Czech Republic).
- Basse-Normandie; Auvergne (France).
- Evrytania; Achaïa (Greece).

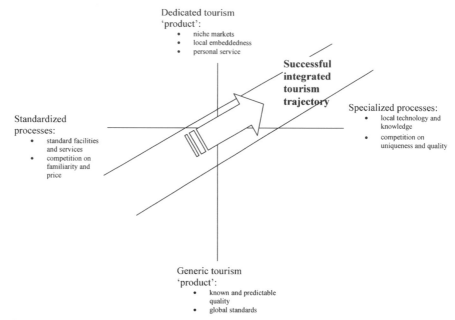

Dedicated tourism
'product':
- niche markets
- local embeddedness
- personal service

Successful integrated tourism trajectory

Standardized processes:
- standard facilities and services
- competition on familiarity and price

Specialized processes:
- local technology and knowledge
- competition on uniqueness and quality

Generic tourism
'product':
- known and predictable quality
- global standards

Fig. 2.1. Theorizing a successful trajectory for integrated tourism (after Kneafsey *et al.*, 2001).

- West (Mayo, Roscommon and Galway); North Midlands (Roscommon, Leitrim, Cavan, Longford and Westmeath) (Ireland).
- North Cataluña; Comunidad Valenciana (Spain).
- England–Wales border region (Herefordshire, Shropshire and Powys); Cumbria (UK).

All 12 destinations are designated as either Objective 1 or 2 ('lagging') regions and are thus characterized by the following: high unemployment or seasonal employment; relative remoteness from centres of economic activity; dependence on a narrow range of farm and non-farm products and services; out-migration; an ageing population. The study regions cover a range of regional circumstances and experiences, enabling a comparative analysis of the differential development of integrated tourism, and differing endowments of resources, products and activities. Preliminary findings from a review of the documentary evidence of the tourism, resources and activities of the regions have been compared against criteria which have been identified from the literature as being significant in the study of integrated tourism. These include: networks; scale; endogeneity; embeddedness; sustainability; complementarity; and empowerment (Jenkins and Oliver, 2001).

2.4.1 Networks

Integrated tourism both implies and requires a focus on networks, relationships and partnerships. Networks and relationships may be historical, providing actors

Fig. 2.2   The SPRITE study regions.

with a sense of attachment to place; or they may take newer forms, providing possibilities for new institutional structures and new types of entrepreneurial activity (Kneafsey, 2001). Further, they may be vertical, involving the formation of extra-local alliances; or they may be horizontal, coordinating local activities and local actor relationships (Murdoch, 2000a). The concept of partnerships and the associated emphasis on stakeholders, community projects and public–private finance initiatives have recently become widespread in policy thinking, along with ideas of devolution and regional development (Courlet and Pecqueur, 1991; Griffin, 1999).

A major purpose of networks which implicate producers, communities and institutions within a locality is to capture an 'organizational rent' for that locality by attracting consumers into the networks and ultimately enhancing the use value of the locality's products and services (Pecqueur, 2001). Such networks seek to create products which are both 'composite' (combining several products) and 'located' (bound to a particular place with its particular culture and history) (Jenkins and Oliver, 2001). The specific role of small and medium-sized tourism enterprises has recently been explored (Halme and Fadeeva, 2000), indicating that benefits provided by network activities (whether personal, firm-related, regional or societal) have important motivational roles in the process of sustainable development.

The SPRITE regions are characterized by a rich natural and cultural resource base and they have a variety of products and activities to offer tourists. However, these are not necessarily linked together as an 'integrated' or 'composite' group of products (Jenkins and Oliver, 2001). Although linked to a specific rural desti-nation (i.e. bound to a specific place with its particular culture and history), these products and activities may lack the involvement of institutional networks and local partnerships which constitute important mechanisms to enable economic and social integration. In other words, they just 'happen' to be offered in the same place (Esparcia *et al.*, 2002). The documentary evidence suggests that these rural destinations differ significantly in their degrees of institutional devel-opment, in their number of tourism-related partnerships and in the extent of their promotional activities. However, in recent years, EU LEADER (Liaisons Entré Actions de Développement de l'Economie Rurale) initiatives have effectively promoted cooperation and participation by local actors in the development of tourism in several of these regions, especially those with less well-established traditions of tourism, such as the Irish North Midlands and the England–Wales border (Esparcia *et al.*, 2002).

2.4.2 Scale

Scale refers to the size and extent of tourism resources and the volume and impact of tourism activities in relation to the existing economic, social, cultural and resource base. Tourism provision can range from small-scale (for example, specialized niche market tourism) to large-scale (for example, low-cost facilities relying on scale economies). Soft tourism is centred on a sense of place involving local destinations, products and communities, with limited impacts on local societies and natural environments (Jenkins and Oliver, 2001). The natural and cultural resources which characterize the SPRITE regions are inexorably linked to small-scale 'soft' tourism, and typified by small and 'micro' businesses, which are often family-run. Although sometimes making relatively little impact economically, this small-scale industry helps to preserve the vernacular architecture and tradi-tional sociocultural events which attract tourists to these cultural destinations in the first place (Fiallo-Pantziou *et al.*, 2002).

Tourism activities and resources may be spatially manifest in a number of ways: they may be concentrated at specific places; along lines (such as roads or rivers); or widely distributed throughout an area (Wall, 1997). Many of the SPRITE regions have a range of tourism products which are a widely distributed. This contributes to the dispersal of tourists, although visitors are frequently concentred at tourism 'hot spots'. For example, the ski stations in the Catalonian Pyrenees, the Auvergne, Achaïa, Evrytania and the Šumava Mountains; specific paths and routes, such as those in Cumbria, where most of the tourism resources are located within the Lake District National Park, and where the more severe visitor impacts to the destination require regular restoration; the 'mass' tourism of the Basse Normandie littoral, which contrasts with small-scale activity inland;

the Arran Islands and other specific sites on the 'tourist circuit' in the west of Ireland; and towns in inland Valencia which receive a high influx of visitors during the summer months and during local festivals. The economic benefits of such attractions can be confined to a particular place rather than being evenly distributed throughout an area (Esparcia *et al.*, 2002). However, some large-scale attractions coexist with small-scale tourist activities and infrastructure, and they effectively complement each other in terms of seasonality. For example, in the Catalonian Pyrenees, while snow tourism dominates in the winter months, nature-based and cultural activities occur during the rest of the year (Esparcia *et al.*, 2002).

2.4.3 Endogeneity

Endogenous or 'bottom-up' development strategies include those which focus on distinctive economic, environmental and cultural aspects of a destination. Developing products and services derived from such resources usually means a strong local participation, which may, in turn, increase awareness of local cultural identity (Ray, 2000; Jenkins and Oliver, 2001).

Endogeneity tends to characterize destinations with longer traditions of tourism, where local structures for promotion or development have matured. For example, in the west of Ireland, where there is an established tradition of tourism, local ownership and involvement are marked, although beneficial linkages exist with externally owned hotels, coach tour companies and craft outlets (Commins *et al.*, 2001). In the Lake District, romantic imagery has been linked to tourism since the middle of the eighteenth century (Crawshaw and Urry, 1997), and partnerships there promote local products, which are linked to place. For example, 'Made in Cumbria' promotes local goods at events within and beyond the county through their website http://www.madeincumbria.co.uk/ (Clark *et al.*, 2001).

Quality products have the potential to contribute to place distinctiveness in terms of their specific place-related characteristics, such as style, ingredients and production methods. While there is no generally agreed definition of 'quality products and services', important aspects of the concept are the satisfaction of consumer needs and a consistent level of performance and taste (Ilbery and Kneafsey, 1998; European Commission, 1999). The marketing of such products may be enhanced through labelling schemes which seek to promote particular products, usually within a defined area and often according to prescribed, but not necessarily traditional, processing techniques. Such initiatives are often associated with regions with long-established quality product markets, particularly in France (Morris *et al.*, 2001). In recent years, while traditional forms of tourism have seen a decline, such as the spa tourism in the Auvergne, shifting patterns in consumer habits have resulted in a growth in demand for quality products, which are often perceived as being inherent in more 'local' and 'natural' products (Nygard and Storstad, 1998; Morris *et al.*, 2001). In the Auvergne, cheeses that are native to specific geographical areas and 'Le Puy green lentil' (the first vegetable to receive an Appellation d'Origine Contrôlée (AOC) label) are marketed through the creation of strong local imagery and labels, such as AOC and the European Union's Protected Designation of Origin (PDO) scheme (Mamdy *et al.*, 2001).

Endogeneity is a key factor in facilitating integrated tourism. However, external agencies, actors and resources can also be critical in bringing funding, new organizational patterns and skills that may contribute to its development in a region, for example, by encouraging associations which bring together local producers and tourist service providers, or organizing training courses for those involved in tourism businesses. However, exogenous resources can also cause revenue leakages, such as in the ski regions, where facilities and services are usually operated by externally owned companies. Thus, while a combination of endogenous and exogenous forces appears to produce the optimum potential for integrated tourism, obtaining a balance is critical in making it a reality (Jenkins and Oliver, 2001; Esparcia *et al.*, 2002).

2.4.4 Sustainability

Sustainable development is a multidimensional concept: interpreted in its broadest sense, it has economic, sociocultural, political, geographical and ecological aspects (McCool and Moisey, 2001). The sustainable harnessing of resources and activities tends to lead to economic viability, resource and sociocultural conservation, while the unsustainable harnessing of resources and activities tends to lead to high rates of business failure and a deterioration of the rural destination. In many respects, 'integrated tourism' overlaps with 'sustainable tourism', recent definitions of which are becoming increasingly holistic (Swarbrooke, 1999). However, sustainable tourism remains a somewhat passive concept, concerned with minimizing tourism's impacts rather than optimizing its benefits. Integrated tourism, on the other hand, is concerned with energizing local development through the creation of new partnerships and networks which link previously disparate activities and resources (Jenkins and Oliver, 2001).

In sociocultural terms, the use of local resources by tourism brings benefit to areas by helping to sustain local cultures, traditions and heritage. In Cumbria, arts events organized by local authorities have become important in sustaining the cultural life and the dynamism of the area (Clark *et al.*, 2001). However, in the same way that tourism can contribute to the sustainability of the cultural destination, it can also play a role in its demise. In Achaïa, for example, developments relating to snow tourism are having a negative visual impact on the area's traditional architectural landscape (Esparcia *et al.*, 2002), while, in the west of Ireland, the influx of day-trippers to the Arran Islands is having a detrimental effect on traditional lifestyle (Commins *et al.*, 2001).

Tourism can have a potentially negative impact on local ecosystems and this represents one of the greatest challenges for the tourism industry. Although tourism can bring economic and social benefits to local communities, together with an improved quality of life, tourism inevitably transforms the rural destination. For example, the snow sport industry can have a negative impact upon the local living costs and lifestyles of different stakeholder groups, as well as having detrimental effects on species that cannot tolerate such widespread human disturbance (Perdue, 2004). The quality of a resource may be particularly threatened where tourism is dependent upon a limited product range, such as angling and boating along the waterways of the Irish North Midlands (Commins *et al.*, 2001). Designation can be an effective way of promoting an area for tourism while at the same time ensuring its sustainability, although, ironically, it may draw too much attention to a specific place (Hewison, 1992); for this reason, integrated approaches which focus on the wider destination are likely to be significant in preserving the future of these rural areas.

Seasonality affects the potential sustainability of tourism in economic, environmental and cultural terms. In destinations where tourism is highly seasonal, tourism tends to be concentrated during specific periods of the year, while infrastructure remains underused during the rest of the year. Thus natural and cultural resources can suffer negative impacts during a high season, while the economic viability of small tourism businesses and the stability of the local labour market can be threatened during the 'low' tourism season. The current growth in off-peak short breaks (between one and three nights' duration) in Europe, which are often independently organized, may help to ameliorate this situation. This trend is facilitated by the liberalization of air-transport markets and increased competition between surface-transport operators (British Tourist Authority, 2000; Barker, 2001).

2.4.5 Embeddedness

Embeddedness implies that resources or activities are directly linked to place, and that relationships are formed within particular sociocultural contexts in particular localities (Hinrichs, 2000; Murdoch, 2000b). Embeddedness can be said to exist where tourism activities are a part of local social and recreational life; when products enhance and commodify the local landscape; and where attractions are based on the existing natural, built, historical and cultural heritage of a region. In the SPRITE regions, examples of embedded tourist resources include local museums and ethnographic visitor centres; arts, crafts and music festivals; nature-based sports and activities; and cultural, historic and gastronomic sites and trails. The links between producers, place, products and consumers can be explicit, such as through the direct marketing technique of 'farmers' markets' that are run in some Cumbrian towns and through produce that is labelled with a specific place name (for example, 'Grasmere gingerbread'; Clark *et al.*, 2001).

Embeddedness exists when linkages appear between producers, communities, consumers and institutions and tourist resources and activities. Tourism providers and producer structures emerge in order to enhance local products and develop strategies for their management and delivery. Some of these strategies require collaboration between different actors and activities. For example, in the Auvergne 'La Route des Métiers' is an association of handcrafters, retailers, museums, châteaux and farmers which was created for the Livradois-Forez Park; this association revalorizes local products, which can be bought directly from the producer, and encourages tourism that is closely linked to territory (Mamdy *et al.*,

2001). However, embeddedness can also limit the market reach of a local tourism 'product', which will then remain marginal in relation to the globalized tourism sector. For example, in the Irish North Midlands the reliance on water-based tourism activities limits the region's attractiveness to a wider tourism market. In contrast, the west of Ireland is known for its quality foods and traditional way of life, which are preserved in the offshore islands; a number of cultural events; and the operation of summer colleges for language learning, since Gaeltacht designated areas, in which Irish is the everyday spoken language, are found along the western seaboard (Stocks, 2000). This diverse range of products attracts both national and international visitors (Commins *et al.*, 2001). Tourism needs to be both embedded and disembedded in order to remain socio-economically sustainable and viable in the long term.

2.4.6 Complementarity

Tourism itself may be complementary (for example, it may take place alongside traditional agriculture on a farm where appropriate resources for tourism are available) or substitutional (for example, it may replace farming entirely, as with caravan sites on some small coastal farms). Tourism activities may also be complementary (for example, conservation-related tourism in a protected area) or substitutional (for example, a foreign-owned all-inclusive tourist resort may conflict with local activities and lifestyle) (Jenkins and Oliver, 2001).

Cooperation between tourism stakeholders exists within the SPRITE study regions; some establish partnerships specifically to encourage this. In the Pyrenees region, traditional activities such as farming and handicrafts complement new ones such as rural tourism. The snow sport industry is becoming increasingly integrated with these other activities and skiers frequently prefer to rent houses in local villages rather than to stay in the large hotels (Esparcia *et al.*, 2002). In Cumbria, where the environment's protection is a main objective in regional policy, visitors are encouraged to become involved in conservation activities (Clark *et al.*, 2001). However, conflicts also exist between, for example, those wishing to develop the tourism sector and those wishing to maintain the traditional use of local resources. For example, in the Auvergne, there are those who wish to preserve the region's traditional economy based on cheese production, and who see the development of tourism as a threat to this traditional way of life. Tensions exist where natural resources are restricted and protected, such as in the Šumava Mountains, where local communities and businesses often perceive the National Park as restrictive and there is conflict between nature conservation initiatives and local development plans (Cudlínová *et al.*, 2001).

2.4.7 Empowerment

Empowerment is the manifestation of local control over resources and activities, the potential for which may be enhanced if products are tied or embedded to a particular place (Jenkins and Oliver, 2001). In regions where development most strongly depends on the use of local resources and products, local people tend to be more involved in the control of these resources and in the decision making processes. This is particularly evident in relation to sociocultural heritage and gastronomy. In the England–Wales borders, recent trends towards the promotion of locally based quality products, crafts and skills by the county councils are leading to the empowerment of local communities and, in Cumbria, local communities have been empowered through the organization of agricultural shows and other types of events (Clark *et al.*, 2001). The empowerment of local communities through the development of tourism in rural destinations is manifest in three key ways: (i) a greater control of local resources by local actors/structures; (ii) participation of local stakeholders in decision making relating to the development of tourism and the wider rural landscape; and (iii) an increase in communities' self-esteem (Esparcia *et al.*, 2002). For example, in inland Valencia, local communities have become encouraged by the economic potential of their region, and this is being reflected in a higher number of people deciding to stay in the area to initiate their own businesses (Esparcia *et al.*, 2002); and, in the west of Ireland, small-scale partnerships, such as LEADER initiatives, allow communities to become involved in local rural development. Business associations and voluntary and non-profit groups are also playing key roles in facilitating community participation in the decision making processes in these regions (Commins *et al.*, 2001; Esparcia *et al.*, 2002).

2.5 Conclusions

Preliminary findings from the SPRITE project indicate that a successful integrated tourism trajectory is that which moves towards dedicated and specialized (as opposed to generic and standardized) production, where non-industrial and non-commercial conventions are paramount. Niche markets, local embeddedness, personal service, local technology and knowledge, and competition on uniqueness and quality all characterize such production.

In addition, seven key characteristics of integrated tourism have been identified: networks; scale; endogeneity; embeddedness; sustainability; complementarity; and empowerment. The first of these is especially critical in the context of rural development; however, as tourism networks are established and consolidated, the distinction between 'local' and 'extra-local' and between 'endogenous' and 'exogenous' becomes less of a priority. Instead, it is cooperation (as opposed to competition) between stakeholders in these regions that enables the achievement of wider development goals. Many destinations have already developed, or strive to develop, mechanisms which facilitate participation and cooperation among a wide range of stakeholder groups. None the less, significant competition also exists between, for example, those wishing to develop the tourism sector and those aiming to maintain the traditional uses of local resources.

Acknowledgements

This chapter is based on a collaborative programme of research funded under the EU's Quality of Life and Management of Living Resources programme (QLK5-CT-2000-01211 – SPRITE) and undertaken by the Universities of Wales (Aberystwyth) (coordinators: Tove Oliver and Tim Jenkins), Caen, Patras, Ireland (Galway), Valencia, Lancaster and Coventry, together with the Institute of Landscape Ecology (České Budějovice), CEMAGREF (Clermont-Ferrand) and Teagasc (Dublin). The authors particularly wish to thank Brian Ilbery, Moya Kneafsey and Gunjan Saxena of Coventry University, for their valuable contributions towards the SPRITE conceptual framework.

References

British Tourist Authority (2000) *Digest of Tourism Statistics*, 23. British Tourist Authority, London.

Barker, L. (2001) *Short Break Holidays*. Key Note Market Report, September 2001. Available on-line at: http://www.keynote.co.uk

Butler, R.W. and Clarke, G. (1992) Tourism in rural areas: Canada and the UK. In: Bowler, I.R., Bryant, C.R. and Nellis, M.D. (eds) *Contemporary Rural Systems in Transition*. CAB International, Wallingford, UK, pp. 166–183.

Clark, G., Chabrel, M., Ilbery, B., Saxena, G. and Kneafsey, M. (2001) *Analytical Reviews of Tourism: United Kingdom (SPRITE Deliverable 3)*. Lancaster University, Lancaster.

Commins, P., Hunter, B., McDonagh, P., Cawley, M., Gillmor, D., Keane, M. and Kelly, R. (2001) *Analytical Reviews of Tourism: Ireland (SPRITE Deliverable 3)*. Teagasc, Dublin.

Courlet, C. and Pecqueur, B. (1991) Local industrial systems and externalities: an essay in typology. *Revue: Entrepreneurship and Regional Development* 3, 305–315.

Crawshaw, C. and Urry, J. (1997) Tourism and the photographic eye. In: Rojeck, C. and Urry, J. (eds) *Touring Cultures*. Routledge, London, pp. 176–195.

Cudlínová, E., Bartoš, M., Kušová, D., Lapka, M., Maxa, J. and Těšitel, J. (2001) *Analytical Reviews of Tourism: Czech Republic (SPRITE Deliverable 3)*. Academy of Sciences of the Czech Republic, České Budějovice.

Esparcia, J., Buciega, A., Pitarch, M. and Pérez, M. (2002) *Consolidated Analytical Review of Tourism (SPRITE Deliverable 5)*. Universitat de València, Valencia.

European Commission (1999) *Towards Quality Rural Tourism: Integrated Quality Management of Rural Tourist Destinations*. European Commission, Brussels.

Fiallo-Pantziou, E., Petrou, A. and Skuras, D. (2002) *Consolidated Analytical Review of Resources and Activities (SPRITE Deliverable 4)*. University of Patras, Patras.

Griffin, K.A. (1999) The inter organisational relationships in Irish tourism: the case of Lough Derg. *Irish Geography* 32, 58–72.

Halme, M. and Fadeeva, Z. (2000) Small and medium-sized tourism enterprises in sustainable development networks: value added? *Greener Management International* 30, 97–113.

Hewison, R. (1992) The future of the pastoral. In: Council of Europe (ed.) *Management of Public Access to the Heritage Landscape*. European colloquy jointly organized by the Council of Europe and the Office of Public Works (Ireland), Dublin, 16–18 September 1991. Council of Europe, Strasburg, pp. 49–54.

Hinrichs, C. (2000) Embeddedness and local food systems: notes on two types of direct agricultural market. *Journal of Rural Studies* 18, 295–303.

Hopkins, J. (1998) Commodifying the countryside: marketing myths of rurality. In: Butler, R.W., Hall, C.M. and Jenkins, J.M. (eds) *Tourism and Recreation in Rural Areas*. Wiley, Chichester, UK, pp. 139–156.

Ilbery, B. and Kneafsey, M. (1998) Product and place: promoting quality products and services in the lagging rural regions of the European Union. *European Urban and Regional Studies* 5, 329–341.

Jenkins, T. and Oliver, T. (2001) *Integrated Tourism: A Conceptual Framework (SPRITE Deliverable 1)*. University of Wales, Aberystwyth.

Kneafsey, M. (2001) Rural cultural economy: tourism and social relations. *Annals of Tourism Research* 28, 762–783.

Kneafsey, M., Ilbery, B. and Jenkins, T. (2001) Exploring the dimensions of culture economies in rural west Wales. *Sociologia Ruralis* 41, 296–310.

Long, P. and Lane, B. (2000) Rural tourism development. In: Gartner, W.C. and Lime, D.W. (eds) *Trends in Outdoor Recreation, Leisure and Tourism*. CAB International, Wallingford, UK, pp. 299–308.

McCool, S.F. and Moisey, R.N. (2001) *Tourism, Recreation and Sustainability*. CAB International, Wallingford, UK, 355 pp.

McIntyre, G. (1997) *Développement d'un tourisme durable: Guide à l'intention des planificateurs locaux*. World Tourism Organization, Madrid.

Mamdy, J. F., Marsat, J. B., Pitot, B., Tirard, D., Bensliman, O. and Legac, G. (2001) *Analytical Reviews of Tourism: France (SPRITE Deliverable 3)*. Cemagref, Clermont-Ferrand.

Mitchell, R.E. and Eagles, P.F.J. (2001) An integrative approach to tourism: lessons from the Andes of Peru. *Journal of Sustainable Tourism* 9, 4–28.

Morris, C., Buller, H., Ilbery, B., Kneafsey, M. and Maye, D. (2001) *Foreign Product Labelling Schemes and their Applicability to the UK*. University of Gloucestershire, Cheltenham, UK.

Murdoch, J. (2000a) Networks: a new paradigm of rural development? *Journal of Rural Studies* 16, 407–419.

Murdoch, J. (2000b) Quality, nature and embeddedness: some theoretical considerations in the context of the food sector. *Economic Geography* 76, 107–125.

Nygard, B. and Storstad, O. (1998) Deglobalisation of food markets? Consumer perceptions of safe food. *Sociologia Ruralis* 38, 35–53.

Page, S.J. and Getz, D. (1997) The business of rural tourism: international perspectives. In: Page, S.J. and Getz, D. (ed.) *The Business of Rural Tourism*. International Thomson Business Press, London, pp. 3–37.

Pecqueur, B. (2001) Qualité et développement territorial: l'hypothèse du panier des biens et de services territorialisées. *Économie Rurale* 261, 37–49.

Perdue, R.R. (2001) Sustainable tourism and stakeholder groups: a case study of Colorado ski resort communities. In: Crouch, G.I., Perdue, R.R., Timmermans, H. and Uysal, M. (eds) *Consumer Psychology of Tourism, Hospitality and Leisure*, Vol. 3. CAB International, Wallingford, UK, pp. 253–264.

Ray, C. (2000) *Endogenous Socio-Economic Development and Trustful Relationships*. Centre for Rural Economy, Newcastle, UK.

Salais, R. and Storper, M. (1992) The four worlds of contemporary production. *Cambridge Journal of Economics* 16, 169–193.

Sharpley, R. (2000) Tourism and sustainable development: exploring the theoretical divide. *Journal of Sustainable Tourism* 8, 1–19.

Slováčková, P. (2000) Vacation smelling of manure – ecological tourism. *Ekonom* 44, 48–49 (in Czech).

Stabler, M.J. (1997) *Tourism and Sustainability*. CAB International, Wallingford, UK, 381 pp.

Stocks, J. (2000) Sustaining tourism and culture in the Donegal Gaeltacht. In: Robinson, M. Long, P., Evans, N., Sharpley, R. and Swarbrooke, J. (eds) *Expressions of Culture, Identity and Meaning in Tourism*. Centre for Travel and Tourism and Business Education, Sunderland, UK, pp. 375–384.

Storper, M. and Salais, R. (1997) *Worlds of Production: the Action Frameworks of the Economy*. Harvard University Press, Cambridge, Massachusetts, 370 pp.

Swarbrooke, J. (1999) *Sustainable Tourism Management*. CAB International, Wallingford, UK, 371 pp.

Wall, G. (1997) Tourism attractions: points, lines, and areas. *Annals of Tourism Research* 24, 240–243.

3

The Peripherality, Tourism and Competitiveness Mix: Contradictory or Confirmed?

FIONA WILLIAMS[1] AND MARSAILI MACLEOD[2]

[1]Land Economy Research, Scottish Agricultural College, Aberdeen, UK;
[2]Department of Geography, Aberdeen University, Aberdeen, UK

3.1 Introduction

Although peripheral regions may possess characteristics that have traditionally been considered a constraint on economic activity (such as the high cost of travel, lack of agglomerative advantages, distance from markets), the economic dimension of tourism demands destination features often associated with remote areas. On the one hand, the material nature of the production and consumption of tourism converts peripheral characteristics into components of socio-economic development, to be used as a means of reducing or overcoming peripheral disadvantage. Conversely, the symbolic nature of the tourist production and consumption system means that conventional peripherality and its associated characteristics can acquire a distinct meaning and, in certain situations, can constitute the basis of specific tourist products or represent an added value for certain tourist activities (Gomez Martin and Lopez Palomeque, 2001).

This chapter illustrates the contribution of peripherality to the competitiveness of tourism in rural regions using empirical data from two contrasting areas in Scotland: East Ayrshire, a relatively accessible region, and the Shetland Islands, a peripheral region. The objectives are twofold: first, to demonstrate the extent to which peripherality is associated with characteristics which are positively perceived by consumers; and secondly, to explore to what degree such peripheral characteristics can add value to the tourism product.

We begin by briefly considering the issue of competitiveness with respect to tourism in rural areas and that of differentiation based on peripherality. After outlining the key aspects of the methodological approach, a selection of findings relating to the Scottish case study areas are presented, namely:

- The nature of the tourism product in each study area.
- The conventional characteristics and barriers for tourism development associated with peripheral and accessible locations.

©CAB International 2005. *Tourism SMEs, Service Quality and Destination Competitiveness*
(eds E. Jones and C. Haven-Tang)

- The experiential and cultural characteristics associated with peripheral location by consumers.
- A comparison of the above with the perceived characteristics associated with a relatively more accessible location.
- A discussion relating to the wider processes, structures and issues bearing influence on the development of the tourism product in the study areas.

3.2 Tourism and Rural Competitiveness

Tourism development necessitates a number of prerequisites: resources and attractions, infrastructure, investment, labour and promotion. When these are present, different processes of development occur which are associated with contrasting spatial patterns and forms, varying levels of concentration and dispersal of tourists in different geographical contexts (Williams, 1998). While it is fully acknowledged that not all peripheral areas are rural and not all rural areas are peripheral, much of that written with respect to peripherality and tourism is set within the rural tourism field.

As a rule, conventional peripherality is not associated with the types of tourism that draw upon inner cities or old industrial sites – though such areas may suffer from sociological marginality. Hall and Jenkins (1998) refer to the emergence of geographically marginal peripheral areas as a major regional and rural subtype which is increasingly distinct from the more viable core regions.

Wanhill (1997: 2) also refers to 'rural' when he describes areas that are indicative of peripherality within the tourism context – 'sparsely populated: small towns or villages in rural or coastal locations that are relatively isolated'. Indeed, as far as the European Union (EU) is concerned, peripheral areas are equated with 'rural and agricultural areas' (Richardson, 2000: 59). Here we take a broad view to encompass the many ways in which tourism manifests itself in peripheral areas. In other words, we refer to tourism that is to all extents and purposes reliant on the natural and cultural resources present in peripheral areas; such resources are also characteristic of rural areas and are therefore commonly described as 'rural' in tourism literature.

In a climate of rural restructuring, tourism is increasingly establishing itself as a vehicle for economic development – an outcome of which is a fiercely competitive market place for rural tourism products. Marketing aimed at realizing the potential market value of rural resources is increasingly viewed as an important tool for rural development but is often considered as the weak link in the development and diversification process. An indifference to marketing frequently arises from the costs involved, the small scale of individual producers and the undifferentiated nature of their products.

The issues of marketing and market performance are linked inextricably to the concepts of 'competitive advantage' and 'competitiveness'. The former represents the potential of an enterprise, sector or economy to perform better than its competitors, while in the context of relatively free markets, competitiveness can be defined as a sustained ability to profitably gain and maintain market share (Martin *et al.*, 1991).

If an industry or a region is competitive, it is because its constituent businesses have competitive advantages (Porter, 1985). These may take the form of low costs, which provide the ability to compete through low prices or by differentiation (being different from the competition in a manner which consumers value and for which they are prepared to pay). Rural enterprises, by their very nature, tend to follow a differentiation approach and frequently focus on a particular niche or segment of the market. Differentiation can either be 'supply-side' or 'demand-side' based (Craig and Grant, 1993). Supply-side differentiation comes through a firm's ability to add uniqueness to the products or services it supplies. These opportunities arise through the methods of production or delivery, the quality of the human resource, the level of customer service or the quality of management activities including marketing. Demand-side differentiation relies on a firm's ability to understand customer and consumer demand and to match a demand for difference with its own product or service and associated marketing mix (features of the product, its pricing, promotion and means of sale). It is therefore dependent on an understanding of customers and consumers and their needs and wants, and this may be gained through either formal or informal market research.

3.3 Perspectives on Peripherality and Competitiveness

A classification provided by Copus (2001) is a useful means by which to consider the spatial peripherality issues present in the tourism literature. Conventional concepts of peripheral disadvantage are classified into three broad groups: the causal, contingent and associated. Causal elements include increased travel or transport costs and the absence of agglomerative advantage, both as a result of remoteness relative to the main population centres or hubs of economic activity. Contingent elements of peripheral disadvantage are consequential upon the causal elements, such as the high cost of service provision. Finally, the third group of elements are associated with peripherality, although the causal links are less direct.

Tourism authors frequently adopt supply-side perspectives on tourism and often describe peripheral areas as possessing certain (seemingly objective) characteristics, in particular, the existence of a number of development barriers accruing from the destination's location. Such characteristics fit neatly into the classification provided by Copus (2001).

First, consider the causal elements of the classification in relation to the tourism literature. There have been attempts to model transport mode selection (see, for example, Mill, 1992) and identify common decision variables (such as availability, frequency, cost/price, speed/time and comfort/luxury). The inhibitive aspects of the distance decay function on travel decisions are incorporated in such models. For example, Prideaux (2000) concludes that increased distance generally leads to increased transport access costs and assumes greater importance within the total holiday cost. Absence of agglomerative advantage has also been cited as a barrier to tourism development in remote locations – the latter characterized by firms that are predominantly small to medium in size (small and medium-sized enterprises (SMEs)). Wanhill (1997) highlights a number of weaknesses in tourism SMEs that can be attributed to lack of agglomerative advantage, thus acting as barriers to tourism development. These include transaction and information costs inhibitive to obtaining knowledge, and supply dominated by family businesses with limited business skills.

Secondly, contingent elements include limited market opportunities or markets in decline, limited ability to appreciate market needs and demands, little statistical information or market research and a lack of strategic management (Wanhill and Buhalis, 1999). Finally, barriers associated with peripherality include seasonality coupled with poor climate, a lack of tourist infrastructure, and that tourism alternatives are usually primary resource economies with small manufacturing bases.

On the other hand, the very aspects considered prohibitive to tourism development in the literature can actually form the basis of the tourism resource. Distance itself may become a function of a destination's popularity. There are positive characteristics contingent upon a region's distance from centres of population, namely, remote natural environments. Furthermore, embedded in peripheral localities are local identities which form the 'culture' or 'essence' of an area and effectively provide further resources available for development by local actors (Ray, 1999). These resources are inextricably linked with the local territory and can be strategically used to add value to local products and services and to create positive images that motivate people to visit. Therefore, many of the conditions of marginal territories embody features which act as a product plus and have the potential to be beneficial to tourism development.

These issues have implications for tourism in marginal areas. Changes in the needs and tastes of demand in the sector and the consolidation of new types of tourism mean that elements previously rejected are now recognized as tourist resources. Gomez Martin and Lopez Palomeque (2001: 1) attribute this to a 'process of social and cultural re-evaluation' of the attributes of marginality.

In response to the discussion above, we argue that peripherality can be defined, and behaviour influenced by the subjective perceptions of a place and not just by objective criteria, i.e. distance from the core. Fennell (1996: 826) suggests that the 'periphery may be represented by experiential, environmental or cultural phenomena or symbols, which may include lochs, mountains, wind, solitude, barrenness, a rainforest, or lack of banking machines'. The purpose of this research is to develop our understanding of how positive perceptions of peripheral areas held by potential consumers can be used to gain competitive advantage, with a view to ameliorating the commonly associated negative implications of peripherality.

3.4 Methodology

The findings reported here draw upon integrated case study fieldwork of a European Fifth Framework Project entitled, 'Aspatial Peripherality, Innovation and the

Rural Economy' (AsPIRE). The AsPIRE project explores a range of processes increasingly emerging to compound or distort the handicaps conventionally associated with remote locations through a range of themes: social capital; business networks; governance; information and communications technology, and tourism. The methodological instruments utilized formed part of the AsPIRE project's case study work, undertaken in the six countries represented in the research team.[1] Three primary data collection instruments were used in each of the case study areas: a visitor survey, business survey and organizational survey (Table 3.1).

A face-to-face visitor survey was conducted with 50 visitors in each Scottish study area. Consequently this questionnaire was relatively short (intended to take no longer than 10 minutes to dispatch) and the questions were largely closed. Both factual and perceptual information was sought from visitors with questions targeted at the collection of behavioural and attitudinal data and those for purposes of classification. Likert rating scales (relating to designative attributes of the areas) and verbal bipolar scales (relating to evaluative attributes of the areas) were included.

There was limited information available regarding the numbers and nature of visitors to the study regions, i.e. there was no all-encompassing, coherent sampling frame. Hence the surveys were dependent on using a range of sample sources available in the study areas, namely visitor attractions, transport terminals and accommodation providers. These sample sources are obviously subject to seasonality constraints and visitor movements. A combination of quota and purposive sampling techniques was adopted. A distinction was made (as far as available information allowed) between different segments of the market and, given the information available, an approximate representative (quota) sample was used. Interviews were 'staggered' as far as possible, in season and to encompass weekends and weekdays.

The business survey utilized a questionnaire for face-to-face interviews with entrepreneurs in the study areas. A total of ten tourism-related enterprises was surveyed in each area. The organizational survey was designed to encompass both public/statutory, quasi-public and third-sector organizations involved with the promotion and/or development of tourism in the study regions. The questionnaire was semi-structured, consisting of open and closed questions. Some of the questions were attitudinal and involved Likert rating scales.

Table 3.1. Type and number of interviews.

Survey type	No. of interviews	
	Shetland	E. Ayrshire
Visitor	50	50
Business	10	10
Organization	3	4

3.5 Tourism Management in Scotland

Prior to introducing the case study areas, it is useful to provide a brief outline of the current structure of tourism promotion and development within Scotland. The management of tourism in Scotland has undergone and continues to undergo rapid change as the requirements of consumers and businesses change. Widening access to Internet information, centralized booking systems, cheaper travel and the assertion of niche marketing have influenced a reorganization process within public-sector tourism structures. The recently rebranded VisitScotland (the former Scottish Tourist Board) is the dedicated national organization responsible for tourism development and for the delivery of the National Tourism Strategy. A network of 14 area tourist boards (ATBs) undertakes the marketing and promotion of tourism at the regional level, with a responsibility for leading the delivery of area tourism strategies in partnership with the tourism industry. Shetland Isles Tourism and Ayrshire and Arran Tourist Board are the respective tourist boards for Shetland and East Ayrshire. The ATBs are currently funded by grant aid from VisitScotland and local authorities, combined with commercial income. The business development, marketing and training function for tourism lies with the Local Enterprise Companies.

The functionality of the existing Scottish ATB network is currently under scrutiny. As part of an ongoing Scottish Parliament Inquiry into Tourism in Scotland, an ATB Review is currently being undertaken at the request of the Minister for Tourism, Culture and Sport. The ATB Review has been instigated by disquiet within the trade about the effectiveness of ATBs, common concern regarding the geographical levels at which tourism-related functions are delivered, and the cost-effectiveness of current delivery systems. Indubitably, the outcomes of the Review will affect the delivery of tourism development and support within the two case study areas.

3.6 The Study Areas

3.6.1 Shetland

The Shetland Isles (study area A) is the most peripheral unitary authority area within the UK, closer to Bergen than to the Scottish capital of Edinburgh. In terms of straight-line distance it is situated almost 1000 km from London, and it lies on latitude 61° north, equitable with Helsinki. A total population of 22,740 occupies 16 of the 100-plus islands in the archipelago (Shetland Islands Council, 2001). Although sparsely populated by UK or European standards, Shetland supports twice the number of inhabitants per square kilometre than the Highlands and Islands region (with a land mass of 1468 km^2). The population is concentrated in the main seaport town of Lerwick (7270) and the remainder is dispersed across the traditional crofting settlements and larger villages (Shetland Islands Council, 2001).

The main sources of economic activity are the fisheries and aquaculture sector, the North Sea oil industry, tourism and agriculture. Like many other rural regions, public services are also a significant employer. Despite numerous physical handicaps, Shetland has a consistently low unemployment rate, currently 1.5% (NOMIS, 2002); yet its continued success is strongly reliant on cost-efficient internal and external transport links necessary to sustain its fragile industries. Existing external sea and air links to the Scottish mainland, through the Lerwick ferry terminal and Sumburgh airport, are vital for the heavy traditional industries transporting heavy goods and raw materials and for supporting potential growth in the tourism industry.

An estimated 458 people are employed in the Shetland tourism accommodation sector, and a further 500 work in tourism-related enterprises (MacPherson Research, 2001). The islands have developed a low-volume/high-value tourism product which is strongly dependent upon the areas rich natural environment, the flora and fauna and prehistoric remains. Foremost attractions include the National Nature Reserves of Hermaness and Noss and the designated bird reserve of Sumburgh Head, followed by prehistoric settlements, the Broch of Mousa and the multi-period settlement Jarlshof. A burgeoning number of community-managed built attractions provide an ancillary service product, though on a relatively small scale. The 2000 Visitor Survey states that 47,179 visitors injected some £11.91 million into the island economy, of which business visitors generated over 40%. There is a degree of seasonal variation in the composition of visitors, with holiday visits concentrated between May and July, with a corresponding drop in business travel. Distance from markets and high transport costs are considered significant handicaps for all aspects of the islands' economic activity, but, from a tourism perspective, improving accessibility of the islands to key visitor market segments (Fig. 3.1) is considered fundamental for utilizing the natural and cultural resources to their full potential.

3.6.2 East Ayrshire

By way of contrast, the unitary authority area of East Ayrshire's (study area B) tourism potential is derived from its relative closeness to the main centres of population in Scotland and northern England. The area is located within 35 km south-west of the Glasgow conurbation, linked by good-quality rail and road networks, and some 500 km from London. Neighbouring North Ayrshire also

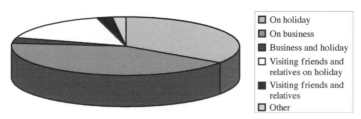

Fig. 3.1. Purpose of visit to Shetland (2000).

hosts Glasgow Prestwick International Airport. The industrial town of Kilmarnock is the main administrative centre, with a population of approximately 31,000. Outside Kilmarnock, in the neighbouring Irvine Valley and southern Cumnock and Doon Valley areas, smaller traditional textile and ex-mining settlements account for the majority of the remaining 89,900 inhabitants (Mittial Research, 2000).

Historically, coal mining, iron and steel smelting and textiles dominated the East Ayrshire economy. Decades of decline during the latter half of the last century, however, eradicated the coal, iron and steel-making industry and today only associated engineering companies and a few specialist textile and clothing companies remain. During the latter half of the 1990s East Ayrshire suffered significant job losses of 35% in the manufacturing sector and, despite inward investment by major international companies in growth sectors (tourism, pharmaceuticals, micro-electronics, civil aviation), job losses continue to exceed job creation (Ayrshire Economic Forum, 2000). At 71%, gross domestic product (GDP) per capita is a fifth below the UK average, and the area suffers from consistently high unemployment rates – currently 5.6%.

Tourism continues to be perceived as a growth industry in East Ayrshire, as it can potentially benefit from close proximity to traditional Ayrshire coastal resorts, golf attractions and business tourism generated from Prestwick airport. Contrary to other areas of the Ayrshire and Arran Tourist Board area (East Ayrshire is one of three local authority areas which fall under the jurisdiction of the Tourist Board), East Ayrshire's tourism product is less well developed. The product derives its main iconic appeal from the area's industrial heritage and the national poet Robert Burns. In addition, East Ayrshire has relatively undeveloped natural resources, including natural lochs, woodlands and internationally significant moorland areas. Figures available for Ayrshire and Arran as a whole state that, in 2000, 1 million people visited the region; yet little is known about the distribution of tourists throughout the region, which includes East Ayrshire. Figures (ScotExchange, 2000) reveal that the majority of tourists visit the Ayrshire and Arran region for holiday purposes (Fig. 3.2); however, the East Ayrshire market is dominated by day visitors either from people on holiday on the Ayrshire coast or from residents on day-trips from nearby population centres. Main attractions include Deans Castle and Country Park in Kilmarnock town (the most visited attraction in Ayrshire, which 295,000 people visited in 2000), the Dunaskin Visitor Centre, an industrial heritage site, and Loudoun Castle theme park.

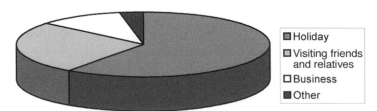

Fig. 3.2. Purpose of visit to Ayrshire and Arran (2000).

In addition to only a narrowly based tourism product, East Ayrshire's specific problems in terms of competitiveness relate to:

- Deficiencies in the range and quality of tourist accommodation and facilities.
- A lack of tourist attractions in rural areas.
- A lack of recognition of the area as a tourist destination in its own right, with many potential visitors passing through *en route* to the Ayrshire coast.

As a result of the above, although tourism-related employment accounts for 9% of all employment in Ayrshire and Arran, it is thought to be substantially lower for East Ayrshire. Consequently, although data are not available, the share of the estimated £171 million expenditure per annum spent in Ayrshire and Arran is expected to be disproportionate and heavily in favour of North and South Ayrshire.

3.7 Indicative Findings

3.7.1 The nature of visitors to the study regions

The Scottish element of the AsPIRE visitor survey highlighted significant differences in the purpose of visit to the two areas (Fig. 3.3). In Shetland, 43 of the visitors interviewed were away from home on holiday, whereas 20 of those interviewed in East Ayrshire were on a day-trip. Consequently, the length of stay reflected this, with the group of visitors to Shetland either being on a short break (2–5 nights) or a main holiday (7 or 14 nights), staying in self-catering or serviced accommodation. In East Ayrshire, of those staying overnight (often in other parts of Ayrshire as opposed to East Ayrshire), there was a propensity towards staying with friends or relatives.

In both areas, travelling as a couple or family was most prevalent, though there was a greater number of families in the East Ayrshire sample (29 as compared with ten in Shetland). Eleven visitors were travelling alone in Shetland. As can be seen in Fig. 3.4, the majority of interviewees in Shetland fell into

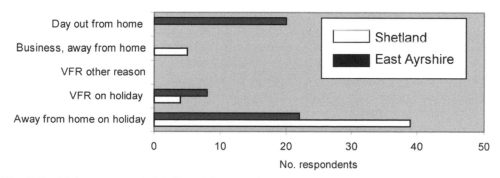

Fig. 3.3. Main purpose of visit (Scottish survey).

the 65+ age category, with the remainder being fairly evenly distributed among the other age categories. In East Ayrshire the most prominent age group was 35–44, with nearly half the sample belonging to this group. Higher earners (incomes) were evident in Shetland (Fig. 3.5) with ten of the sample having a combined income of between £41,000 and £55,000 and an additional nine between £56,000 and £70,000+. Fourteen of the Shetland sample preferred to quote 'retired' as opposed to giving an income figure. In East Ayrshire, the majority of the sample fell into the lower income brackets (£10,000–40,000).

Almost half of the visitors to Shetland interviewed were of the opinion that goods and services on the island were inexpensive and four-fifths considered they were getting value for money (40/50). A greater number of the East Ayrshire sample (33/50) considered the area to be expensive, though these visitors were strongly of the opinion that they were getting value for their money.

What we see in the results is a reflection of the type of tourism present in the study areas. As stated previously the Shetland Islands have developed a low-volume/high-value tourism product, targeted at those segments with greater spending power (tending to be older empty-nesters). Conversely, East Ayrshire tends to cater for the day visitor and predominantly family market, drawing upon the large population centres nearby.

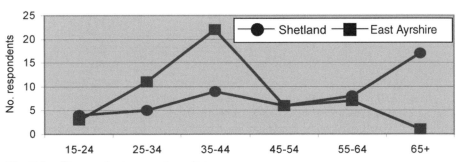

Fig. 3.4. Respondent age categories.

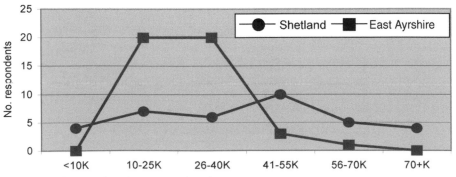

Fig. 3.5. Respondent income categories.

3.7.2 Aspects of accessibility to the study areas

Transport infrastructure both to and on the Shetland Isles is well developed, largely because of the investments made as a result of the levies imposed on oil-related activity related to the Sullom Voe oil terminal. While such investment has obviously benefited the islands' economy, the business generated by the construction and operation of the terminal, combined with an absence of airline competition, has inflated the cost of air travel. The type of transport used for travel strongly reflected the location of the two areas and the origin of the visitors. The vast majority of visitors to East Ayrshire had arrived by private car (44), whereas visitors interviewed in Shetland had arrived by plane (25) and/or boat/ferry (28), either hiring cars (18) or taking private cars (13) across with them.

Respondents in both study areas were asked to consider whether the area that they had visited was 'accessible'. Visitors to Shetland were somewhat divided in opinion, as shown in Fig. 3.6. The cost of access, however, shifted the balance more towards inaccessibility, with the majority of respondents considering the area to be costly to travel to.

> It's easy to get here as long as you have the cash.
>> (English visitor, Shetland, 2002)

> The cost of getting here is astronomic . . . It is one of the most expensive places to come to [in the world].
>> (English visitor, Shetland, 2002)

> All it is is a plane ride over [but] you could go to New York for half the cost of coming up here.
>> (American visitor, Shetland, 2002)

The vast majority of respondents in East Ayrshire considered that study area to be very accessible, if somewhat costly in terms of travel. Therefore, while in conventional terms Shetland is a peripheral region, visitors to the area did not consider it inaccessible as such; rather, it was perceived as expensive to travel to the island (Fig. 3.6). Despite the majority of visitors to East Ayrshire using their private car for transport, as opposed to costly ferry and air services, the cost of travel was still deemed to be expensive.

Accessibility (in terms of cost) was recognized by local tourism enterprises interviewed for the business survey in Shetland. Indeed, every tourism business interviewed cited the high cost of travel to Shetland as the most significant barrier to development.

> It's not a problem when they're here – it's getting them here.
>> (Boat trip operator, Shetland, 2002)

> The cost of travel is strangling tourism business and tourist markets. It's inaccessible in terms of cost.
>> (Hotelier, Shetland, 2002)

> We've had people cancel because of the cost of getting here.
>> (Self-catering provider, Shetland, 2002)

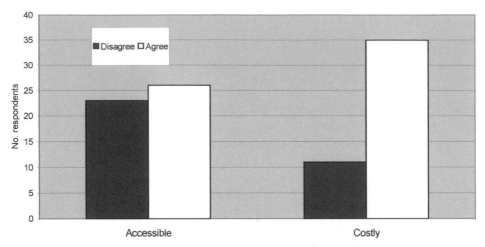

Fig. 3.6. Perceptions of accessibility among visitors to Shetland.

However, it was in many cases acknowledged that the high costs of access did deter mass-market activity (the cruise market aside) and tended to encourage higher income, older and more specialist market segments. Indeed, the results of the visitor survey would appear to support such an argument, as did the institutions in Shetland with a remit for tourism development (namely, the ATB, the Local Enterprise Company (LEC) and the Island Council). Wildlife, archaeology, history and music were given as examples of particular product categories targeted at such specialist markets.

> Shetland can never be mainstream, it is not a family destination. It will attract AB's and 'empty nesters', we have to tap into that. What we need to sell are things such as wildlife – a very mature and specialist market.
>
> (LEC, Shetland, 2002)

3.7.3 Peripherality and the tourism product

The association between distance/cost and specialist markets brings us to the associated characteristics of peripherality. From the perspective of businesses and institutions, the unique selling features of Shetland were seen as wildlife, landscape and natural beauty, archaeology, history and cultural identity.

> It's tranquil and unspoilt . . . it's not for the weather, let's face it. Nature wise, archaeological Viking heritage – it's a unique place to sell.
>
> (Hotelier, Shetland, 2002)

> There are all sorts of angles – birds, crafts, music . . . it's fascinating.
>
> (Tour Guide, Shetland, 2002)

Any relationship between these attributes and Shetland's peripheral status is subject to further analysis. However the feeling of being away from mainstream population bases (and elements associated with the core) was apparent within the visitor survey.

I wanted to come somewhere where there wasn't a MacDonald's [*sic*].

(American visitor, Shetland, 2002)

Do you know what is great about here – there are no coffee bars, no Costa's and no Starbuck's.

(American visitor, Shetland, 2002)

With reference to perceptions of the product offerings, a significant number of visitor interviewees in Shetland were in strong agreement with statements about Shetland such as 'attractive natural heritage; appealing historic sites; interesting local culture and traditions; friendly local people; and interesting wildlife'. As seen in Table 3.2, with the exception of 'friendly local people' and 'attractive natural heritage', responses from the East Ayrshire visitors were less conclusive. 'Interesting wildlife' and 'interesting industrial heritage' did not score highly, nor did 'interesting local culture and traditions'. Compared with Shetland, however, the visitors to East Ayrshire considered the scope of sporting activities and recreational opportunities to be greater.

Inclement weather and seasonality are elements commonly associated with peripherality and tourism in peripheral areas, and such elements were considered to be obstacles in the development and promotion of tourism in Shetland. However, particular activities, projects and approaches to development were going some way towards alleviating these problems. The season is extended through the means of various festivals and events, the traditional 'Up Helly Aa' (the Viking Festival held in March to signify the transition from winter to spring), the Shetland Folk Festival (May) and the Walking Festival (September) being

Table 3.2. Visitor survey results – attractions and activities statements (A, Shetland; B, Ayrshire).

Attractions/activities statements	Disagree strongly		Disagree slightly		Agree slightly		Agree strongly	
	A	B	A	B	A	B	A	B
Good recreational opportunities	1	–	3	1	15	21	16	25
Good sporting activities	–	–	3	1	10	22	7	19
Attractive natural heritage	–	–	–	–	8	19	40	31
Interesting industrial heritage	1	3	5	22	23	13	0	0
Appealing historic sites	–	1	1	2	16	24	31	21
Interesting local culture and traditions	–	3	–	10	12	24	33	11
Friendly local people	–	–	2	1	–	6	47	43
Interesting wildlife	–	–	–	7	2	30	46	7
Appealing summer climate	2	12	11	28	23	8	8	2
Appealing winter climate	10	13	5	27	2	6	2	1

examples of this. Community tourism also has an important role to play in the maintenance and support of local business (leisure and tourism) activities and attractions throughout the winter months.

While poor weather was played down in promotional activities, it was widely accepted that, providing visitors could arrive in Shetland (which has a reputation for summer fog), they were not always in anticipation of good weather. Interestingly enough, visitors interviewed in Shetland were more likely to perceive Shetland as having an appealing summer climate than their counterparts in East Ayrshire (Table 3.2).

3.7.4 Peripherality and 'the experience'

The final group of attributes to consider are those 'attractive' to visitors in an experiential sense. In addition to the more tangible products and services cited by businesses and tourism development organizations, other more subjective selling features were cited.

Peace, quiet, lack of pollution.

(Café owner, Shetland, 2002)

Clean, fresh air, beautiful, safe, lack of pollution, safe and interesting . . . not full of louts.

(Tour guide, Shetland, 2002)

Escape, a little bit different, the break, a change.

(Self-catering provider, Shetland, 2002)

Unique, in that houses won't be locked and no one locks their cars.

(Hotelier, Shetland, 2002)

Indeed, these attributes were supported by the initial results from the visitor survey, when visitors were asked what attracted them to Shetland.

I wanted something remote and tranquil.

(Scottish visitor, Shetland, 2002)

I like wild places.

(English visitor, Shetland, 2002)

Its remoteness.

(Australian visitor, Shetland, 2002)

For the natural world and the environment.

(Italian visitor, Shetland, 2002)

Visitors to both regions were asked to consider the evaluative attributes of each area on a bipolar scale (1–5) with opposing descriptors at each end of the scale, for example 'relaxing' as opposed to 'distressing'. The data (Fig. 3.7) for Shetland visitors was strongly biased towards relaxing, fascinating, pleasant, safe, uncrowded and solitude. Conversely, the equivalent descriptors for East Ayrshire did not rank as highly (Fig. 3.8).

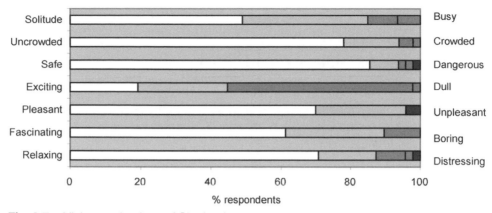

Fig. 3.7. Visitor evaluations of Shetland.

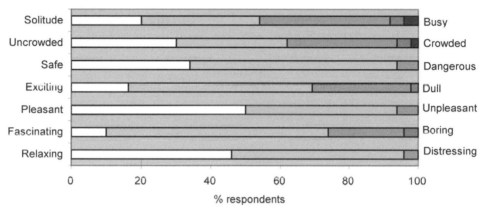

Fig. 3.8. Visitor evaluations of East Ayrshire.

There were some among the institutional representatives that considered that such angles on the Shetland product could be promoted more heavily. A Tourist Board Director was quoted as being of the opinion that low crime, escape and getting away from it were promotional messages that required more attention. Existing promotion focused upon the themes of 'the natural world', 'outdoor adrenalin rush', 'ancient echoes' and 'clean and green'. Such positional characteristics were deemed less relevant in the East Ayrshire area, with a greater emphasis on fun-packed family entertainment and value for money. This is again indicative of the nature of the product and corresponding markets in the two areas.

In the AsPIRE project, peripheral and more accessible area(s) data are available from another five countries, allowing for a larger data set that has been subjected to more rigorous data analysis, using multivariate analysis techniques (factor and cluster analysis). In this chapter, elements of the organizational and business surveys undertaken in Scotland have been used to provide contextual information and illustrate some of the points made.

While what has been undertaken is a very basic analysis, some indicative findings can be drawn from these results, which would appear to favour the proposed hypotheses. Thus the findings suggest that our peripheral study region can and does draw upon 'local identity' to add value to its tourism product and that this identity is a function of the area's peripherality. In addition, visitors associate particular destination attributes with perceived distance from the core. Also, perceptions of peripherality differ between market segments and this leads to different propensities to visit the periphery. By investigating these issues further, we hope to understand more fully the subjective perceptions of peripherality and how they can be harnessed for purposes of economic development.

In the next section we place the initial results into the context of competitive advantage, and conclude with a proposed structure from which to consider elements worthy of further analysis.

3.8 A Marketing Perspective on Peripherality and the Sourcing of Competitive Advantage

In an increasingly competitive rural tourism marketplace new ways are emerging as means to differentiate tourism products and services. While peripherality is a complex notion, what is important in terms of tourism is that peripherality or associated attributes can contribute towards 'positional' characteristics, i.e. those that can give goods and services (or companies, or destinations) a competitive advantage over rivals.

Previous research has shown that peripherality as a concept is subject to different interpretations and, although a number of indicators exist that relate to conventional peripherality (such as accessibility indicators derived from travel time and cost models), measurements of other characteristics of peripherality are less prevalent. Figure 3.9 attempts to categorize peripheral elements into three main groups (ranging from the objective, as in conventional peripherality, to the subjective, as in those area attributes associated with peripherality). Linkages between each of these can be termed substantive, in that they are objective and easily identifiable, or subjective, in that they are experiential, lying in the eye of the beholder.

As discussed in section 3.2 (Tourism and Rural Competitiveness), peripherality characteristics can also be considered in terms of their supply-side or demand-side orientation. For example, classifying a product according to location and distance from main markets will generate characteristics that are fixed and dependent on the product being available at that location. Alternatively, characteristics aiming to generate attraction, such as relaxation, safety and solitude, are market-oriented and, as such, are dependent on the producer's ability to understand their consumer. There is clearly a linkage between these categories. For example, features of attraction designed to generate a feeling of well-being and getting away from it all may originate from the location or environment of the attraction or provider. Thus the sourcing of competitive advantage from supply-side phenomena cannot always be seen as distinctive and separate from demand-side issues.

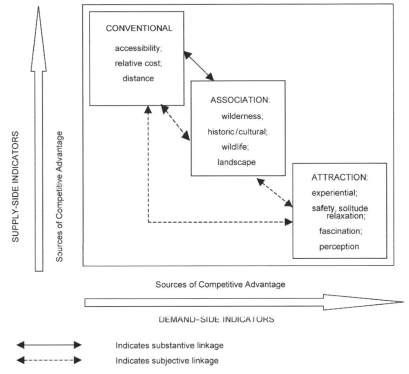

Fig. 3.9. Peripherality and the sourcing of competitive advantage.

Given an increasingly competitive marketplace, there is a need to establish new ways of constructing competitive advantage. While the utilization of 'local identity' in development is not new, only more recently have such tactics been strategically used as a means of product differentiation (particularly for rural products) as the spending power and growth in new markets becomes increasingly apparent.

The Shetland case study, contrasted with East Ayrshire, supports the premise that peripherality and its associated features and experiences, can be important assets in gaining competitive advantage for tourism providers. In comparison, the more accessible East Ayrshire region pays less attention to local identity in selling and promoting its products, and likewise the experiences of the visitors to East Ayrshire are distanced from the local milieu and, as such, perceptions of the area are not as pronounced. Thus it is evident that the embedded resources in Shetland can add value to the tourism product, and that particular destination attributes within Shetland are associated with the perceived distance from the core. Association, either geographically, historically or appealing to cognitive aspects, has the potential to influence consumer perceptions. A distinctive image can be created through the subtle use of signs and symbols which may be indicative of aspects of peripherality while appealing to the intrinsic motivations of individuals. The forging of links between products and a region's landscape, culture and heritage (embodied in an area's peripherality) can assist in adding value to products, with a view to ultimately satisfying the needs and wants of individuals.

Although this in itself is of importance for understanding tourism in the periphery, ultimately the fundamental goal is to explain how positive perceptions of peripherality can be harnessed for development. Although this is beyond the remit of this chapter, these issues have formed the basis of a second line of inquiry within the AsPIRE project, where we examine the differing endogenous and exogenous approaches to the development of tourism in the periphery. Finally, underpinning concepts that attempt to explain the various influences that affect tourist behaviour apply equally to other consumers of the periphery. Businesses, residents and the public sector (within both the periphery and the core) also hold individual perceptions of peripherality. In particular, potential entrepreneurs may base business location decisions on subjective perceptions, in addition to or over and above economic factors.

Although spatial peripherality indicators may go some way towards measuring objective factors, they do not encompass all aspects of the decision making environment, which, as we have seen is much influenced by the subjective perceptions of peripherality. By investigating the features of peripherality as they are interpreted by consumers and by studying the 'gap' between reality and perceptions, we hope, first, to begin to understand the deficiencies of conventional indicators and, secondly, to propose new indicators that demonstrate the potential of an area for gaining competitive advantage through aspects of peripherality.

Note

[1]This chapter derives from the EU FP5 project 'Aspatial Peripherality, Innovation and the Rural Economy', AsPIRE (Contract QLK5-2000-00783). The collaborating laboratories are as follows: Scottish Agricultural College, Aberdeen, Scotland (coordinator), Irish Agriculture and Food Development Authority (TEAGASC) Rural (Dublin) and National University of Ireland (Galway) (Ireland), University of Valencia (Spain), University of Patras (Greece), University of Dortmund (Germany), University of Helsinki (Finland).

References

Ayrshire Economic Forum (2000) *Ayrshire Strategy for Jobs*. Ayrshire Economic Forum, UK.

Copus, A.K. (2001) From core–periphery to polycentric development: concepts of spatial and aspatial peripherality. *European Planning Studies* 9(4), 539–552.

Craig, J.C. and Grant, R.M. (1993) *Strategic Management – Resources, Planning, Cost-efficiency, Goals*. Kogan Page, London, 167 pp.

Fennell, D.A. (1996) A tourist space-time budget in the Shetland Islands. *Annals of Tourism Research* 23(4), 811–829.

Gomez Martin, B. and Lopez Palomeque, F. (2001) Tourism, territory and marginality: principles and case studies. In: *The Annual Conference of IGU Commission on*

Evolving Issues of Geographic Marginality in the Early 21st Century World, Stockholm, 25–29 June.

Hall, C.M. and Jenkins, J.M. (1998) The restructuring of rural economies: rural tourism and recreation as a government response. In: Butler, R., Hall, C.M. and Jenkins, J. (eds) *Tourism and Recreation in Rural Areas*. John Wiley and Sons, New York, pp. 43–67.

Labour Force Survey (2002) extracted from NOMIS, http://www.nomisweb.co.uk

Martin, L., Westgren, R. and Duren, E. (1991) Agribusiness competitiveness across national boundaries. *American Journal of Agricultural Economics* 73, 1456–1464.

MacPherson Research (2001) Shetland Visitor Survey 2000, prepared for Shetland Islands Tourism, Shetland Islands Council, Highlands and Islands Enterprise, Shetland Enterprise, VisitScotland, Inverness.

Mill, R.C. (1992) *The Tourism System*, 2nd edn. Prentice Hall Inc, New Jersey.

Mittial Research (2000) *Ayrshire, Scotland as a Location for Call and Contact Centres*. Report for Enterprise Ayrshire, UK.

Porter, M.E. (1985) *Competitive Advantage – Creating and Sustaining Superior Performance*. Macmillan, London, 557 pp.

Prideaux, B. (2000) The role of the transport system in destination development. *Tourism Management* 21, 53–63.

Ray, C. (1999) Endogenous development in the era of reflexive modernity. *Journal of Rural Studies* 15(3), 257–267.

Richardson, T. (2000) Discourses of rurality in EU spatial policy: the european spatial development perspective. *Sociologia Ruralis* 40(1), 53–71.

ScotExchange (2000) *Tourism in Ayrshire and Arran 2000*. Available from: http://www.scotexchange.net

Shetland Islands Council (2001) *Shetland in Statistics 2001*. Shetland Islands Council Development Department, Lerwick, UK.

Wanhill, S. (1997) Peripheral area tourism: a European perspective. *Progress in Tourism and Hospitality Research* 3, 47–70.

Wanhill, S. and Buhalis, D. (1999) Introduction: challenges for tourism in peripheral areas. *International Journal of Tourism Research* 1, 295–297.

Williams, S. (1998) *Tourism Geography*. Routledge, London, 212 pp.

4 Policy Options for the Development of an Indigenous Tourism SME Sector in Kenya

GEOFFREY MANYARA AND ELERI JONES

Welsh School of Hospitality, Tourism and Leisure Management, University of Wales Institute, Cardiff, UK

4.1 Introduction

As a leading foreign exchange earner, generating 18% of the total foreign exchange earnings (Dieke, 2000) and contributing about 10% of the gross domestic product (Government of Kenya, 2003a), the tourism industry is extremely important to the Kenyan economy. Kenya has been a major force to reckon with in the African tourism industry, especially in sub-Saharan Africa where Kenya is arguably the most developed tourist destination (Sindiga, 1999a). However, this prime position has been usurped by South Africa, with Kenya now taking second position. One could argue that Kenya would have maintained her position ahead of post-apartheid South Africa had certain developments (e.g. broadening of the product range, market diversification, effective planning and management) been undertaken. However, little effort has been made to align tourism development with global developments and, as a result, Kenya's tourism industry experienced a downturn in the 1990s (Akama, 1999). Sindiga observes that:

> The crisis facing Kenya's tourism industry may be summarised as follows: breakdown in physical infrastructure; environmental degradation of natural resources especially national parks and reserves; a narrow tourism product and source markets for tourists; uneven distribution of tourism benefits to local communities; low foreign exchange earnings per capita and a low rate of retention of foreign exchange earnings within the country; mass tourism; foreign ownership; and management of tourism enterprises.
>
> (Sindiga, 1999a: 110)

This chapter analyses the current scenario for tourism development in Kenya, identifying that the extant model of tourism development is based on an anachronistic 'colonial' model, with tourism receipts by foreign-owned companies leaking from Kenya rather than contributing to in-country poverty

©CAB International 2005. *Tourism SMEs, Service Quality and Destination Competitiveness*
(eds E. Jones and C. Haven-Tang)

alleviation. The chapter goes on to describe an 'ideal scenario', with tourism development owned and controlled by Kenyans, and places special emphasis on the potential role of indigenous small and medium-sized enterprises (SMEs), in line with the United Nations Development Programme's (UNDP) sustainable livelihoods approach (UNDP, 1999) and the criteria for poverty alleviation developed by the World Tourism Organization (WTO) (WTO, 2002) to achieve appropriate community linkages leading to poverty alleviation. Obstacles to the achievement of the ideal scenario are identified and discussed. In addressing these obstacles, it is evident that there needs to be a policy framework for tourism development that is integrated into wider country-building strategies to achieve the optimum exploitation of tourism resources for Kenya.

4.2 Tourism and Poverty Alleviation

Poverty in Kenya has been and still is a serious problem. Since independence, the Kenyan government has been committed to fighting poverty through various policies and initiatives. However, despite these efforts, poverty has been on the increase, especially in the 1990s, due to a decline in economic growth that, significantly, was attributed to the decrease in tourism activity over the same period (Government of Kenya, 2000). Due to the increase in poverty, several multinational and local organizations have joined the government in its efforts towards poverty alleviation. One strategy that has been proposed, especially by the UNDP, is the sustainable livelihoods approach – an approach to poverty alleviation that is derived from people's capacity to access options and resources and use them to earn a living in such a way as not to foreclose for others, either now or in the future (UNDP, 1999).

WTO (2002) suggests that tourism can be a tool for poverty alleviation in developing countries with significant advantages over other sectors: tourism is comparatively labour intensive; it employs a high proportion of women; it can be developed in remote areas without alternative viable economic activities; and it has minimal trade barriers. However, while the WTO suggests that tourism has a higher potential for linkage with local enterprises and also that tourism products can be built on the local resources that the poor have, it does not adopt a sustainable livelihoods perspective.

In the light of its economic contribution and growth potential, the tourism industry would seem the obvious tool for the Kenyan government to use in the war against poverty. However, in using tourism as a tool for poverty alleviation, the emphasis must be not only to achieve tourism growth and hence increase the revenue from tourism, but also to ensure that there are clear strategies for linking tourism receipts to local communities to achieve the goal of poverty alleviation and achieve sustainability. Awareness is now growing in terms of the sustainability of tourism and several projects, e.g. Conservation of Biodiverse Resource Areas (COBRA) and Lewa Downs Conservancy, which are based on very different models of sustainability, are now in place to increase the involvement of the local communities in tourism development (Sindiga, 1999b).

4.3 An Anachronistic Model of Tourism Development

One of the major factors hindering tourism development in Kenya is the extant model of development, which follows an anachronistic colonial model based on the now infamous 'safari' of the then US President Theodore Roosevelt in the 1900s and designed to meet the needs of an elite ex-metropolitan European clientele. Legislation supported the development of game reserves to protect wildlife resources and promote organized recreational activities, e.g. hunting (Akama, 1999). This legislation has clearly disadvantaged indigenous communities that share natural resources with wildlife by restricting the movement of indigenous people through extrinsic rather than natural forces. Local communities were and still are scarcely involved in tourism development, which focuses on wildlife and coastal products. Today, Kenya's prime tourist market remains Western Europe, with real control of tourism resources vested in the hands of a few Western investors whose main interests are profit-driven.

Safari and coastal tourism products have been instrumental in the development of Kenya's tourism, especially in the 1980s, when arguably the industry was at its best. However, safari and coastal tourism products, unlike the Egyptian pyramids, are not unique and are easily substitutable in consumer destination choice sets (Goodall and Ashworth, 1988). Significantly, due to the failure of traditional industries such as agriculture, many sub-Saharan countries, e.g. South Africa, Namibia, Zambia, Zimbabwe, Mozambique, Botswana and Tanzania, are now turning to tourism as a vehicle for economic development and offering similar tourism products, increasing competition and challenging Kenya's lead. Despite comments by the Minister of Tourism and Information in the Kenyan media about development and promotion of domestic tourism and assertion by the new government that tourism is high on the agenda (Government of Kenya, 2003a), the Kenyan government has, to date, either ignored the redefinition of tourism policy objectives or not publicized them. The government has none the less identified tourism development as crucial to poverty alleviation in the new unveiled Economic Recovery Strategy for Wealth and Employment Creation for the period 2003–2007 (Government of Kenya, 2003b), but has to date not clearly spelt out how this can be achieved.

One of the key relatively unexplored areas of the Kenyan tourism industry is the identification of alternatives to traditional international markets. For example, the apparently lucrative international tourism market adumbrates the development of regional and domestic markets. This reliance on a single tourist market makes the Kenyan tourism industry very vulnerable to externalities, such as war and terrorism. Many destinations, e.g. the UK and China, have vibrant domestic markets, with turnover exceeding that from international markets. Countries such as South Africa are now emulating this approach to tourism development and their domestic market has grown considerably. The development of domestic and regional tourism markets should be enhanced in Kenya, not only because of revenue but also because of the potential for regional integration and distribution of wealth. Moreover, these markets would enable the establishment and growth of Kenyan-owned tourism SMEs. As Ritchie and Crouch stress:

> generally the supply of tourism is driven by domestic or local demand that is typically stable and reliable and less fickle than demand from distant markets. Hence, solid domestic demand provides a healthy competitive environment and the critical mass of demand necessary to support a thriving tourism and hospitality sector.
>
> (Ritchie and Crouch, 2003: 24)

4.4 A Paradigm Shift for Tourism Development in Kenya

4.4.1 Lack of a sound tourism policy, unsystematic tourism planning and unclear roles and responsibilities

Obstacles to tourism development in Kenya originate from the lack of sound tourism policy, as emphasized by the Chief Executive of the Tourism Trust Fund (TTF) in an interview published in *The East African* in February 2003. In fact, the government can, in this regard, be seen as an obstacle in itself for failing to develop an appropriate tourism policy. The consequences of this have been that tourism development in Kenya has been haphazard (Akama, 1999) and local communities within Kenya's tourism regions have continued to languish in poverty. Moreover, the government's tourism policy relies on the exploitation of the traditional safari and coastal tourism products and advocates for foreign investment, without any strategy for the development of local communities or the development of indigenous tourism SMEs.

Furthermore, planning and management of tourism in Kenya appears unsystematic despite the National Tourism Master Plan (NTMP). Before the Japanese Development Agency (JICA) funded NTMP, itself a contentious document, tourism planning in Kenya relied on 'letting things just happen'. Even with NTMP, there is no clear synchronization of its agenda with the numerous district development plans, rendering its implementation suspect. Tourism development has no clear guidelines or regulations and no public agency is charged with the responsibility of implementing the NTMP. The suggestion, therefore, by the TTF's Chief Executive Officer that emphasis should now be in the formulation of a robust tourism policy is timely and must incorporate the involvement of all stakeholders – local communities, private businesses, government officials, universities and lobby groups.

Moreover, there is potential conflict between the roles of various national organizations and even ministries. For instance, it is not clear which ministry is charged with the responsibility of formulating the tourism policy or how tourism development would be integrated with wider development strategies. Should infrastructural developments with tourism potential be addressed to the Ministry of Tourism and Information or the Ministry of Planning and National Development? How do the roles and responsibilities of Kenya's two main national tourism organizations – the Kenya Tourism Development Corporation (KTDC) and the Kenya Tourist Board (KTB) – overlap? Initially, KTDC was the sole tourism organization charged with, as the name suggests, tourism development in Kenya, and marketing and promotion activities were in the hands of the Ministry for Tourism and Information. KTB was established in the 1990s to take over the marketing and promotional activities from the ministry and is more oriented to the private sector. KTB currently appears more active and its role has evolved to encompass new product development. It is therefore not clear what the role of KTDC is, and the private-sector orientation of the KTB suggests that the local communities most in need of help may not benefit.

4.4.2 Lack of tourism awareness

Very little research has been done on the issue of tourism awareness – perhaps due to the assumption that everybody knows what tourism is. While this might be true for developed countries, where tourism-related material has a high profile in the media, the same is not true for Kenya. Although not generally discussed, tourism awareness is the key to tourism development in Kenya and consequently tourism SME growth. Ideally, there should be campaigns to inform people what tourism is all about, how it affects them, what opportunities exist, what the rights of local communities are – for example, in terms of property rights – as well as the positive and negative impacts of tourism. Sirakaya *et al.* (2002) observe that increased tourism awareness can lead to increases in local community support for tourism development initiatives.

Lack of tourism awareness in Kenya persists at all levels – from the government to the grass-roots levels – and is evidenced through a range of indicators, including: lack of clear definitions of what tourism is and who is a tourist; the concept of a domestic tourist; understanding how tourism development can be optimized; and facilitating the planning and management of tourism resources. In order to effectively plan, manage and formulate appropriate tourism policy, a destination should develop its own tourism indicators, e.g. in terms of arrivals and receipts or use of tourism satellite accounting (Fretchling, 1999; Millington, 2003), to be able to set realistic tourism development targets and ensure that the full potential of tourism development is exploited.

4.4.3 Misperceptions and misinformation

Insecurity and bad publicity in the traditional Western tourist markets have been blamed for the decline in the tourism industry in Kenya. However, although Kenya experienced limited political and civil unrest in the 1990s, this was insignificant compared with other tourism destinations. Many African countries are now stigmatized by incessant civil unrest – a problem exacerbated by bad publicity and media bias. Furthermore, Kenya's plight has been compounded by recent terrorist activities targeting American and Israeli interests, resulting in travel adviseries and even travel bans, such as the one by the British government in May 2003. Situations in other countries, such as Rwanda, Burundi and Democratic Republic of Congo, have resulted in bad publicity for Kenya, partly because of limited understanding by potential tourists of the geography of Africa. It is not uncommon for Kenya to be mistaken as part of the Republic of South Africa. The main problem here is not only making Kenya a secure destination, but also how to respond to potential bad publicity. While South Africa and Egypt are potentially less secure than Kenya in terms of crime and terrorism, their tourism industries remain vibrant. It is therefore clear that crisis management and media management strategies should be developed and implemented.

4.4.4 The need for product diversification

Reliance on the 'big five' game experience (elephant, leopard, lion, rhino and buffalo) and coastal tourism products spatially restricts tourism activity. Kenya's top tourism destination areas are located in the coastal and Maasailand regions, an areal manifestation of tourism that persists in modern-day tourism development despite the potential of the whole of Kenya for tourism development. Localization of the tourism industry has minimized and restricted tourism development, not only in terms of infrastructure and facility development, but also in terms of diversification of the tourism product and tourist markets. Thus, some Kenyan destinations, such as Amboseli National Park and Maasai Mara Game Reserve, have experienced haphazard tourism development that is almost near saturation point, raising concerns about environmental issues, such as pollution and destruction of habitat.

Development of new products, e.g. authentic cultural tourism products – local cuisine, entertainment, architecture, medicine and art, in which the local communities would be advantaged is key to tourism development and tourism SME growth in Kenya. Culture is one of the most important characteristics of any given destination (Ritchie and Crouch, 2003) and it is therefore ironic that it does not play a major role in tourism development in developing countries in general and Kenya specifically.

New products open up opportunities to exploit alternative markets. Targeting of specialist niche markets and/or new markets that appreciate the concept of authenticity is seen as a way forward for tourism development. Exploitation of such markets will require the establishment of strategic partnerships with like-minded organizations and businesses. Cultural tourism products would also lay the foundation for other forms of tourism (Ritchie and Crouch, 2003), and also provide an atmosphere conducive to the growth of indigenous tourism SMEs.

4.4.5 Preventing leakage by indigenous ownership

The government has for some time favoured and encouraged private and, to a large extent, foreign ownership of tourism resources, and therefore indirectly discouraged the development of tourism SMEs. As a result, almost 80% of the tourism resources are in the hands of foreign investors (Dieke, 2000). This has in most cases not only meant higher leakages of tourism revenue, but also minimal benefits to local communities. Strategies for enhancing local community ownership of tourism resources are encouraged. These may revolve around models of development used for agriculture, whereby Kenyan farmers own SMEs and further form associations to manage key functions, e.g. marketing. This is a form of share scheme that could be integrated into tourism development.

Foreign individuals and organizations own tourism businesses in Kenya, resulting in a tourism development agenda skewed in favour of external interests. Consequently, local community involvement in tourism development has been minimal. WTO emphasizes the importance of local linkages in reducing leakages of tourism revenue (WTO, 2002). Linkage of the Kenyan tourism industry is low, and consequently there is high leakage through repatriation of profits, employment for foreign expatriates, purchase of goods and services from abroad and use of foreign-owned airlines. Factors attributable to low level of linkages between tourism and the agricultural sector, for instance, are insufficient and inadequate local agricultural development and lack of value-added agro-processing facilities, information and marketing (Torres, 2002). Most of these leakages could easily be minimized through consideration of the supply chain and the procurement of local raw materials and food products for the hospitality sector; yet most hospitality establishments import raw materials.

Parker (2003) highlights the issue of ownership of tourism resources by asking 'Who owns wildlife?' Land ownership, especially in tourism regions, is not clearly defined. Most of the national parks and game reserves were carved out from lands traditionally owned by local communities such as the Maasais; yet today it is not clear whether they still own any land or whether this has become government property. Furthermore, it is not clear how local communities have been compensated or what property rights they possess in terms of the use of these lands. Land is exploited, especially by private foreign organizations, and local communities have not benefited. Notwithstanding that, it is clear who pays for environmental degradation; it is the local communities that bear the brunt of such negative impacts. Moreover, tourism development, e.g. in Mombasa, has put land values beyond the means of local communities.

The WTO argues that stronger linkages within the local economy are crucial not just to minimize leakages, but also to maximize tourism benefits (WTO, 2002). Emphasis on the use of locally produced raw and processed materials would enhance the output multiplier effect of tourism (Cooper *et al.*, 1998) and foster the growth of SMEs in other sectors, such as the agricultural sector. The output multiplier is mainly concerned with the amount of additional output generated with increase in tourist expenditure. The assumption in this case is that an increase in tourist expenditure will lead to an increase in output and therefore a higher output multiplier as goods and services are sourced from the local economy. Although some scholars (e.g. Sindiga, 1999a,b) argue that tourism development should not be seen as a panacea for development in developing countries, effective tourism policy formulation, planning and management, can ensure that tourism contributes to the general development of a developing country by encouraging intersectoral growth.

4.4.6 Conflicts resulting from competition for scarce resources

Kenya's safari products showcase a vast range of wildlife in their natural habitats. Most of these are also suitable for either pastoralism or farming, e.g. the Maasai Mara area is one of the leading producers of wheat in Kenya. Competition for scarce resources results in conflicts between humans and wildlife (with wild animals attacking and destroying the local communities' livelihoods or vice versa) and land encroachment ('illegal' acquisition of land for agricultural purposes from areas reserved for wildlife). Many conflicts result from tourism benefits not reaching the local communities so that there is no incentive for local communities to support tourism development.

4.4.7 Capacity building in indigenous communities

Local communities must be equipped with the necessary skills and knowledge to take advantage of both direct and indirect opportunities that will arise from tourism development. Tourism is a labour-intensive industry (WTO, 2002). Growth of tourism SMEs would create additional employment opportunities. However, innumeracy and illiteracy are major obstacles to the employability of persons from local communities. While the government has made efforts to improve literacy and numeracy in general, it is, however, not clear if any efforts are being made towards tourism-specific capacity building. Addressing this issue in a tourism development strategy would enable local communities to take advantage of tourism development opportunities. In a Utopian Kenyan tourism scenario, strategies should be in place to ensure that local communities are equipped with basic numeracy and literacy skills, supplemented with more tourism-specific skills and knowledge. This could be achieved through a national education policy integrating the development of tourism-specific and entrepreneurial skills and knowledge into wider educational initiatives to achieve an inclusive capacity-building approach to support tourism development.

4.4.8 Knowledge exploitation and technology transfer

The link between public and private organizations and institutions of higher learning within the tourism industry in Kenya is very weak. In the UK, for example, the Wales Tourist Board is in constant consultation with higher institutions of learning in matters pertaining to tourism development in Wales. In Kenya this link is almost non-existent, although institutions such as Moi University have a myriad of research projects that would be beneficial to tourism development. In contrast, the agricultural sector has benefited greatly from knowledge exploitation and technology transfer with university researchers. Thus, in the case of tourism, the government of Kenya relies on external initiatives by funding agencies such JICA and the European Union (EU) for tourism development projects. External agencies subcontract foreign consultants to carry out most projects promoting Kenyan tourism development.

4.4.9 Quality standards

In a competitive global economy, the issue of standards and quality is increasingly important for destination competitiveness. Unlike developed destinations, Kenya does not have clear guidelines for maintaining standards and quality within the tourism industry. Furthermore, unlike the manufacturing sector in Kenya, which has the Kenya Bureau of Standards as its quality body, it is not clear which national body is charged with the maintenance of quality within the tourism industry and what measures are taken to ensure quality. Regulation of existing tourism enterprises through licensing arrangements is, however, vested in the Ministry of Tourism and Information. The tourism accommodation sector in Kenya has been left solely to private investors who run and own classified tourism accommodation facilities. Smallholder accommodation facilities, such as those common in Europe, are an area that has not been exploited and provides ample opportunity for Kenya tourism SME development. However, in developing tourism SMEs in Kenya, the issue of internationally recognizable quality and standards should be given a high priority. Cooper *et al.* (1998) note that the issue of classification and grading is mostly applied to the accommodation sector and rarely the tourism product in general. The responsibility of classification and grading of the tourism SMEs in Kenya should be charged to an independent national tourism organization that will enforce strict measures to ensure high qualities and standards of Kenyan tourism products. Currently the onus of enforcing quality and standards is on the government through the Ministry of Tourism and Information.

4.4.10 Networks and partnerships

The WTO emphasizes that partnerships are crucial for any poverty alleviation strategy. Whereas this is important, the bone of contention is in the type of partnership being advocated. For instance, the WTO suggests that local communities should form partnerships with established tourism enterprises. This strategy will only perpetuate the giant–dwarf relationships whereby the local communities are at the mercy of the goodwill of these enterprises, thereby enforcing dependency. This is in fact against the goals of sustainable livelihoods approach that seeks to enhance independence.

Adoption of a different approach alongside the WTO's partnership approach is therefore essential. An equal partnership approach is preferred, whereby local SMEs and the existing tourism enterprises complement and cooperate with each other rather than compete, as they will be offering different tourism products. In addition, partnerships that seek to empower local communities and foster independence must be nurtured. In this regard, partnerships with organizations and businesses that seek to enhance community development initiatives, support fair trade efforts, support responsible tourism and appreciate authentic tourism products are encouraged.

4.4.11 Legislative protection for local communities

In an ideal Kenyan tourism scenario, the tourism legislative framework should be developed and implemented. This framework should ensure protection for local communities and Kenyan-owned SMEs and, most crucially, emphasize the definition of property rights. In addition, labour laws will have to be redefined and enforced such that preference is given to the employment of local communities in tourism development. Although this approach may go against the doctrine of globalization in that there are protectionist connotations (Fayed and Fletcher, 2002), it is important to note that any long-term poverty alleviation strategy must embrace protectionism to some extent. Local communities in Kenya, for example, have not benefited from tourism development; yet the private sector has had almost a free hand in running its affairs.

4.5 An Ideal Scenario for Tourism Development in Kenya

Analysis of key dimensions of the prevailing scenario for tourism development in Kenya is made in Table 4.1 and juxtaposed against an ideal scenario for tourism development. Appropriate policy formulation would address the issues associated with low awareness of the concept of tourism by local communities alongside the development of tourism-specific skills complementing wider educational objectives aimed at raising numeracy and literacy levels. Development of entrepreneurial skills would foster Kenyan-owned business start-ups. The WTO argues that the SME sector has played and still plays a significant role in tourism development in Europe; the same could be expected for Kenya (WTO, 2002). New product development would support market diversification and the development of domestic and regional markets. As a result of this, enhanced tourism receipts and an emphasis on support of Kenyan-owned SMEs would reduce leakage. Increased linkage to local communities and development of supply chains linking to non-tourism Kenyan SMEs would promote interdependence between tourism and other sectors, e.g. agriculture. Fostering Kenyan-owned SMEs would build confidence and enable the development of complementary partnerships between Kenyan businesses and regional/international partners.

Table 4.1. Extant anachronistic model versus potential idea scenario for Kenya tourism development.

Extant anachronistic model	Potential ideal scenario
Lack of appropriate policy, planning and management	Emphasis on appropriate policy formulation, planning and management
Lack of tourism awareness in local communities	Enhanced tourism awareness through, e.g. media campaigns
Lack of skills and knowledge by local communities	A national education policy focusing on basic numeracy and literacy skills alongside an all-inclusive tourism-specific capacity-building strategy
Narrow range of products, i.e. safari and coastal	Broad range of products from natural to cultural
Focus on traditional Western markets	Focus first on domestic, then regional and diverse international markets
High leakages through foreign ownership and control	Low leakages as emphasis is on Kenyan-owned SMEs and domestic tourism
Low linkages within the local economy	High linkages due to intersectoral interdependence for raw and processed materials
Minimal and unequal partnerships	Complementary partnerships between Kenyan-owned SMEs and local and international organizations

4.6 Tourism Policy Recommendations for the Kenyan Government

Addressing the development issues outlined in section 4.5 requires the involvement of the government in achieving eight key objectives: raising tourism awareness; new product development; definition of new markets; sound legislative framework; capacity building; development of quality management systems; investment in tourism development and the promotion of indigenous tourism SMEs; achievement of a high multiplier effect.

- *Raising tourism awareness*
  There needs to be enhanced awareness of the positive and negative impacts of tourism and their management throughout the tourism hierarchy from government to grass-roots level. This could involve a media campaign approach using promotional materials and educational documentaries both on radio and television to educate local communities and to change perceptions. This approach should seek to reassure local communities both that they are capable of enjoying the tourism resources in the country and that they can exploit opportunities arising from tourism development.
- *New product development*
  Innovation of new culturally based products, e.g. cuisine and entertainment requiring local expertise, would help to redefine Kenyan tourism not in terms

of wild animals and beaches but in terms of its people and culture. This would differentiate Kenya from the ever-increasing competition from other African countries while maximizing benefits for local communities.

- *Definition of new markets*
  Dependency on the Western market has meant that the industry is very vulnerable to conditions set by the West, such as travel bans, with detrimental impacts. The government should therefore seek to redefine its tourism markets by looking into more stable markets, such as domestic and regional tourism markets.

- *Sound legislative framework*
  A sound legislative framework should focus on: the establishment and implementation of employment laws to protect local communities from exploitation; the redefinition of property rights, especially in relation to the exploitation of natural resources; and ensuring local community ownership and effective compensation, where applicable.

- *Capacity building*
  The government should integrate its tourism capacity development strategy into its general education policy focusing on developing basic numeracy and literacy skills as a basis for capacity-building strategies. The more specific tourism agenda will promote not just basic operational skills but also the managerial and entrepreneurial skills necessary to empower local communities to run and manage tourism businesses.

- *Development of quality management systems*
  The government will need to establish a national standards organization to uphold quality and standards in the industry. A grading system would promote the incremental improvement of quality, increase consumer confidence in the product and enhance destination competitiveness.

- *Investment in tourism development and promotion of indigenous tourism SMEs*
  In its endeavour to develop indigenous SMEs, the government will need to implement mechanisms to facilitate access to financial resources by local communities, e.g. through the development of an easily accessible credit system. Differential taxation systems for foreign-owned and Kenyan-owned establishments would favour the development of Kenyan-owned businesses.

- *Achievement of a high multiplier effect*
  The government should introduce measures to ensure that existing tourism establishments purchase goods and services locally and employ Kenyans. Promotion of indigenous business will ensure Kenyan ownership of tourism development, promoting linkage and reducing leakage. Procurement of raw and processed materials from Kenyan sources results in a high multiplier effect.

4.7 Conclusions

The tourism industry is extremely important in Kenya and a key area for boosting overall economic development and alleviating poverty. Tourism development in Kenya is, however, modelled within the precincts of an anachronistic colonial model, mainly involving foreign investors, to the detriment of the development of indigenous tourism SMEs. Consequently, tourism benefits have been minimal to local communities and, in addition, tourism development has hardly had significant impacts on poverty alleviation, a major problem facing the country.

A paradigm shift is therefore urgently needed to redefine Kenyan tourism in a way that maximizes benefits for local communities. This scenario should seek to build on the strengths of the local communities, while at the same time emphasizing strategies for turning weaknesses into strengths and threats into opportunities. The ideal scenario should therefore seek to ensure the creation of Kenya-owned SMEs, which will enable more effective linkage with the local economy and will support complementary partnerships. In order to achieve this, an all-inclusive capacity-building strategy will need to be adopted, tourism awareness will have to be broadened, a legislative framework put in place, the tourism infrastructure developed, tourism products and markets diversified and standards and quality upheld.

To achieve this, there are a number of obstacles that have to be tackled to promote the involvement of local communities in tourism development in Kenya. The government should therefore develop an appropriate tourism policy to tackle these obstacles and enable the development of a robust tourism industry in which Kenyan-owned tourism SMEs would play an increasingly significant role.

References

Akama, S. (1999) The evolution of tourism in Kenya. *Journal of Sustainable Development* 7(1), 6–25.

Cooper, C., Fletcher, J., Gilbert, D. and Wanhill, S. (1998) *Tourism: Principles and Practice*, 2nd edn. Longman, Harlow, UK, 530 pp.

Dieke, P.U.C. (2000) *The Political Economy of Tourism Development in Africa*. Cognizant Communication Corporation, New York, 355 pp.

Fayed, A.H. and Fletcher, J. (2002) Globalisation of economic activity: issues for tourism. *Tourism Economics* 8(2), 207–230.

Fretchling, D.C. (1999) The tourism satellite accounts: foundations, progress and issues. *Tourism Management* 20, 163–170.

Goodall, B. and Ashworth, G. (1988) *Marketing in the Tourism Industry: the Promotion of Destination Regions – 2nd International Workshop*. Croom Helm, London, 244 pp.

Government of Kenya (2000) *Kenya Interim Poverty Reduction Strategy Paper 2000–2003*. www.imf.org/org/external/NP/ken/01/index.htm Accessed on 7 October 2002.

Government of Kenya (2003a) *Draft National Tourism Policy*. Government Press, Nairobi.

Government of Kenya (2003b) *Strategy for Economic Recovery: A Discussion Paper for the Ministry of Planning*. Government Press, Nairobi.

Millington, K. (2003) From safari to satellites: building the statistics base in Botswana. In: Lennon, J.J. (ed.) *Tourism Statistics: International Perspectives and Current Issues*. Continuum, London, pp. 59–65.

Parker, I. (2003) Who owns wildlife? The law does not say. *The East African* 15 September. http://www.nationaudio.com/News/EastAfrican/15092003/Features/Magazine 1509200329.html

Ritchie, J.R.B. and Crouch, G.I. (2003) *The Competitive Destination: A Sustainable Tourism Approach*. CAB International, Wallingford, UK, 272 pp.

Sindiga, I. (1999a) *Tourism and African Development: Change and Challenge of Tourism in Kenya*. African Studies Centre, Leiden, The Netherlands, 214 pp.

Sindiga, I. (1999b) Alternative tourism and sustainable development in Kenya. *Journal of Sustainable Development* 7(2), 108–127.

Sirakaya, E., Teye, V. and Sönmez, S. (2002) Understanding residents' support for tourism development in the central region of Ghana. *Journal of Travel Research* 41(1), 57–67.

Torres, R. (2002) Toward a better understanding of tourism and agricultural linkages in Yucatan: tourist food consumption and preferences. *Tourism Geographies* 4(3), 282–306.

United Nations Development Programme (UNDP) (1999) Towards operationalisation of sustainable livelihoods approach in Kenya. www.undp.org/sl/documents/country-specific/kenya_psd.htm Accessed on 6 February 2003.

WTO (2002) *Tourism and Poverty Alleviation*. World Tourism Organization, Madrid, 115 pp.

5 Quality Issues for the Family Business

DONALD GETZ,[1] JACK CARLSEN[2] AND ALISON MORRISON[3]

[1]Haskayne School of Business, University of Calgary, Canada; [2]Curtin Business School, Curtin University of Technology, Western Australia; [3]Scottish Hotel School, University of Strathclyde, UK

5.1 Introduction

There are many impediments to quality that are inherent to family business, but also there is ample scope for the dreams, talents and tireless efforts of owner-operators to create high-quality experiences for customers. The propensity for both failure and excellence in family businesses in tourism and hospitality is high, with individual circumstances making a huge difference. Understanding of the human and family elements in these businesses is essential if quality is to be improved.

This chapter[1] provides an overview of quality issues within family businesses, including business/product quality, service quality and impacts on destination quality and competitiveness. The importance of family business as a distinct form of management has been only lately recognized by academics (e.g. Gersick et al., 1997; Chua et al., 1999) and has been paid very little attention by tourism and hospitality scholars. Owner-operators and family-owned businesses have been lumped into the categories of small and medium enterprises (SMEs), which ignores the fact that ownership makes a huge difference. Many are small for very personal, deliberate reasons, and a large proportion are 'micro' in size. Consequently, little is known about the management of the family business in tourism and hospitality. What has been demonstrated repeatedly, in many countries and settings, is that tourism and hospitality attracts many investors for lifestyle and autonomy reasons, including the desire to be self-employed and the opportunity to remain in or move to attractive rural and resort areas. And there are many unique opportunities for individual entrepreneurship and family business within the industry.

The motives, goals and business behaviour of owner-operators are generally different from those of other business managers and corporations. Businesses owned and operated by individuals and families are typically not grown for the sake of getting bigger, nor are they managed as if profit-making were the sole objective. Family issues intrude on all aspects of the business, especially with regard to sharing responsibilities, involving the children, and succession (inheritance) within the family. Tourism/hospitality businesses impose a number of special challenges on the family, particularly seasonality of demand causing cash-flow fluctuations, a high level of host–guest contact, almost unlimited demands on operators' time and the intrusion of guests into family space and time.

Chua *et al.* (1999) argue that the theoretical essence of a family business lies in the vision of its dominant family members. The vision must be to use the business for the betterment of the family – potentially across more than one generation. Birley (2001: 75) also concludes that 'owner-manager attitude is a more productive approach to describing and understanding the family business sector than the more traditional methods of equity or managerial control'. In this approach the vision (or motives and goals) and behaviour of the firm are differentiated from those of non-family businesses and businesses in which family involvement makes no difference to its operations or future development.

Children in family businesses often reject taking over the family business because of perceptions of hard work and low profitability. Our research in several countries has found a very low level of involvement of children in family businesses and a very low rate of inheritance and succession planning by owners. Parents are quick to point out many of the hardships and constraints making it difficult or undesirable for children to get involved or take over. Consequently, most 'family businesses' in this industry are in fact operated by sole proprietors and couples (called 'copreneurs').

5.2 Framework for Evaluating Quality in the Family Business

The conceptual framework illustrated in Fig. 5.1 is derived from research and constitutes a set of propositions regarding the family business perspective on quality. Three applications of quality must be considered: the product (nature and viability of the business); service as delivered to guests (including the direct influence of owners and family members); and impacts on destination quality and competitiveness.

The conceptual framework places the family and its family vision in the centre, as this determines fundamental goals such as the degree of profit and growth orientation. Surrounding the family core is an inner ring of fundamental concerns that apply to most family businesses, all of which can act to limit overall innovation and growth in this sector of tourism and hospitality. Many owner-operators will be less concerned with quality than with the major task of merely sustaining the business to support the family. Without growth it is difficult to increase profits sufficiently to introduce (or buy) new products or tap new markets. Growth is also likely to be necessary to achieve major quality improvements such as by adding and training staff or upgrading the standard of service.

Lifestyle and location factors are important and in many cases in tourism and hospitality are a preoccupation of the owners. So too are autonomy/control

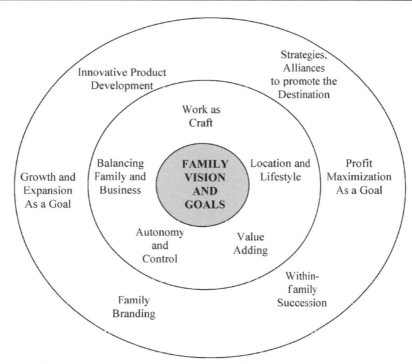

Fig. 5.1. Dominant family business concerns affecting product, service and destination quality. Inner ring: core vision and goals. Middle ring: basic family business concerns (generally limiting innovation, growth and quality). Outer ring: hallmarks of exceptional family businesses (all these factors should positively affect the quality of the business and destination).

and the desire for independence, including an aversion to debt. Balancing family and business is essential and, although some owners are more family-oriented than others, it is an inescapable factor even in most sole-proprietor enterprises. The fourth concern, the notion of work as craft, is applicable to many – and indeed motivates them to establish or buy a business. This is certainly true for arts and crafts producers, but also applies to chefs, tour operators interested in nature or hospitality providers who take delight in producing quality goods and/or services. In some cases, however, the craft orientation results in business excellence and a devotion to quality service. Together, these inner-ring concerns often act to restrict the growth orientation of family businesses. Even though owners typically pursue higher profits, it is often by way of value adding (e.g. adding technology, improved marketing or physical improvements) rather than growth of the core business.

The outer ring specifies attributes of the exceptional family businesses. A small minority in tourism and hospitality aggressively pursue profit and growth, and these entrepreneurs are much more likely to pursue innovation and alliances to promote the destination. Innovative product development on the part of owners provides competitive advantages for destinations, but most family business owners purchase existing businesses and keep them the same, or they copy established business types and practices because they cannot afford to take a major risk. Those family businesses passed on to the next generation in some ways are exceptional as they must be sustainable in financial and marketing terms, so it can be expected that succession within the family (as opposed to a sale to another family) will be advantageous for the destination. Finally, those families that explicitly and effectively engage in family branding are making a quality statement that should have a favourable impact upon the destination.

From the destination's perspective, these interdependent factors are major criteria for family businesses that can make a real difference. This is not to denigrate the importance of the vast majority, as they often constitute the core of an area's tourist infrastructure. It is to suggest that, if the destination desires growth, to reposition itself or to base its appeal on exceptional quality, then in most cases only a small subset of family business entrepreneurs will be involved.

5.3 Evaluation of Factors Affecting Quality in Family Businesses

In this section, each of the three applications of quality are discussed in greater detail, starting with the business (or product) itself, then service quality and finally impacts upon destination quality and competitiveness.

5.3.1 Business quality

The nature and viability of the business itself is a primary consideration, as many fail outright or consistently underperform in terms of profitability. Owner-operators are often criticized or denigrated for perceived failures, notably highly variable or poor product and service quality. To some people the family company still carries a stigma of amateurism and nepotism. Taylor *et al.* (1998: 59), in discussing the financing of small tourism and hospitality businesses, conclude that 'debt finance should be used cautiously by these firms'. Apparently many owners understand the need for caution because they tend to be very debt-averse, taking it on only when absolutely necessary. Consciously or unconsciously, they are sacrificing growth potential and increased quality for a less risky strategy. Shaw and Williams (1998), drawing on their own earlier work in Cornwall, UK, as well as other studies of the industry, concluded that many owners were 'non entrepreneurs' or 'constrained entrepreneurs'. Undercapitalization was a serious constraint, resulting in little, if any, improvement or development of small accommodation businesses, and business failure is frequently observed to be high in this sector. Shaw and Williams also characterized small-scale entrepreneurs in tourism in these ways: having little or no formal qualifications; using mostly family resources and labour; lacking business planning and growth strategies; doing little if any marketing; and possessing non-economic motives. Typically such owners moved to resorts for semi-retirement and other lifestyle reasons. 'True entrepreneurship' was associated with non-personal sources of capital and innovative management skills.

5.3.1.1 Motives and goals: lifestyle and autonomy versus entrepreneurship

Although motives for establishing or purchasing a family business can be complex, research has demonstrated that lifestyle and autonomy factors are predominant in the tourism and hospitality sectors (Bransgrove and King, 1996; Ryan, 1998; Shaw and Williams, 1998; Ateljevic and Doorne, 2000; Getz and Carlsen, 2000; Andersson *et al.*, 2002; Nilsson *et al.*, 2003). When the primary reason for being in business is not profit maximization or growth of the business, one might suspect that service delivery could suffer. A majority of owner-operators in this industry do not appear to meet the minimum criteria to be considered as 'entrepreneurs', even though there does not exist an accepted, universal definition of 'entrepreneur' or 'entrepreneurship' (Ucbasaran *et al.*, 2001), let alone agreement on the existence of particular subtypes. A dominant theme focuses on the entrepreneur's personality traits, although many authors (e.g. Sexton and Kent, 1981; Gartner, 1988; Brockhaus, 1994; Risker, 1998) have rejected the personality traits approach, concluding that it has failed to identify a set of common traits for entrepreneurs or to differentiate them from managers.

Within the personality traits theme, Katz (1995) identified 'growth entrepreneurs' as those who measure their success by business size and growth, and contrasted these people with 'autonomy'-seeking business owners, the kind who want to be their own boss or occupy their own place. Smith (1967) separated 'craftsmen' from 'opportunistic' entrepreneurs, with major differentiating factors being the 'craftsman's' aversion to risk, less growth and a focus on making a comfortable living. Small business owners are often portrayed as being 'craftsmen' or 'lifestyle entrepreneurs' and family businesses in particular are frequently assumed to be risk averse because they must place family security ahead of potential growth. The desire for autonomy – to be one's own boss – and for family independence appears to be a basic and unchanging human trait. This motivating factor accounts for many career-switching entrepreneurs who start tourism and hospitality businesses to escape what they dislike about their existing work and to steer their own economic future. The need for autonomy drives many entrepreneurs, and control-related motives and goals are found to be very important among owners of tourism and hospitality businesses. Autonomy also leads many people specifically to service-sector ventures where they can manage an establishment in a hands-on fashion. Autonomy and lifestyle motives are closely bound.

5.3.1.2 Microbusinesses

Undoubtedly a majority of family businesses in this industry are 'micro' in size (employing fewer than ten persons), and many consist only of the owner, couples or owners plus children (Middleton, 2001). Micro-enterprises, like bed and breakfast, guesthouse, small hotel and farm-stay accommodation, tour guiding and numerous other personal services, frequently do not have the potential to grow or excel, given their inability to generate large revenues or to sustain a viable cash flow. Furthermore, many are attached to the family farm or home and it becomes difficult or even impossible to separate the business assets from the family property. In these cases, inheritance of land might mean the end of the tourism/hospitality business. In rural areas in particular, the family business is often established to provide a secondary source of income, and typically these are founded and operated by women. Seasonality of demand is such a determining factor that many owners do not event think of their business as being permanent. In such circumstances, improving the quality of the business or core product might very well be impossible.

5.3.1.3 Seasonality

The often extreme nature of seasonality of demand in this industry can severely limit profitability, cause cash-flow problems and result in a lack of money for reinvestment or growth. The outcome, as demonstrated on the Danish island of Bornholm, is that many owners do not establish their business with all-year operations in mind, but treat it as a source of supplementary income or even as a hobby. Those that decide to 'combat' seasonality engage in a number of strategies, including the pursuit of dual markets (domestic and tourism) and the export of manufactured goods (Getz and Nilsson, 2004).

5.3.1.4 Control, communications and decision making within the family

How families in business communicate and make decisions is an important factor in shaping quality. It is common for the founder in male-dominated businesses to employ a paternalistic or autocratic form of control, which does not necessarily result in high levels of morale and service quality. On the other hand, we found that many copreneurs (i.e. owner-operator couples) deliberately sought consensus and work of equal value. Involving children early in their lives is considered by many experts to be necessary for eventual succession, and this requires attention to how they can increase their contribution and responsibility over time and how they can overcome perceptions that the business is not attractive. Where decision making is slowed by family dynamics or consensus becomes impossible to achieve, quality in the business might suffer. Typical disputes among family members include risk-taking versus financial conservatism, long-term asset-building versus taking money out of the business to meet immediate family needs, and uncertainty about possible succession or inheritance within the family. Indeed, only a small minority of family businesses in tourism and hospitality survive the founders. When there is unanimity on purpose and methods, the family can act as a very effective team in delivering quality experiences. Satisfaction expressed by customers will then feed back directly to the family and further motivate them.

5.3.1.5 Innovation

Although many owners claim to be innovative, we found that much of this was in terms of value adding to improve revenues or cut costs. In other words, owners are likely to keep the basic business concept and concentrate on ways to make it more appealing and generate more profit, as opposed to developing new concepts. Most owners who purchase or start a business in this industry are following well-established business models – to do otherwise is risky.

5.3.2 Service quality

This section examines the quality of service as provided to customers, and it is highly dependent on the owners and their family, who provide most of the service directly. This relates as much to the goals and motives of owners as it does to physical facilities or the nature of the business. Referring to three Baltic islands that possess high levels of local ownership and control, Twining-Ward and Baum (1998) concluded that all three had entered a period of decline and were suffering from the ill effects of seasonally low demand. The problems are augmented by a dominance of small, family enterprises 'which in many cases lack the professional training required to secure a high quality of service' (Twining-Ward and Baum, 1998: 135).

5.3.2.1 Inseparability of product, service and family

In many family businesses the family is part of the product. Indeed, being in close contact with guests and delivering personal, hands-on service is a primary motive for entering a tourism or hospitality enterprise. From the guest's point of view, interacting with an owner or the owner's family can be an important part of the experience. Consequently, it is not possible to speak of service and product quality as being separate issues. Even where staff are employed in family businesses, their morale, attitudes and actions are likely to be directly affected by the owners, who take a personal hand in every aspect of the business. This might result in service that is quite different from that obtained in large, impersonal establishments.

5.3.2.2 Family branding

The most prominent family-dependent issue in marketing is that of exploiting the family-firm status, or the family name, for competitive advantage. The term 'family branding' can be used to describe a family of brands, such that the same brand name is used on *every* product the company makes or *every* service it offers. If the overall brand name has value in terms of acceptance by customers, then all the products and services using that name should be well received. On the other hand, if a brand associated with quality is later applied to a low-price product, the consumer might begin to think that the entire family of brands has lowered its standards. Dunn (1995: 21), based on analysis of successful Scottish family businesses, concluded that some of them used their family status for marketing purposes to imply quality, care and special attention to customers. Because the 'brand' is often the family name, it should ideally communicate all the following brand attributes:

- Quality and value (service; good value for money; reliability) based on past performance and the assumption that a family takes pride in all it does.

- Tradition (we have a long history; we are rooted in the community; and we care about you).
- Personality (we are a family, different from corporations, with our own way of doing things; we offer all our clients customized experiences and a personal touch; we are always ethical in our business dealings).

In some cases the attributes can also signify culture or tradition, as in an ethnic business. Whatever the name, customers should be made to feel they personally know and understand the family behind it.

5.3.2.3 Balancing family and business

Couples running a business and owner-operators with children can face numerous and serious challenges for balancing work and family – especially where there is physical overlap between home and the space devoted to visitors (as in many small accommodation enterprises in particular). Women in particular might be expected to run the home, care for children and provide guest services simultaneously. Accordingly, family roles and responsibilities, whether established formally or by implicit understanding, will influence the customer's experience.

5.3.2.4 The art and craft of owner-operators

Resorts and other recreational environments attract a lot of people interested in pursuing their favourite sports, while hospitality businesses afford operators the opportunity to pursue lifelong interests in a creative environment (e.g. cooking, arts and crafts, flowers, catering, decorating, events production). Many owner-operators fit the classic 'craftsman' label (Smith, 1967). In these businesses there are many more females than males. Special interests and skills held by owners should lead to quality experiences for the guest, as the service providers will take pride in their work and seek to innovate.

5.3.3 Destination quality

Middleton (2001), on the subject of small business owners in tour and hospitality, stated that, at the leading edge, they embody the entrepreneurial spirit and vitality of places, but, at the trailing edge, many exist on the fringes of the industry, damaging the environment of the destination in which they are located, reducing visitor satisfaction and the perceived quality of the overall experience. This is a vital issue in tourism, because so many rural areas and resorts in particular are dominated by the small, family-business sector. As they go, so does the destination. On the one hand, it is easy for owners to get into this industry and often easy to fail. On the other, there are profit and growth-oriented entrepreneurs who can help grow and position their community as an attractive destination.

5.3.3.1 Ease of entry

Part of the explanation for an over-representation of family businesses in rural areas (Westhead and Cowling, 1998: 44) is the fact that many types of tourism and hospitality business are easy to enter. Either they do not require special skills, lengthy experience or large amounts of capital, or entrepreneurs think they do not. Naïvety and over-optimism seem to be commonplace in small family businesses in these sectors. One result is that many such businesses fail to meet owners' performance standards or fail outright. A high turnover rate among small businesses can be damaging to the destination, in several ways. First, family stability across the generations allows for capital and knowledge accumulation, plus commitment to the area and leadership in its marketing. Although family businesses when sold are likely to be acquired by other owner-operators, the business is often unchanged and the problems perpetuated. Tourism and economic development agencies should not indiscriminately assist the start-up of small businesses in the mistaken belief that this creates jobs or competitive advantages; rather, they must find specific ways to help small business owners overcome the many difficulties facing them, while at the same time attracting and cultivating investors with skills, capital and the motivation to grow and prosper.

5.3.3.2 Profit- and growth-oriented entrepreneurs

The 'growth entrepreneurs' identified by Katz (1995) exist as a minority among owners of family businesses in the tourism and hospitality industry. In the Danish and Canadian samples they exhibited significantly different goals and attitudes from lifestyle- and autonomy-oriented owners, including the explicit goal to keep growing their business. Many of these growth-oriented entrepreneurs were purchasers, and they tended to acquire certain types of businesses (i.e. accommodation and restaurants), which undoubtedly were perceived to present better opportunities for profit and growth. What is of great interest is that the profit- and growth-oriented entrepreneurs are also motivated by lifestyle and autonomy preferences. Although it remains an untested hypothesis, it is suggested that this subset of family business owners is most likely to emphasize and achieve high quality in their business, in terms of customer service, and in overall destination quality and competitiveness. This is not to deny the importance of those perennially small, lifestyle businesses in which owners are motivated and able to create high-quality experiences.

5.4 Case Studies Illustrating Quality Management

Several case studies from Canada, Australia and New Zealand are summarized below (taken from Getz *et al.*, 2004), revealing that many family businesses do stress quality of business, product and service.

Alborak Stables, Canada: The founding family had a long history on the land and involvement with horses, so they understood the need to build a quality business from the very start. Their competition consisted of 12 to 15 other English-style riding and breeding stables in the region. This led them to decide to build a top-quality facility in order to stand out immediately. Plans included the addition of bed and breakfast accommodation and other leisure pursuits on their land.

River Valley Ventures, New Zealand: The owners aimed to position this business firmly at the top of their industry segment (backpacker and up-market accommodation plus outdoor adventure) both in profitability and in quality of product. This means River Valley has had to create and continuously promote itself as a destination in its own right. An ambitious deal with a backpacker transport company enabled the owners to expand the operations and achieve higher profitability.

Wild Over Walpole (WOW), Australia: WOW's mission statement is 'To be leaders in sustainable nature-based environmental tourism offering our clients a blend of ecological, cultural and adventure opportunities.' WOW's objectives are to provide visitors with high-quality experiences based on the natural environment, to implement best practice in environmental management and to expand, protect and restore the land and wildlife.

Minnewanka Tours, Canada: Rather than undertaking physical expansion, the company has been active in improving the quality of its equipment and service. Boats get refitted and replaced, and all equipment is kept up to date. Increasing numbers of tourists, in line with growing visitation to Banff National Park in general, have put pressure on the provision of service but also generated more revenue.

Henry of Pelham, Canada: Their dedication to high quality in viticulture and oenology has been rewarded with over 50 international awards. The family winery offers a tasting bar and cellar store, and in 2002 they opened the Coach House Café adjacent to the cellar door saleroom. Winery tours, picnic areas, art exhibitions and events are part of the winery experience, and an annual Shakespearean performance is popular among visitors from Toronto.

Rivendell, Australia: The owners' vision to create and operate this winery has been pursued with a passion since the early 1980s. During that time there have been a number of partnerships, with family members and non-family partners, lease arrangements and equity funding that provided the much needed capital. However, this also limited the control that the owners had to protect the integrity of the business and the quality of food, wine and preserves which is associated with the name Rivendell.

O'Reilly's Rainforest Guesthouse, Australia: A good example of how a successful family brand, developed through four generations, has not only been extended into new product lines (including merchandise and wines) but has had a positive effect on destination image as well. It is not uncommon to hear people say they are going to O'Reilly's for a holiday or short break – as opposed to saying they are going to Lamington National Park, where it is situated, or to the Gold Coast hinterland. Their overall emphasis on quality is reflected in the obtaining of Advanced Accreditation under the Nature and Ecotourism Accreditation Program.

Crystal Creek Rainforest Lodge, Australia: This accommodation business is situated on a 2000 ha subtropical rainforest property adjoining a World Heritage listed nature reserve in eastern Australia. It features pristine surroundings, luxury bungalows, walking trails, fine cuisine and a small functions centre. In keeping with the theme of peace and tranquillity, accommodation is limited to seven couples at any one time, and each bungalow provides total privacy amidst the rainforest. Bungalows have all modern facilities and guests can order fine cuisine prepared on the property by the owners, Ralph and Judy. This couple established the business in 1992 after retiring from their professional careers. They explicitly sought a natural location because of Ralph's lifelong interest in wildlife and nature, while Judy brought with her a love of art and cooking. Professionals were hired to design the development, which has won several environmental tourism awards.

Most businesses we have studied did not have a focus on customer service, even though it was implicit in all of their business activities and in one case improving customer service was stated as a business goal. Personal service is sometimes promoted as a unique selling point of family businesses, where the customer knows that they are dealing with the people that both own and operate the business. There can also be a market perception that family businesses are unique and offer a different product or service from that offered by a non-family businesses. This belief that it is better to be unique than to try and compete with existing businesses was apparent, with one owner claiming 'it is better to be different, than it is to be better'. When there is a high degree of social interaction with visitors, the privacy of family members is lost and it can also make it difficult to complete the daily tasks of running the business. However, one business does give priority to social interaction and customer service ahead of the other tasks in the running of the business. The owner said that he did not mind if it 'takes one and a half hours to empty the rubbish bins' if he is socializing with visitors around the caravan park.

5.5 Conclusions

Quality is a major issue in the family business sector, considering specific aspects of the owners' motives, goals and family dynamics. There are many inherent factors that act against quality of business and service in family businesses in tourism and hospitality, all of which also have a negative impact on destination quality and competitiveness. There are also inherent factors that, in special family businesses, generate superb experiences and successful businesses. Additionally, there are a minority of owner-operators who pursue profit and growth, who can therefore be expected to help realize goals for economic development and destination competitiveness.

The conceptual model put forward in this chapter places family vision at the core, as the majority of tourism and hospitality businesses appear to be started for lifestyle and autonomy reasons, thereby precluding or limiting growth. A focus on the owners' lifestyle, location and internal (family-first) goals might very well have a negative impact on quality, whereas a strong desire for hands-on work and a craftsperson's special interest (such as cooking, guiding, decorating) might also be expected to result in an emphasis on product and service quality. For those exceptional family businesses that grow and profit under entrepreneurial guidance by the owners, the outer ring of the model suggests that innovation, family branding and a destination orientation will follow. These are also the businesses most likely to be inherited.

Case studies and other research findings reported in this chapter point to practical implications for family businesses, support agencies and destinations. Owner-operators who are primarily oriented towards autonomy and lifestyle might find it a struggle to sustain a viable business, let alone improve it in terms of quality. They need the ongoing support of economic development and tourism agencies, first in terms of developing sound business management practices, then in terms of quality enhancements and value adding. However, agencies seeking employment growth and destinations pursuing aggressive competitive or repositioning strategies will probably find that the majority of small, family businesses do not contribute. In those cases it is desirable to identify, attract and cultivate profit- and growth-oriented entrepreneurs.

Considerably more research and experimentation are necessary to better understand the family business in tourism and hospitality as it affects quality. What incentives and support systems will work best for the lifestyle and autonomy seekers as opposed to the profit- and growth-oriented owners? Can destinations and development agencies find practical ways to attract and cultivate those who will maximize quality and competitiveness? Perhaps the biggest challenge is to find effective ways to reach and convince the majority of small, family-business owners with appealing programmes for continuous quality improvement.

Note

[1]In this chapter we have drawn from our book *The Family Business in Tourism and Hospitality* (2004, CAB International, Wallingford, UK).

References

Andersson, T., Carlsen, J. and Getz, D. (2002) Family business goals in the tourism and hospitality sector: case studies and cross-cases analysis from Australia, Canada, and Sweden. *Family Business Review* 15(2), 89–106.

Ateljevic. I. and Doorne, S. (2000) 'Staying within the fence': lifestyle entrepreneurship in tourism. *Journal of Sustainable Tourism* 8(5), 378–392.

Birley, S. (2001) Owner-manager attitudes to family and business issues: a 16-country study. *Journal of Small Business Management* 26(2), 63–76.

Bransgrove, C. and King, B. (1996) Strategic marketing practice among small tourism and hospitality businesses. In: Thomas, R. (ed.) *Spring Symposium Proceedings of*

International Association of Hotel Management Schools. Leeds Metropolitan University, Leeds, UK, pp. 29–38.

Brockhaus, R. (1994) Entrepreneurship and family business: comparisons, critique, and lessons. *Entrepreneurship Theory and Practice* Fall, 25–38.

Chua, J., Chrisman, J. and Sharma, P. (1999) Defining the family business by behaviour. *Entrepreneurship Theory and Practice* 23(4), 19–37.

Dunn, B. (1995) Success themes in Scottish family enterprises: philosophies and practices through the generations. *Family Business Review* 8(1), 17–28.

Gartner, W. (1988) 'Who is the entrepreneur?' is the wrong question. *American Journal of Small Business* 12, 11–32.

Gersick, K., Davis, J., Hampton, M. and Lansberg, I. (1997) *Generation to Generation: Life Cycles of Family Business.* Harvard Business School Press, Boston, 302 pp.

Getz, D. and Carlsen, J. (2000) Characteristics and goals of family and owner-operated businesses in the rural tourism and hospitality sectors. *Tourism Management* 21, 547–560.

Getz, D. and Nilsson, P. (2004) Responses of family businesses to extreme seasonality in demand: the case of Bornholm, Denmark. *Tourism Management* 25(1), 17–30.

Getz, D., Carlsen, J. and Morrison, A. (2004) *The Family Business in Tourism and Hospitality*, CAB International, Wallingford, UK, 214 pp.

Katz, J. (1995). Which track are you on? *Inc.* 17, 27–28.

Middleton, V. (2001) The importance of micro-businesses in European tourism. In: Roberts, L. and Hall, D. (eds) *Rural Tourism and Recreation: Principles to Practice.* CAB International, Wallingford, UK, pp. 197–201.

Nilsson, P., Petersen, T. and Wanhill, S. (2003) *Public Support for Tourism SMEs in Peripheral Areas: the Arjeplog Project, Northern Sweden.* Centre for Regional and Tourism Research, Bornholm, Denmark.

Risker, D. (1998) Toward an innovation typology of entrepreneurs. *Journal of Small Business and Entrepreneurship* 15(2), 27–41.

Ryan, C. (1998) Dolphins, canoes and Marae: ecotourism products in New Zealand. In: Laws, E., Faulkner, B. and Moscardo, G. (eds) *Embracing and Managing Change in Tourism.* Routledge, London, pp. 285–306.

Sexton, D. and Kent, C. (1981) Female executives versus female entrepreneurs. In: Vesper, K. (ed.) *Frontiers of Entrepreneurship Research: The Proceedings of the 1981 Babson Conference on Entrepreneurship.* Babson College, Wellesley, Massachusetts, pp. 40–45.

Shaw, G. and Williams, A. (1998) Entrepreneurship, small business, culture and tourism development. In: Ioannides, D. and Debbage, K. (eds) *The Economic Geography of the Tourist Industry: a Supply-side Analysis.* Routledge, London, pp. 235–255.

Smith, R. (1967) *The Entrepreneur and the Firm.* Bureau of Business and Economic Research, Michigan State University, East Lansing, Michigan.

Taylor, S., Simpson, J. and Howie, H. (1998) Financing small businesses. In: Thomas, R. (ed.) *The Management of Small Tourism and Hospitality Firms.* Cassell, London, pp. 58–77.

Twining-Ward, L. and Baum, T. (1998) Dilemmas facing mature island destinations: cases from the Baltic. *Progress in Tourism and Hospitality Research* 4, 131–140.

Ucbasaran, D., Westhead, P. and Wright, M. (2001) The focus of entrepreneurial research: contextual and process issues. *Entrepreneurship Theory and Practice* Summer, 57–80.

Westhead, P. and Cowling, M. (1998) Family firm research: the need for a methodological rethink. *Entrepreneurship Theory and Practice* Fall, 31–56.

6

Capability-based Growth: the Case of UK Tourism SMEs

MARCJANNA M. AUGUSTYN[1] AND JOHN PHEBY[2]

[1]Department of Leisure, Tourism and Hospitality, School of Sport, Performing Arts and Leisure, University of Wolverhampton, Walsall, UK; [2]Department of Strategy and HR, Luton Business School, University of Luton, Luton, UK

6.1 Introduction

Why do some tourism enterprises continuously grow while others experience stagnation, decline or fluctuations in growth? It can be argued that external barriers to growth, such as limited access to financial resources, government regulations, barriers to entry, existing and potential competition, political unrest or cataclysms, are chief among the factors hindering the growth of tourism enterprises. While these external barriers to growth can partly explain the differences in performance of tourism enterprises operating in differing external environments (e.g. in geographical locations of varied socio-economic and political environments), they do not sufficiently explain the reasons for the diverse performance levels of tourism enterprises that operate within similar external environments.

The search for gaining a greater understanding of the reasons for the diverse performance levels of tourism firms directs our attention towards considering internal barriers to growth. The major internal factors that hinder the performance of tourism enterprises include their inability to attract and retain good quality staff, their inability to attract new customers or retain existing customers, their inability to manage supply chains and their inability to develop effective distribution channels. All these internal barriers to growth are related to either the lack of adequate resources or the inability of the firm to convert these resources into distinctive organizational capabilities. Indeed, it is increasingly being argued that, for enterprises to succeed and sustain growth, they need to achieve a capabilities-based competitive advantage. The development of specific capability platforms that enable firms to launch themselves on to a growth trajectory constitutes an integral part of this process.

This chapter investigates the ways in which UK tourism small and medium-sized enterprises (SMEs)[1] convert their resource base into distinct capability platforms that give them a competitive advantage and enable them to grow. The types of growth-enabling capabilities within this sector are also discussed. The factors constraining growth as well as the factors that contribute towards the growth of tourism SMEs are identified. A dynamic McKinsey Consultants' model that seeks to analyse growth over differing time horizons in relation to capability platforms that underpin growth at each stage of the firm's development is deployed in this study as an analytical framework.

6.2 Capabilities-based Competitive Advantage

The strategic focus on analysing industry external environment and competitive positioning, grounded in the work of Michael Porter (1980, 1985), enabled many organizations to achieve competitive advantage and growth. However, the value of these approaches to gaining competitive advantage and growth was eroded in the 1990s due to greater market fragmentation and proliferation, changing customer preferences, shorter product life cycles and globalization (Stalk *et al.*, 1992; Grant, 2002). In searching for alternative approaches to gaining sustainable competitive advantage the attention of scholars and practitioners focused on the internal environment of the firm, and particularly on the effective use of the firm's resources. Consequently, a new paradigm for competition, known as the resource-based view (RBV) of the firm, was developed.

Central to the RBV is the assumption that the firm is a pool of resources and capabilities which are the primary source of its profitability and as such should be the primary determinants of the firm's strategy (Wernerfelt, 1984). Advocates of the RBV stress, however, that resources[2] rarely create value on their own and that it is the development of organizational capabilities[3] that leads to a firm's growth in today's dynamic business environment (e.g. Barney, 1991; Rumelt, 1991; Peteraf, 1993; Hamel and Prahalad, 1994; Collis and Montgomery, 1995; Man *et al.*, 2002; Jones and Tilley, 2003). Outcomes of recently conducted empirical research across various economic sectors confirm this thesis (e.g. Rangone, 1999; Spanos and Lioukas, 2001; Afuah, 2002; Lerner and Almor, 2002; Schroeder *et al.*, 2002).

Capabilities-based competition assumes, therefore, that the firm's competitive advantage stems from a strategy that is built around the unique combination of the firm's key business processes, organizational routines, knowledge and skills, which are transformed into strategic organizational capabilities (Stalk *et al.*, 1992). It should be noted, however, that not all abilities of an organization are of strategic value but only those that deliver value to the customer, possess collective and cross-functional character, are valuable across multiple products or markets and are unique[4] in relation to other firms (Stalk *et al.*, 1992; Hamel and Prahalad, 1994; Teece *et al.*, 1997; Besanko *et al.*, 2004). Organizational capabilities possessing the above attributes constitute an essential source of competitive advantage, as they represent the hidden or invisible assets of an organization that cannot be easily imitated by a competitor (Prahalad and Hamel, 1990; Mintzberg *et al.*, 1998).

Establishing capabilities-based competitive advantage involves formulating and implementing strategies that exploit the firm's internal differences through converting resources into distinctive, scarce and valuable capabilities. The strategic focus is placed on developing capabilities rather than products. Hamel and Prahalad (1994) believe that capabilities are the roots of the firm's competitiveness while individual products are the fruits.

The RBV paradigm for competition, which defines a firm in terms of what the firm is capable of doing better than its competitors, may provide the firm with a much more durable basis on which to build its competitive position and grow within a constantly changing environment. This is mainly due to the fact that the non-product-specific organizational capabilities enable a firm to diversify by reapplying its experience and best practice from one setting to another and to contribute to the competitiveness of a range of products offered by the firm (Makadok, 2001).

6.3 Building Capability Platforms

The process of developing strategic organizational capabilities entails converting the firm's resources into hierarchical capability platforms, where more general, broadly defined capabilities are formed from the integration of more specialized resources and capabilities (Grant, 2002). There are two stages in the process of developing hierarchical capability platforms (Fig. 6.1), according to Turner and Crawford (1994) and Militello and Schwalberg (2002). The first step in this process involves the creative blending of the firm's tangible, intangible and human resources into unique lower-order foundation capabilities, i.e. those minimum capabilities that the firm commands for its competitive performance. The second step in this process comprises the merging of the firm's resources and foundation

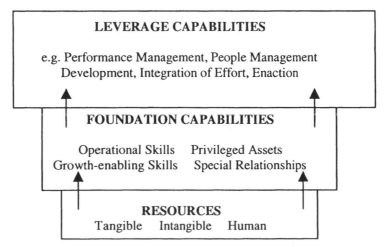

Fig. 6.1. The process of building capability platforms (based on Turner and Crawford, 1994; Baghai *et al.*, 1999; Militello and Schwalberg, 2002).

capabilities into higher-order leverage capabilities, i.e. capabilities that confer upon the firm its growth and sustainable competitive advantage.

A useful framework for classifying foundation capabilities for growth is offered by McKinsey Consultants (Baghai et al., 1999), who identify four categories of capabilities: operational skills, privileged assets, growth-enabling skills and special relationships. Operational skills refer to issues such as how well the company operates management information systems, research and development and product and service design (Baghai et al., 1999).

Privileged assets, both tangible and intangible, are those assets that are unique to the organization and that are valuable. According to Collins and Montgomery (1995), an asset is valuable if it is hard to copy (measured by its physical uniqueness, its accumulation path dependency, its causal ambiguity and its economic deterrence), if it is durable (measured by its depreciation time), if it is appropriate (measured by the ability to capture the value that the asset creates), if it cannot be easily substituted by a different asset and if it is competitively superior. Examples of privileged assets include distribution networks, brands and reputation, customer information, infrastructure and intellectual property.

Growth-enabling skills include acquisitions skills, financing and risk management skills and capital management skills. Finally, special relationships – for example, with existing customers and suppliers, powerful individuals, businesses and governments – can unlock growth opportunities that would otherwise not be available (Baghai et al., 1999).

The changing and tacit[5] nature of leverage capabilities makes it difficult to provide a full list of such capabilities. Nevertheless, some typologies of capabilities that the literature provides may assist firms and researchers in identifying leverage capabilities. The typologies developed by Ulrich and Lake (1990), Turner and Crawford (1994) and Spanos and Lioukas (2001) were of particular use in interpreting the primary data in this study (Table 6.1). These three approaches to categorizing capabilities demonstrate both similarities and differences. While Ulrich and Lake (1990) as well as Spanos and Lioukas (2001) classify capabilities in broad, functional terms, the classification of Turner and Crawford (1994) provides mainly an insight into cross-functional capabilities.

Apart from these three generic typologies of capabilities, Man et al. (2002) identified four types of leverage capabilities that are typical for SMEs:

- Innovation, i.e. the ability to innovate in new products, services and processes.
- Quality, i.e. the ability to maintain or achieve high quality in products or services, which leads to the firm's good image and reputation.
- Cost-effectiveness, i.e. the ability to achieve cost-effectiveness so as to set a competitive price.
- Organicity, i.e. the ability to create and maintain flexible, organic organizational structures and systems for achieving production speed and responsiveness (Man et al., 2002).

The literature stresses, however, that the value of organizational capabilities changes over time as the business environment changes and what once constituted leverage capability may become a foundation capability (Hamel and

Table 6.1. Typologies of capabilities.

Ulrich and Lake (1990)	Turner and Crawford (1994)	Spanos and Lioukas (2001)
Financial capability, i.e. the ability of a business to produce the good or service at a lower cost than its competitors; the ability of a business to manage the costs and financial systems more effectively than its competitors through lower supplier costs or lower overhead costs	*Performance management*, i.e. the ability of a firm to monitor performance against clearly set goals within a strategic framework and to reinforce or adjust activities in response to current outcomes and circumstances with a view to improving current performance and initiating positive incremental change	*Management capability*, i.e. the ability to encompass managerial competencies, knowledge and skills of employees together with efficient organizational structure, organizational culture, efficient mechanisms of coordination, strategic planning procedures and ability to attract creative employees
Strategic/marketing capability, i.e. the ability of a firm to offer products that the customers perceive as having added value and that differentiate the firm from its competitors	*Resource application*, i.e. the ability of a firm to ensure that suitable resources work together to best support the organization's strategic intent and to maximize the benefit gained from the assets available	*Marketing capability*, i.e. the ability to combine building privileged relationships with customers and suppliers with market knowledge, control over distribution channels and a strongly installed customer base
Technological capability, i.e. the ability of a firm to utilize technological advancements in order to offer innovative products	*People management*, i.e. the ability of a firm to motivate staff to achieve willingness and the intent to work in ways consistent with the firm's objectives	*Technical capability*, i.e. the ability to convert input into outputs, including efficient production and the ability to create economies of scale

continued

Table 6.1. *Continued*.

Ulrich and Lake (1990)	Turner and Crawford (1994)	Spanos and Lioukas (2001)
	Integration of effort, i.e. the ability of a firm to coordinate the actions of the firm's members and to ensure coherence among the firm's practices, systems and policies so that the firm's efforts are focused on achieving its objectives and counter-productive or wasted effort is prevented	
	Enaction, i.e. the ability of a firm to carry decisions into action in a timely and effective way	
	Pathfinding, i.e. the ability of a firm to identify, crystallize and articulate achievable new directions for the firm to find new avenues for survival and profit	
	Development, i.e. the ability of a firm to change the firm's assets in order to enhance their relevance to the firm's activities and directions over time with a view to increasing the firm's capability to perform effectively in the future through the creation of assets well suited to its future circumstances	

Prahalad, 1994; Turner and Crawford, 1994). For example, while some of the leverage capabilities typical for SMEs (Man *et al.*, 2002) are genuine differentiators within this sector (e.g. quality and cost-effectiveness), they are routine advantages in the case of successful large organizations. Consequently, organizations must take a dynamic approach to capability development, which assumes that, once capability platforms have been built, they need to be occasionally reconfigured (including the development of new capabilities) to address the changing internal and external environments (Teece *et al.*, 1997; Eisenhardt and Martin, 2000).

The lifespan of capabilities depends on whether they can be easily imitated by competitors or whether they are mobile between firms (Grant, 2002). The more difficult it is for rival companies to acquire or imitate a capability, the longer the durability of this capability is in terms of its potential for conferring sustainable competitive advantage. In building capability platforms, it is therefore necessary to ensure that they cannot be easily transferred across firms. Grant (2002) identifies several sources of capability immobility, including geographical immobility of natural resources, complementarity of resources and capabilities, accumulation of resources and capabilities over a long period, imperfect information concerning the organizational processes, and context-specific performance of individuals and teams embedded in organizational routines and culture.

6.4 Capability Platforms and the Sustained Growth of Firms

Based on extensive international primary research of over 100 companies, McKinsey Consultants argue that the sustained growth of a firm results from the firm's ability to build an incremental growth staircase. Development of appropriate capabilities underpins each step on this growth staircase. These capability platforms launch a firm on to the next stage of its growth trajectory (Baghai *et al.*, 1999).

Such a systematic approach to growth enables firms to address two major risks associated with the dynamic nature of the business environment: market uncertainty and capability gaps (Baghai *et al.*, 1999). The risk of market uncertainty is reduced by taking one step at a time; the step that enables a firm to respond to a particular characteristic of the business environment at that time. Such a sequential approach to growth also enables the firm to capture the opportunities that have arisen in the business environment at that time. Furthermore, every step on the growth staircase is associated with learning new skills and extending the portfolio of the firm's unique and hard to imitate capabilities, which can lead a firm to gaining a lasting competitive advantage (Baghai *et al.*, 1999).

McKinsey Consultants' approach to sustained growth is therefore associated with the concept of incremental organizational learning, as the capability platforms developed at each step of the firm's growth staircase represent a synthesis of learning across individual organizational units and individual members of the organization (Hamel and Prahalad, 1994). Indeed, as Teece *et al.*

(1997) stress, capabilities are the unique and idiosyncratic processes that emerge from path-dependent histories of individual firms, their experience and learning processes. Thus, the McKinsey Consultants' model provides a useful framework for analysing a firm's growth over differing time horizons and for gaining an insight into the types of capability platforms that facilitate each step on the firm's incremental growth staircase.

6.5 Methodology

A study aimed at investigating the ways in which UK tourism SMEs convert their resource base into distinct capability platforms that give them a competitive advantage and enable them to grow was conducted in 2002. This entailed a detailed investigation into the existing resources and capabilities of those firms. It was also necessary to establish which distinctive capabilities contributed to the growth of a particular firm at each stage of its growth history. The factors constraining growth as well as the factors that contribute towards the growth of tourism SMEs were also identified.

Given the detail necessary to consider such issues, a comparative case study approach was adopted. Criterion-based sampling was employed in the process of selecting the case study subjects from the population of UK private tourism SMEs. In particular, the enterprises should have:

1. Been in business for at least 10 years.
2. Enjoyed sustained growth over a period of at least 5 years.
3. Employed fewer than 50 people at the beginning of their operation.[6]

Furthermore, the data necessary for the attainment of the aim of the study needed to be accessible and comparable.

An on-line directory of UK Registered Companies (FAME[7]) constituted the sampling frame from which the case study subjects were drawn. A search for the firms relevant to this study was conducted using the FAME advanced search criteria. The total number of UK private tourism SMEs featured in this directory amounted to 2645 firms. To ensure availability of the firms' performance data, the search was then limited to only those firms that were active and supplied updated reports. This process identified 126 firms (4.8% of the total number of tourism SMEs within the sampling frame). As the database provides extensive information on the financial performance of companies, the reports of all 126 firms were scrutinized against the first two criteria for the choice of the case study subjects. Only seven firms satisfied the criteria established for the purpose of this study. Based on the results of an extensive analysis of the growth indicators of these seven firms, the firms were ranked in order from the best performing firm and then contacted in the same order. The top three firms identified in the ranking agreed to participate in the study. However, in one case (the second firm) the interviewee did not represent the senior management so the information needed for the study was partial. A fourth firm was thus contacted, which agreed to participate in the study.

The case studies are based on material derived mainly from primary data that were collected using the technique of semi-structured in-depth telephone interviews with senior managers of the selected firms. Secondary sources of information were used only to broaden the researchers' knowledge of the firms' backgrounds.

The data were analysed against the McKinsey Consultants' model (Baghai *et al.*, 1999), which seeks to analyse growth over different time horizons in relation to capability platforms that underpin growth at each stage of the firm's development. The terminology used in describing the firm's capabilities originates mostly, but not exclusively, from Turner and Crawford's (1994) typology of capabilities.

6.6 The Experience of UK Tourism SMEs

6.6.1 Profiles of the case study subjects

The three case study subjects selected for this study (labelled the Hotel, the Coach Operator and the Events Organizer) demonstrate a number of differences and similarities in their profiles (Table 6.2). The main characteristics that differentiate these firms include the sector of the tourism industry that they represent (tourist accommodation, travel services and events organizers) and consequently

Table 6.2. Profiles of the case study subjects.

Firm attribute	The Hotel	The Coach Operator	The Events Organizer
Year of starting the firm	1897	1956	1987
Employees (no. in 2002)	80	135	85
Type of business	Private limited (family)	Private limited (family)	Private limited
Location (county)	Powys	Northamptonshire	West Yorkshire
Trade description	Hotel with restaurant	Coach and bus services	Organization of events and training
1992 SIC UK code	5511	6023	7484
Main services	Accommodation Catering Special events Health treatment Other	Supplier of transport to the travel trade, local authorities, schools Tailored tours Holidays Excursions Corporate transport Coach hire	Events management Incentive programmes Business travel Team-building sessions Other

the main type of services that they offer. Furthermore, these three firms differ in terms of their age (ranging from 105 years in the case of the Hotel to 15 years in the case of the Events Organizer) and in terms of the location of their operation (different parts of the UK).

Despite these differences, the three firms demonstrate a number of similar characteristics. First, they are all private limited companies, with the Hotel and the Coach Operator also being family businesses. Secondly, they have been continuously growing since their inception and joined the league of the leading firms within the sectors they represent and within their regional (the Hotel and the Coach Operator) or national (the Events Organizer) markets. Indeed, the growth of these firms enabled them to move from the category of small businesses (employing fewer than 50 people) to the category of medium-sized businesses (employing fewer than 250 people). The most impressive growth in terms of the numbers of employees was recorded by the Events Organizer (from 18 employees in 1998 to 85 employees in 2002). It should be noted, however, that more recently the Coach Operator recorded a slight decline in the numbers of people employed (Table 6.3). Nevertheless, the overall performance of the company between 1999 and 2002 was positive with all but one (i.e. net sales) performance indicators demonstrating the growth of the firm. Similarly, the performance of the Hotel and the Events Organizer between 1999 and 2002 was highly positive (Table 6.3).

While the similar characteristics of the case study subjects provide an essential comparative basis for this analysis, the major differences between the firms are important for the process of data interpretation.

6.6.2 Converting resources into capability platforms

In order to examine ways in which UK tourism SMEs convert their resource base into distinct capability platforms that give them a competitive advantage and enable them to grow, it was first necessary to identify the essential resources of the case study subjects. As indicated in Table 6.4, the three firms possess a

Table 6.3. Key performance indicators[a] of the case study subjects.

Firm indicator	The Hotel	The Coach Operator	The Events Organizer
Employee number	0	−9[b]	+48
Net sales	+15	−2[b]	+39
Net sales per employee	+15	+7[b]	−6
Operating income	+14	+175	+23
Net income	+85	+36	+23
Total assets	−24	+14	+29
Remuneration per employee	+6	+11[b]	+23
Profits before tax	+141	+25	+30
Profits after tax	+84	+30	+23

[a]Percentage growth (+)/decline (−) over 3 years (base: 1999).
[b]Over 2 years (base: 2000).

Table 6.4. Key resources of the case study subjects.

Firm resources	The Hotel	The Coach Operator	The Events Organizer
Tangible	Grand building	Travel shop	Two offices in the UK
	Location	Variety of coaches	One office in the USA
	Diverse facilities		
Human	Experience	Experience	Experience
	Professionalism	Professionalism	Professionalism
	Employee commitment	Management commitment	Employee commitment
	Management continuity	Management continuity	Knowledge and expertise (know-how)
	Networking skills of the owner	IT skills	
Intangible	High standard of service	High standard of service	High standard of service
	Established customer base	Established customer base	Established customer base
	Member of Best Western	Member of five trade associations	Member of three trade associations
	External recognition (IiP)	External recognition (awards)	External recognition (awards)
			Organizational culture

number of similar resources, particularly within the area of human and intangible resources (the types of services that the firms offer explain the differences in the types of tangible resources). The firms identified experience and professionalism as the most important human resources. Indeed, the senior manager of the Hotel stressed during the interview: 'If I could bottle the professionalism of the staff here and sell it, I would be a millionaire.'

The commitment of the employees or management was also seen as an important human resource. While the Hotel and the Coach Operator stressed the significance of management continuity, the Events Organizer identified knowledge and expertise across the whole range of disciplines as another important human resource. In terms of skills, the Hotel emphasized the importance of the owner's networking skills while the Coach Operator identified IT skills as an important human resource.

The intangible resources that the firms possess are similar and include a high standard of service, membership of professional bodies, external recognition and an established customer base. The only exception occurs in the case of the Events Organizer, who also identified organizational culture (i.e. the firm's values, traditions and social norms) as an important intangible resource.

What foundation capabilities have these three firms developed using the resources that they possess? It is interesting to note that, despite a very high level of similarity in the type of resources that each firm possesses, the types of foundation capabilities developed by each firm differ to a greater extent than their resources do (Table 6.5). The greatest level of similarity occurs within the group of privileged assets, where all firms possess flexibility of infrastructure or service, reputation, customer loyalty and value distribution networks. Within the group of operational skills, all firms developed the capability of responding to trends and, within the group of growth-enabling skills, the capability of leadership. The capability of developing special relationships with customers and access-conveying bodies is also present in all firms studied.

The study shows, however, that some foundation capabilities characterize only two firms. These capabilities include product enhancement in the case of the Hotel and the Coach Operator and discovering new competitive arenas in the case of the Coach Operator and the Events Organizer. A number of similar foundation capabilities were developed by the Hotel and the Events Organizer, including the ability to attract quality staff, the ability to motivate and enthuse staff, the ability to develop staff and the ability to establish special relationships with their suppliers and with powerful individuals (Table 6.5).

Using similar resources (Table 6.4), the firms subject to this analysis also developed unique foundation capabilities that other firms studied did not. For example, in terms of operational skills, the Hotel developed the capability of creating a 'wow' factor and the capability of delivering effective customer service, the Coach Operator developed the capability of cost reduction and the Events Organizer developed the capability of attention to detail. In terms of growth-enabling skills, the Coach Operator developed the capability of acquisition-based expansion, while the Events Organizer developed the capability of merger-based expansion. Finally, the Hotel also developed special relationships with overseas labour markets as a unique foundation capability.

The similarities between the three case study subjects in terms of the types of foundation capabilities that the firms developed indicate that the same foundation capabilities contribute to the firms' competitiveness despite the sectors they represent. The differences indicate that the firms can convert a similar resource base into unique foundation capabilities that enable these firms to compete within their specific sectors.

Through the process of creative integration of similar resources and partly different foundation capabilities, the firms developed unique higher-order leverage capabilities that lay behind the growth of each firm at each stage of their growth history, as explained below.

6.6.3 Staircases to growth of the case study subjects

McKinsey Consultants' model (Baghai et al., 1999) was used to analyse the growth of the firms over various time horizons and to identify the types of leverage capabilities that underpinned the firms' growth processes.

Table 6.5. Key foundation capabilities of the case study subjects.

Firm capabilities	The Hotel	The Coach Operator	The Events Organizer
Operational skills	Responding to trends Product enhancement Attracting quality staff Motivating and enthusing Creating a 'wow' factor Effective customer service	Responding to trends Product enhancement Discovering new competitive arenas Cost reduction	Responding to trends Discovering new competitive arenas Attracting quality staff Motivating and enthusing Attention to detail
Privileged assets	Infrastructure/service flexibility Reputation Customer loyalty Value distribution network	Infrastructure/service flexibility Reputation Customer loyalty Value distribution network	Infrastructure/service flexibility Reputation Customer loyalty Value distribution network
Growth-enabling skills	Leadership Staff development	Leadership Geographical expansion Acquisition-based expansion	Leadership Geographical expansion Staff development Merger-based expansion
Special relationships with:	Customers Access-conveying bodies Suppliers Powerful individuals Overseas labour markets	Customers Access-conveying bodies	Customers Access-conveying bodies Suppliers Powerful individuals

6.6.3.1 The Hotel's staircase to growth

While ensuring guest comfort and enjoyment has been the Hotel's priority since the beginning of its operation and management continuity was the major growth-enabling factor throughout the Hotel's history, there were five distinctive steps on the Hotel's staircase to growth, each underpinned by specific leverage capabilities (see Fig. 6.2). In the first period of the Hotel's operation (1897–1960s), product innovation enabled the growth of the Hotel. This process involved several stages of the Hotel's enlargement, which have led to the increase in its capacity from 40 to 200 guests. New facilities were also added (e.g. a swimming-pool was opened in 1935), existing facilities refurbished and new events introduced.

The operational skills that the Hotel acquired in the first 60 years of its operation, and particularly the product enhancement and the Hotel's ability to respond to market trends, contributed to the further growth of the Hotel in the 1970s. In particular, the Hotel's refurbishment programme of that time included the transformation of the existing rooms into *en suite* rooms. The Hotel also opened its Leisure Suite in 1977, which incorporated a Health Suite that offered comprehensive treatment for the guests. The Hotel's capabilities of development and resource application constituted the essential platforms that took the firm to the next step on its growth staircase.

The Hotel's ability to monitor its performance against a clear set of strategic goals and to adjust its activities with a view to improving its performance (i.e. performance management capability) underpinned the Hotel's growth in the 1980s. The Hotel's established image, reputation and customer loyalty, as well as good relationships with important stakeholders, greatly facilitated this process.

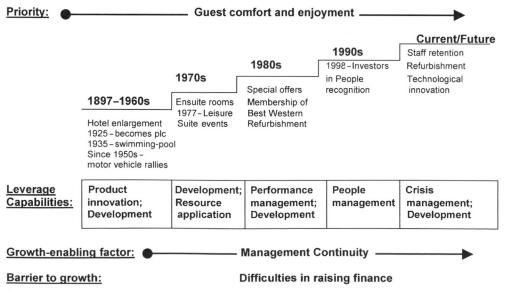

Fig. 6.2.   The Hotel's staircase to growth and leverage capabilities.

In the 1990s, the Hotel capitalized on its ability to attract quality staff, including quality temporary foreign staff, through the Hotel's well-established relations with overseas labour markets, its ability to motivate and develop staff and its strong leadership. Indeed, people management was the Hotel's leverage capability of that time, as the firm appreciated the value of the human aspect of the services it offered. Indeed, the Hotel gained Investor in People (IiP) recognition in 1998, which constituted a big stimulus to the further growth of the firm.

The Hotel continues to build upon this strength and its commitment to people management was reflected in the fact that despite a significant loss of £250,000 that the Hotel incurred due to the foot-and-mouth disease, it did not lay off any staff. The organizational capabilities developed throughout the history of the Hotel enabled the company to recover quickly from the crisis of the early years of the twenty-first century. The Hotel is currently reapplying its capability of development to launch itself on to the next step on its growth trajectory. The major changes to the Hotel's assets include incorporating technological innovation into the operations of the Hotel and as an important component of the product offered as well as the development of the state-of-the-art conference and restaurant facilities. Potential difficulties in raising finance are, however, perceived by the senior management of the firm as the major barrier to the future growth of the Hotel.

6.6.3.2 The Coach Operator's staircase to growth

The firm identified the highest standard of service and reliability as its major priority and management continuity as the essential growth-enabling factor. The Coach Operator's staircase to growth also consists of five steps, underpinned by the capabilities that have enabled the firm to grow for nearly 50 years (Fig. 6.3).

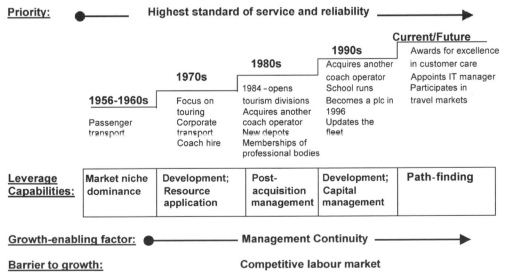

Fig. 6.3. The Coach Operator's staircase to growth and leverage capabilities.

The firm was established in 1956 with a view to offering passenger transport. Market niche dominance enabled the firm to grow throughout the 1950s and 1960s. However, the increasing competition within the passenger transport industry in the 1970s, combined with the firm's flexible infrastructure and its ability to enhance product and respond to market trends, encouraged the Coach Operator to shift its original focus of operation to the new area of offering touring services. Additionally, the company started to offer corporate transport services and coach hire. The capabilities of development and resource application thus facilitated the firm's growth in the 1970s.

While the Coach Operator continued to be successful in serving the tourism market and opened two specialized tourism divisions in 1984 (a tailored tours division and a travel shop), the major factor that stimulated the firm's growth in the 1980s was the acquisition of another coach operator and the firm's ability to effectively manage post-acquisition relations. In particular, a comprehensive training programme for drivers was introduced at that time.

The next decade in the Coach Operator's growth history was also associated with its significant growth. This success was partly associated with acquiring another coach operator. However, the dominant factor that underpinned the Coach Operator's growth in the 1990s was the reapplication of the development capability that proved to significantly enhance the company's performance in the 1970s. This time, however, the firm's focus shifted to offering school-run services as they proved to be very profitable. Although the touring services were still offered by the company, they no longer constituted the major area of the firm's activity. The firm's growth in the 1990s was also underpinned by its capital management capability and significant investment in updating the fleet.

Despite very impressive and sustained growth between the 1960s and 1990s, the performance of the Coach Operator was slightly worse at the beginning of the twenty-first century, particularly in terms of the decline in employment (Table 6.3). The firm explains this decline in employment by the competitive nature of the labour market due to the shortage of drivers, a trend that characterized this industry in the 1990s. The firm's inability to retain good staff also contributed to this decline. However, the initiatives for the future, which include appointing an IT manager and the firm's participation in travel markets, which are underpinned by the development of a path-finding capability, do not directly address the barriers to growth that the firm identified.

6.6.3.3 The Events Organizer's staircase to growth

Although the youngest of the three firms analysed in this study, the Events Organizer has been continuously growing since being formed. The firm was established from the merger of two successful events organizers that operated independently between 1987 and 1997. Resource application conferred growth on both companies in that period. The geographical synergy of these two firms (one was operating in the south and the other in the north), their complementary activities and their well-established customer bases led to the merger of these two companies in 1998 (Fig. 6.4).

The major priority for the Events Organizer is to deliver creative, experimental solutions that inspire improved performance and knowledge in teams and

Priority: **Delivering creative, experimental solutions that inspire improved performance and knowledge** ➤

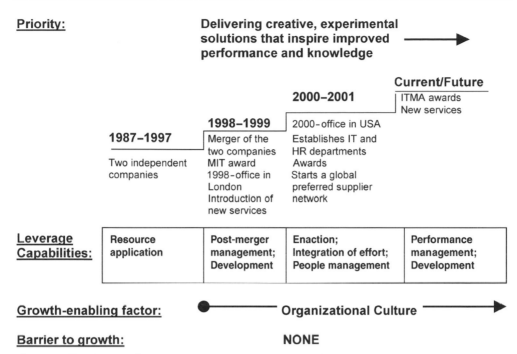

Fig. 6.4. The Events Organizer's staircase to growth and leverage capabilities.

individuals. Following the merger, the firm focused on introducing new services, which included web event solutions, experimental training and event communication. Thus, post-merger management and development were the leverage capabilities that underpinned the firm's growth between 1998 and 1999.

The Events Organizer's growth between 2000 and 2001 was attributed to the firm's ability to carry out its plans (enaction), its ability to integrate the efforts of the firm's business partners and staff and its ability to manage people. Indeed, the firm opened an office in the USA, started a global preferred supplier network and established an IT department and a human resources department. The establishment of the human resources department was of particular importance in the firm's development of the people management capability. The efforts aimed at the development of this capability proved to be effective as they enabled the firm to retain its experienced and well-qualified staff, one of the main assets of the company. A range of staff retention techniques were utilized in this process, including the firm's focus on developing staff and promoting from within through structured career paths, allowing people to grow and develop at their own pace, rewarding staff commitment with tangible and intangible benefits, monitoring progress through staff appraisal and motivating staff through job rotation and job enrichment.

Although the excellent performance of the Events Organizer has already been recognized externally (e.g. Incentive Travel and Meeting Association awards for Best Overseas Events and Best Use of Venue's Facilities), the firm sees its future growth in deploying its performance management capability and development. Apart from leverage capabilities, the Events Organizer identified organizational culture (i.e. a clear business definition, values and reputation) as the major growth-enabling factor throughout its growth history. The firm does not currently recognize any barriers to growth; instead, the Events Organizer aims to achieve a 20% growth per year for the next 10 years.

6.6.4 Comparison of the firms' staircases to growth

The sustained growth of tourism SMEs discussed in this study resulted from the firms' ability to build incremental growth staircases underpinned by the development of appropriate capabilities. While the firms are characterized by different growth histories, the development and resource application capabilities contributed to the early expansion of each firm. The leverage capabilities that underpinned the further growth of these firms differ in terms of either the type of capabilities developed or the step on the firms' growth staircases at which they were deployed. Some leverage capabilities are unique to individual organizations (e.g. crisis management in the case of the Hotel, capital management and path-finding in the case of the Coach Operator and enaction and integration of effort in the case of the Events Organizer). Other leverage capabilities were deployed by only two firms (e.g. performance management and people management by the Hotel and the Events Organizer or post-acquisition/merger management by the Coach Operator and the Events Organizer). Such diversity in the types of leverage capabilities deployed by these firms is desirable as leverage capabilities normally respond to the specific needs of a company at a specific point in time.

It is also worth noting that, except for innovation, none of the capabilities identified by Man *et al.* (2002) as typical for SMEs contributed in any major way to the growth of the three UK tourism SMEs. It may be argued that, due to the dynamic nature of capabilities, cost-effectiveness, quality and organicity are no longer sufficiently strong or unique for the firms studied to constitute leverage capabilities. Indeed, some elements of these capabilities were present in the analysis of the firms' foundation capabilities (Table 6.5).

The dynamic character of capabilities is also confirmed in this study by the fact that the firms were building new leverage capabilities to address the changing internal and external environments. Some capabilities were, however, successfully reapplied (although they might have been reconfigured), which indicates the durability of some of the firms' leverage capabilities. For example, the Hotel frequently reapplies its capability of development. Indeed, this capability underpins the Hotel's growth at each step of its growth history except the step of the 1990s. The immobility of physical resources fully justifies reapplication of this capability by the Hotel, particularly as the deployment of the capability of development was accompanied by the development of another capability relevant to the characteristics of the specific step on the Hotel's growth staircase. The capability of development is also reapplied by the Events Organizer and the Coach Operator but less frequently than in the case of the Hotel.

In terms of barriers to growth, only two firms identified them. The Hotel perceives the difficulties in raising finance as the major obstacle to its future growth while the Coach Operator sees the competitive labour market as its potential barrier to growth. Although both barriers are classed as external barriers to growth, their negative impact could be reduced if the firms developed appropriate capabilities that would enable them to grow in spite of these external barriers. In the case of the Hotel, the development of a capital management capability could facilitate this process while, in the case of the Coach Operator, the development of a people management capability could prove useful. Indeed, the example of the Events Organizer indicates that a people management capability could contribute to the retention of high quality staff and subsequently to the firm's growth.

A number of variables may explain the differences in the types of leverage capabilities that the three firms have had at their disposal at each stage of their growth histories and in their perceived barriers to growth. These variables include the priorities set by these firms, the different industry environments within which the firms operate and the different learning experiences that the firms acquired throughout the processes of their development.

6.7 Conclusions

This chapter has argued that enterprises need to achieve a capabilities-based competitive advantage to succeed and sustain growth. The development of hierarchical capability platforms that enable firms to launch themselves on to a growth trajectory constitutes an integral part of this process. Using three cases of UK tourism SMEs, the ways in which these firms convert their resource base into lower-order foundation capabilities and then higher-order leverage capabilities have been analysed.

This study has indicated that each of the three firms achieved a sustained capability-based growth. In each case, this growth has been incremental and underpinned by the development of leverage capabilities specific to the circumstances of a particular firm at a particular time. Despite a great similarity of these firms' resources and partial similarity of their foundation capabilities, most of the leverage capabilities have varied from firm to firm. Factors constraining or facilitating the firms' growth have also been identified and some ways in which firms could reduce the potential negative effects of these obstacles to growth have been suggested.

As this incremental process of building capability platforms has led the firms to learning many new skills and extending their portfolio of capabilities, it can be hoped that these firms will continue to grow and gain a lasting capabilities-based competitive advantage.

Notes

[1]The sector of tourism SMEs (i.e. tourism-related enterprises which employ up to 250 people, where enterprises which employ up to 50 people are classified as small firms)

is highly diverse in terms of their long-term aspirations and goals, ranging from life-style firms, i.e. firms whose owner-managers are not interested in developing their businesses but are content with the steady income that their businesses generate (Deakins, 1999), to growth-oriented firms, i.e. firms that aim to confer their competitive advantage and gain superiority over their rivals. This chapter focuses on growth-oriented tourism SMEs.

[2]Resources include the tangible and intangible assets owned or controlled by a firm (Amit and Schoemaker, 1993).

[3]Organizational capabilities are long-lasting bundles of creatively integrated resources that work together to form a unique set of abilities that enable a company to undertake a particular productive activity and provide a particular benefit to customers (Ulrich and Lake, 1990; Hamel and Prahalad, 1994).

[4]An organizational capability is unique if it cannot be easily imitated by other firms and for which ready substitutes are not available (Hamel and Prahalad, 1994).

[5]The tacit nature of leverage capabilities means that the capabilities cannot be easily formalized, are practical and are context-specific (adapted from the characteristics of tacit knowledge discussed in Ambrosini, 2002).

[6]The current number of people employed could exceed the limit of 50 as the number of people employed could have increased as the company grew.

[7]FAME contains detailed information on public and private companies in the UK and Ireland. It is available on CD-ROM, DVD-ROM and the Internet (Bureau van Dijk Electronic Publishing, 2002).

References

Afuah, A. (2002) Mapping technological capabilities into product markets and competitive advantage: the case of cholesterol drugs. *Strategic Management Journal* 23, 171–179.

Ambrosini, V. (2002) Resource-based view of the firm. In: Jenkins, M. and Ambrosini, V. (eds) *Strategic Management. A Multi-Perspective Approach*. Palgrave, Basingstoke, UK, pp. 132–152.

Amit, R. and Schoemaker, P.J.H. (1993) Strategic assets and organisational rent. *Strategic Management Journal* 14, 33–46.

Baghai, M., Coley, S. and White, D. (1999) *The Alchemy of Growth. Kickstarting and Sustaining Growth in Your Company*. TEXERE Publishing, London, 250 pp.

Barney, J.B. (1991) Firm resources and sustained competitive advantage. *Journal of Management* 17, 99–120.

Besanko, D., Dranove, D., Shanley, M. and Schaefer, S. (2004) *Economics of Strategy*, 3rd edn. John Wiley & Sons, New York, 632 pp.

Bureau van Dijk Electronic Publishing (2002) FAME, ww.bvdep.com/FAME.html

Collins, D.J. and Montgomery, C.A. (1995) Competing on resource strategy in the 1990s. *Harvard Business Review* July–August, 118–128.

Deakins, D. (1999) *Entrepreneurship and Small Firms*, 2nd edn. McGraw-Hill, London, 278 pp.

Eisenhardt, K.M. and Martin, J.A. (2000) Dynamic capabilities: what are they? *Strategic Management Journal* 21, 1105–1121.

Grant, R.M. (2002) *Contemporary Strategy Analysis. Concepts, Techniques, Applications*, 4th edn. Blackwell Publishers, Malden, Massachusetts, 551 pp.

Hamel, G. and Prahalad, C.K. (1994) *Competing for the Future. Breakthrough Strate-gies for Seizing Control of Your Industry and Creating the Markets of Tomorrow*. Harvard Business School Press, Boston, 329 pp.

Jones, O. and Tilley, F. (2003) *Competitive Advantage in SMEs. Organising for Innova-tion and Change*. John Wiley & Sons, Chichester, UK, 275 pp.

Lerner, M. and Almor, T. (2002) Relationships among strategic capabilities and the per-formance of women-owned small ventures. *Journal of Small Business Management* 40, 109–125.

Makadok, R. (2001) Toward a synthesis of the resource-based and dynamic capability views of rent creation. *Strategic Management Journal* 22, 387–401.

Man, T.W.Y., Lau, T. and Chan, K.F. (2002) The competitiveness of small and medium enterprises. A conceptualisation with focus on entrepreneurial competencies. *Journal of Business Venturing* 17, 123–142.

Militello, F.C. and Schwalberg, M.D. (2002) *Leverage Competencies*. Financial Times/ Prentice Hall PTR, Upper Saddle River, New Jersey, 231 pp.

Mintzberg, H., Ahlstrand, B. and Lampel, J. (1998) *Strategy Safari. A Guided Tour Through the Wilds of Strategic Management*. Prentice Hall Europe, Hemel Hempstead, UK, 406 pp.

Peteraf, M. (1993) The cornerstones of competitive advantage: a resource-based view. *Strategic Management Journal* 14, 179–191.

Porter M. (1980) *Competitive Strategy. Techniques for Analysing Industries and Competitors*. The Free Press, New York, 397 pp.

Porter M. (1985) *Competitive Advantage. Creating and Sustaining Superior Performance*. The Free Press, New York, 557 pp.

Prahalad, C.K. and Hamel, G. (1990) The core competence of the corporation. *Harvard Business Review* May–June, 79–91.

Rangone, A. (1999) A resource-based approach to strategy analysis in small and medium-sized enterprises. *Small Business Economics* 12, 233–248.

Rumelt, R. (1991) How much does industry matter? *Strategic Management Journal* 12, 167–185.

Schroeder, R.G., Bates, K.A. and Junttila, M.A. (2002) A resource-based view of manu-facturing strategy and the relationship to manufacturing performance. *Strategic Management Journal* 23, 105–117.

Spanos, Y.E. and Lioukas, S. (2001) An examination into the causal logic of rent genera-tion: contrasting porter's competitive strategy framework and the resource-based perspective. *Strategic Management Journal* 22, 907–934.

Stalk, G., Evans, P. and Shulman, L.E. (1992) Competing on capabilities: the new rules of corporate strategy. *Harvard Business Review* March–April, 57–69.

Teece, D.J., Pisano, G. and Shuen, A. (1997) Dynamic capabilities and strategic manage-ment. *Strategic Management Journal* 18, 509–533.

Turner, D. and Crawford, M. (1994) Managing current and future competitive perfor-mance: the role of competence. In: Hamel, G. and Heene, A. (eds) *Competence-based Competition*. John Wiley & Sons, Chichester, UK, pp. 241–263.

Ulrich, D. and Lake, D. (1990) *Organizational Capability. Competing from the Inside Out*. John Wiley & Sons, New York, 339 pp.

Wernerfelt, B. (1984) A resource-based view of the firm. *Strategic Management Journal* 5, 171–180.

7

Producing Hospitality, Consuming Lifestyles: Lifestyle Entrepreneurship in Urban Scotland

MARIALAURA DI DOMENICO

Judge Institute of Management, University of Cambridge, UK

7.1 Introduction

An area of enquiry that remains comparatively under-researched and under-theorized is that which concerns the business values and orientations of entrepreneurs with small-scale or micro tourism businesses. More research into and understanding of the sector-specific nature of small tourism enterprises in different contexts are needed. This chapter examines the notion of 'lifestyle' as an orientation for small business owners in the tourism sector. Lifestyle orientation has been previously identified as a factor contributing to a lack of business success defined in terms of economic growth criteria (Shaw and Williams, 1987; Morrison *et al.*, 1999). Using the social scientific conceptual framework of symbolic interactionism, this chapter explores the results of research into lifestyle entrepreneurs who hold predominantly non-economic business values and orientations and define business success using a broad range of criteria. Therefore, rather than conceptualizing tourism entrepreneurship purely in terms of economic-driven business models, it is argued that it is necessary to broaden our analytic approach.

By using the actors' own definitions of business success and accounts of their own orientations and values, a more enlightened understanding of the individual as entrepreneur is ensured through an appreciation of both sector-specific and contextual issues. Moreover, the rejection of an overtly growth- or profit-driven motive as an entrepreneurial style can also be seen to afford opportunities for greater product individuality and service differentiation. The specific empirical study which is considered in this chapter is of the views and business orientations of 30 guesthouse owners in the two Scottish urban locations of Dundee and Inverness. It is used to develop a coherent profile of this particular entrepreneurial type in order to advance our understanding of the self-defined roles of those individuals who are involved in tourism business and destination development.

This chapter first explores the notion of 'lifestyle entrepreneurship' against a backdrop of relevant studies in the area. Through this process, the dominant foci in the literature are highlighted. These have tended to be around studies within the rural context and on those using survey research methods. There is an apparent lack of interest on the part of researchers in examining lifestyle indices to explore urban as opposed to rural contexts. It is argued here that there is indeed a need to explore the influence of lifestyle orientation on the operators of such tourism small and medium-sized enterprises (SMEs) in the urban context. This leads to a review of the way in which this Scottish comparative research study was able to provide the guesthouse owners interviewed with a 'voice'. This was done by employing qualitative rather than quantitative techniques, and by employing the symbolic interactionist conceptual framework in order to give the methodology a firm theoretical underpinning. The aim was to uncover the entrepreneurs' self-definitions rather than merely imposing upon them the researcher's own generated definitions. The latter strategy tends to be more prevalent in tourism studies of entrepreneurship to date. It is argued that a challenge facing researchers, policy makers and those responsible for destination development is to find out more about those individuals who set up and operate their own tourism businesses in an effort to understand their self-ascribed goals, needs and motivations, and therefore their impact on their business and geographical contexts.

The importance of the guesthouse operation must be understood in terms of its position within the hospitality sector as a key segment of the broader tourism industry, which is dominated by such small businesses. It is often stressed that in order to ensure the most appropriate form of tourism development there should be an emphasis on local initiatives, local values and key stakeholders in the community. Taking such an approach, the small-scale guesthouse proprietors should be considered as key players in a particular locality. They can be considered as the 'foot-soldiers' of the industry, undertaking highly interactive customer-facing roles. They are charged with the delicate task of managing and influencing the views and experiences of the tourist. They are often the 'live-in' owners of the 'corner guesthouse' and are encouraged by the national and regional tourism bodies to present to the visitor an image of their society and their local area which reflect the traditions and expectations of, in the present case, Scottish or Highland hospitality. It must therefore be of considerable interest to policy makers as well as to tourism academics to explore their views and self-defined characteristics.

7.2 The 'Lifestyle Entrepreneur' in the Tourism Literature

In order to place the discussion in context, the first aim must be to reach an understanding of the key concept of 'lifestyle entrepreneur', which is associated with small-scale accommodation providers and the types of business context in which they are placed. This process facilitates an understanding of their self-images and definitions of their situations presented later in the chapter.

The two concepts of 'entrepreneur' and 'lifestyle' can be combined to form the concept of 'lifestyle entrepreneur', which is complex and more than the sum of its parts. The concept of business growth is fundamental to many definitions of entrepreneurship. However, business growth cannot be seen as an only or necessary factor, as starting up a business may represent many different things to different people belonging to different groups within society. For example, 'for some, starting a business represents an escape from the control of others' (Scase and Goffee, 1987: 33). This was the finding of Bechhofer *et al.* (1974) in their study of small-scale Edinburgh 'petit bourgeois' shopkeepers. Also, 'incentive' is very much a function of the total social, cultural and economic environment in which small-scale business people live. In particular, the social structures and cultural contexts in which people operate, and in reference to which they make decisions, are particularly important (Ateljevic and Doorne, 2003). It is one thing to be positively disposed to the business role, but it is another to assume that role in preference to all other competing roles. The former requires a certain predisposition towards the role, whereas the latter involves actual 'real' behaviour, often requiring the catalyst of particular incentives under favourable conditions. Again, different opportunities and different obstacles are presented by particular environments, and these would affect different groups, with different skills and capacities, in different ways. Thus, the sector must be considered (e.g. the service sector), the particular industry (e.g. the tourism industry) and the geographical location of the business (e.g. urban Scotland), besides the socio-economic characteristics of particular individuals, the roles they play and the views they display.

It is also necessary to explore the different developmental patterns of the business enterprise, which again can often be linked to the motivational patterns and categories of the proprietor. Although profit and business growth and development may appear as complementary business aims to some, the growth of a small-scale operation, as well as not being realized, may not even be part of the original motives or objectives of a particular group. Curran (1986) reviewed several studies from 1971 to 1986 which show that owners of small businesses are not necessarily motivated by the desire to grow and indeed many may deliberately avoid growth. This observation does not fit in neatly with generally accepted 'ideal-typical' definitions of the entrepreneur, as the desire for profit may exist independently from the desire for growth.

Although entrepreneurs of small tourism and hospitality firms can be viewed to some extent in the same manner as those running small businesses in other sectors, significant distinguishing factors can be identified in that start-ups involve businesses that tend to be small in size. The growth potential for the business is often limited, and adopting a growth-oriented strategy would often render the original operational and managerial capacities of the entrepreneur obsolete. Owners of tourism SMEs may be female or male, or couples, but will be similarly oriented by a desire to be in control of business decisions. Their businesses may be run, for example, by the owners as a part-time activity, or by married women or retired people to supplement their income. Therefore, the appeal of this type of business is linked to the size, flexibility, relatively low levels of required capital investment and low barriers of entry and exit inherent in the hospitality sector as a whole (Williams *et al.*, 1989; Shaw and Williams, 1990; Dewhurst and Horobin, 1998; Andrews *et al.*, 2001). Such proprietors can only fit into the broad concept of 'entrepreneurship' if one adopts a broad definition in terms of such benchmark criteria as the conception and start-up of a new business by the entrepreneur and sustained direct business ownership by the original founder.

The concept of 'lifestyle' is difficult to define, as it implies a quality of life that is subjectively defined by each individual and includes aspects of work, family and gender and their relationship to each other. Status is also expressed through 'lifestyle', which is marked by symbols such as type of housing and occupation as well as consumption patterns. As Giddens (2001: 296) points out, 'individual identities are structured to a greater extent around lifestyle choices'. The choice of setting up or running a business venture may involve a change in lifestyle. Kuratko and Hodgetts (1998: 362) state that lifestyle ventures appear to have as driving forces the linked notions of independence, autonomy and control: 'Neither large sales nor profits are deemed important beyond providing a sufficient and comfortable living for the entrepreneur.'

Within the context of the tourism and hospitality industries, 'lifestyle' proprietors, or so-called 'ubiquitous entrepreneurs' (Morrison *et al.*, 1999), are likely to be concerned with survival as opposed to being overtly growth-driven. They desire profit, but this is only one of a multitude of business goals and is manifested in terms of acquiring sufficient income to ensure a certain style of living. Therefore, the lifestyle entrepreneur is seen as someone who regards the business as a means of obtaining desirable comforts, such as a substantial home and the ability to reside in a scenic or preferred location. However, such an individual is also concerned with intangible benefits, such as increased time to devote to leisure pursuits or the ability to control the organization of work and leisure. It is for this reason that such an individual may not be interested in a business opportunity that might involve perceived problems related to growth, or extensive financial or time commitments. Reid *et al.* (1999: 55) argue that, based on the results of their research sample of 234 Scottish and Irish small family businesses, a considerable number of small concerns 'may be lifestyle as opposed to growth-oriented businesses'. Similarly, Ateljevic and Doorne (2000: 379) acknowledge that, in the context of small tourism firms operating in New Zealand, lifestyle entrepreneurship comprises 'quality of life, the pursuit of individualistic approaches and constrained business growth'.

A study which comes up with different conclusions from those described earlier was that carried out by Buick *et al.* (2000: 120) into small Scottish hotel proprietors, in which they argue that there has been the 'death of the lifestyle entrepreneur' as they conclude that respondents in their survey sample were 'definitely interested in the survival and growth of the business . . . This is contrary to the definition of the lifestyle entrepreneur.' This finding contrasts starkly with those of other studies linking the lifestyle-oriented small business proprietors to a lack of growth orientation (Goffee and Scase, 1985; Curran, 1986; Reid *et al.*, 1999). The Buick *et al.* (2000) study was also not supported by the research described here. It is argued that the desire for growth and the desire for business survival are very different types of orientations. Therefore, the proposition is put forward that one may be a lifestyle entrepreneur and at the same time also desire business survival, but not necessarily embrace the goal of business growth. It can be seen, therefore, that the criteria used by Buick *et al.* (2000) display problematic contradictions, as a distinction must be made between aspirations towards business survival and business growth. The claim that there has been the 'death of the lifestyle entrepreneur' (Buick *et al.*, 2000) is refuted for this reason. As will be shown in the next section, none of the proprietors interviewed during the qualitative depth interviews, which were an integral part of the research described in this chapter, desired business growth. Lifestyle was identified by the proprietors as the principal determinant of business orientation and decision making. In fact, as is shown through an appreciation of the collective 'voice' of the proprietors concerned, growth is even seen as a direct threat to the 'lifestyle' benefits, which incorporate the ideals of flexibility and 'hands-on' operating control, as essential characteristics of running an owner-occupied guesthouse.

It can be surmised that, in the tourism and hospitality sectors, the lifestyle entrepreneur often exhibits a desire for social relationships and enjoys playing host. They also usually enjoy owning the type of property that would normally be outside their income range if they were not in the tourism industry. These individuals tend to play an important social and economic role in their communities, which are often set in naturally scenic surroundings. Indeed, the owner-occupiers often wanted to leave the 'rat race' of modern life once they had an independent income, which was often derived from retirement packages or inheritance. Sometimes, one spouse could continue working in order to receive a steady income while the other could take a chance on operating a business, which could be integrated into the desired family lifestyle and enable leisure opportunities for the operators in the off-season period.

7.3 Giving the Lifestyle Entrepreneur in Dundee and Inverness a 'Voice' through a Symbolic Interactionist Framework and In-depth Interviews

The research outlined in this chapter is derived from a comparative investigation of the views and self-definitions of small-scale hospitality providers who operate their business concerns in the two Scottish urban settings of Dundee and Inverness (Di Domenico, 2003). A picture of the self-definitions and images of these proprietors is provided in this chapter through a review of some of the findings from 30 in-depth interviews conducted with the proprietors during 2001. Comments derived from interview transcripts have been selected and are used in the next section of this chapter to provide a 'voice' for the individuals involved in the study, and to further support those findings presented herein. Before discussing the methodological framework orienting the study, it is necessary to set the account in context by effectively locating the lifestyle entrepreneurs in the Scottish urban areas of which they are a part.

Most Scottish towns and cities have adopted development strategies which include a focus on tourism. However, there is a 'Scottish divide' in terms of tourism development. Edinburgh tends to be taken as a unique case in that it has always been advantaged by being the capital and having a well-established historic-tourist status (Ashworth and Tunbridge, 1990). Areas outside the central belt and away from the key Scottish urban centres of Edinburgh and Glasgow have often been ignored, not only by academics but also by policy makers and, in some cases, such as, for example Dundee, even by tourists. Although rivals in certain respects, both dominant cities of Edinburgh and Glasgow benefit from cumulative causation effects, not the least of which is their geographical, economic, social and symbolic proximity to Scotland's institutional apparatus. However, Scotland consists of a geographical, social, cultural and political diversity, which is certainly not reflected solely by the towns and cities of the central belt area. Thus, the interest in Dundee and Inverness is predicated on the relative lack of attention that has been paid to such areas.

New thinking in the tourism industry in Scotland has recently introduced an increased vitality into urban centres which have not been subjected to much in-depth analysis. Dundee and Inverness are similar in certain important aspects while also forming contrasting pictures. They are both affected by Scottish east-coast cultures deriving from a wide spectrum, which covers similarity of local dialect and geographical locations, although neither can be defined as the dominant north-east urban location, an honour normally bestowed on Aberdeen. However, they also contrast with each other in terms of their destination imaging and symbolic heritage. Dundee's legacy of urban deindustrialization (McCarthy and Pollock, 1997), combined with its continued population decline, has directed the city towards tourism as well as teaching and technology in renewed development efforts. This compares to the established 'tourist-historic' city of Inverness, which has been the scene of rapid population growth in recent years when it managed to establish itself firmly on the main tourist trail in Scotland as the capital of the Highlands. Consequently, by focusing upon the nature of lifestyle orientation for guesthouse owners in these two Scottish cities, the research sought to fill a geographical gap in the literature as well as making a less than conventional linking between urban setting and lifestyle entrepreneurship.

The conceptual orientation of symbolic interaction was used to provide a framework for giving a voice to the guesthouse owners of Dundee and Inverness. The 'social action/interaction' reference frame helped give useful insights throughout the study into the ways in which the proprietors viewed themselves and their contexts. This orientation involves the variety of meanings which the proprietorship of a guesthouse has for the owner. It is firmly established in the social sciences as an orientation which takes the actors' definitions of the situation in which they are engaged as a starting-point in order to understand better their actions and viewpoints. In the present instance, the methodology, using this approach, was to elicit from the proprietors their definitions of their situations, using the in-depth interview as the central process of data collection.

There is a reciprocal relationship between the symbolic interactionist frame of reference and the qualitative, interpretative methodological approach used in this study. Symbolic interactionism as an action theory (Ritzer, 1996) does not allow us to view society as an entity over and above the individuals who compose it, or as something that can be analysed independently of the actions of which it is constituted. It concentrates on face-to-face social interactions. Thus, while structural or systems approaches in the social sciences begin from the assumption that social behaviour is conditioned or shaped by forces at the levels of the 'society' or the 'organization', action theorists tend to argue that individuals act rather than organizations or even societies (Cassell, 1993). They point to the connection between actions and meanings, and argue that people choose, interpret and intend their actions and do not simply react to external constraints or stimuli. Therefore, with action approaches, 'society' is recognized as a series of interactions between and among individuals, although they are still seen as constrained by the social processes, which emanate from the organizational structures that have been created (Layder, 1994; May, 1996).

As a conceptual orientation, therefore, symbolic interactionism emphasizes the individual rather than the structure of the society or the organizations within which people act, in order not to dehumanize people into sterile factors of analysis. It can be termed a humanist perspective, taking a 'ground-up' approach. The 'top-down' structuralist approaches are viewed as robbing people of their essential characteristics as actors in social processes. For the researcher adopting a symbolic interactionist perspective, social life is con structed by individuals themselves in their interactions with others, and not produced by some more impersonal entity which exists externally from their experience (Cassell, 1993). Symbolic interactionism is not a tightly integrated theoretical school (Ritzer, 1996) but rather a perspective which is useful as a research orientation. In its variety of forms it has inspired and been inspired by differing methodologies with both quantitative and qualitative underpinnings. However, the present research used a qualitative strategy as this approach was better suited to the research questions. Moreover, a qualitative approach ensured that the voice of the proprietor would be heard, rather than buried beneath other interpretations, a danger exemplified by much of the large-scale survey research conducted in this area to date.

Justification for this research orientation is argued on three levels. First, it relates to the need to achieve a satisfactory methodological 'fit' that reflects an intrinsic empathy with the nature and characteristics of the small hospitality business and the proprietor. The proprietor is typically involved in on-site dealings, daily interactions and transactions. Furthermore, as hospitality transactions are by their nature highly personal and interactive, social acts function as a firmly rooted part of everyday life (Di Domenico and Morrison, 2003). These characteristics are in sharp contrast to large multi-site businesses, which generally have more detached owners and formalized structures of action. Secondly, although tourism and hospitality research in general tends to draw upon various models adapted from both business and social science disciplines, the focus has tended to date to be on an understanding of the configuration of a hospitality organization using business-based structural models often derived from a large business context (for example, Davidson *et al.*, 2001). Thus, it is argued here that the application of such models at the level of the individual small business may be deemed inappropriate. Finally, a symbolic interactionist orientation enables the 'voice' of the small business proprietor to be heard. This is with respect to how they view and negotiate their social worlds, interact, symbolize associations and meanings, and present, interpret and manipulate the various aspects of the 'self' in their encounters and experiences with others (Goffman, 1959). Therefore, it is proposed that, within the context of the small hospitality business, focusing on the actions and behaviours of the proprietors, a symbolic interactionist approach has considerable merit. Furthermore, it provides greater understanding from a grounded, micro-level perspective of wider tourism dynamics prevalent in their individual 'worlds'.

7.4 The 'Voice' of the Lifestyle Entrepreneur

The objectives of the empirical research carried out in the two chosen urban locations of Dundee and Inverness were to highlight the perspectives of the participants in terms of the ways in which they define their own realities. Therefore, the research objectives that specifically sought to determine their business orientations and the significance to them of lifestyle-related criteria were twofold. Namely, they were: first, to explore the extent to which the business was used as a vehicle for fulfiling defined lifestyle needs/choices and how elements of their lifestyle are integrated with their business activities; and, secondly, to determine their objectives and future plans in relation to their businesses.

7.4.1 Lifestyle orientation and business choice

All proprietors interviewed emphasized the importance of non-economic and lifestyle considerations in terms of business choice. It was evident from the analysis that the owner-occupiers regarded the concept of 'lifestyle' as incorporating both work and non-work activities, each of which was seen to affect and be affected by the other. Therefore, positive orientations to own a guesthouse were found to be determined primarily by lifestyle goals. It is argued that the strength of this orientation is further enhanced by the specific nature of the owner-occupied business, where there is overlap between the home and the business and consequently a complexity and meshing of business and personal goals. This is exemplified by the comments of a Dundee-based proprietor: 'You work for yourself which is . . . great. It suits me because I'm at work but I'm in my home. So it's nice being at home . . . plus it's your workplace.'

The analysis highlighted that the needs of the proprietors interviewed were complex and broad and could not be conveniently reduced into easily definable criteria, such as a desire for profit or a high need for achievement. What was evidenced was that the proprietors desired a certain 'way of life' as determined by their specific needs and wants, with the business being used as an enabling tool to acquire this 'way of life'.

The relationship between the lifestyle preferences of the proprietor and the nature of work involved in running a guesthouse needs to be viewed against the backdrop of the proprietors' life histories and narratives about their back-grounds. The majority of female proprietors identified their ability to look after children and family commitments as elements of lifestyle circumstances making such a business an attractive option. It is interesting, therefore, that the nature of their positive orientations towards setting up and running a guesthouse were all based on lifestyle issues and the perception of, among other factors, increased flexibility and personal control. However, such lifestyle orientations can be fur-ther segmented into lifestyle preferences and lifestyle circumstances. Descriptions of the former indicate that the proprietors' orientations are seen to derive from self-defined goals or wants, the adoption of which is essentially voluntary in nature. Descriptions of the latter, on the other hand, indicate that their orienta-tions derive from externally imposed or current circumstances, such as family commitments, which necessitate and restrict certain actions being taken. Each of these lifestyle orientations greatly influences the views held towards the nature of work, in terms of whether that work is seen by the proprietors to be proactively embraced as a preference or passively accepted through force of circumstances based on the perception of limited alternative options.

In terms of lifestyle preferences and the preferred nature of work, a common theme among proprietors was the desire not to hire staff for day-to-day tasks on a formal basis in order to avoid any potential problems which could occur. Those who did employ the services of a cleaner or similar helper did so mainly on an informal basis. The nature of lifestyle preferences and the desire to avoid situations and responsibilities contradicting this notion are exemplified by the comments of a Dundee-based proprietor:

> We wanted to try something which didn't have as much responsibility and was less stressful. Yes, downsizing as they say. It isn't as hectic as the hotel, where we always had to have the bar open on time, and closed on time and we were always clock-watching and watching the staff.

Therefore, regardless of the potential profit to be made, the research findings revealed that the proprietors desired sufficient profit in order to ensure their life-style preferences, but avoided activities, such as the employment of staff, where these were seen to reduce their quality of life, regardless of the potential increase in earnings.

7.4.2 Future plans for business and self

A highly significant finding was that none of the owner-managers interviewed as part of this research desired business growth. The research showed that they did not measure business success in terms of growth criteria. Rather than concluding that such microbusinesses lacked the ability to grow in financial or resource terms, it became apparent that their owners did not demonstrate any ambition to do so and therefore did not put measures in place to facilitate growth opportuni-ties. This strengthens the view that the dominance of personal goals on the part of the small business entrepreneur was not always in keeping with rational eco-nomic decision making. Proprietors did, however, express a desire for profit and financial success. This is indicative of the fact that the desire for profit was seen to exist independently of business growth. The findings demonstrate that the objectives of the guesthouse owner/manager are based on ensuring a balance between income and profit acquired through the business and expenditure of effort in order to ensure or maintain a desired lifestyle. Other objectives include maintenance of personal control and direct business ownership and achieving job satisfaction.

The interview findings show the proprietors' self-definitions of business growth are in terms of what it means to them and to their businesses. They defined business growth as involving the following three main implications: an increase in the actual size of the operation; an increase in the range of services to be provided for guests; and an increase in the need to employ staff. All of these factors were deemed generally to be undesirable, regardless of financial viability, opportunity or potential profits. According to the individuals interviewed, reasons cited for this lack of growth orientation included a perceived decline in their overall quality of life which could result from the growth of the business. Other important factors identified as growth disincentives were the expected decrease in free time and personal comfort; perceived loss of personal control; expected loss of actual physical space on the premises for the proprietor and family; and a possible need for the proprietor to vacate the premises and reside elsewhere, whereby the property would fulfil the role of 'business' and no longer that of 'home'. Proprietors discussed their fears regarding business growth as involving significant disruption to the business and premises in the short term with a negligible expected increase in profit levels. A recurring theme was the overt desire to maintain their current ability to provide the level of personalized service, which is seen as their distinct competitive advantage over larger budget hotel chains. Consequently, in the eyes of the lifestyle entrepreneur, business growth would carry with it increasing 'detachment' from the 'hands-on' daily running of the business and in effect alter the essential character and desired image of intimacy projected by the business.

Therefore the needs of the business are seen as important by the proprietors, but only where these do not significantly impede their desired quality of life in terms of personal comfort, space and time. In all cases, it can be thus surmised that lifestyle needs are seen by the actors to be a higher priority than business needs if possible conflicts between the two are envisaged. The business is run mainly in order to support and enable an improvement in the owner's desired style of living.

An interesting finding while 'in the field' was that in one particular case in Inverness the proprietors decided to 'downsize' and reduce the number of letting rooms available from three to only two. Although this was the only case in which a decision to reduce the physical size and space of the business had been taken, as opposed to maintaining their existing level of operation, it does nevertheless support the argument that such individuals lack a real orientation towards growth of the business: 'Well, it's now reduced to two so you see we're not too big . . . and that suits us . . . but we still chose the house to set up the business . . . and also because we liked it.'

A reduction in the number of services previously being made available to guests was also evident in some cases. This typically involved withdrawing the provision of evening meals. Although this did not involve a change in the actual size of the business, it does indicate an important feature which encompasses a certain definition of business growth. This involves the range of services provided for guests. Due to their definitions of growth, it could reasonably be argued that such individuals have also downsized and reduced their business operations. Another interesting feature when downsizing was identified to have taken place was that in every relevant case the additional services had been provided at the start of the business life cycle. This indicates that lifestyle orientations remain dominant throughout the life cycle of the business.

All those interviewed identified personal control over daily business activities as a highly valued characteristic. Personal control is defined in terms of 'hands-on' dealings, physical presence and daily business actions/interactions. Although many had help from family members or employed the limited assistance of a cleaner to help with tasks, none expressed a desire to expand or grow to a level where their daily 'hands-on' involvement in the running of the business would no longer be required. The small size of the business therefore enabled a high level of business contact and face-to-face interaction, a characteristic that was highly valued by all those interviewed as this facilitated personal control. It is surmised, therefore, that such individuals would not thrive in the role of detached business owner-manager of a larger operation, as this does not coincide with their definitions of business 'control'.

Linked to the findings of a lack of growth orientation among the guesthouse proprietors and the corresponding desire for direct rather than indirect control are the findings relating to business inheritance and ownership. Interestingly, unlike what might be the case with family-run small businesses in other sectors of the economy, there is no evidence of a desire to pass on the business to children or other family members. Even in the cases where there were found to be complementary roles between the proprietor(s) and other family members, the idea that the business would be carried on by children or other relatives after the retirement of the owner was not something that was contemplated, as the business was seen as a home as well as a business. The identity of the business can therefore be seen to be a function not only of its size, location and type, but also of the owners and their personal plans. Some owner-managers did express a desire to sell the business as a going concern before moving to a different location. Others, who tended to let fewer rooms, wished to remain on the premises and had plans to convert the property for their sole use as a family home after their retirement.

7.5 Conclusions

This chapter has drawn upon research focusing on the Scottish guesthouse owner-manager. It describes a comparative depth study at the micro level of urban hospitality business enterprises. This is an area which has been little researched to date. This is reflected in the literature on the small business proprietor in general and, more specifically, on the 'lifestyle entrepreneur' in the tourism and hospitality sectors. The concept of 'lifestyle entrepreneur' has been shown to be a complex one, which results in difficulties of definition creation. It has been demonstrated that the concept of 'entrepreneur', although useful on a broad level, remains ambiguous and lacks the precision to be applied effectively to tourism SME operators, as reflected by the views of the participants in this research. Although the literature can be used to provide justification for the use of the concept, it can also be said that it 'carries a lot of baggage' with it and requires further refinement in this instance. Contemporary views of 'entrepreneurship', for example, appear to embrace a particular view of business growth as fundamental to the concept. This is the aspect of 'entrepreneurship' which is generally a research focus. However, in the present study, growth was not assumed as a goal, and business success seems to imply more complex orientations than just profit. The findings of the study illustrate that the owner-managers of 'lifestyle' firms consciously reject what are often taken to be the key benchmarks in determining business success, such as the desire for business growth. Self-defined success factors place the ability to acquire and maintain a chosen lifestyle as of higher value than so-called rational economic business growth objectives. Arguably, this leads to a redefining of definitions of entrepreneurship to encompass and recognize sociocultural orientations and values as important and equally valid dimensions of business success.

It is demonstrated that it is important to understand the 'world-views' of the SME owner-managers. However, although the small-scale accommodation provider can be viewed generally in the same manner as other small-scale entrepreneurs, there appear also to be significant distinguishing factors in this business sector. The needs of the guesthouse owner-occupier are broad and complex, not easily reduced to the profit motive or to a 'high need' for achieving anything more than a certain 'way of life'. They desire independence and achieve it through private enterprise, which they define in terms of its desired nature and limitations.

The conclusion drawn from this analysis is that 'lifestyle' implies a subjectively defined quality of life, which includes aspects of work, family and gender, as well as patterns of consumption, and how they relate to each other. It is considered vital to explore the characteristics of those individuals, the 'lifestyle' proprietors, who have been somewhat ignored to date by those not concerned with tourism or hospitality businesses. For those concerned with tourism businesses and destination development, it is important that the goals, orientations and daily realities of owner-managers of small lifestyle businesses are duly considered and understood. In an increasingly service-oriented postindustrial future, these 'lifestyle' businesses may become more of the norm, rather than the profit-oriented, impersonal hotel chains which have begun to grow in dominance over the past 50 years. The latter may arguably be stimulating the provision of a more anonymous and standardized service. However, this can lead to a loss of individuality, context specificity, and therefore a more alienating and less authentic experience for the tourist.

References

Andrews, R., Baum, T. and Morrison, A. (2001) The lifestyle economics of small tourism businesses. *Journal of Travel and Tourism Research* 1, 16–25.

Ashworth, G. and Tunbridge, J. (1990) *The Tourist-Historic City*. Belhaven, London, 296 pp.

Ateljevic, I. and Doorne, S. (2000) 'Staying within the fence': lifestyle entrepreneurship in tourism. *Journal of Sustainable Tourism* 8(5), 378–392.

Ateljevic, I. and Doorne, S. (2003) Unpacking the local: a cultural analysis of tourism entrepreneurship in Murter, Croatia. *Tourism Geographies* 5(2), 123–150.

Bechhofer, F., Elliot, B., Rushforth, M. and Bland, R. (1974) The petits bourgeois in the class structure: the case of the small shopkeepers. In: Parkin, F. (ed.) *The Social Analysis of Class Structure*. Tavistock, London, pp. 103–128.

Buick, I., Halcro, K. and Lynch, P. (2000) Death of a lifestyle entrepreneur: a study of Scottish hotel proprietors. *Journal of Applied Hospitality Management Praxis* 2(2), 114–125.

Cassell, P. (1993) *The Giddens Reader*. MacMillan, London, 368 pp.

Curran, J. (1986) *Bolton Fifteen Years On: a Review and Analysis of Small Business Research in Britain 1971–1986*. Small Business Research Trust, London, 64 pp.

Davidson, M., Manning, M. and Timo, N. (2001) Are customer satisfaction and performance in hotels influenced by organisational climate? In: Pforr, C. and Janeczko, B. (eds) *Capitalising on Research: Proceedings of the CAUTHE Capitalising on Research Conference*. University of Canberra, Canberra, Australia, pp. 40–56.

Dewhurst, P. and Horobin, H. (1998) Small business owners. In: Thomas, R. (ed.) *The Management of Small Tourism and Hospitality Firms*. Cassell, London, pp. 19–38.

Di Domenico, M. (2003) Lifestyle entrepreneurs in the hospitality sector: guest house owner-occupiers. PhD thesis, University of Strathclyde, Glasgow, UK.

Di Domenico, M. and Morrison, A. (2003) Social action research and small hospitality firms. *International Journal of Contemporary Hospitality Management* 15(5), 268–273.

Giddens, A. (2001) *Sociology*. Polity Press, Cambridge, UK, 768 pp.

Goffee, R. and Scase, R. (1985) *Women in Charge: the Experiences of Female Entrepreneurs*. Allen & Unwin, London, 163 pp.

Goffman, E. (1959) *The Presentation of Self in Everyday Life*. Penguin, Harmondsworth, Middlesex, 255 pp.

Kuratko, D. and Hodgetts, R. (1998) *Entrepreneurship: a Contemporary Approach*. The Dryden Press, Fort Worth, 608 pp.

Layder, D. (1994) *Understanding Social Theory*. Sage, London, 240 pp.

McCarthy, J. and Pollock, S. (1997) Urban regeneration in Glasgow and Dundee: a comparative evaluation. *Land Use Policy* 14(2), 137–149.

May, T. (1996) *Situating Social Theory*. Open University Press, Buckingham, UK, 272 pp.

Morrison, A., Rimmington, M. and Williams, C. (1999) *Entrepreneurship in the Hospitality, Tourism and Leisure Industries*. Butterworth-Heinemann, Oxford, UK, 288 pp.

Reid, R., Dunn, B., Cromie, S. and Adams, J. (1999) Family orientation in family firms: a model and some empirical evidence. *Journal of Small Business and Enterprise Development* 6(1), 55–67.

Ritzer, G. (1996) *Sociological Theory*. McGraw-Hill, New York, 864 pp.

Scase, R. and Goffee, R. (1987) *The Real World of the Small Business Owner*. Routledge, London, 176 pp.

Shaw, G. and Williams, A. (1987) Firm formation and operating characteristics in the Cornish tourism industry – the case of Looe. *Tourism Management* 8(4), 344–348.

Shaw, G. and Williams, A. (1990) Tourism, economic development and the role of entrepreneurial activity. In: Cooper, C. (ed.) *Progress in Tourism, Recreation and Hospitality Management*, Vol. 2. Belhaven, London, pp. 67–81.

Williams, A., Shaw, G. and Greenwood, J. (1989) From tourist to tourism entrepreneur, from consumption to production: evidence from Cornwall, England. *Environment and Planning A* (21), 1639–1653.

8 Modelling the Integration of Information and Communication Technologies in Small and Medium Hospitality Enterprises

HILARY C. MURPHY

Swansea Business School, Swansea Institute of Higher Education, UK

8.1 Introduction

Although many small and medium-sized enterprises (SMEs) share problems in relation to the diffusion of information and communications technologies (ICTs) (Dixon *et al.*, 2002), which have only recently been explored in any great depth (Shiels *et al.*, 2000), a blanket approach to ICT diffusion across all SMEs has been criticized (Martin and Matlay, 2001; Dixon *et al.*, 2002; Henry-Crawford, 2003). Fallon and Moran (2000) comment on the heterogeneity of sector-specific ICT capability, e.g. retailing and finance. While small and medium hospitality enterprises (SMHEs) share some characteristics with SMEs in other sectors, SMHEs experience distinctly different forces in relation to technology, including: the dominant technology role of a key supply chain partner – the destination management system (DMS); market 'pull' by Internet customers; peripherality, which contributes to a reduced technology infrastructure; and the lifestyle/occupational characteristics of SMHE owner-managers (Buhalis, 1993; Blackburn and Athayde, 2000; Thomas *et al.*, 2000; DTI, 2001).

This chapter seeks to explore the special case of ICT adoption in SMHEs using Paul Gamble's model (Gamble, 1984). Gamble's model (see Table 8.1) suggests that the adoption of technology by hotels proceeds through stages relating to traditional management functions from Stage 0 – pre-computer – to Stage 3 – tactical. Progression from one stage to the next signifies an increase in integration and thus efficiency and productivity, with Stage 3 reflecting the introduction of hospitality organizations into the electronic marketplace where technologies will integrate the entire hospitality and tourism industry. Gamble's model is used, initially, as a baseline for evaluating the diffusion of technology within SMHEs and is developed throughout this chapter. Other models of adoption were considered, e.g. the Ladder of Adoption (DTI, 2001) and the e-SME curve (Local Futures Group, 2001). However, they are recently

©CAB International 2005. *Tourism SMEs, Service Quality and Destination Competitiveness* (eds E. Jones and C. Haven-Tang)

Table 8.1. Conceptual framework: diffusion of IT in the hotel industry (from Gamble, 1984).

	Characteristics

STAGE 0
  Pre-computer
	Paper-based office system
	  Photocopiers, telex, Private Automatic Branch Exchange (PABX), electric typewriters, adding machines, calculators, electric registers and guest accounting machines

STAGE 1 Clerical Hotel Computer	Stand-alone back office system Stand-alone front office system Food and beverage control
STAGE 2 Administrative Hotel Computer	Integrated front office, food and beverage control
STAGE 3 The Tactical Hotel Computer	A totally integrated system which goes beyond ordinary business functions to allow access to external information on markets, consumer behaviour, links to travel agents, tour operators

developed, linear, web-oriented models that presuppose an ordered and sequential progression in diffusion and adoption. They do not correspond to the time period considered in this chapter and are already under criticism (Fallon and Moran, 2000; Martin and Matlay, 2001). Gamble's model (Gamble, 1984) is appropriate for the range of skills, business processes and technical competences of the SMHE and provides an initial, conceptual framework for this chapter. While Gamble's model refers to the hotel industry in general, there seem to be distinct differences in practice between the adoption of ICTs by large, affiliated, chain hotels and small, independent hotels.

Thus, this chapter develops a new matrix model to highlight ICT diffusion in SMHEs identifying factors that influence the adoption of data and technology building on Gamble's 1984 model. Four phases of ICT adoption by SMHEs are identified:

- Phase 1 – the environmental phase – in the early 1990s explores ICT exploitation in both domestic and international contexts. It reveals the need to include a much wider set of environmental variables that affect the diffusion of technology in the hospitality sector.
- Phase 2 – the strategic or collaborative phase – in the mid-1990s locates ICT in an organizational context and explores the feasibility of adoption of a collective or collaborative approach to information retrieval and use, and the constraints and opportunities of developing collective responses to the market. In doing so, Gamble's model loses some explanatory force and the inherent complexity of diverse influences produces a much more varied response than anticipated.

- Phase 3 – the management phase – of the late 1990s examines the impact of electronic commerce (e-commerce) on ICT exploitation and reassesses the longitudinal changes identified in Phases 1 and 2. To some extent Gamble's model holds up, though external forces often prove more critical to ICT adoption than internal ones.
- Phase 4 – the innovative phase – focuses on present and future prospects and examines the role of direct marketing and the special case of viral marketing, through investigation at destination level, and signposts future positioning for SMHEs.

The matrix model provides a new framework to contextualize the diffusion of ICTs in SMHEs over the last decade and reveals a clearer representation of the critical forces that act upon SMHEs.

8.2 Research Methodology

This chapter brings together the author's research over a 10-year period contextualized against relevant literature reflecting the work of other researchers and incorporates a number of quantitative and qualitative methods (see Fig. 8.1). Phase 1 measures the diffusion of technology within SMHEs and is designed to shed light on the factors that influence the diffusion of technology (or lack of it) against the proposed diffusion in Gamble's model. It then proceeds to a comparative study against similar data collected in other regions that are primarily descriptive in nature and further investigates if there are relationships between variables that affect diffusion/adoption of ICTs. This initial study evolves into a longitudinal study at a later stage in the research process. The major methodology at this stage is primarily a survey approach that leads to predictions, explanations and an understanding of the nature of the data. The approach is both descriptive and analytical, which allows a broader, complementary view of the diffusion of ICTs. This initial stage of the research results in a wealth of statistical evidence and the focus proceeds to Phase 2 to research on the meaning rather than the measurement. 'Indeed, one of the ways in which quantitative research may facilitate qualitative research is in the judicious selection of cases for further study' (Bryman, 1988: 136). In Phase 2 a more phenomenological approach is incorporated into the theoretical

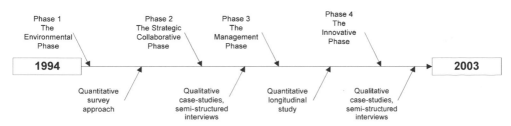

Fig. 8.1. Stages of research approaches.

perspective at this stage. Qualitative data are collected and small samples and cases are examined. The external forces and environmental changes at this time reveal that certain drivers are forcing change on SMHEs and the next stage of the research process revisits the original population in the form of a longitudinal study, and a more positivistic approach predominates. In Phase 3, the aims are to research the changes that may have occurred during the past decade and allow an examination of the changes within the social, economic, governmental and market context. The methodology of surveys and question-naires are similar to the first stage with similar statistical tests and analyses applied to the data for comparative purposes. Phase 4 focuses again on a more phenomenological perspective. The case study is adopted as an overall meth-odological approach and is experimental in design and aims not only to explore certain phenomena but also to understand them within a particular context (Yin, 1994). The phenomena investigated are the possibility of apply-ing web-based marketing techniques to tourism and hospitality products within the context of a destination.

8.3 Diffusion of ICTs in SMHEs

8.3.1 Phase 1 – the environmental phase

Whitaker (1986) provided some evidence for low adoption of ICTs by SMHEs, although little substantive quantitative research had been undertaken in this sec-tor at this time regarding diffusion of ICTs. A survey in 1994 (Main, 1994) revealed that only half of independent hotels used any form of information tech-nology (IT). Smaller hotels were less likely to use IT, with only 26% of those hotels with fewer than 20 rooms being users. There also appeared to be a rela-tionship between formal education qualifications and the use of IT. It would seem that this sector has no evident source of independent information about IT, which should be addressed via education and training within the sector. Addi-tionally, Lee-Ross (1998) carried out similar studies in Australia, which support the observation that SMHEs tended to be undercapitalized and have limited finances for marketing and issues in relation to price sensitivity, seasonality and product perishability, in addition to low adoption of IT.

Also, at this time small enterprises were not using IT to the same extent as larger firms and Doudikis *et al.* (1994) revealed that small enterprises focused on operational rather than strategic issues. This was particularly true of SMHEs, where 'emphasis was on clerical and administrative functions; especially accounting or inventory that addresses primarily what might be called "overhead considerations"' (Gamble, 1994: 274).

There was a lack of direction, guidance and infrastructure from the tourist boards towards the development of integrated systems. Many regionally inte-grated systems were in their infancy in this era in the late 1980s/early 1990s and most could be described as costly mistakes or outright failures (Mutch, 1996). Buhalis (1993) suggested that survival for SMHEs required regional integrated computer information reservation management systems (RICIRMS) to support the consumer and provide economies of scale and scope and direct marketing opportunities for SMHEs. Government agencies lacked the finance to develop regional systems and there was a continued resistance from SMHEs to cooperate, which were frequently viewed as an infringement of their independence status. Large hotel operators were extensively adopting computer reservation systems (CRSs) or global distribution systems (GDSs) to distribute and book products, supported by videotex technology. However, most of the GDSs and CRSs were designed to deliver to tour operators and the business traveller, not the traditional markets that are attracted to small and medium-sized hotels, and thus further lack of representation acts against the SMHE sector, which was not represented on GDSs/CRSs (Buhalis, 1993). After initial investigation, it became clear that not only internal factors inherent in the owner and hotel but also external forces played a vital role in the diffusion of technology. Hence strategic partners, such as intermediaries and suppliers, could force SMHEs to incorporate ICTs and to be represented in e-commerce.

During this period, there was also a growing awareness of the role of SMHEs in the wider economy, which resulted in a number of studies as to how governments could help in their creation and management, particularly within the European Union (EU) (Lowyck and Wanhill, 1992; Wanhill, 1993). Costa and Eccles (1996) identified the relative influence of the EU in gaining wider recognition for hospitality and tourism and particularly the performance of hospitality firms. Poon (1994) predicted the end of mass consumption and the advent of the 'new tourism revolution', driven by advances in technology, although there is still no real evidence of this. Other authors' work (Gamble, 1994; Glancey and Pettigrew, 1997; MacVicar and Main, 1998) also suggested that there were inherent problems in the human resource management and culture of small organizations, which exacerbated the slow adoption of ICTs. Hankinson (1990) found little evidence of marketing strategies in his survey, conducted in the late 1980s, of small hotels in Bournemouth and that any investment undertaken was reactionary and geared towards survival. Overall he discovered little evidence of any business planning or strategy for development.

However, other research in the USA at this time commented on the early use of the Internet and offered a different viewpoint – i.e. that it does not currently justify the resources necessary to initiate and maintain a presence and that business use of the web would far outstrip consumer activity. Technical problems continued to hinder Internet developments and the future was unclear, with management functions the least utilized (Murphy *et al.*, 1996). The lack of technology infrastructure for SMHEs, the inherent characteristics of SMHEs and their managers, the inability of key stakeholders to cooperate and coordinate and make progress and lack of funding all played key roles in impeding the adoption of technology in this sector. External factors were also critical, e.g. private financing, public funding and IT suppliers. At this early level of adoption, a 'piecemeal' approach appeared to permeate the SMHE sector. As indicated in Fig. 8.2, it was clear that adoption would be slow, even stagnant. Gamble (1994) observed

Stages of Gamble's Model	Time Frame	IT Applications and Infrastructure	Markets and Customers	Funding and Finances	Channels of Distribution	Human Resources
Stage 0 Pre-computer	1985	Property Management Systems, Word Processing and Accounting	Mass Markets Customers not Connected	Economic Recession	Fragmented and Lengthy	Embedded Culture
Stage 1 Clerical hotel computer	1990	Global Distribution Systems Computer Reservation Systems (GDS/CRS)		Little Capital Investment Government Funding Low		Lack of Training Poor Strategic Skills No IT Training Entrepreneurship Low
Stage 2 Administrative computer	1995					
Stage 3 Tactical computer	2000					
Stage 4 Creative connected computer						

Fig. 8.2. Matrix model of diversity of diffusion at the end of Phase 1.

that strategic change to maximize ICT adoption required boldness and visionary change and 'that the indicators are that a two to seven year period is needed' (Gamble, 1994: 280).

8.3.2 Phase 2 – the strategic or collaborative phase

The key to successful and efficient management of any organization, not just in the hotel industry, lies in the utilization of information and the ability to access available information and manipulate that information to the advantage of the business. Additionally, in a service industry such as the hotel industry, not only is it important to have information about the business environment in which one operates but the more information (or better market profile) one has of potential and existing customers and markets the higher the chance of delivering the kind of service to the customer that matches his/her needs. However, 'data collection is problematic, mainly because a great deal of data, much of it soft, much of it external to the firm, is involved' (Gamble, 1994: 274). In 1997 there were few historical, internal data stored, and external data were both limited and expensive (Main and Buhalis, 1997).

The hospitality and tourism sector has traditionally been at the forefront of efforts to monitor and track guest preferences (O'Connor, 1996). Customer loyalty is recognized as the dominant factor in a business organization's success. As a mature industry, the aim is for market share gains, rather than market growth. This can be achieved by acquiring more information on customers and deeper customer knowledge. Two technological developments in particular have had a great effect on how guest history data can be used: first, the reduction in the cost of data storage and, secondly, the growth in the amount of processing power that is economically available. As a result, extensive data about customer profiles and purchasing behaviours can be stored, e.g. using smartcard technology, and the same card could be used for a variety of different functions (Main and O'Connor, 1998).

SMHEs, however, tend not to be users of technology, and their lack of marketing knowledge has consistently been identified as a key weakness (Hankinson, 1990; Buhalis, 1993). An effective two-way flow of information between an enterprise and its customers is needed for both effective yield management and a marketing information system (MKIS) (Anderson, 1997). Wood (2001) indicated in her findings on hospitality and tourism SMHEs in Yorkshire and Humberside that MKIS mainly concentrated on internal and immediate operating environment data. An MKIS would provide the necessary information system to build up a database of external and internal information, where predictive modelling and the analysis of historical data would enhance decision making for SMHE operators (Main, 2000). Marvel (2001) further suggested that yield management may offer another possible strategy for smaller hotels to improve profitability. However, Marvel also points out that small family-run firms were often resistant to innovation in general. Scarce resources meant that limited funds were not available to fulfil the necessary tasks to operate a yield management system such as tracking 'unconstrained demand', which can be a time-consuming process.

'Immediate opportunities are for greater "low-tech" yield management' (Main, 2000: 162).

Brown *et al.* (1994) summarized a number of studies and concluded that the service sector tended to be less marketing-oriented, with less use of external information than the manufacturing sector. A later empirical study by Li (1997) showed that service organizations were less likely to possess a marketing information system. Main (2000) also revealed that there was little use of external sources of data, consultancies, trade associations or tourist boards. They (SMHEs) made little use of loyalty schemes to encourage repeat business and there seemed to be no effective measurement in terms of cost-effectiveness of marketing activities – they were 'too busy being busy' (Main, 2000: 164).

However, adoption of IT in small enterprises was not initiated solely by owner-managers but also by other actors (Dabinett and Graham, 1994). Perceptions of all employees of the technology, the situation, managers and individual characteristics constitute a base for the strategic disposition of IT in small enterprises. Other authors highlighted the importance of the human resource element in introducing and optimizing technology (Goldsmith and Nickson, 1997). Every organization has a culture of its own and SMHEs are dominated by the prevailing attitudes of the owner-manager and the consequent influence over their employees' attitudes, behaviour and performance. If the owner-manager has an aversion to new technology then 'it is unlikely that IT will penetrate the organization' (Proudlock *et al.*, 1998: 241). Notwithstanding the level of entrepreneurship, a strong, highly resistant culture becomes an obstacle to the integration and adoption of technology.

The rise of the DMS and more collaboration between software developers and tourist boards were representative of this period. The growing interest in community tourism development was paralleled within the EU by a switch of emphasis away from large automatic grants to attract inward investment projects, towards small firms and indigenous development. The EU, through grant assistance, provided 'incentives for tourism SMEs to work with it in a partnership arrangement' (Wanhill, 2000: 145). Several authors (e.g. Buhalis, 1993; Main, 1994) concurred on the proposition that collaboration within destinations was essential to produce meaningful information for marketing and strategic management knowledge acquisition. DMSs were going through a second phase of development and redevelopment, with EU funding giving support to research and development with a focus on SMHEs.

At this time tourism customers were gradually becoming aware of new distribution channels and the benefits of dealing more directly with tourism/hospitality suppliers. Progressive SMHEs at this time were forming consortia and/or joining with independent web providers and commercial portals and positioning themselves for the future. However, there existed a 'digital divide' between the information-rich who are making best use of all available technologies and the information-poor who have little technology and representation in electronic marketplaces.

Highlighted in this phase were the failures to use data effectively and the human resource issues that emerged as impediments to adoption. Employers needed to invest in the long term; they often lacked entrepreneurial skills and adopted a passive attitude, preferring to use old familiar management tools and techniques. Travel agencies and tour operators were reluctant to share their information and feared being bypassed in the buying process and losing commission. It is difficult to assess the position for SMHEs at this time in the context of Gamble's model. Certainly, it was not progressing seamlessly through the traditional management functions as first proposed (see Fig. 8.3). External influences and stakeholders started to play a more influential role in pushing technology to SMHEs. Early adopters of technology seemed to progress to a more tactical and strategic use of technology (Gamble's Stage 3 of the model), leaving others on the wrong side of the 'digital divide' (Gamble's Stage 1 or 0).

8.3.3 Phase 3 – the management phase

The turn of the millennium saw paradigm shifts in the adoption of technology, with the Internet becoming a standard platform for both customers and suppliers in the tourism and hospitality sector. There had clearly been an increase in the uptake of technology in this sector (Main, 2002b). In the past 5 years, the role of the DMS has changed and the relevance and importance of technology as a business driver has been recognized by the Tourist Boards (Main, 2000). However, 'a paucity of training is undertaken by small firms in spite of evidence of its value to SME management and employees' (Proudlock *et al.*, 1998: 243).

Sangster (2001) suggested that at the outset the Internet was heralded as offering a level playing-field for independent operators. However, the reality of the Internet is that size increasingly matters and rather than being an enabler for smaller hotels, the Internet may accelerate their decline. This may be due to the relatively large costs involved in delivering an Internet-enabled business. Nevertheless, surveys in 2000 and 2001 revealed that over 60% advertise and receive bookings through the Internet (Main, 2002c). Marvel (2001) suggested that to neglect the potential of the Internet may open the breach for competitors to collect and exploit useful client information and that appropriate affiliations will assure effective management of a hotel's Internet exposure. Teo (2002) commented that, with the advent of e-commerce, many companies are reviewing the way they do business. Some researchers propose that consumers' own characteristics play an important role in their propensity to engage in Internet transactions (Sheth and Parvatiyar, 1995; Jarvenpaa and Traxtinsky, 1999), with purchasers of tourism and hospitality products being a particularly good fit.

Technology offers significant advantages for SMHEs in operational, tactical and strategic management (Gilbert and Hudson, 1999). Distribution networks and partnerships with other tourism product providers might also offer SMHEs wider distribution networks and partnerships with complementary products (Palmer and McCole, 2000; O'Connor, 2001). Increasingly the use of IT is a major prerequisite in forming strategic alliances, developing innovative distribution methods, communicating with consumers and partners and satisfying consumer demand. Both customers and partners tend to place a greater value on organizations that utilize ITs than on their competitors (Thomas, 1998). However, there is still variability in the perception by managers of the

Stages of Gambke's Model	Time Frame	IT Applications and Infrastructure	Markets and Customers	Funding and Finances	Channels of Distribution	Human Resources
Stage 0 **Pre-computer**	1985	Property Management Systems, Word Processing and Accounting	Mass Markets Customers not Connected	Economic Recession	Fragmented and Lengthy	Embedded Culture
Stage 1 **Clerical hotel computer**	1990	Global Distribution Systems Computer Reservation Systems (GDS/CRS)		Little Capital Investment Government Funding Low		Lack of Training Poor Strategic Skills No IT Training Entrepreneurship Low
Stage 2 **Administrative computer**	1995	Outsourcing Application Software Rise of the Destination Management System	Digital Customers and Market Space Evolving	Growth of EU Funding DGXXIII	Dis-intermediation Re-intermediation	Manager's Aversion to Technology
Stage 3 **Tactical computer**	2000					
Stage 4 **Creative connected computer**						

Fig. 8.3. Matrix model of diversity of diffusion at the end of Phase 2.

advantages in their strategic attitudes to IT (Camison, 2000). There is also some confusion in the channels of distribution for customers and hotel managers as the Internet introduces more intermediaries into the arena. Hotels have their own web sites, use specialist Internet service providers (ISPs) to distribute their product, and the DMSs provide on-line booking plus various other links and sites (O'Connor, 2001). Several barriers hinder adoption and prevent SMHEs from capitalizing on IT and the Internet. These include the accelerating pace of change, the perceived usefulness of IT systems and past poor experiences of technology, in addition to the barriers identified throughout this chapter (see Fig. 8.4). There is a diversity of diffusion and Gamble's model needs to be re-evaluated for SMHEs.

8.3.4 Phase 4 – the innovative phase

Consumers are increasingly confident of transactions over the Internet and are incorporating the Internet into their tourism buying behaviour, particularly at the information-seeking stage, looking to the Internet to provide instant gratification of their purchasing requirements. 'The Internet is ubiquitous and media rich and forms an ideal channel through which viral marketing can travel and . . . utilize "peer to peer conversations"' (Main, 2002a: 293). We are entering an era of permission-based and one-to-one marketing where customers, inundated with direct product offerings, seek to discriminate on the basis of carefully targeted marketing messages. However, getting the timing and frequency of contact is essential. Main (2002a) indicates that the breadth and depth of data collected via the websites are not being exploited. Web statistics are limited to those of general trends, hits and page impressions. A more detailed analysis of logging files and customer tracking files would produce more meaningful statistics for marketing purposes, e.g. exit information and time spent on page, would all assist designing websites to meet customer criteria and build lifetime customer value (Main, 2002b).

For most tourism marketers, the goal of direct marketing would be to connect with individual customers to obtain permission to engage in direct communication with him/her, generate lasting relationships and increase customer lifetime value. Murphy (2003) investigates how destinations are utilizing marketing data on behalf of their members. As buyers become more sophisticated in the use of the Internet when purchasing travel and tourism products, the wealth, breadth and depth of information collected as a result of site visits become massive. Therefore, the careful mining of these data becomes crucial to matching customers and product offerings. However, destinations seem to utilize direct marketing to fill up spare capacity, whereas a better approach might be to be customer focused and use direct marketing campaigns that match their customer needs (Mitchell, 2002). Poor planning and a lack of core competences in Internet management persist in many tourism and hospitality businesses (Carson and Sharma, 2001). As the digital economy develops hotels increasingly need greater technology, regardless of their size. There is abundant evidence that many medium-sized hotels have moved away from the clerical use of IT and

Stages of Gamble's Model	Time Frame	IT Applications and Infrastructure	Markets and Customers	Funding and Finances	Channels of Distribution	Human Resources
Stage 0 Pre-computer	1985	Property Management Systems, Word Processing and Accounting	Mass Markets Customers not Connected	Economic Recession	Fragmented and Lengthy	Embedded Culture
Stage 1 Clerical hotel computer	1990	Global Distribution Systems Computer Reservation Systems (GDS/CRS)		Little Capital Investment Government Funding Low		Lack of Training Poor Strategic Skills No IT Training Entrepreneurship Low
Stage 2 Administrative computer	1995	Outsourcing Application Software Rise of the Destination Management System	Digital Customers and Market Space Evolving	Growth of EU Funding DGXXIII	Dis-intermediation Re-intermediation	Manager's Aversion to Technology
Stage 3 Tactical computer	2000	Web-based Applications, ASPs, Destination Management Systems, New Roles for GDS	Customized and Niche Products Connected and Mobile Customers	Continued EU Support UK Initiatives	Direct Channels Customer Choice Additional Channels	
Stage 4 Creative connected computer						

Fig. 8.4. Matrix model of diversity of diffusion at the end of Phase 3.

have begun to use it in decision making and for creative marketing. The Internet and web-based applications have enabled, and perhaps forced, dramatic changes in the way of doing business. Hospitality application service providers (ASPs) offer remotely hosted hospitality software applications for hotels over an Intranet or the Internet, charging them a negotiated monthly fee for their use. ASPs offer cheaper high-end applications with specialized IT support and expertise, though a recent study showed that there are perceived weaknesses in the ASP model (Paraskevas, 2003).

A good, clean, well-maintained customer database is arguably any company's best asset. Once in place, it opens up a wealth of possibilities for marketing purposes, enabling the segmentation of markets according to types of products of interest, time of year they are likely to buy, their purchasing history and demographic profiles (Murphy, 2003). However, destinations that glean data effectively from their websites and databases seem reluctant to make direct contact with their customers. Concern was expressed about 'pestering' the customer too frequently. They also felt their customers suffered from information overload in general. This makes profiling more important and gaining permission to contact them crucial, via 'opt-in' rather than the destination's choice of 'opt-out'. More creative use of technology by destinations and their members is, however, limited and Main (2002a) examines viral marketing in the context of city marketing. The concept of viral marketing is very simple: create a piece of marketing collateral that customers will want to pass via e-mail on to their friends and acquaintances. The research shows that individual tourism and hospitality enterprises, cities and destinations have yet to adapt to creative tools, such as 'virals'. They are collecting data from their websites but fail to use it creatively: 'Customers have indicated in this research that they are receptive to permission-based marketing and . . . would make this type of direct marketing a realistic proposition' (Main, 2002a: 294).

As the digital economy develops, hotels increasingly need greater technology, regardless of their size (IH&RA, 2000). There is abundant evidence that many medium-sized hotels have moved away from the clerical use of IT, e.g. record keeping and word processing, and have begun to use it in decision making, e.g. yield management and data management (Paraskevas, 2003). As technology becomes more sophisticated, we are seeing more creative use of technology in utilizing SMS (short message systems) and MMS (multimedia message systems) in other business sectors. According to KPMG (2003), there are 100 million digital wireless devices with capabilities beyond voice communication. These devices, e.g. personal digital assistants (PDAs) and mobile phones, are increasingly used to deliver direct marketing messages into the palm of the hotel customer. The use of ambient technology and wearable technology are also being researched for application to this sector. With the proliferation and information-gathering capacity of websites, we can expect to witness more sophisticated databases and data mining to acquire guest intelligence and target hospitality consumers accurately.

This makes the case for developing beyond Gamble's model, which is referred to as 'Stage 4: Creative, Connected Computer' in the matrix model, or abandoning it in preference to a model that better relates to the SMHE – a model that reflects the diversity of diffusion and the critical external, environmental factors. The new, revised model (see Fig. 8.5) illustrates the critical drivers within the SMHE sector in terms of adoption of technology and attempts to highlight the critical factors over the last decade. Far from being a simple stage-by-stage progression in the adoption of technology, as indicated in Fig. 8.1, the new model reveals that the adoption of ICTs by SMHEs is complex, influenced not only by internal factors but by uncontrollable external factors. More recent factors include the growth of dynamic packaging, where customers can put together their own travel/tour package in one visit, the exploitation of the Internet, the growth of the digital economy (e-commerce and mobile commerce (m-commerce)), the 'technically savvy' 'wired' consumer and consequent demand-side pull, and the increasing technology role of the DMSs. An analysis of the complexity and strength of external forces is not attempted, or of the causal relationships, which will be the focus of future research.

8.4 Conclusions

The model was populated with emergent, cumulated and grounded data informing the generation of a new matrix model and outlines a more complex view of inhibitors and motivators for the adoption by SMHE, which inevitably influences current ICT decision making. It contextualizes the events over a 10-year time frame and avoids the limited and limiting vision of linear models, which do not recognize the inherent diversity and complexity of the SMHE. The quantitative/longitudinal data give measurement and reflection of the penetration of ICT and the qualitative case study approach provides a basis for building more descriptive models and a richer picture of the SMHE.

The matrix model highlights the critical socio-technical relationship that has an impact on owner-managers and avoids a deterministic view of diffusion. It highlights the importance of human capital, the proactive or reactive approach of managers to rapid technological developments and the imperative that SMHEs should carry out both internal and external audits in order to map, match and develop ICTs to organizational resources and market needs. The matrix model allows for expansion in all dimensions, provides an incremental approach to measure, map and predict diffusion and presents an opportunity for SMHEs to define where they currently are, from both an operational and strategic perspective, and position themselves to exploit ICTs.

SMEs play a crucial role in European competitiveness and job creation, not only because they represent the overwhelming majority of enterprises in Europe and create two-thirds of all employment but also because they are the source of dynamism and change in new markets. European studies show that SMEs, in general, have to innovate both from a technological and an organizational perspective and build partnerships with other organizations in order to address strategic opportunities and challenges successfully (Dutta and Evrard, 1999). As far as the hospitality sector is concerned, it can be argued that they have little choice and must either enter into IT-motivated strategic alliances or risk being sidelined (Morrison et al., 1999). 'Impediments to

Stages of Gamble's Model	Time Frame	IT Applications and Infrastructure	Markets and Customers	Funding and Finances	Channels of Distribution	Human Resources
Stage 0 **Pre-computer**	1985	Property Management Systems, Word Processing and Accounting	Mass Markets Customers not Connected	Economic Recession	Fragmented and Lengthy	Embedded Culture
Stage 1 **Clerical hotel computer**	1990	Global Distribution Systems Computer Reservation Systems (GDS/CRS)		Little Capital Investment Government Funding Low		Lack of Training Poor Strategic Skills No IT Training Entrepreneurship Low
Stage 2 **Administrative computer**	1995	Outsourcing Application Software Rise of the Destination Management System	Digital Customers and Market Space Evolving	Growth of EU Funding DGXXIII	Dis-intermediation Re-intermediation	Manager's Aversion to Technology
Stage 3 **Tactical computer**	2000	Web-based Applications, ASPs, Destination Management Systems New Roles for GDS	Customized and Niche Products Connected and Mobile Customers	Continued EU Support UK Initiatives	Direct Channels Customer Choice Additional Channels	
Stage 4 **Creative connected computer**		Ambient Technology E-COMMERCE and	Dynamic Packaging M-COMMERCE		Strategic Alliances	Web-based Learning

Fig. 8.5. Matrix model of diversity of diffusion at the end of Phase 4.

achieving improved business performance may be exacerbated by poor planning and a lack of core competences in Internet management in many tourism and hospitality businesses' (Carson and Sharma, 2001: 116).

The issues of training still need to be addressed, perhaps through the Internet itself, by web-based learning, which would accommodate SMHE managers, who can only rarely afford to take time away from their businesses. Tourist boards and government must acknowledge the characteristics of the SMHE when they develop DMSs and be inclusive in their consultation and developments for destination websites. Successful bids for funds (e.g. under DGXXIII 6th Framework Programme) should be coordinated in collaboration with appropriate stakeholders, which must include SMHEs, who are collectively a significant proportion of regional tourism, and a strategy of 'coopetition' should be encouraged.

None the less, the question of whether SMHEs are too small to benefit from technology must be considered. Some SMHEs have few rooms and cannot guarantee the release of inventory to web-based retailers. Peacock and Evans (1999) and Baker et al. (1999) propose a similar viewpoint in that technology has still much to prove in terms of reducing costs and increasing productivity. Also, from a business culture and entrepreneurial viewpoint, adoption of technology could be in complete conflict with the 'lifestyle' choice that Morrison et al. (1999) identify as a key characteristic of the SMHE owner-manager. It is also mooted that the Internet and web-enabled technologies may prove to be merely 'intermediate technologies' and that mobile technology will be the future platform, with diffusion of mobile technology surpassing that of Internet-based technology in 2001.

Despite these considerations, the pervasion of technology appears to be relentless; therefore maximizing the benefits of technology is crucial and continuous. As we move towards a more mobile marketplace, SMHEs need now to be in a position to reach their wired, mobile customers and operate in the digital economy.

References

Anderson, A. (1997) *Yield Management in Small and Medium Sized Enterprises in the Tourist Industry*. Publication of Directorate General XXIII, Tourism Unit, European Commission Brussels, 17 pp.

Baker, M., Sussman, S. and Meisters, M. (1999) The productivity paradox and the hospitality industry. In: Buhalis, D. and Schertler, W. (eds) *Proceedings of the International Conference in Information and Communications Technology in Tourism*. Springer-Verlag, Vienna, pp. 300–309.

Blackburn, R. and Athayde, R. (2000) Making the connection: the effectiveness of Internet training on small businesses. *Education and Training* 42, 4–5

Brown, S., Fisk, R. and Bittner, M. (1994) The development of services marketing thought. *International Journal of Service Industry Management* 5(1), 21–38.

Bryman, A. (1988) *Quality and Quantity in Social Research*. Routledge, London, 592 pp.

Buhalis, D. (1993) RICIRMS as a strategic tool for small and medium enterprises. *Tourism Management* 14(5), 366–378.

Camison, C. (2000) Strategic attitudes and information technologies in the hospitality business, empirical analysis. *International Journal of Hospitality Management* 19(2), 125–143.

Carson, P. and Sharma, P. (2001) Trends in the use of Internet Technologies. *World Hospitality and Tourism Trends* 2(3), 116–128.

Costa, J. and Eccles, G. (1996) Hospitality and tourism impacts: an industry perspective. *International Journal of Contemporary Hospitality Management* 8(7), 11–19.

Dabinett, G. and Graham, S. (1994) Telematics and industrial change in Sheffield, UK. *Regional Studies* 28(6), 605–617.

Dixon, T., Thompson, B. and McAllister, P. (2002) *The Value of ICT for SMEs in the UK: a Critical Literature Review.* College of Estate Management, Small Business Service, Reading, UK, 49 pp.

Doudikis, G.I., Smithson, S. and Lybereas, T. (1994) Trends in information technology in small businesses. *Journal of End User Computing* 6(4), 15–25.

DTI (2001) *Business in the Information Age: International Benchmarking Report.* UK Department for Trade and Industry, London, 68 pp.

Dutta, S. and Evrard, P. (1999) Information technology and organization within European small enterprises. *European Management Journal* 17(3), 239–251.

Fallon, M. and Moran, P. (2000) Information communications technology (ICT) and manufacturing SMEs, 2000. In: *Small Business and Enterprise Development Conference, 10–11 April.* Manchester University, Manchester, UK, pp. 100–109.

Gamble, P. (1984) *Small Computers and Hospitality Management.* Hutchison, London, 185 pp.

Gamble, P. (1994) Strategic issues for the management of information services from the tourism to the hospitality industry – lessons for the future. *Progress in Tourism Recreation and Management* 5, 273–288.

Gilbert, D. and Hudson, S. (1999) Tourism constraints: the neglected dimension in consumer behaviour research. *Journal of Travel and Tourism Marketing* 8(4), 69–78.

Glancey, K. and Pettigrew, M. (1997) Entrepreneurship in the small hotel sector. *International Journal of Contemporary Hospitality Management* 9(1), 21–24.

Goldsmith, L. and Nickson, D. (1997) *Human Resource Management for Hospitality Services.* International Thomson Business Press, London, 235 pp.

Hankinson, A. (1990) The small hotel's approach to capital investment. In: *Proceedings of the Small Business Research Conference.* University of Nottingham, UK, pp. 38–47.

Henry-Crawford, S.-M. (2003) *E-Business Developments in UK SMEs: the Road to the Emerald Isle.* Small Business Research Centre, Kingston University, London.

IH&RA (2000) The hospitality industry and the digital economy. In: *Think Tank on Technology, 2000.* IH&RA Publication, Lausanne, pp. 1–25.

Jarvenpaa, S.L. and Traxtinsky, N. (1999) Consumer trust in an Internet store. *Information Technology and Management* 1(1/2), 45–72.

KPMG (2003) *Mobile Internet 'Any place, any time, everything'* http://www.kpmg.co.uk/kpmg/uk/image/mobileint.pdf Accessed on 12 April 2003.

Lee-Ross, D. (1998) Comment: Australia and the small to medium sized hotel sector. *International Journal of Contemporary Hospitality Management* 10(5), 177–179.

Li, E.Y. (1997) Marketing information systems in small companies. *Information Resources Management Journal* 10(1), 27–35.

Local Futures Group (2001) *E-London and the London Plan.* A Report to the GLA from Local Futures Group, London, 43 pp.

Lowyck, E. and Wanhill, S. (1992) Regional development and tourism within the European community. In: Cooper, C. and Lockwood, A. (eds) *Progress in Tourism, Recreation and Hospitality Management.* Belhaven, London, pp. 227–244.

MacVicar, A. and Main, H. (1998) Desktop: how culture in an international multi-locational travel organization affects technology decisions in business process re-engineering. In: Buhalis, D., Tjoa, A. and Jafari, J. (eds) *Proceedings of the International Conference in Information and Communications Technologies in Tourism*. Springer-Verlag, Vienna, pp. 139–149.

Main, H. (1994) The application of information technology in independently owned hotels. MPhil thesis, University of Wales, UK.

Main, H. (2000) The use of marketing information systems and yield management in the hospitality industry. In: Ingold, A., McMahon-Beattie, U. and Yeoman, I. (eds) *Yield Management Strategies for the Service Industries*, 2nd edn. Continuum, London, pp. 162–179.

Main, H. (2002a) Developing the use of viral marketing in the context of web-based communications strategy for city destinations. In: Wober, K. (ed.) *Proceedings of the International City Tourism Conference 2002*. Springer-Verlag, Vienna, pp. 286–296.

Main, H. (2002b) The expansion of technology in small and medium hospitality enterprises with a focus on net technology. *Information Technology and Tourism* 4(3/4), 167–175.

Main, H. (2000c) The use of the Internet by hotels in Wales – a longitudinal study: 1994–2000. *International Journal of Hospitality and Information Technology* 2(2), 35–45.

Main, H. and Buhalis, D. (1997) Catalysts in introducing information technology in small and medium sized hospitality organizations. In: Tjoa, A. (ed.) *Proceedings of ENTER – International Conference on Information and Communication Technologies in Tourism*. Springer-Verlag, Vienna, pp. 275–285.

Main, H. and O'Connor, P. (1998) The use of smartcard technology to develop a destination-based loyalty/affinity scheme for SMEs in tourism and hospitality. In: Buhalis, D., Tjoa, A. and Jafari, J. (eds) *Proceedings of ENTER – International Conference on Information and Communications Technologies in Tourism*. Springer-Verlag, Vienna, pp. 7–16.

Martin, L. and Matlay, H. (2001) 'Blanket' approaches to promoting ICT in small firms: some lessons from the DTI ladder adoption model in the UK. *Internet Research: Electronic Network Applications and Policy* 11(5), 399–410.

Marvel, M. (2001) Improving performance in small and medium sized hotels: the Swiss experience. *Travel and Tourism Analyst* 5, 43–61.

Mitchell, A. (2002) In one to one marketing, which one comes first? *Interactive Marketing* 1(40), 354–367.

Morrison, A., Rimington, M. and Williams, C. (1999) *Entrepreneurship in the Hospitality, Tourism and Leisure Industries*. Heinemann, Oxford, UK, 288 pp.

Murphy, H. (2003) An investigation into how data collected by destinations websites are utilised as a direct marketing tool. In: Frew, A., Hitz, M. and O'Connnor, P. (eds) *Proceedings of ENTER – International Conference on Information and Communications Technologies in Tourism*. Springer-Verlag, Vienna, pp. 316–328.

Murphy, J., Forrest, E.J., Wotring, C.E. and Brymer, R. (1996) Hotel and management on the Internet: analysis of sites and features. *Cornell Hotel and Restaurant Quarterly* 37(3), 70–82.

Mutch, A. (1996) The English Tourist Network Automation Project: a case study in inter-organizational system failure. *Tourism Management* 17(8), 603–609.

O'Connor, P. (1996) *Using Computers in Hospitality*. Cassell, London, 240 pp.

O'Connor, P. (2001) The changing face of hotel electronic distribution. *Travel and Tourism Analyst* 5, 61–78.

Palmer, A. and McCole, P. (2000) The role of electronic commerce in creating virtual tourism destination marketing organizations. *International Journal of Contemporary Hospitality Management* 12(2/3), 198–204.

Paraskevas, A. (2003) Application service providers and hospitality SMEs in Greece. International Journal of Hospitality and Information Technology 3(2), 61–73.

Peacock, M. and Evans, G. (1999) A comparative study of ICT and tourism and hospitality SMEs in Europe. In: Buhalis, D. and Schertler, W. (eds) *Proceedings of the International Conference in Information and Communications Technology in Tourism.* Springer-Verlag, Vienna, pp. 247–257.

Poon, A. (1994) The new tourism revolution. *Tourism Management* 15(2), 91–92.

Proudlock, M., Phelps, B. and Gamble, P. (1998) IT adoption strategies. *Journal of Small Business and Enterprise Development* 6(3), 240–252.

Sangster, A. (2001) The importance of technology in the hotel industry. *Travel and Tourism Analyst* 3, 43–56.

Sheth, J.N. and Parvatiyar, A. (1995) Relationship marketing in consumer markets: antecedents and consequences. *Journal of the Academy of Marketing Science* 2(3), 255–272.

Shiels, H., McIvor, R. and O'Reilly, D. (2000) Understanding the implications of ICT adoption: insights from SMEs. *Logistics Information Management* 16(5), 312–326.

Teo, T.S.H. (2002) Attitudes toward on-line shopping and the Internet. *Behaviour and Information Technology* 21(4), 259–271.

Thomas, R. (1998) An introduction to the study of small tourism and hospitality firms. In: Thomas, R. (ed.) *The Management of Small Tourism and Hospitality Firms.* Cassell, London, pp. 1–16.

Thomas, R., Lashley, C., Rowson, B., Xie, G., Jameson, S., Eaglen, A., Lincoln, G. and Parsons, D. (2000) *The National Survey of Small Tourism and Hospitality Firms: 2000.* Centre for the Study of Small Tourism and Hospitality Firms, Leeds Metropolitan University, Leeds, UK.

Wanhill, S. (1993) European regional development funds for the hospitality and tourism industries. *International Journal of Hospitality Management* 12(1), 67.

Wanhill, S. (2000) Small and medium tourism enterprises. *Annals of Tourism Research* 27(1), 132–147.

Whitaker, M. (1986) Overcoming the barriers to successful implementation of information technology in the UK hotel industry. *International Journal of Hospitality Management* 6(4), 229–235.

Wood, E. (2001) Marketing information systems in tourism and hospitality small and medium sized enterprises: a study of Internet use for market intelligence. *International Journal of Tourism Research* 3/4, 283–299.

Yin, R.K. (1994) *Case Study Research: Design and Methods.* Sage, Beverly Hills, 232 pp.

9 Business Goals in the Small-scale Accommodation Sector in New Zealand

C. MICHAEL HALL AND KRISTY RUSHER

Department of Tourism, University of Otago, Dunedin, New Zealand

9.1 Introduction

Small business is usually regarded as the cornerstone of employment and wealth generation in the New Zealand economy. Small and medium-sized enterprises (SMEs) account for 35% of New Zealand's economic output and for a greater amount of employment than in other international economies. According to the New Zealand Ministry of Economic Development (2001), 84.9% of New Zealand businesses are small enterprises, defined as those that employ five or fewer FTEs (full-time equivalent employees) and 11.6% are medium-sized enterprises (businesses that employ six to 19 FTEs). Nevertheless, despite their supposed significance, there has been no comprehensive study to date on the overall business profile, management characteristics and entrepreneur profile of small businesses in New Zealand (Hall and Rusher, 2004).

The New Zealand tourism industry is also dominated by SMEs, although estimates vary on the exact number (Hall and Rusher, 2004). According to the Tourism Industry Association (TIA) of New Zealand (2002), the tourism industry has ten publicly listed companies and about 16,500 small to medium enterprises (interestingly, these figures also indicate that only approximately 20% of tourism businesses are members of TIA). The New Zealand Tourism Strategy 2001 estimates that the tourism industry has 'between 13,500 and 18,000 SMEs, approximately 80% of which employ less than 5 people' (Tourism Strategy Group, 2000: 7), of which approximately 34% are accommodation providers. The New Zealand Tourism Strategy 2001 recognized that SMEs lie at the heart of tourism, even though they 'have limited ability to invest in its development' (Tourism Strategy Group, 2000: Foreword), with the Strategy Group observing that, among other factors, 'upskilling and capability building of sector participants, particularly small and medium sized businesses' was 'critical to the success' of the New Zealand Tourism Strategy 2001.

As with small businesses in New Zealand generally, the understanding of the actual business behaviour of tourism SMEs is extremely limited (Page *et al.*, 1999), particularly when it is claimed that the strategies of some tourism SMEs may well be aimed as much towards maintaining the desired lifestyles of the owners as they are towards profit maximization or growth-oriented strategies (Ateljevic and Doorne, 2000, 2004; Getz and Carlsen, 2000; Hall and Kearsley, 2001; Miciak *et al.*, 2001). For example, as Hall and Rusher (2004) observed, little is known of the risk tolerance and uncertainty management behaviour of tourism SMEs which are associated with business decision making and activities, including business entry and exit strategies, even though it is a major theme within the wider small business and entrepreneurship literature (e.g. Brockhaus, 1980; Palich and Bagby, 1995; Busenitz, 1999; Thomas, 2000). Arguably, the one exception to the lack of knowledge of small business behaviour is in the food and wine tourism sector where substantial research has been undertaken on collaboration and network relations and contribution to regional development (Hall, 2003, 2004). However, even here, substantial gaps remain in terms of knowledge of intersectoral behaviours and the reasons for not collaborating. This chapter indicates the profile of one sector in New Zealand's tourism industry, that of the bed and breakfast (B&B) sector. As with comparable Canadian research (Miciak *et al.*, 2001), this chapter seeks to provide a basic profile of New Zealand B&B businesses in order to identify the owners' management attitudes and operational decision making. The chapter particularly focuses on some of the issues associated with lifestyle entrepreneurship, as well as posing questions about the degree to which members of the sector engage in behaviours that may assist in destination competitiveness.

9.2 The Bed and Breakfast Sector

A B&B is a small business where the owners rent out a small number of rooms in a private home to travellers on a short-term basis (Angowski Rogak, 1995). The B&B sector has gained an important international profile in recent years through the growth of more personal forms of travel, with the B&B providing accommodation in friendly, intimate surroundings, where the visitor is welcomed into the host's home (Mangin and Collins, 2001). For example, in examining the motivations which surround choice of lodging in New Zealand, Johnston-Walker (1998) observed that B&B guests place far more emphasis on social interaction than hotel guests. Internationally, research on B&Bs has also grown (e.g. Warnick and Klar, 1991; Vallen and Rande, 1997; Zane, 1997), with lifestyle motivations being noted as a significant factor in business development (e.g. Miciak *et al.*, 2001).

In New Zealand, lifestyle concerns have been demonstrated to be significant in the development of rural home-stay accommodation (Høgh, 1998; Oppermann, 1998; Warren, 1998; Hall and Kearsley, 2001). However, such developments have at times not come without perceived negative or unexpected consequences. Although not solely concerned with rural home-stay businesses, Warren's (1998) survey of rural businesses echoes a number of concerns found in the New Zealand and international literature regarding the development of rural B&Bs and the relationship between business and lifestyle issues (see Tables 9.1 and 9.2).

Table 9.1. Changes in personal life from tourism business (from Warren, 1998: 13).

	Main ($n = 430$)		Secondary ($n = 324$)	
	Number	%[a]	Number	%[a]
Increased personal income	102	24	86	27
Greater social contact with visitors	302	70	68	21
Meeting people from other cultures	210	49	100	31
Something to do/hobby	94	22	51	16
Loss of personal space	87	20	91	28
Loss of personal time	152	35	98	30
Loss of social contact with family and friends	91	21	67	21
Increased stress	100	23	70	22
Enabling home improvements	43	10	52	16
Increased travel opportunities	40	9	52	16
Decreased travel opportunities	58	14	58	18
Increased employment opportunities	50	12	42	13
Decreased employment opportunities	7	2	11	3
Enjoyment/satisfaction	4	1	3	1
Other	15	4	5	2

[a]Multiple responses.

Table 9.2. Changes in family life from tourism business (from Warren, 1998: 14).

	Main ($n = 430$)		Secondary ($n = 324$)	
	Number	%[a]	Number	%[a]
Increased personal income	92	26	59	24
Greater social contact with visitors	182	52	72	29
Meeting people from other cultures	145	41	62	25
Something to do/hobby	46	13	40	16
Loss of personal space	76	22	61	24
Loss of personal time	120	35	59	24
Loss of social contact with family and friends	67	19	55	22
Increased stress	75	21	41	16
Enabling home improvements	26	7	33	13
Increased travel opportunities	25	7	35	14
Decreased travel opportunities	32	9	25	10
Increased employment opportunities for family	44	13	54	2
Decreased employment opportunities for family	3	1	7	3
Other	7	2	3	1

[a]Multiple responses.

The exact number of B&Bs operating in New Zealand is extremely hard to ascertain (Hall and Rusher, 2004). Many B&B businesses are unregistered while some are also 'casual' or 'hobby' businesses, operating only at times of peak demand or at convenient times for the owners (Cheyne-Buchanan, 1992). The perceived low entry costs of B&B start-ups, particularly with respect to ownership of existing rural property with unoccupied bedrooms as a result of either children having left home or because of changes in farm employment structures (Oppermann, 1998), reflects wider research on the attraction of low entry costs for encouraging business start-up in other sectors (Amit et al., 1995), although the social opportunities offered through contact with visitors have also been recognized as a very significant factor in farm-stay start-ups (Oppermann, 1998). On the other hand, it should also be emphasized that there is an equally low exit barrier and the hosts could essentially decide on a seasonal or even daily basis to terminate their involvement in the provision of accommodation (Cheyne-Buchanan, 1992), a situation that reinforces the perception from some members of the tourism industry, as well as policy makers, that many B&Bs are an 'informal' tourism sector that may actually cause damage to the destination by not being available to provide services when tourists demand them (Hall and Rusher, 2004).

The growth in the number of B&B accommodation businesses has also coincided with the overall development of international tourism in New Zealand, as changes in the leisure and holiday structures of domestic travellers increasingly emphasize short breaks, while it should also be noted that growth in tourism in rural New Zealand is also a response to massive economic restructuring. An analysis of telephone books, advertising in Visitor Information Centres and other tourism media suggests that in early 2002 there were at least 640 self-described B&B businesses in New Zealand, although this figure is likely to be a substantial underestimation (Hall and Rusher, 2004). However, it is extremely difficult to accurately estimate how B&B operations have contributed to either SME economic activity or even the tourism industry given that B&B businesses usually do not formally register themselves with the Companies Office, unlike other business types. Therefore, it is not possible to accurately monitor the emergence, decline, economic activity or contribution of these particular enterprises. A second difficulty in measuring the activity in this sector is that New Zealand's domestic and international tourism and accommodation surveys only include a very small number of the total of B&B operations. For example, the director of a regional tourism organization in one region in New Zealand where accommodation surveys are undertaken reported that, while only seven B&Bs participated in the survey, he believed that, at his last count, there were at least 70 others!

9.3 Methodology

A survey of B&B operators in New Zealand was undertaken between February and December 2002. The questionnaire consisted of 147 questions in a mixture of discrete and scaled quantitative questions plus open-ended qualitative questions.

Eligible businesses were selected for participation in the survey by mailing a copy of the questionnaire to owner-manager's address listings from a purpose-built database. The database was compiled from several accommodation guide sources, and included properties listed on the Internet and in print publications (Travelwise, 2002; Jasons Travel Guide, 2002; AA Accommodation Guide, 2002; New Zealand Yellow Pages, 2002). For inclusion in the database, the business must have been advertised or listed in the electronic and/or print media as a B&B enterprise. This resulted in identifying 1110 B&B businesses that were operating in this region. However, it must be emphasized that a major difficulty with achieving a representative sample of B&B operators was that some of these businesses rely solely on word of mouth or a sign outside the property to generate business, and therefore do not advertise and cannot even be recognized as accommodation from a telephone directory. Questionnaires and a reply-paid envelope were mailed to the identified B&B businesses. A second questionnaire was mailed to those businesses that did not respond to the first mailing. There were 347 usable responses, equating to a final response rate of just over 30%.

Upon telephone contact with non-respondents, several significant non-response biases were found. A number of non-respondents declined to participate because they did not wish to supply the information requested by the questionnaire, in particular information relevant to the profitability of their business, even though confidentiality was guaranteed and responses would only be used in an aggregate form. A number of B&B businesses were in the process of being sold or had recently been taken over, so their owners did not wish to participate because they had insufficient knowledge regarding the details required, or they had no interest in receiving the report that summarized the survey findings from survey participants. Some non-respondents also declined to participate because they perceived that answering the questionnaire was too time-consuming and would interfere with the normal functioning of their business or the enjoyment of their lifestyle. A small number of respondents also indicated that they were required to complete a Statistics New Zealand survey form each month requesting details about guests who stayed, and completing an additional survey was too onerous. The remaining non-respondents indicated a broad variety of other reasons for not participating in the survey; some examples included that 'the survey had been completed but not yet mailed', recent illness, or that the owners perceived that 'the survey was not relevant to them as they operated their business as a hobby' and were therefore 'not a true business' or 'too small' to be considered.

9.4 Characteristics and Issues

As anticipated, the business structure of respondents was relatively informal. Only 15% of respondents had registered their business with the Companies Office, although 67% were registered for goods and services tax (GST). Almost 83% of respondents described themselves as a family business, with around the same percentage of businesses having been established since 1995. There was no significant relationship between business structure and date of establishment.

However, there was substantial variability in the amount that income from accommodation provided compared with the total income of respondents. For 32% of respondents, accommodation income provided less than 10% of all income (with a total of almost 47% earning less than 20% from accommodation), while for 18% it provided between 91 and 100% of all income. There are two very significant clusters of business types in relation to dependence on accommodation for income. For the majority of respondents, income from accommodation represented a very small portion, with over 50% of respondents earning 30% or less of their total income from accommodation; at the other extreme, almost 24% of respondents depended on accommodation for 80% or more of their income. Clearly, such clustering may have significant implications for business strategies. Interestingly, there were no significant relationships between these clusters and other business characteristics, except with days open per year and the possible exceptions of age of respondent and information about other investment and incomes, indicating the possible use of retirement or other investment funds as sources of income and perhaps emphasizing a social or 'pocket money' function in running an accommodation business. Indeed, from conversations with some B&B owners, the notion of having guests for pocket money, e.g. spending money that would otherwise not be available and which was usually cash in hand and therefore not declared for taxation purposes, arose several times. This observation is supported when it is noted that the mean gross revenue for the 2000–2001 financial year for respondents was between NZ$5500 and NZ$11,000; only 19 respondents earned more than $100,000; 23 between $50,000 and 100,000; and 49 between $26,000 and $50,000. The clustering of businesses was also indicated in the extent to which personal savings had been invested in the business: 99 respondents had invested less than 10% of their personal savings while 58 respondents had invested over 90% of their personal savings in the business.

Although B&B is highly seasonal, with the highest occupancy in summer, 32% of businesses claimed to be open 365 days a year. On average, each business has just over three double beds and almost four single beds. The average number of bed-nights sold per respondent in 2001 was 499.25, although it should be noted that almost 40% of businesses do not keep information on occupancy rates and bed-nights. Interestingly, respondent estimates of the value of the business and of fixed assets were also quite low, between $26,000 and $50,000. This was extremely surprising, given house and land costs even in rural New Zealand, and is regarded as a substantial underestimation. The businesses are self-managed, with only 13 respondents noting they employ management staff and only 47 respondents indicating that they would employ extra staff in the coming 12 months, to whom less than half of the respondents stated that they would offer any formal training. In terms of time commitment in peak season, 56% of respondents claimed they spent 36 hours a week or more in work related to the B&B, with that dropping substantially to 18% in terms of low season commitment. Only 35% had previous experience in the tourism and hospitality industry, although almost 58% had previously owned a business and just under half had completed a business course of some description. Thereby perhaps supporting the impression that B&Bs represent an easy sector in which to enter.

This impression was only reinforced by the very limited business research undertaken by respondents, although exactly 50% have sought business advice in one form or another.

Relationships with other parts of the industry are generally weak. Only 35% of respondents use wholesalers to access markets and only slightly more engage in cooperative marketing with other operators. The main form of promotion is brochures (77% of respondents) – usually placed at the local Visitor Information Network (VIN) centre (72%) – and websites (70%). Not surprisingly, given the means by which the sample population was generated, the New Zealand Bed & Breakfast Guide was also significant (62%). Nevertheless, connections with the formal business and tourism sectors are extremely poor. Only nine respondents are members of the local Chamber of Commerce, 17 respondents are members of accommodation associations in New Zealand, and five are associated with Conferences and Incentives New Zealand. Only a third of respondents are members of TIA. Arguably such poor connections only serve to reinforce negative images of the informal nature of the B&B sector in the institutions that substantially influence tourism policy in New Zealand at the national and local levels. Moreover, the ease with which operators can place brochures in their local VIN office or have information placed on a website can serve as much to limit information flows between operators and other parts of the industry as it does to promote them, as is often claimed by the advocates of information technology in improving network developments in the tourism industry (Buhalis, 2002).

A number of questions were also asked with respect to the importance of various goals when starting the business (see Table 9.3). The most significant responses related to issues of lifestyle as well as the desire for social interaction. Earning income is not a significant necessity (slightly more than a third of all respondents). At first glance this might support the idea that such operations are developed only for lifestyle considerations and are therefore not well managed according to business principles. However, a series of further questions regarding such perceptions clearly indicate that this is not the case. The vast majority of respondents see profit as being extremely significant and there is also a strong desire to keep the business growing, although this is also matched by enthusiasm

Table 9.3. Reasons for getting involved in business.

Rank	Reason	No. of respondents
(1)	To meet people	251
(2)	Desire to balance lifestyle with occupation	205
(3)	Desire to work at home	185
(4)	Appealing lifestyle	154
(5=)	Money/security/investment	126
(5=)	Retirement programme	126
(7)	Minimal costs/spare room	119
(15)	Recover debt on acquired land	25
(16)	Desire to involve family in business	22

for lifestyle gains and job satisfaction. As Hall and Rusher (2004) noted, such twinning of goals may cause tensions but it does not mean that B&B operations are any less well managed or customer oriented than in the formal tourism sector. Indeed, the social motivations of running a B&B clearly indicate the potential for stronger customer orientations than in those businesses with staff who are not so interested in making social connections with their consumers. Moreover, in terms of attitudes towards government assistance, there was very little support for the notion that such support was essential for business growth.

However, one of the most interesting responses to reasons for getting involved in business is the low rating of the desire to involve family in the business. Less than 10% of respondents indicated that their children were moderately to fully involved in running the business. Yet, as noted above, the majority of respondents described themselves as a family business. Clearly such a situation raises fundamental questions about the notion of family businesses, particularly as there was only limited support (just under 30%) for the statement that the business was an important means of keeping a property in the family. Although it is clearly debatable as to what exactly a family unit consists of, it would seem appropriate that the role of couples as entrepreneurs is far more important than the notion of a family business that is operated on an intergenerational basis. Therefore, the idea of copreneurship (Marshack, 1994) would seem to be an extremely useful avenue by which to investigate such businesses and others like them in the tourism industry, as part of a life-course approach to examining businesses development and entrepreneurial behaviour (Hall, 2005).

9.5 Conclusions

Along with a previous regional study (Hall and Rusher, 2004), this national study found that respondents strongly indicated that the risks and responsibility of operating a B&B business were worth the perceived gains in lifestyle. An examination of the attitudes of owners to the issues of applying strict business principles to a business that is known for its lifestyle benefits has shown that there is evidence of a strong business philosophy being balanced against the personal goals of the business owners to enjoy a good lifestyle. These characteristics are consistent with those exhibited by small family-owned tourism enterprises (e.g. Getz and Carlsen, 2000) and extremely consistent with research that has been undertaken on motivations for operating farm stays (Hall and Kearsley, 2001). However, in the context of New Zealand's small business environment, these B&B businesses present some unique insights into understanding the business goals and entrepreneurial behaviours of tourism SMEs, particularly with respect to the situation that fulfiling the lifestyle goals of the owners is almost equally important to meeting more traditional business goals and objectives. Indeed, for the vast majority of the respondents, lifestyle is a strategic business objective. Therefore, these findings illustrate the need to incorporate lifestyle goals within the development of models of the entrepreneurship process within tourism and, arguably, within much small business knowledge overall (e.g. Gibb and Davies, 1990, 1992; Glancey, 1998; Perren, 1999; Greenbank, 2001).

Interestingly, at least five other consequences emerge from understanding the importance of lifestyle as a strategic business objective of small tourism businesses. First, our understanding of small business performance and entrepreneurial success needs to incorporate quality-of-life measures as an important component of entrepreneurial decision making (Hornaday and Aboud, 1971; Keats and Bracker, 1988).

Secondly, lifestyle and amenity factors also become a significant factor in decision making regarding the location of new small tourism business ventures. Therefore, in terms of broader issues of regional development and place promotion, the location of business and the attraction or retention of individuals for lifestyle reasons may be extremely significant and may have positive implications for regions beyond simply that of being available as tourism service providers to relatively small numbers of tourists.

Thirdly, in looking at entrepreneurship and business development issues of small firms, it becomes important to look at the entrepreneur's stage in their life-course or, more probably in the case of many of the businesses investigated in the current study, the life-course of copreneurs (Marshack, 1994; Hall, 2005), given that the businesses tend to be run by couples in a relationship who are also partners in a business setting (Also see on the issue of gender and entrepreneurship Rosa et al., 1996; Baines and Wheelock, 1998; Chell and Baines, 1998; Cliff, 1998; Lynch, 1998). The utilization of concepts of copreneurship are also useful in distinguishing some of the business motivations and attributes of some small tourism enterprises from others that fit the category of being a family business.

Fourthly, it is important to recognize that because of the capacity of many of the small firms in the study to successfully undertake business promotion without participating in collective marketing activities, there are not necessarily any incentives to join formal tourism networks. Indeed, the ease with which a small firm may develop Internet capacities may actually even work against collaborative developments in some situations. From discussions with some B&B operators it was noted that they have never been asked. Comments from some members of the 'formal' tourism sector may actually be discouraging and the value often assumed to exist in cooperative promotional networks by members of those networks might not be seen to accrue to an individual business that is successfully able to reach its market without such membership.

Finally, the study suggests that, despite comments often heard to the contrary about the business skills of the 'informal accommodation sector' from regional tourism organizations and from some members of the formal accommodation sector, there is substantial business acumen among the respondents. The desire to make a profit from the business was important but it was a business goal combined with other goals, such as lifestyle, which should rightly be classified as a small business objective as much as making money. Moreover, in the case of many of the B&B operators in this survey, it should be emphasized that the desire for social interaction as a goal of business start-up may well make such operations much more service oriented than many other businesses in tourism destinations, thereby providing for a significant addition to the tourism value chain and the desire to be a competitive location.

References

AA Accommodation Guide (2002) http://www.nz-accommodation.co.nz/ Accessed on 12 January 2002.

Amit, R., Muller, E. and Cockburn, I. (1995) Opportunity costs and entrepreneurial activity. *Journal of Business Venturing* 10, 95–106.

Angowski Rogak, L. (1995) *The Upstart Guide to Owning and Managing a Bed and Breakfast.* Upstart Publishing, Chicago, 224 pp.

Ateljevic, I. and Doorne, S. (2000) 'Staying within the fence': lifestyle entrepreneurship in tourism. *Journal of Sustainable Tourism* 8(5), 378–392.

Ateljevic, I. and Doorne, S. (2004) Diseconomies of scale: a study of development constraints in small tourism firms in central New Zealand. *Tourism and Hospitality Research* 5, 5–24.

Baines, S. and Wheelock, J. (1998) Working for each other: gender, the household and micro-business survival and growth. *International Small Business Journal* 17(1), 16–35.

Brockhaus, R.H. (1980) Risk taking propensity of entrepreneurs. *Academy of Management Journal* 23, 509–520.

Buhalis, D. (2002) *eTourism: Information Technology for Strategic Tourism Management.* Prentice Hall, Harlow, 376 pp.

Busenitz, L. (1999) Entrepreneurial risk and strategic decision making: it's a matter of perspective. *Journal of Applied Behavioral Science* 35, 325–340.

Chell, E. and Baines, S. (1998) Does gender affect business 'performance'? A study of micro-businesses in business services in the UK. *Entrepreneurship and Regional Development* 10, 117–135.

Cheyne-Buchanan, J. (1992) Issues of marketing and promotion in farm tourism: a case study of the Manawatu region of New Zealand. *Australian Journal of Leisure and Recreation* 2(3), 15–19.

Cliff, J.E. (1998) Does one size fit all? Exploring the relationship between attitudes towards growth, gender, and business size. *Journal of Business Venturing* 13, 523–542.

Getz, D. and Carlsen, J. (2000) Characteristics and goals of family and owner-operated businesses in the rural tourism and hospitality sectors. *Tourism Management* 21, 547–560.

Gibb, A. and Davies, L. (1990) In pursuit of frameworks for the development of growth models of the small firm. *International Small Business Journal* 9(1), 15–31.

Gibb, A. and Davies, L. (1992) Methodological problems in the development of a growth model of business enterprise. *Journal of Entrepreneurship* 1(1), 3–36.

Glancey, K. (1998) Determinants of growth and profitability in small entrepreneurial firms. *International Journal of Entrepreneurial Behaviour and Research* 4(1), 18–27.

Greenbank, P. (2001) Objective setting in the micro-business. *International Journal of Entrepreneurial Behaviour and Research* 7(3), 108–127.

Hall, C.M. (2003) Wine and food tourism networks: a comparative study. In: Pavlovich, K. and Akoorie, M. (eds) *Strategic Alliances and Collaborative Partnerships: a Case Book.* Dunmore Press, Palmerston North, pp. 262–268.

Hall, C.M. (2004) Small firms and wine and food tourism in New Zealand: issues of collaboration, clusters and lifestyle. In: Thomas, R. (ed.) *Small Firms in Tourism: International Perspectives.* Elsevier, Oxford, UK, pp. 167–181.

Hall, C.M. (2005) *Developing Tourism: Rethinking the Social Science of Mobility.* Prentice Hall, Harlow.

Hall, C.M. and Kearsley, G. (2001) *Tourism in New Zealand: An Introduction.* Oxford University Press, Melbourne, 324 pp.

Hall, C.M. and Rusher, K. (2004) Risky lifestyles? Entrepreneurial characteristics of the New Zealand bed and breakfast sector. In: Thomas, R. (ed.) *Small Firms in Tourism: International Perspectives*. Elsevier, Oxford, UK, pp. 83–97.

Høgh, L. (1998) Farming the tourist: the social benefits of farm tourism in Southland, New Zealand. In: *Pacific Rim Tourism: Past, Present and Future*. Centre for Tourism, University of Otago, Dunedin, pp. 43–48.

Hornaday, J.A. and Aboud, J. (1971) Characteristics of successful entrepreneurs. *Personnel Psychology* 24, 141–153.

Jasons Travel Guide (2002) http://www.jasons.co.nz/country.cfm?country=nz&CFID= 67567&CFTOKEN=77860685 Accessed on 18 January 2002.

Johnston-Walker, R. (1998) The accommodation motivations and preferences of international free and independent travellers to New Zealand. In: Mitchell, R., Ritchie, B., Thyne, M. and Carr, A. (eds) *Pacific Rim Tourism: Past, Present, Future*. Centre for Tourism, University of Otago, Dunedin, pp. 49–55.

Keats, B.W. and Bracker, J.S. (1988) Toward a theory of small firm performance: a conceptual model. *American Journal of Small Business* Spring, 41–58.

Lynch, P. (1998) Female micro-entrepreneurs in the host family sector: key motivations and socio-economic variables. *Hospitality Management* 17, 319–342.

Mangin, E. and Collins, A. (2001) *An Investigation into Service Quality Variation Within a Tourist Brand: the Case of the Shamrock*. Discussion Paper No. 35, Department of Food Business and Development, National University of Ireland, Cork.

Marshack, K.J. (1994) Copreneurs and dual-career couples: are they different? *Entrepreneurship: Theory and Practice* 19(1), 49–70.

Miciak, A.R., Kirkland, K. and Ritchie, J.R.B. (2001) Benchmarking an emerging lodging alternative in Canada: a profile of the B&B sector. *Tourism Economics* 7(1), 39–58.

New Zealand Ministry of Economic Development (2001) *SMEs in New Zealand: Structure and Dynamics*. New Zealand Ministry of Economic Development, Wellington.

New Zealand Yellow Pages, Telecom Directories Ltd. (2002) http://www.yellowpages. co.nz Accessed on 15 January 2002.

Oppermann, M. (1998) Farm tourism in New Zealand. In: Butler, R., Hall, C.M. and Jenkins, J. (eds) *Tourism and Recreation in Rural Areas*. Wiley, Chichester, pp. 225–235.

Page, S.J., Forer, P. and Lawton, G. (1999) Small business development and tourism: *terra incognita*? *Tourism Management* 20(4), 435–460.

Palich, L.E. and Bagby, D.R. (1995) Using cognitive theory to explain entrepreneurial risk-taking: challenging conventional wisdom. *Journal of Business Venturing* 10, 425–438.

Perren, L. (1999) Factors in the growth of micro-enterprises (Part 1): developing a framework. *Journal of Small Business and Enterprise Development* 6(4), 366–385.

Rosa, P., Carter, S. and Hamilton, D. (1996) Gender as a determinant of small business performance: insights from a British study. *Small Business Economics* 8, 463–478.

Thomas, R. (2000) Small firms in the tourism industry: some conceptual issues. *International Journal of Tourism Research* 2, 345–353.

Tourism Industry Association of New Zealand (2002) *Key Facts and Figures*. Tourism Industry Association of New Zealand, Wellington. http://www.tianz.org.nz/ind/ind01.htm Accessed on 3 April 2002.

Tourism Strategy Group (2000) *New Zealand Tourism Strategy 2001*. Office of the Minister of Tourism/Tourism Strategy Group, Wellington.

Travelwise (2002) *Charming Bed and Breakfast in New Zealand*. Travelwise, New Zealand.

Vallen, G. and Rande, W.L. (1997) Bed and breakfasts in Arizona: demographics and operating statistics. *Cornell Hotel and Restaurant Administration Quarterly* August, 62–66.

Warnick, R.B. and Klar, L. R., Jr (1991) The bed and breakfast and small inn industry of the Commonwealth of Massachusetts: an exploratory study. *Journal of Travel Research* 29(3), 17–25.

Warren, J. (1998) *Rural Tourism in New Zealand*. Centre for Research, Evaluation and Social Assessment, Wellington.

Zane, B. (1997) The B&B guest: a comprehensive view. *Cornell Hotel and Restaurant Administration Quarterly* 38(4), 69–75.

10 The Future of the Tourism and Hospitality Workforce Begins at Home

CLAIRE HAVEN-TANG AND DAVID BOTTERILL

Welsh School of Hospitality, Tourism and Leisure Management, University of Wales Institute, Cardiff, UK

10.1 Introduction

> Parents can be quite forceful sometimes. My dad wanted me to be a plumber and we were going to do a partnership thing, and I sort of told him that I didn't want to and wanted to do something else, so he got quite stroppy [sic] and says 'you are wasting your time doing all that', so you sort of are getting pressure from your parents but then other people say 'you do what you want to do'. It can be quite confusing.
>
> (Excerpt from a focus group of Year 11 school students, Mid Wales)

> Parents [account for the] first 89–90% [of] influence on career decisions, then it is peer pressure, then it is probably general society pressure, bottom of the pile is probably the careers adviser!!
>
> (Excerpt from a focus group of career advisers, North Wales)

An area that is under-researched is that of parental attitudes towards careers in tourism and hospitality, particularly in the light of the influence parents exert on the career decision making (CDM) processes of young people. To ensure that, in the future, the tourism and hospitality industry is able to access a skilled and qualified workforce, who have selected the tourism and hospitality industry as a first-choice career, more research into and understanding of parental attitudes towards the tourism and hospitality industry and parental influence in the CDM process are required. This chapter reports on the findings of an investigation into parental attitudes in Wales towards careers in tourism and hospitality by drawing on the findings of a much wider study into the problem of attracting suitably qualified people into the tourism and hospitality industry in Wales (Haven, 2002).

This chapter first explores the problems faced by the tourism and hospitality industry in Wales in the light of a number of studies on employment characteristics and the nature of the tourism and hospitality industry in Wales. This sets the scene in terms of the future quality and competitiveness of the industries in

Wales from a human resource perspective. The chapter then examines relevant literature on the role of parents in the CDM process and how attitudes represent a predisposition to behaviour. After outlining the methodological approach to this investigation, the findings of parental attitudes towards careers in tourism and hospitality and the CDM process are presented, specifically:

- The key groups considered to be influential and those with no influence in the CDM process.
- Important career factors and factors provided by careers in tourism and hospitality.
- Selection of the tourism and hospitality industry as a potential career for their child.

The implications of this research for the tourism and hospitality industry are that, if parents are misinformed about careers within tourism and hospitality, it is likely that their attitudes and subsequent behaviour will be misdirected, bringing serious consequences for the future tourism and hospitality workforce in Wales.

10.2   The Nature of the Problem Facing the Tourism and Hospitality Industry in Wales

10.2.1   Background to the Welsh tourism industry

DTZ Pieda Consulting (1998) report constant increases in investment in Welsh tourism and hospitality projects, resulting in substantial increases in the demand for a quality workforce. Forecasts suggested that an extra 10,000 tourism workers would be required by 2003 (DTZ Pieda Consulting, 1998). Airey and Frontistis (1997) identify that very little is known about what potential recruits think of the industry in order to establish a basis from which to attract the best possible workforce. Furthermore the inherent problems of attracting a suitably qualified workforce in order to meet these labour demands are likely to be exacerbated, as labour demand is exhausting labour supply. Hence, the promotion of tourism and hospitality careers as first-choice careers in Wales is problematic.

Previous research into employment and training in the tourism sector in Wales (DTZ Pieda Consulting, 1998) identified a number of issues pertinent to Wales. Remuneration is traditionally low in the industry, which often leads to high turnover and a limited labour catchment area, which in turn undermines the ability to attract and retain quality workers. Displacement is also an issue, with employees being attracted away from tourism and hospitality into other sectors, as well as new facilities recruiting from existing labour supplies (DTZ Pieda Consulting, 1998). A tourism industry survey in 2000 by Tourism South and West Wales (TSWW) identified that 52% of respondents believed that they had experienced recruitment difficulties due to a lack of qualified people, while 43% felt that their recruitment difficulties were due to the negative image of the industry. Young people in particular were found to have negative perceptions of the tourism and hospitality industries (DTZ Pieda Consulting, 1998). Many young people experience the tourism and hospitality industry through temporary holiday jobs or work experience placements, which are, by their very nature, quite restricted in their scope and can distort perceptions of the industry.

10.2.2 Employment profile

The employment profile of the hospitality industry in particular is such that it employs a disproportionate number of young people, with 40% below the age of 25 and the number of people working in hospitality below the age of 20 more than four times the national average (HtF, 2001). DTZ Pieda Consulting (1998) suggest that negative perceptions may be initiated at the school and career service level, which may not promote a very positive image of tourism employment as a result of the school and career service perception of service industries. Baum (1995) also discusses the portrayal of the tourism and hospitality industries as a young person's industry, in order to create an image of energy and enjoyment, especially within organizations attempting to match staff image with their client profile. Prior studies, such as Purcell and Quinn (1996), found that many higher education students possessing qualifications within tourism and hospitality do not obtain employment in these sectors and, while a certain level of leakage can be expected, there is a concern that this may be higher than normal due to negative perceptions of the industry among students.

10.2.3 Cultural perceptions

Research has identified negative cultural perceptions of the industry in some areas of Wales (DTZ Pieda Consulting, 1998). These negative cultural perceptions can be attributed to the varying nature, structure and scale of the tourism industry in the different regions of Wales. Part-time workers were found to account for 51% of employees in the tourism sector, with 74% of these part-time employees in the hotel, bar and restaurant sectors (DTZ Pieda Consulting, 1998). Wales also has a significantly higher proportion of self-employment in the tourism sector than the national average for Great Britain. To a certain extent, this can be explained by the fact that Wales has a high number of small establishments, many of which employ fewer than ten employees (DTZ Pieda Consulting, 1998). This is supported by TSWW (2000), who found that 71% of tourism industry businesses in Wales employed fewer than ten members of staff.

The short tourism season is a defining characteristic of tourism in Wales and seasonality is a particular issue in parts of West Wales and North Wales, which are dominated by coastal tourism. Additionally, although some rural areas, such as parts of Mid Wales, possess an established tourism sector, it is geographically dispersed, characterized by small-scale operations and lacks the tourism support infrastructure of the more urbanized areas. As a result, career progression may be restricted and the career opportunities obscured. The requirement for flexible labour sources to address the seasonality issue creates a lack of long-term attachment, which can act as a disincentive to training, subsequently reducing the level and quality of skills within the industry (DTZ Pieda Consulting, 1998). Sensitive cultural issues surrounding perceptions of tourism were also identified, with tourism activity being seen to undermine the 'Welshness' of local communities in some areas of Wales, which can deter local people from entering the industry. Such issues hamper the development of a suitably skilled workforce.

10.2.4 Qualifications and trends in educational participation

Access to the tourism and hospitality industries is relatively easy, with few demands for specific qualifications. *Tourism: Competing with the Best* (Department of National Heritage, 1996) states that the fact that no qualifications are required to do particular occupations might give those occupations an image of low status. Comparisons between the qualification attainment levels of tourism and hospitality employees and other employees within the UK demonstrate that the proportion of staff within the tourism and hospitality industries with no qualification was above average. This does not appear to be the case in other European countries. A benchmarking study (CBI, 1995) discovered that a higher proportion of staff had vocational qualifications in France and Germany than in Britain. Similarly, Baum (1995) emphasizes the tradition of training and education in relation to tourism and hospitality employment within other countries in Europe. As a result, more able young people in Wales who have the potential to attain qualifications are less likely to be attracted to employment within the tourism and hospitality industries.

The structure of the population is changing, with fewer young people entering the labour force, due to a reduction in the number of births. This is creating an ageing labour force, which conflicts with the traditional pattern of employing younger people and therefore may restrict the potential labour supply for the tourism and hospitality industries. The changing trends within full-time education compound changes in the industrial structure and demographics of the workforce. The increased time duration of the transition from school to work is a trend that is highlighted in a survey of pupil destinations from schools in Wales (Career Service Association of Wales, 1999). Year 11 pupils from schools in Wales continuing in full-time education stood at 71.4% in 1998 (total number in cohort 35,651 pupils), compared with 69.9% in 1995 (total number in cohort 35,520 pupils). The high number of Year 11 pupils remaining in full-time education is a trend also identified in other regions of the UK. Lifetime Careers (2000) found that 71% of students surveyed expected to remain in full-time education.

Although there has been a long-term focus towards increasing educational participation, the transition towards massification in post-16 education creates many issues that are likely to have an impact upon the future tourism and hospitality workforce. Increased educational participation creates skill shortages within different occupational areas from previously and is linked to structural change within industrial sectors. Higher levels of educational attainment are likely to create a more highly qualified workforce with career aspirations that exclude industries perceived to be low skilled or unskilled, such as the tourism and hospitality industries. Baum (1995) asserts that the participation rate in post-compulsory education has implications for the status of tourism and hospitality employment. Specifically, in cases where participation is high, the demand for low skills, which is prevalent within the industries, may not be met, as a significant proportion of young people will be overqualified for such work. Conversely, where participation rates are low, higher proportions of school students are likely to consider the tourism and hospitality industries as viable career options. This supports the earlier work of Pizam (1982), who states that growing participation rates in higher education produce an educated workforce that is reluctant to consider employment in semi-skilled and unskilled career areas. As a result, the absence of structured routes into managerial occupations within the tourism and hospitality industries only serves to compound this problem.

10.2.5 Why investigate parental attitudes in Wales towards careers in tourism and hospitality?

At the outset of the wider study, it was assumed that attitudes towards the tourism and hospitality industry were negative and that there were specific groups of influencers in the CDM process, with career professionals being the most important, due to the statutory requirement to provide careers education and guidance in secondary schools as a result of the 1997 Education Act. A series of exploratory qualitative research methods were used initially to explore the assumption that career professionals were the most influential, as well as to establish the attitudes of school students and career professionals towards careers in the tourism and hospitality industries.

Findings from the exploratory qualitative phase of the wider study included: describing the industries from a consumer perspective; career professionals effectively discounting themselves as influencers in the CDM process; a belief that the media were a significant tool in terms of influencing and informing career choice; less negativity from the school students than from the career professionals about tourism and hospitality as possible career choices. Analysis of the exploratory research with career professionals and school students clearly demonstrated that parental influence was perceived to be extremely significant within the CDM and career guidance process. Therefore, parents were a group of influencers that had to be approached and a survey to investigate their attitudes was deemed essential to the wider study.

10.3 Parents: Career and Attitude Literature

10.3.1 Parental influence

Super (1953) suggests that the nature of the career pattern is determined by the individual's parental socio-economic level, mental abilities, personality characteristics and the opportunities to which they are exposed. It has been established that children begin to acquire social attitudes and values from an early age, initially from their parents and subsequently from their peers. This suggests that children who identify with their parents and their subculture are likely to develop preferences for the types of occupations that their parents value (Super, 1957).

Family members have been shown to be of considerable importance as they represent a credible information source. Hemsley-Brown (1998) found that students who had a parent or close relation working in a field often had a clearer idea about what the job encompassed. Similarly, Lankard (1995) states that family influence is an important force in the preparation for work, and attitudes about work and careers are a result of family interaction. However, family members are not always best equipped to offer advice as their occupational experience may be restricted and their attitudes towards work may be biased or outdated. Previous research has indicated that non-tourism industry workers tend to have negative perceptions of tourism industry jobs (Choy, 1995). Similarly, Getz's study of the Spey Valley in Scotland (1994a) encountered parental bias in terms of career advice. He found that careers in tourism and hospitality had an extremely undesirable image, despite high levels of parental involvement in the hotel and tourism industry.

Paul (1962, cited by Hayes and Hopson, 1971) recommends that parental attitudes towards work be classified under four headings: the 'silent attitude', which describes homes where work is never openly discussed; the 'resentful attitude', where only grievances about work are disseminated; the 'participating attitude', which describes homes where work is discussed by enthusiastic parents; and the 'candid attitude', where all aspects of work, including advantages and disadvantages, are discussed openly. Similarly, Middleton and Loughead (1993) present three types of parental involvement in the career development of young people: positive involvement, non-involvement and negative involvement. They suggest that young people feel higher levels of anxiety about their career decisions in relation to the negative involvement of parents. Parents within this category are purported to be controlling and domineering in their interactions with their children. As a result, the children often pursue careers selected by their parents rather than those they prefer, in order not to disappoint their parents. This relates to the literature on the theory of planned behaviour (Ajzen and Madden, 1986), whereby the opinion of others and the consequences of complying or not complying with these opinions are considered prior to an action being carried out.

10.3.2 Changing attitudes

Previous attitudinal research (LaPiere, 1934, cited by Gross, 1996) demonstrates how the attitudes people say they have may be quite different from the attitudes implied by their behaviour. As a result, attitudes may be deemed to be only one determinant of behaviour. Although they represent a predisposition to behaviour, how individuals actually act in a particular situation will be dependent upon the immediate consequences of that behaviour, in particular how others are perceived to evaluate actions and habitual ways of behaving.

The 'theory of planned behaviour' (Ajzen and Madden, 1986) was designed to take account of voluntary and non-voluntary behaviours by including the concept of perceived behavioural control. This reflects the ease or difficulty that an individual attaches to the performance of the necessary behaviour based on past experience and current obstacles (Arnold *et al.*, 1995; Gross, 1996). Research has demonstrated that adding the perceived behavioural control variable can often improve the predictability of intention and behaviour (Hogg and Vaughan, 1995; Jonas *et al.*, 1995), as perceived behavioural control is thought to influence behaviour directly and also indirectly through intentions (Arnold *et al.*, 1995). Therefore, the theory of planned behaviour asserts that intentions are determined by attitudes, subjective norms and perceived behavioural control, while behaviour is determined by intentions and perceived behaviour control. However, although perceived behavioural control is important in determining the extent to which an individual believes they can perform the necessary behaviour in any given situation, the usefulness of perceived behavioural control will be limited if the individual's perception of the object is unreliable or inaccurate.

Unlike opinions, attitudes do not change quickly (Getz, 1994b). Predicting behaviour is possible without having an understanding of the factors that cause a particular behaviour; however, some degree of comprehension is essential for producing attitude change: 'in order to understand and predict the effectiveness of one person's attempt to change the attitude of another; we need to know who says what in which channel to whom and with what effect?' (Laswell, 1948, cited by Gross, 1996: 440).

Festinger (1957) identifies cognitive dissonance as a major source of attitude change. Cognitive dissonance occurs when two cognitive elements, whether beliefs, attitudes or behaviour, are contradictory. The cognitive element of an attitude comprises beliefs, opinions, knowledge or information held by an individual towards an attitude object. Individuals may acquire beliefs and opinions about a particular attitude object without having any personal experience of that attitude object (Gross, 1996). In order to combat this contradiction, the presence of dissonance is thought to motivate the individual to change one or more cognitive elements, so that they may be able to interpret situations differently. However, those with strong feelings on an issue or object are generally very resistant to messages and information that contradict their beliefs. Messages may be ignored or distorted to conform to their original beliefs.

As message recipients, individuals can influence the persuasiveness of a specific message, based on the attitudes they already possess; furthermore, levels of education and intelligence might affect attitude change, as they often determine the extent to which recipients understand the message (Hayes, 1993). Additionally, if individuals perceive that there are determined efforts to change their attitudes, they often adopt an attitude opposing the one contained in the message. Latitudes of rejection or acceptance vary, depending upon the original position of the individual (Hayes, 1993). 'The greater the discrepancy between the attitude a person already holds and the one which the communicator wants the person to hold, the less likely it is that any shift in attitude will occur' (Gross, 1996: 447). Hence, the more extreme the message, the more likely it is that it will fall outside the recipient's latitude of acceptance, but inside their latitude of rejection.

10.3.3 Why parental influence needs to be appreciated within the career decision making process

Career education and guidance (CEG) has been defined as 'a process of structured intervention aimed at helping individuals to take advantage of the educational, training, and occupational opportunities that are available' (Ginzberg, 1971: 4). Hayes and Hopson (1971) emphasize the importance of a sound understanding of the dynamics of the CDM process to those providing guidance, whether in formal or informal environments. Guidance work implies the existence of favourable conditions, within which competent and knowledgeable individuals can make choices. However, individuals are rarely 'free agents' and may not possess the level of maturity required to secure appropriate choices. Hence, those providing guidance are operating within the constraints that young people have been exposed to. Additionally, Hawthorn (1995 and 1996, cited by Foskett and Hemsley-Brown, 1997: 8) asserted that choice:

> whether free or relatively constrained, is dependent upon personal histories, experiences, perceptions and interpretations of the influence of explicit and implicit socio-economic and cultural pressures, both in the individual's immediate family environment and beyond in the social environment and the global environment portrayed by the media.

Influencers, in the form of parents, shape attitudes towards careers by conveying beliefs and values about the important aspects of careers and different career areas to school students. An attitude can be viewed as an integration of beliefs and values. Beliefs are representative of the information individuals possess about the world, which may be inaccurate or incomplete, while values relate to an individual's sense of what is desirable, good and worthwhile (Gross, 1996). Therefore, influencers shape attitudes by generating beliefs about the important aspects of a career and values about the various types of career areas and professions. If the influencers' levels of comprehension are found to be questionable and misinformed, it is likely that specific attitudes will be misdirected. Furthermore, if the aspects they deem important to a career are not evident in specific attitudes towards tourism and hospitality, it provides a strong indication as to why the tourism and hospitality industries are not perceived to provide first-choice careers.

10.4 Methodology

Marsh (1982, cited by de Vaus, 1996) argues that a survey is not synonymous with a particular technique of collecting information. Although questionnaires are predominantly used, other techniques, such as structured and in-depth interviews, observation and content analysis, are also appropriate. However, de Vaus (1996: 3) asserts that surveys are characterized by:

> a structured or systematic set of data . . . we collect information about the same variables or characteristics from at least two (normally far more) cases . . . For each case, we obtain its attribute on each variable. Because questionnaires are

the easiest way of ensuring this structured data, they are the most common technique used in survey research.

Following the exploratory qualitative research in the autumn of 1999, bilingual questionnaires were distributed to 1860 parents of Year 10, 11 and 12 pupils in 12 schools throughout Wales in December 2000. This comprised four schools in South Wales, three schools each in Mid and West Wales and two schools in North Wales. The exploratory qualitative research with career professionals and school students had produced significant findings and was used to assist the design of a quantitative methodology to evaluate parental attitudes towards careers within tourism and hospitality, specifically. The statements obtained during the qualitative stage were used as attitude statements in order to measure parental responses, together with theories identified in the literature review. The questionnaire respondents were asked to indicate their agreement or disagreement with each statement arranged along a five-point Likert scale. The questionnaire sought to address a number of issues, including:

- Parental influence in the CDM process and how parents rate various other 'influencers'. Which are the most and least influential groups of influencers against those identified in the literature and exploratory qualitative research with career professionals and school students?
- Parental opinions on the importance of a variety of aspects when choosing a career.
- Parental opinions relating to factors provided by a career in tourism and hospitality.

Statistical Package for the Social Sciences (SPSS) was used to analyse the data. Results from the parents in the quantitative stage were used to underpin the findings from the career professionals and school students in the exploratory qualitative stage. The number of questionnaires returned was 463, achieving a response rate of 25%.

10.5 Findings

10.5.1 Parental influence

Parents rated themselves the most influential group in terms of influencing career choices. Of the total respondents, 20.5% rated themselves as 'highly influential' and 53.6% felt that they were 'influential', compared with 18.1% and 4.5% who ranked themselves as 'slightly influential' and having 'no influence', respectively. These figures support the findings obtained from the career professionals and school students in the exploratory qualitative stage, as well as previous studies (Super, 1953; Hodkinson, 1995; Foskett and Hemsley-Brown, 1998; Cothran and Combrink, 1999; Lifetime Careers, 1999). In many cases family members can be credible sources of information. However, family members are not always best equipped to offer advice. Their occupational experience may be restricted and their attitudes to work and career areas may be biased, outdated or misinformed.

10.5.2 Other 'influencers' in the career decision making process

In addition to their own influence, parents rated some other factors as 'influential' in their children's CDM process, as shown in Fig. 10.1. In terms of being 'highly influential' in the CDM process, parents also rated work experience (24.6%) and subject teachers (14.5%). Hence, it would appear that parents have a high regard for the influence of the formal methods and specialist sources of CEG, such as career coordinators, career advisers, subject teachers, careers literature and work experience.

Parental opinions regarding the influence of less formal and non-specialist sources of CEG, such as family members, friends, television and newspapers/magazines, were much lower (Fig. 10.2). Television, in particular, was given much less status in terms of influence on the CDM process, which indicates that too much emphasis may be placed upon the glamour of the media, which might sell a 'lifestyle' instead of a 'career', rather than the influence of social and educational contexts, particularly as individuals often only search for specific information on particular careers if they have a predisposition towards that career. The parental responses contradict the findings of the earlier exploratory research, which found that television, in particular, was a significant tool in terms of influencing and informing career choices.

The low status given to non-specialist sources of CEG and the media is of little surprise. As Hayter (2001) suggests, the fundamental objective of 'fly-on-the-wall' television documentaries is to attract high viewing numbers. Therefore, the focus is on the exploitation of kitchen and hotel life in order to attract the attention of viewers, rather than consideration of the impressions provided of working conditions within the industries.

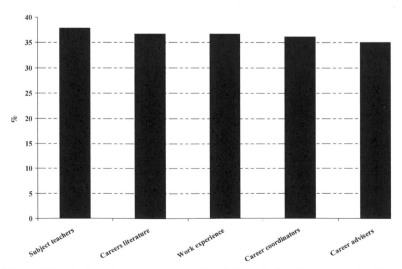

Fig. 10.1. Other factors that parents rated as 'influential' in the career decision making process.

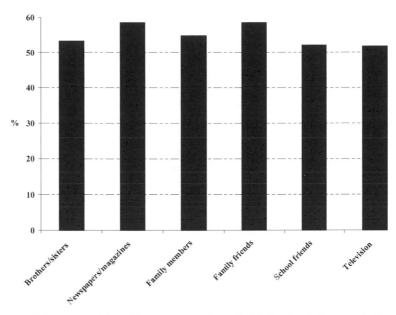

Fig. 10.2. Those considered by parents to have 'slight' or 'no' influence in the career decision making process.

10.5.3 Factors important to careers in general and careers in tourism and hospitality

Parents were asked to rate factors that they considered important to careers in general, followed by factors that they felt would be provided within tourism and hospitality careers. As important and extremely important factors when choosing a career, parents prioritized interest/enjoyment, job security and training opportunities (see Fig. 10.3). When the factors they believed existed within careers in tourism and hospitality were compared with the factors parents had deemed important when choosing a career, it was apparent that a career in tourism and hospitality would incorporate the majority of the important career factors (Fig. 10.4).

Yet, although it appears that a career in tourism and hospitality would incorporate the majority of the career factors considered important by parents, the findings illustrate that attitudes may be deemed to be only one determinant of behaviour, as the attitudes of parents with regard to what they thought a career in tourism and hospitality would provide, based on their earlier response to careers in general, were fairly positive. However, this attitude was not reflected in their behaviour with regard to the selection of tourism and hospitality careers for their children. This suggests that, while parental attitudes towards the general idea of a career in tourism and hospitality are not completely negative, they are unlikely to consciously select that career area for their child (Haven, 2002). This demonstrates that, although attitudes represent a predisposition to behaviour, how individuals actually act in a particular situation will be dependent upon the immediate consequences of that behaviour, in particular how others are perceived to

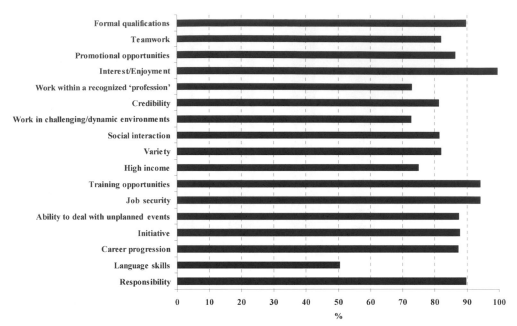

Fig. 10.3. Factors parents consider important in a career.

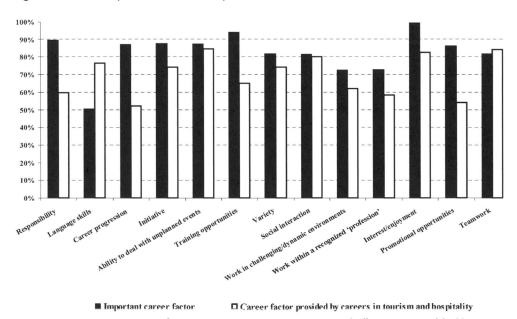

■ Important career factor   □ Career factor provided by careers in tourism and hospitality

Fig. 10.4. Important career factors and career factors parents believe are provided by careers in the tourism and hospitality industry.

evaluate actions, thus illustrating the application of the theory of planned behaviour (Ajzen and Madden, 1986). If two cognitive elements are contradictory, as in this case where discrepancies exist between parental attitudes and behaviour, cognitive dissonance is likely to occur. In order to address this inconsistency, dissonance should motivate the individuals to change one or more cognitive elements, so that they can alter their interpretations. The fairly positive attitudes of parents towards what they believe a career in the tourism and hospitality industries would provide presents a platform from which interpretations can be altered to create more positive behaviour in terms of career choice.

10.5.4 Selection of the tourism and hospitality industry as a potential career

Few parents selected tourism or hospitality as career choices for their child. Of the 463 parents that responded, only 48 selected tourism as a possible career choice for their child, while 24 selected hospitality. Parents who selected tourism and/or hospitality as possible careers for their child generally had no experience of working within those industries. This challenges the findings of previous studies. Murphy (1985) identifies that certain groups of people appear to develop much more positive attitudes towards the tourism industry in any tourism-related community. Residents with a commercial or vocational investment in tourism were found to be more likely to be favourably disposed to the industry than were other community members. Those who owned or operated businesses, as well as those who worked in those businesses, were found to have more positive attitudes to the industry than those who had no direct involvement or perceived that they derived no benefits from tourism. Murphy (1985) concludes that familiarity with the industry tends to generate more favourable overall evaluations. Similarly, Choy (1995) found that non-tourism workers tend to have fairly negative perceptions of tourism industry jobs.

These empirical findings demonstrate that parents with no experience of tourism and hospitality employment are not as negative towards the industries as might have been expected. In fact, it would appear that parents with experience of work within the tourism and hospitality industries are less likely to select tourism and hospitality as career choices for their children. One explanation for this is that they may have developed negative attitudes towards the industries through exposure to their highly seasonal local tourism and hospitality industries, as those selecting tourism or hospitality as the career area in which they had spent most of their working life were predominantly located in Mid, North and West Wales. As message recipients, it may be difficult to change the attitudes of parents with experience of tourism and hospitality employment and to promote tourism and hospitality as first-choice careers (Haven, 2002).

10.6 Conclusions

This investigation into parental attitudes towards careers in tourism and hospitality demonstrates that students are gaining much of their careers information and guidance from non-specialist sources, such as parents, thus illustrating the importance of providing non-specialist deliverers of careers information with accurate and up-to-date information about the tourism and hospitality industry in Wales. Parents are powerful influencers in the CDM process and they acknowledge this influence. As influencers, parents shape attitudes towards careers by conveying beliefs and values. If their levels of comprehension are found to be inaccurate, their attitudes and subsequent behaviour may be misdirected, which may ultimately affect their children's behaviour and career choices. For example, if parents have negative attitudes towards the industries, they are unlikely to encourage their children into tourism and hospitality as a career choice. Parents who lack work experience in the tourism and hospitality industries are not necessarily negative towards the industries as career choices, but parents with tourism and hospitality employment experience are less likely to select tourism or hospitality as a career choice. This has implications for parents as message recipients. If messages about tourism and hospitality careers are in tune with their attitudes towards the industry, the message is more likely to be accepted, as opposed to situations where the message is more extreme in relation to their attitudes. In the case of the latter, messages about careers within the tourism and hospitality industries may well fall outside the parents' latitude of acceptance.

In terms of shaping school students' attitudes towards careers and the role of various influencers, the research illustrates the formal and informal social contexts surrounding the CDM process, which challenges the policies adopted by some high-profile media campaigns designed to change attitudes towards careers in tourism and hospitality. CDM is context-related and cannot be separated from the family background, culture and life histories of school students (Hodkinson, 1995). This demonstrates the conflict that exists within CDM, as policy makers and the industry operate on the assumption that individuals are 'free agents'. An issue that has been highlighted within this research, as well as previous studies (Ginzberg, 1971; Hayes and Hopson, 1971; Hodkinson, 1995), is the need for policy makers, practitioners and the industry to recognize the complexity of the CDM process.

In his longitudinal study of the Spey Valley in Scotland, Getz (1994a) asserts that tourism and hospitality have become the predominant industry in many rural areas where there are few alternative employment opportunities. Moreover, he discusses the importance of cultivating local young people as potential employees, in order to ensure the long-term sustainability of tourism and hospitality in such rural areas and to guard against in-migration and transient workers. This approach should be adopted by the tourism and hospitality industries in Wales in order to enhance service quality and destination competitiveness from a human resource perspective.

The future of a skilled and quality workforce begins at home, with the attitudes of parents towards careers and specifically their attitudes towards tourism and hospitality as a career option. Tourism SMEs and other tourism and hospitality employers need to appreciate this aspect and target career information messages accordingly. However, given the fragmented nature of tourism SMEs, the delivery of accurate and effective career messages depends upon tourism employers working with various public-sector interventions, such as those undertaken by the Careers Service, Tourism Training Forum for Wales and Springboard Wales, to ensure that the benefits of tourism and hospitality employment are emphasized to parents and potential recruits of the industry.

References

Airey, D. and Frontistis, A. (1997) Attitudes to careers in tourism: an Anglo Greek comparison. *Tourism Management* 18(3), 149–158.

Ajzen, I. and Madden, J.T. (1986) Prediction of goal-directed behaviour: attitudes, intentions, and perceived behavioural control. *Journal of Experimental Social Psychology* 22, 453–474.

Arnold, J., Cooper, C. and Robertson, I. (1995) *Work Psychology: Understanding Human Behaviour in the Workplace* 2nd edn. Pitman, London, 418 pp.

Baum, T. (1995) *Managing Human Resources in the European Tourism and Hospitality Industry: a Strategic Approach*. Chapman & Hall, London, 281 pp.

Careers Services Association of Wales (1999) *Pupil Destinations from Schools in Wales*. Careers Services Association of Wales, Flintshire, UK.

CBI (1995) *Filling the Gaps: Skills for Tourism*. Confederation of British Industry, London.

Choy, D. (1995) The quality of tourism employment. *Tourism Management* 16(2), 129–137.

Cothran, C. and Combrink, T. (1999) Attitudes of minority adolescents toward hospitality industry careers. *International Journal of Hospitality Management* 18(2), 143–158.

Department of National Heritage (1996) *Tourism: Competing with the Best – People Working in Tourism and Hospitality*. DNH, London.

de Vaus, D.A. (1996) *Surveys in Social Research*, 4th edn. UCL Press, London, 411 pp.

DTZ Pieda Consulting (1998) *Employment and Training in the Tourism Sector in Wales*. DTZ Pieda Consulting, Manchester, UK.

Festinger, L. (1957) *A Theory of Cognitive Dissonance*. Harper & Row, New York, 291 pp.

Foskett, N.H. and Hemsley-Brown, J.V. (1997) *Career Perceptions and Decision Making among Young People in Schools and Colleges. Report of the Career Perceptions and Decision Making (CAPDEM) Project*. Centre for Research in Education Marketing, University of Southampton, Southampton, UK.

Foskett, N.H. and Hemsley-Brown, J.V. (1998) *Perceptions of Nursing as a Career among Young People in Schools and Colleges – a Report on Behalf of the Department of Health*. Centre for Research in Education Marketing, University of Southampton, Southampton, UK.

Getz, D. (1994a) Students' work experiences, perceptions and attitudes towards careers in hospitality and tourism: a longitudinal case study in Spey Valley, Scotland. *International Journal of Hospitality Management* 13(1), 25–37.

Getz, D. (1994b) Residents' attitudes towards tourism: a longitudinal study in Spey Valley, Scotland. *Tourism Management* 15(4), 247–258.

Ginzberg, E. (1971) *Career Guidance: Who Needs It, Who Provides It, Who Can Improve It*, 1st edn. McGraw-Hill, New York, 356 pp.

Gross, R. (1996) *Psychology: the Science of Mind and Behaviour*, 3rd edn. Hodder & Stoughton, London, 948 pp.

Haven, C.L. (2002) Attitudes in Wales towards careers in tourism and hospitality. PhD thesis, University of Wales Institute, Cardiff, UK.

Hayes, J. and Hopson, B. (1971) *Careers Guidance: The Role of the School in Vocational Development*. Heinemann Educational, London, 260 pp.

Hayes, N. (1993) *Principles of Social Psychology*. Lawrence Erlbaum Associates, Hove, UK, 168 pp.

Hayter, R. (2001) The 'hospitality' branding: a question of impact on the industry's image. *Hospitality Review* 3(1), 21–25.

Hemsley-Brown, J.V. (1998) Career perceptions and decision making. *Newscheck* 9(3), 5–7.

Hodkinson, P. (1995) How young people make career decisions. *Education and Training* 37(8), 3–8.

Hogg, M.A. and Vaughan, G.M. (1995) *Social Psychology: An Introduction*. Prentice Hall, Hemel Hempstead, UK, 550 pp.

HtF (2001) *Labour Market Review 2001 for the Hospitality Industry*. Hospitality Training Foundation, London.

Jonas, K., Eagly, A.H. and Stroebe, W. (1995) Attitudes and persuasion. In: Argyle, M. and Colman, A.M. (eds) *Social Psychology*. Longman, London, pp. 1–19.

Lankard, B. (1995) *Family Role in Career Development* [online], ERIC Digest 164. Available from: http://ericacve.org/docs/dig164.htm Accessed on 18 May 1999.

Lifetime Careers (1999) *The 1998 Attitudes and Aspirations Survey*. Lifetime Careers, Mexborough.

Lifetime Careers (2000) *Attitudes and Aspirations Survey 2000*. Lifetime Careers (Barnsley, Doncaster & Rotherham), Rotherham, UK.

Middleton, E.B. and Loughead, T.A. (1993) Parental influence on career development: an integrative framework for adolescent career counselling. *Journal of Career Development* 19(3), 161–173.

Murphy, P.E. (1985) *Tourism: a Community Approach*. Methuen, London, 320 pp.

Pizam, A. (1982) Tourism manpower: the state of the art. *Journal of Travel Research* 11(2), 5–9.

Purcell, K. and Quinn, J. (1996) Exploring the education-employment equation in hospitality management: a comparison of graduates and HNDs. *International Journal of Hospitality Management* 15(1), 51–68.

Super, D.E. (1953) A theory of vocational development. *American Psychologist* 8, 185–190.

Super, D.E. (1957) *The Psychology of Careers*. Harper and Brothers, New York, 362 pp.

Tourism South and West Wales (TSWW) (2000) *Tourism Industry Survey*. TSWW, Swansea, UK.

11 HRM Behaviour and Economic Performance: Small versus Large Tourism Enterprises

Anne-Mette Hjalager

Advance/1, 8000 Aarhus C, Denmark

11.1 Introduction

For a number of reasons, human resource issues in the tourism sector are attracting increasing attention. Most often, the main focus is quantitative: the creation of jobs and the derived benefits for the countries and regions concerned (Smeral, 1997; Leiper, 1999). The International Labour Organization is concerned not only with employment, but also the quality of work and working conditions, i.e. the creation of jobs of acceptable quality (ILO, 2001). The focus here is on such issues as fair pay, reasonable work security, full-time opportunities, training and career opportunities and the right to join a union (Sinclair, 1997; Royle, 2000). The opening of the European Union's (EU) labour markets and (legal and illegal) immigration patterns are having a considerable effect on tourism labour supply. Policy-making in this labour market has never been easy, and recent developments have only increased the challenges.

The literature has often focused on the labour market realities faced by tourism enterprises. The rapid turnover of personnel in particular is presented as a severe problem, hampering long-term strategic considerations (Johnson, 1985). As tourism is a particularly labour-intensive sector which is dependent on the encounter between employee and customer, the management of human resources is assumed to play a major role for the economic performance of enterprises. Turnover is regarded as a management problem that can be handled along with other personnel issues (Wood, 1994; Iverson, 2000). This has led business advisers and academic researchers, each in their own way, to recommend the adoption of mainstream human resource management (HRM) principles, e.g. retention and wages policies, training, empowerment.

This chapter suggests that HRM in tourism and other sectors differs in significant ways, and that the feasibility of the transfer of HRM practices from the one to the other lacks substantial evidence. Seasonality is a constraint, and the fierce competition that most enterprises in tourism experience makes other types of HRM practices than those usually recommended by the experts desirable. The main hypothesis of the chapter is that value added in the tourism sector does not systematically coincide with mainstream HRM. In other words, we assume that well-managed enterprises with low staff turnover and a high level of formal quali- fications do not necessarily perform better. The chapter will investigate whether, at the end of the day, it is not the most numerically flexible and most pragmatic enterprises which achieve better profits; rather, it is those that adopt other and more theory-consistent strategies. Another key question concerns the difference between small and large enterprises. It is presumed that value added is higher in the latter, but that variations in the stability and qualification profiles have no sig- nificant influence on this. Thirdly, the chapter will present evidence on tenure in the tourism sector, assuming that small enterprises are platforms for careers in larger enterprises and that variation in salary levels is a decisive factor. However, average tenure tends not to be long in large or small enterprises in tourism, and the difference in terms of size is not significant.

11.2 Data Sources and Methods

The study is based on the Danish labour market database (IDA), which contains information on all accommodation, catering and travel service enterprises and their employees (approximately 15,000 enterprises and 60,000 employees). In the case of employees, a large number of socio-economic data are available for research purposes. While the data on employers are not quite as extensive, there is still a substantial number of variables that can be analysed. The most useful facility of the database is that it combines financial performance data on enterprises (acquired from tax registers) with information on employees, e.g. educational background (acquired from various official registers).

Using identification numbers in the database, the behaviour of firms and employees can be followed over time in longitudinal research, thereby allowing consistent and conclusive career tracking and tenure calculation. This extremely useful facility has been of enormous benefit to the research for this chapter. Data for this research are made anonymous by the provider Statistics Denmark, so that enterprises and employees cannot be identified.

For this analysis, the data are subject to a number of limitations, the most important of which are:

- The study covers 1984, 1987, 1990, 1993, 1996 and 1999. However, economic performance data are only available for the two latter years, thus limiting some of the analyses.
- Economic performance is measured by added value per whole employee working year. We thus operate with a labour productivity measure.
- Economic performance data are only available for enterprises with ten or more employees.
- The grouping of employees by education and work position follows – for better or worse – official classifications.

- Employees with very short-term employment and employees with other primary employment are omitted, as are persons who are officially registered as full-time students and school pupils.
- The turnover rates are based on data on retention, new employees and employees who have left.
- The longitudinal analysis comprises only enterprises that exist in both years. New enterprises or enterprises that have shut down are left out of this particular part of the study.

Other methodological issues and data interpretations concerning the various results will be described in further detail below.

11.3 Productivity and Turnover

One of the main issues of this study is the productivity of tourism enterprises and labour turnover. Accession rates, i.e. new employees as a percentage of the total number of employees the previous year, are included in Table 11.1. The bottom row of the table shows very clearly that enterprises are hiring intensively. Even among full-time staff on ordinary contracts, there is an annual turnover of one-third. Over a 3-year period, turnover is 70%. Thus, in Denmark as in most other countries, tourism personnel are extremely mobile, either because the employer requires this or by own choice.

The firms are clustered in groups of average value added per employee. Table 11.1 shows that firms with the lowest productivity have a significantly greater annual access of new personnel. Access rates are gross number, including new jobs as well as job openings created by turnover. This is not a surprising result. The more productive firms are better able to retain staff than those with low value added per employee. The latter are forced to hire and fire to match staff with business volumes as closely as possible.

Compared with most other European countries, there are few restrictions on hiring and firing in Denmark (Fahlbeck, 1998). Only salaried employees have a

Table 11.1. Personnel accession rates (%) in tourism (accommodation, catering and travel services), by value added/employee, 1998–1999 and 1996–1999.

	Accession rate 1998–1999	Accession rate 1996–1999
< DKK 100,000	48	83
DKK 100,000–199,999	41	76
DKK 200,000–299,999	36	71
DKK 300,000–399,999	34	68
DKK 400,000–599,999	31	67
DKK 600,000–999,999	20	61
> DKK 1 million	29	61
All	35	70

Note: Only enterprises with 10+ employees. Only enterprises with positive value added/employee. DKK 100 approximates Euro 13.50.

right to notice, the length of which depends on the duration of employment. Other employees can be dismissed immediately, and without notice, though Denmark has been compelled by the EU to implement regulations guaranteeing notice in cases of mass lay-offs. Even in such cases, however, firms are only 'encouraged' to help dismissed employees find new jobs and to cooperate with the authorities and others in this. The directive concerning documentary evidence of employment has also been interpreted broadly in Danish legislation (Scheuer, 1996).

Part of the explanation for the lack of legislative regulation of severance terms, part-time work and temporary employment can be found in the existence of a relatively fine-meshed, publicly financed social security net (Lind, 1997; OECD, 1997). In this sense, therefore, social legislation, combined with unemployment legislation, supports firms' endeavours to achieve numerical flexibility.

In interpreting the figures in Table 11.1, we must also assume that the legal and collective agreement tradition in Denmark saves many enterprises on the margin of economic sustainability from closure. Whether or not this benefits the tourism sector is debatable.

11.4 Profitability and Turnover in Tourism versus Other Sectors

Table 11.2 shows the difference in turnover between tourism, other services and the rest of the private sector. Over a 3-year period, manufacturing industry, etc., only hired 45% new employees compared with 70% in tourism. The rest of the service sector has a slightly higher turnover, albeit considerably below tourism.

The table also shows that the patterns of accession and value added/employee are similar across the sectors. The low performers experience a higher personnel turnover in all three sectors (Simons and Hinkin, 2002). However, the tendency

Table 11.2. Personnel accession rates (%) in tourism (accommodation, catering and travel services), other service sectors and other segments in the private sector, by value added/employee, 1996–1999.

	Accession rate, 1996–1999, tourism	Accession rate, 1996–1999, other private services	Accession rate, 1996–1999, other segments in the private sector
< DKK 100,000	83	67	59
DKK 100,000–199,999	76	58	53
DKK 200,000–299,999	71	51	45
DKK 300,000–399,999	68	47	43
DKK 400,000–599,999	67	49	44
DKK 600,000–999,999	61	51	47
> DKK 1 million	61	53	58
All	70	51	45

Note: Only enterprises with 10+ employees. Only enterprises with positive value added/employee. DKK 100 approximates Euro 13.50.

to use flexibility as an instrument to compensate for performance deficits is considerably more widespread in tourism than in the other sectors.

It is interesting to note that very high performers in sectors other than tourism tend to hire more staff than enterprises with more modest value added. This might be the outcome of successful expansion strategies. This tends to be reflected in U-formed accession rates, though this is not the case in tourism. Hiring is particularly high among the very low performers and the high performers in other sectors, while there is a more average turnover among the moderate performers. Standard value added might have a stabilizing influence on personnel policies. It is probably not surprising that, while profits are 'safe' and 'average', management will focus on other personnel issues than achieving flexibility through hiring and firing.

11.5 Performance and Composition of Personnel

The trade and research literature stresses the importance of recruiting well-qualified staff, not least people with a formal education (Riley, 1996; Baum *et al.*, 1997). In particular, there is a link between a professional enterprise with a favourable image on the one hand and the competences of the staff on the other. Implicitly, it is often taken for granted that enterprises hiring staff with better qualifications will also benefit in financial terms. Conversely, hiring from the bottom of the labour market is a risky business.

The data on which this study is based challenge the implicit assumption that firm performance and educational levels go hand in hand. Table 11.3 compares tourism with the other segments in the private sector. In the case of tourism,

Table 11.3. Percentage of personnel in tourism (accommodation, catering and travel services), other service sectors and other segments in the private sector with a formal education, by value added/employee, 1999.

	Percentage of staff with formal education, tourism	Percentage of staff with formal education, other private services	Percentage of staff with formal education, other segments in the private sector
< DKK 100,000	48	64	62
DKK 100,000–199,999	51	66	65
DKK 200,000–299,999	52	67	71
DKK 300,000–399,999	53	67	69
DKK 400,000–599,999	47	70	68
DKK 600,000–999,999	54	72	67
> DKK 1 million	27	72	67
All	51	68	69

Note: Only enterprises with 10+ employees. Only enterprises with positive value added/employee. DKK 100 approximates Euro 13.50.

there are no straightforward and logical connections between performance and the composition of labour. The most value-added-creating enterprises do not have a high proportion of staff with a formal education. On the contrary, it seems that the competitive strength of these enterprises is connected with the ability to organize and manage the work of larger numbers of unskilled employees in an efficient way. In the rest of the service sector, there is a clearer indication that qualifications matter. In manufacturing, etc., in the far-right column, the picture is also slightly blurred, with competences not necessarily contributing to firm performance.

An obvious objection to this type of investigation is that, in tourism in particular, firms have to rely much more on informal skills and personality traits that are not necessarily acquired through formal training. Even if this is a correct supplementary explanation to the above, the persisting advocacy for more training in tourism is rather contradictory (Jameson, 2000).

11.6 Retention, Wages and Firm Size

The previous sections have analysed the connections between the retention of staff and financial performance. It is suggested that there is a correspondence between these factors. Managers/owners take the business results into account and hire staff accordingly. It is likely that well-performing enterprises are also better workplaces and that they pay higher wages, 'sharing' the profits with the staff who contribute to them. However, this assumption cannot be tested directly here.

We now turn to another issue related to performance and pay. In the following sections, information on firm size is combined with wage levels and the retention of personnel. It is well documented that turnover is higher in small enterprises than in larger ones (Farber, 1994; Iverson and Deery, 1997). This is partly due to the fact that small enterprises cannot easily reallocate staff between departments and jobs, and variations in the business have to be regulated through the external labour market. Careers can best be pursued in larger firms with a distinct hierarchy; employees from small enterprises often have to apply for jobs in other firms if they want promotion or new challenges. This study supports these findings. Table 11.4 also shows, however, that large tourism enterprises have a considerably higher turnover compared with other sectors.

Table 11.4. Retention rates in the same firm by firm unit, size and sector, 1996–1997.

	1–9 employees	10–49 employees	50–249 employees	250+ employees
Tourism	57	66	72	79
Other services	76	79	81	85
Other industries	75	80	83	85

It is likely that employees are motivated to change jobs because of wage differences between firms (of different sizes) and sectors. Employees in the smallest tourism enterprises have, on the whole, no financial incentive to stay in their jobs if they can find something better – wages are higher in other sectors and in larger enterprises. As can be seen from Table 11.5, the difference in wages between the smallest and the largest enterprises in tourism is 31%, in other services 26%, while in other industries it is only 12%. This is a compelling explanation for lower retention rates in tourism. Thus, it is likely that a high turnover is not only the outcome of management decisions, but also of the individual choice of the employees.

While the general pattern of retention rates and wages has not changed between 1993 and 1999, average hourly wages have risen more in sectors other than tourism, and more in large enterprises than in small. This also contributes to staff turnover.

11.7 Job Changes to Other Sectors and Implications for Hourly Wages

We saw in the previous section that tourism employees have clear financial incentives to change jobs, especially to sectors other than tourism. But do they change sectors, and do they obtain higher wages? In other words: are they and their acquired skills and competences competitive in a larger labour market? Table 11.6 shows the increase in wages for persons who shift sectors versus persons who change jobs but choose to stay in the tourism industry.

Table 11.5. Hourly average wage, by size of employer and sector, DKK, 1999.

	1–9 employees	10–49 employees	50–249 employees	250+ employees
Tourism	134	149	161	175
Other services	162	178	187	204
Other industries	154	158	165	172

Table 11.6. Wages increases, percentage, 1996–1999 for persons who change jobs, those who stay in the tourism industry and those who change to other industries, by educational groups.

	Stay in tourism	Change to other sectors
No formal education	23	24
Vocational training, administration	21	24
Vocational training, other trades	17	12
College education	21	32
Bachelor education	21	36
Master's degree	21	29

The better educated have a much higher wage bargaining power in the labour market. As shown in the table, employees with a college or university education achieve a substantial increase in wages by shifting from tourism to other sectors. This is not the case for those with a vocational education, e.g. cooks and waiters, whose skills are in less demand in other sectors. If cooks and waiters change jobs to other industries (for example, to avoid unsocial working hours), they will often have to take unskilled, lower-paid work. Other groups of professionals have obtained training that is more general and applicable to the needs of other business sectors.

To conclude, wages constitute a powerful explanation for staff turnover in the tourism industry. The industry either cannot or will not motivate the majority of personnel to stay by offering competitive wages (Ohlin and West, 1993), and this supports the excessive turnover.

From the point of view of employees and future students, Table 11.6 clearly shows that a specialized education in tourism does not necessarily pay and that, as regards careers and wages, more generalist types of education seem to be the better bet.

11.8 Job Changes to Firms of Other Sizes and Implications for Hourly Wages

Generally speaking, job changes to larger enterprises are likely to mean a bigger rise in wages than job changes from larger to smaller enterprises. This study confirms earlier findings, both for employees leaving the tourism sector and for those who stay. Table 11.7 shows the implications for wage increases for those who stay in tourism. The money-conscious employee will try to shift jobs away from the smallest enterprises. It is interesting to note that a shift from the largest enterprises does not result in any substantial increase in wages, not even when employees find jobs in the same size group. One explanation for this is that employees are already among the best paid, and above-average wage increases may require something more, such as better qualifications.

The importance of firm size can also be seen in the change from tourism to other sectors. Table 11.8 indicates that employees in the smallest tourism

Table 11.7. Wage increases (%, 1996–1999) for job changes to other jobs in tourism, by firm size in 1996 and 1999. Italics: above average.

	Firm size in 1999			
Firm size in 1996	1–9 employees	10–49 employees	50–249 employees	250+ employees
1–9 employees	16	29	27	48
10–49 employees	21	20	27	22
50–249 employees	18	18	21	25
250+ employees	1	7	10	13

Table 11.8. Wage increases (%, 1996–1999) for job changes to other sectors, by firm size in 1996 and 1999. Italics: above average.

Firm size, tourism, in 1996	Firm size, other sectors in 1999			
	1–9 employees	10–49 employees	50–249 employees	250+ employees
1–9 employees	20	*23*	*31*	*31*
10–49 employees	14	21	18	*36*
50–249 employees	10	21	*26*	*24*
250+ employees	–2	7	11	11

enterprises in particular can increase their wages by shifting to larger units in other industries. However, employees in large tourism enterprises may experience a decrease in income if they move to a job in a very small company outside the tourism sector. Their competitive power *vis-à-vis* other applicants for jobs in large companies is also less.

Job changes can, of course, be due to numerous factors, e.g. ambition, the desire for new challenges, unsatisfactory work conditions and family obligations, and wages are not the only motive. In the Danish egalitarian context, putting too much emphasis on the financial side of a job is normally frowned on. However, this study indicates that, behind the scenes and in spite of the social morale, the possibility for higher wages via job shifts influences behaviour to a considerable degree.

11.9 Conclusions

This chapter discusses some important, but often overlooked, aspects of personnel turnover and economic performance of tourism firms. First, tourism enterprises with low value added experience a systematically higher labour turnover than those with a better economic performance. However, this is not the case in other sectors, where there is a U-shaped relationship between turnover and firm profitability. This supports the idea that tourism utilizes numerical flexibility to a considerable degree, and that strict, even Tayloristic, work management pays better than many firms like to admit. From an employee's point of view, tourism is not the most obvious sector for dedicated and consistent careers.

High performance does not correspond to high educational levels in tourism. The organization of a large number of unskilled and semi-skilled employees can be regarded as a core competence of the most successful enterprises, not the specific and formal skills of the majority of staff. The fact that educational institutions are not particularly successful at establishing good stakeholder relations in tourism can perhaps partly be explained by the poor economic returns on education (Kelley-Patterson and George, 2001).

Not surprisingly, retention rates are significantly higher in large tourism enterprises, as are salary levels. Retention rates are probably not only a matter of seasonality and work organization but also of pay. Employees who change jobs will increase their salary, especially if they leave the tourism sector altogether. Persons with a longer formal education, in particular, will experience high average increases in salary. Career shifts to larger enterprises are also rewarded by significant increases in salary.

What are the implications for HRM policies? Over the past few decades, much emphasis has been placed on the need for more consistent recruiting and management practices in tourism, not least in small and medium-sized enterprises (SMEs)(Jameson, 2000; Krakover, 2000). A high employee turnover is most often regarded as harmful. It has not been possible in this study to determine whether a high employee turnover results from low profitability, or whether low profitability is the result of a high turnover. However, it seems that, although not popular for this, many tourism SMEs proactively try to utilize the wage and recruiting instrument to balance their results close to the margin. It is unlikely that retention programmes will work unless they include a financial incentive. We could claim that, when managers do not behave differently, it is because they do not really have any alternative.

This behaviour can be analysed in a transaction cost perspective. One of the arguments for limiting turnover is that recruitment processes are very risky and costly. Moreover, new employees have to be introduced to and trained in their job functions. The more empowerment, the more training. Until new employees are familiar with the job, they will be less productive for the enterprise. These costs are called transaction costs, and are incurred by firms that want flexible access to the pool of external resources (Loveridge, 1983), in this case the pool of casual labour. Unskilled work, such as cleaning, waiting and operating simple machines, can, to a large degree, be embedded in easily understood routines and technology. The proprietor will estimate whether wages saved during quiet business periods will compensate for recruitment-related transaction costs. The level of turnover and wages found in this study indicates that the transaction costs are tolerable, and that enterprises are organizing work in such a way as to compensate for them.

A system such as the Danish, with easy – and cheap – access to hiring and firing, enhances numerical flexibility, and smooth labour placement services play a supplementary role in constantly high turnover levels. In practice, therefore, the authorities are helping enterprises to reduce their transaction costs.

Compared with other countries, labour regulation in Denmark is limited. Labour deregulation and flexibility are often claimed to go hand in hand (Buultjens and Howard, 2001). However, there is less certainty about whether deregulation will also lead to a financially better performing tourism sector in terms of higher value added. It is likely that labour regulation policies will put greater pressure on SMEs operating at the margins, and that structural development, with a substantial number of closures, can be enhanced by government-imposed restrictions. However, the benefits for consumer prices are more ambiguous, which is a reason for governments to avoid regulation if possible.

For employees, tourism can be regarded as a platform for a career in other sectors. For many groups in the labour market – e.g. immigrants – this is the only available path to more secure and better-paid jobs. However, the high turnover in tourism also includes managers and persons with a dedicated training in tourism (Hjalager and Andersen, 2001), and this study shows that employees have good financial reasons to leave. This should be taken as a warning signal to all those educational institutions that – with the best intentions in the world – continue to qualify large numbers of staff for this particular industry alone.

Acknowledgements

This chapter is produced within the framework of the LOK research programme, Theme 1: Managing and Developing Human Resources in SMEs (www.lok.cbs.dk).

References

Baum, T., Amoah, V. and Spivack, S. (1997) Policy dimensions of human resource management in the tourism and hospitality industries. *International Journal of Contemporary Hospitality Management* 9(5/6), 221–229.

Buultjens, J. and Howard, D. (2001) Labour flexibility in the hospitality industry: questioning the relevance of deregulation. *International Journal of Contemporary Hospitality Management* 13(2), 60–69.

Fahlbeck, R. (1998) *Flexibilisation of Working Life: Potentials and Challenges for Labour Law and International Analysis*. Juristforlaget, Lund, Sweden, 87 pp.

Farber, H. (1994) The analysis of inter-firm worker mobility. *Journal of Labour Economics* 12(4), 554–593.

Hjalager, A. M. and Andersen, S. (2001) Tourism employment: contingent work or professional career? *Employee Relations* 23(1/2), 115–129.

ILO (2001) *Human Resources Development, Employment and Globalization in the Hotel, Catering and Tourism Sector*. ILO, Geneva.

Iverson, K. (2000) Managing for effective workforce diversity. *Cornell Hotel and Restaurant Administration Quarterly* April, 31–38.

Iverson, R.D. and Deery, M. (1997) Turnover culture in the hospitality industry. *Human Resource Management Journal* 7(4), 71–82.

Jameson, S.M. (2000) Recruitment and training in small firms. *Journal of European Industrial Training* 24(1), 43–49.

Johnson, K. (1985) Labour turnover in hotels – revisited. *Service Industries Journal* 5(2), 135–152.

Kelley-Patterson, D. and George, C. (2001) Securing graduate commitment: an exploration of the comparative expectations of placement students, graduate recruits and human resource managers within the hospitality, leisure and tourism industries. *Hospitality Management* 20, 311–323.

Krakover, S. (2000) Partitioning seasonal employment in the hospitality industry. *Tourism Management* 21, 461–471.

Leiper, N. (1999) A conceptual analysis of tourism-supported employment which reduces the incidence of exaggerated, misleading statistics about jobs. *Tourism Management* 2(5), 605–613.

Lind, J. (1997) *The Social Benefits and the Deficits of Flexibility: Unemployment and Non-standard Work*. CID, Handelshøjskolen, Copenhagen.

Loveridge, R. (1983) Contingency, control, and risk – the utility of manpower planning in a risky environment. In: Edwards J. (ed.) *Manpower Strategy and Techniques in an Organisational Context.* John Wiley & Sons, London, pp. 133–153.

OECD (1997) *Employment Outlook,* OECD, Paris.

Ohlin, J.B. and West, J.J. (1993) An analysis of the effect of fringe benefit offerings on the turnover of hourly housekeeping workers in the hotel industry. *International Journal of Hospitality Management* 12(4), 323–336.

Riley, M. (1996) *Human Resource Management. A Guide to Personnel Practice in the Hospitality and Tourism Industry.* Butterworth-Heinemann, Oxford, UK, 219 pp.

Royle, T. (2000) *Working for McDonald's in Europe. The Unequal Struggle.* Routledge, London, 248 pp.

Scheuer, S. (1996) *Fælles aftale eller egen kontrakt i arbejdslivet. Udbredelsen af kollektive overenskomster, faglig organisering og skriftlige ansættelsesbeviser blandt privatansatte.* Nyt fra samfundsvidenskaberne, Copenhagen.

Simons, T. and Hinkin, T. (2002) The effects of employee turnover on hotel profits: a test across multiple hotels. *Cornell Hotel and Restaurant Administration Quarterly* 42(4), 65–69.

Sinclair, M.T. (1997) *Gender, Work and Tourism.* Routledge, London, 244 pp.

Smeral, E. (1997) *Volume, Structure and Characteristics of Employment in Tourism: Implications in Terms of Strengths and Weaknesses of Tourism Activity.* Report for the Conference of the European Commission, 'Employment and Tourism: Guidelines for Action', Luxemburg, 4–5 November 1997. European Commission, Luxemburg.

Wood, R.C. (1994) *Organisational Behaviour for Hospitality Management.* Butterworth-Heinemann, Oxford, UK, 226 pp.

12 Insights into Skill Shortages and Skill Gaps in Tourism: a Study in Greater Manchester

CONRAD LASHLEY

Nottingham Business School, Nottingham Trent University, Nottingham, UK

12.1 Introduction

Recognizing the potential benefit of hosting the Commonwealth Games in 2002, tourism managers in Greater Manchester were keen to explore potential skill shortages and skill gaps that might present barriers to the future development of tourism after the games. They commissioned a report in the summer of 2001 and this chapter discusses some of the findings from the research (Lashley *et al.*, 2002). In particular, this chapter suggests that supposed recruitment difficulties due to skill shortages mask some fundamental deficits in management skills and training.

The tourism sector is a major driver of growth in the Greater Manchester area. A recent report (Questions Answered, 2001) suggested that the sector now accounts for 6% of Manchester's gross domestic product and directly employs in excess of 32,000 permanent employees, more than the total numbers employed in both manufacturing and construction combined. Tourism is estimated to be worth approximately £1.5 billion to Greater Manchester, and the pace of growth shows no sign of reaching maturity. Tourism planners and policy makers recognized that the Commonwealth Games would provide a platform for the further development of tourism in the area and identified skill shortages and skill gaps as a potential barrier to this development. They recognized, in particular, that the performance of front-line staff and management has an immediate impact on the tourist experience, and thereby Manchester's reputation as a quality tourist destination.

Planners and policy makers wanted a clear understanding of trends, together with skill levels and employment dynamics, in the tourism, hospitality and leisure retailing sectors. To this end, the research discussed here was commissioned to enhance understanding of current employment and trends and to identify current skill shortages and gaps in the tourism sector. The research was also required to examine employer responses; highlight labour retention and staff turnover issues;

explore employer perceptions of future skills needs; assess the skills supply infrastructure within the region; and make recommendations for action.

12.2 Skill Shortages and Skill Gaps in Tourism Businesses

The significance of skills and training to business performance is contentious (Eccles, 1991; Geanuracos and Meiklejohn, 1993; Baum, 1995; Brander, Brown and McDonnell, 1995; Stone, 1996; Garavan, 1997; Eaglen *et al.*, 1999; Thomas and Long, 2001). The skill levels of employees and a commitment to training is not in itself a guarantee of business success, but, all things being equal, training does produce an array of business benefits. There is a close association between an organization's orientation to training and the other central managerial activities that influence competitiveness (Eaglen and Lashley, 2001). Thus, it seems that employers' attitudes to skills development and utilization are likely to be indicative of a particular outlook relating to other aspects of organizational practice. Those that emphasize employee development are likely, for example, to engage in, or at least be concerned with, developing a suitable means of ensuring quality, promoting the enterprise and controlling costs.

The 2002 *Labour Market Review* provided by the Hospitality Training Foundation (HtF) (2002) offers a useful national-level snapshot to complement the Manchester study. They note, for example, that young people dominate the sector (40% of employees are younger than 25 years old), and that the number of employees below the age of 20 is about four times the national average across all industries. Women remain numerically preponderant (67%) but their number has fallen proportionately to men by some 3% since 1995. The proportion of minority ethnic groups employed in the hospitality sector is – at 8% – slightly higher than average for all sectors (7%). Approximately half of all workers in the hotels and restaurants sector are employed by the 99% of the sector that are defined as small and medium-sized enterprises (SMEs) (employing fewer than 50 employees); furthermore 45% of them are micro-firms employing fewer than ten employees. The picture that emerges from another national survey of small firms (Thomas *et al.*, 2000) suggests that, since small tourism and hospitality firms, like those in other sectors, are characterized by informality, it is not surprising that few (7%) of them have formal written training plans. Small firm owner managers also present barriers to their own development, because a considerable number are running these businesses for motives that are not exclusively commercial. Owners who are running a tourism business because they 'enjoy this life' or 'want to be my own boss' are not always primarily concerned with developing their business management skills (Thomas *et al.*, 2000).

12.2.1 Skill shortages

Recruitment difficulties are frequently referred to in the tourism sector research literature (Pizam and Ellis, 1999; Jameson, 2000). Debate tends to centre upon the extent to which recruitment difficulties are endemic (or not), accounted for by skill-related issues or by high labour turnover, poor pay and image. Recent studies have examined these issues by reference to employer perceptions. Thus, Thomas *et al.* (2000), in what remains the most comprehensive survey of smaller enterprises in tourism and hospitality (with 1396 participating firms), found that more than 30% of firms had experienced recruitment difficulties during the past 12 months.

The two most commonly cited reasons for recruitment difficulties were lack of skills and lack of experience among applicants. Of the 426 firms in the survey who perceived that they had difficulties recruiting staff during the past 12 months, 213 felt that this was due to a lack of skills among applicants and 210 that this was the result of a lack of experience among applicants. When the respondents that claimed a lack of skills among applicants was causing a major recruitment problem were broken down by sector, the two sectors that appeared to have the biggest problem were hotels and travel agents. One surprising result from the question on recruitment difficulties was that the level of pay on offer was not perceived to be a major reason for recruitment difficulties.

Skill difficulties have been commonly associated with the tourism and hospitality industries for many years. The national training organization for the hospitality industry (HtF) found that 50% of vacancies in the hospitality industry were perceived as hard to fill (HtF, 1999). The HtF suggests that one of the main reasons for this is related to skills shortages. In fact, in its previous guise as the Hotel and Catering Training Company (HCTC) in 1995, this agency claimed that skill shortage was the main reason for recruitment difficulties (HCTC, 1995).

More recent assessments of skill shortages undertaken by the HtF (2001a,b,c) and others (for example, DfEE, 2000) offer insight into specific occupational skill shortages. Although it would be inappropriate to attempt to be precise about the levels of shortage, a clear picture emerges as to the areas of activity. The main areas of shortage revealed by employer surveys were chefs/cooks, followed by bar staff, then waiters/waitresses and catering assistants. In some sectors, problems appear to be acute. For example, some 70% of pubs with hard-to-fill vacancies reported difficulty recruiting bar staff, while some 60% of hotels with hard-to-fill vacancies made similar observations about chefs/cooks (HtF, 2001b). It is important to recognize that, if the preceding discussion does point to skill shortages, these are predominantly at the operative level (some 90% of hard-to-fill vacancies).

Keep and Mayhew (DfEE, 1999) provide a counter-argument to the positions outlined above. They claim that, with the possible exception of chefs, there are no serious skills shortages in the leisure (hospitality) sector. They argue that the nature and causes of recruitment difficulties within the sector are not the result of genuine skills shortages but may be a reflection of the sector's reputation for offering relatively poor employment conditions and low pay.

Findings from interviews with tourism employers, recruitment agencies, training providers and trade associations in Greater Manchester confirm many of these national-level observations, but also extend understanding of the nature of skill shortages across the sector (Table 12.1). In fact, there is little evidence of a general recruitment problem across all tourism sectors in Manchester. The reporting of

Table 12.1. Firms registering difficulty in filling jobs.

Sector	Reported difficult to fill jobs
Hotels, serviced and non-serviced accommodation	Night porters, chefs, kitchen staff, reception staff, housekeeping staff
Restaurants and cafes	Head chefs, kitchen staff generally
Bars, pubs and nightclubs	Technical projectionist (cinema)
Museums and cultural activities	Conservators (museum)
	Specialist restorers (gallery)
	Events planners (exhibition centre)
	Marketing people (opera-house)
Sports, recreational activities	Maintenance staff, catering staff
Travel agencies and tour operators	Temporary management staff, booking clerks
Retailing (Trafford Centre only)	General part-time staff, kitchen staff in restaurants

recruitment difficulties varied between firms and job categories. Although 25 of the 41 employers interviewed reported some recruitment difficulties, this is far from being a general problem. The overall impression gained from the interviews with the 41 employers was that there was no general skills shortage across all firms making up the tourism offer.

The accommodation, restaurant and bar sectors did report recruitment difficulties associated with some specific jobs: chefs, kitchen assistants, receptionists and night porters were frequently mentioned. In the main, firms that involved more intensive service work tended to experience recruitment difficulties. Hotels, restaurants, pubs, travel agents and Trafford Centre retailers were more likely to report difficulties recruiting people with the skills required than were museums and cultural activities; sport and recreational activities; or tour operators and airlines. Even in the hospitality sectors, employers were often able to meet general staffing requirements, though problems occurred in specific skill areas. One pub manager reported, 'No, we always have people on file and applicants waiting to start.' Another employer reported that an advertisement for staff in the restaurant window for a week 'brought in 70 applications'. Where employers report difficulties, staff retention was an influential factor. In other words, recruitment difficulties were a by-product of churning employees into and out of these firms, which resulted in the need for a permanent flow of recruits to replace staff who had now left the organization.

As with national studies (I ItF, 2001a, 2002), specific skill difficulties were associated with 'chefs', where there were several skill levels involved and some hotel and restaurant employers complained that they had difficulty recruiting appropriately skilled chefs, though the situation is complex due to skill variations required in different kitchens.

At its simplest, 'cooking' involved prepared foods that were reheated through a microwave oven or cooked through a one-step process such as frying or grilling. The skills required of 'up-market' hotels and restaurants were likely to need pre-trained chefs capable of an array of culinary tasks. National studies often fail to capture the subtleties of the 'chef' market. The variations in skill levels required and the need to supply chefs/cooks to suit this variety of skill levels are frequently missed and driven by an agenda set by the upper end of the market. The 'snip and ping' food preparation and menus requiring one-step cooking are recruiting from different labour markets. Training and qualification provision and employment practice can cause confusion for employers and applicants alike. Managers in 'cuisine style' restaurant and hotels frequently complained that they received applications and interviewed applicants who were clearly not capable of working in their type of operation. They were dismissed as 'not real chefs, cooks at best who are used to cooking by numbers'.

The report stated that many of the interviewees were not really looking for skilled people, indeed many employers were said to have 'low skills expectations; they merely sought to recruit basic social skills that were employable' (Lashley *et al.*, 2002: 10). Several interviewees in the hospitality sector specifically reported that jobs in their organization had been 'deskilled' in recent years. The overall impression was that most firms recruited to posts that were 'routine unskilled jobs'. Recruitment difficulties were in part a consequence of deskilling, which had the effect of lowering barriers to entry for new recruits and thereby reducing potential pay rates, but which meant that employees could find work in competitor firms or sectors where pay is marginally better. The report pointed to several instances of staff leaving one employer for a few extra pennies per hour. In firms such as J.D. Wetherspoon employment strategies aimed to outperform competitors. At the time of the survey, the local Wetherspoon pub paid 70 pence per hour above the national minimum. Most importantly, they claimed to have no recruitment difficulties and staff turnover was well below the average for this sector and most other respondents in the survey. This is an important insight, because many respondents registered a low level of understanding of the wages rates being paid in competitor sectors in Manchester.

Consideration of the supply of labour into the tourism sectors in Manchester suggests that three types of situation need to be considered. First, there are key specialist jobs where there are limited numbers of well-qualified, skilled people and barriers to entry are high, but pay rates and conditions of employment are perceived, by recruits, as being appropriate. Some of the more skilled jobs in the museums and galleries, sports, recreational activities, travel agencies and tour operator organizations are sometimes difficult to fill but do attract recruits eventually. Significantly they usually have a good level of staff retention, so recruitment problems are not, therefore, exacerbated by high levels of staff turnover.

The second group of jobs is typically low-skilled and poorly paid with low barriers to entry. Here there is a potentially high level of supply, often through young people new to the labour market or students working in part-time casual or temporary posts. Pay rates are either on the national minimum wage or pitched at a point close to the legal minimum wage rate. For younger employees, the pay rate is below the national minimum wage rate. Opportunities to find alternative employment, on the part of the employee, and alternative employees, on the part of employers, tend to lead to high levels of staff turnover. In these circumstances managers do not see staff turnover as a major problem because labour is easily replaced, and it can be a useful means of managing workforce flexibility. Total numbers employed can be reduced by just not replacing leavers. Firms in the traditional hospitality sectors and retailing sector represent examples of firms that operate this approach. Some of the best-practice firms pitch pay and employment conditions above these minimal levels because they are able to pick and choose staff, and labour stability tends to be higher, as is the investment in staff training.

The third group relates to the relatively small number of jobs in these low-paid sectors that are skilled and where there is competition for skilled employees. Chefs across hotels, restaurants and pubs and hotel receptionists tend to be able to attract better pay because of the relative rarity of the skill. A recent HtF report (2002) claimed that chefs' pay had risen on average by 12%. In part the rise in chefs' pay has been driven by the competition for their skills that has often caused poaching by one employer from another or plentiful opportunities for a dissatisfied employee to find another job. The skill gap factor is clearly an issue here, where the demand for 'cooking skills' covers a range of competence levels from simple to complex. At the simple end, jobs require basic training in health and safety and food hygiene, together with the immediate preparation and service standards required. Potentially, the barriers to entry are low, but work can be monotonous and boring. At the more skilled end, the work is often linked to complex operations and an ability to apply a wide range of cooking techniques and skills. It is these more complex cooking jobs that have attracted better rates of pay, particularly for qualified and experienced personnel.

12.2.2 Skill gaps

HtF recently noted that skill gaps vary from skill shortages because they relate to a lack of the required skills among existing employees: 'A skill gap is an internal problem. It means that the company requires a certain type of skill and nobody in the organisation currently has that skill. Skill gaps can be solved through recruitment or training' (HtF, 2001b: 35). The same report continues by pointing out that some 14% of employers in their survey felt that a skill gap existed in their organization. This equates broadly with the 19% of smaller firms across the wider tourism sector that made a similar observation (Thomas *et al.*, 2000) but is lower than 26% reported by Ttento (2001). *The National Survey of Small Tourism and Hospitality Firms* (Thomas *et al.*, 2000) found that almost 70% were satisfied with the skill levels of their employees, with a further 19% dissatisfied. Predictably, bed and breakfasts (B&Bs) and guesthouses were least likely to identify skill gaps, probably as a result of the scale of activity and the 'domestic' nature of the service offered, with tour operators and hotels the most likely, at 30% and 27%, respectively (Thomas *et al.*, 2000). The same study asked employers to identify the skill gaps.

This confirms some expectations but also raises interesting areas of contrast. It is not surprising, for example, that there are few perceived language skill deficiencies among small travel agents, B&B/guesthouses, self-catering accommodation, fast-food/take-away operators and public houses/bars that perhaps predominantly serve local markets. It is interesting, however, that languages are seen as a significant skill gap among small tour operators. It is also revealing that small hotels, public houses and restaurants have relatively high proportions of businesses noting a deficiency of suitable customer care skills among their staff. Although various development agencies may express disappointment at such a picture, it may also suggest that some enterprises are now taking the issue of customer interaction more seriously than in the past.

Only 11 of the 41 employers interviewed in the Manchester study stated that they were aware of skill gaps in their workforce. This represents 27% of the employers interviewed and compares with the HtF's industry average of 14% (HtF, 2001a: 35). Most stated that they provided training as a means of rectifying any problems. One pub employer stated:

> No, there are not many skill gaps in our workforce, if you can call them a skill we sometimes find that people find it difficult to communicate with customers, other than that timekeeping and absenteeism are the biggest problem I'm facing with employees. To be quite frank skill gaps is the last of my worries.

Other employers echoed the point that retention was the problem and that in-house training was used to correct performance shortcomings. An employer from an art gallery also confirmed the importance of training: 'No, not at the moment and in the cases where skill gaps have been identified, the person concerned is encouraged to get the appropriate training of one sort or another.' In other cases the correction of any individual skill gaps was a less formal response but none the less a response aimed at correcting the problem within the firm: 'I just pull them to one side and tell them and show them myself how to do it. I find myself telling them the same thing over and over but eventually the message gets through.' The design of jobs to reduce skill needs and the use of technology were factors influential in reducing the perception of skill gaps for many employers, because new recruits could be easily shown 'the ropes'.

12.2.3 Labour turnover and staff retention

The 'churning' of staff through some tourism jobs has an impact on the high recruitment volumes experienced by employers. Labour turnover was reported to be an issue in 20 firms who were included in the survey. These were mostly in the 'hospitality' sectors, covering hotels, restaurants and bars. In fact, when two restaurant firms in the sample from the Trafford Centre Retail Park are included, 16 of the 20 firms registering staff turnover as a concern are in this sector. The opera-house also registered staff turnover as a problem chiefly among similar jobs: 'The area with the highest labour turnover is the front of house staff, i.e. the catering and the stewards.' Two of the leisure travel agent firms registered it as an issue of concern: 'Our Manchester City branch might turn over 40% or 50% but that's the nature, there are so many travel agencies in such a small space.'

Sixteen of the interviewees were able to quote labour turnover statistics as it applied to their unit. In many cases staff turnover just was not seen as a problem. The level of staff turnover in establishments that were able to quote a figure ranged from 5% in one of the airlines to 115% in a fast food restaurant at the Trafford Centre. Often interviewees were not able to quote a figure because staff turnover was not seen as a problem. The company did not formally record the flows of people into and out of their firm, or a figure was kept at head office and this was not seen as a matter of concern for immediate unit management. Prior studies (Lashley and Rowson, 2000) suggest that a low perception of staff turn-over as a management problem was no guarantee that staff turnover was low. Firms frequently just did not record it and, providing they could find replace-ments, did not see it as a problem. A fatalistic acceptance of this being 'just the way things are' was found to exist in some firms.

Interviewees recording staff turnover levels in their unit or business were generating demand for 677 recruits needed to support 1179 jobs. This repre-sents an average staff turnover in the sample of 57.42%. This figure needs to be set against other research that has suggested that staff turnover can be much higher in hospitality occupations. A study of 30 licensed retail firms by Lashley and Rowson (2000) identified an average rate of 188% across the 30 firms and, in one case, a firm recorded over 300% staff turnover per annum. In many cases, firms were experiencing high levels of staff turnover, but were not recording it, so these findings may well mask a much higher level of staff turnover in Greater Manchester. Furthermore, it is estimated that staff turnover for 'unskilled and routine' work costs £500–1000 per head (Lashley and Rowson, 2000). The report suggested that, even at these levels reported in the case study firms, labour turnover was likely to be costing firms in the tourism sector in Manchester an estimated £25 million.

Interestingly, only three employers mentioned pay issues as a reason for staff leaving, and these were in the travel agency sector. Not one of the employers in the hospitality sector firms experiencing high levels of staff turnover mentioned pay levels as a problem. Yet Lashley and Rowson (2000) suggest that 80% of staff felt a chance to improve pay would be an important reason for leaving their existing employer. One of the recruitment agencies in Manchester provided an insight into the pay levels and their view as to why staff leave:

> Mainly about pay, these are the worst paid professions. We pay £4.10 per hour but that's for staff over 18. A lot of the vacancies we have are filled by young adults about 16 years old who don't qualify for that amount of pay.

This potential misunderstanding by employers of the significance of pay levels and their failure to understand the perceptions of their employees are factors relevant to overcoming high levels of staff turnover and thereby recruitment difficulties.

12.2.4 Determining pay

Ten of the interviewees claimed to use the national minimum wage (NMW) as the basis for determining pay of general unskilled employees. One of the inter-viewees based in a fast food restaurant in the city centre summed up the approach: 'Depending on age but in most cases it's the NMW of £4.10 per hour but that's going up soon but our base rate is the same as the NMW.' One of the chain pubs also used the minimum wage as the flat rate: '£4.10 per hour everyone is on that except the chef and the assistant managers and me.' The use of the NMW as an initial starting point that was then enhanced with experience and based on manager discretion was mentioned by several interviewees. For under-18s the rate quoted was generally lower: 'we pay the under-18s £3.50 per hour that's the standard rate'. Of the firms working to the NMW, seven were hospitality sector employers (six in the City and one at the Trafford Centre). This is consistent with national research findings that 'Government statistics still show the industry hosts four of the ten lowest paid jobs in Great Britain – kitchen porters, bar staff, catering assistants and waiting staff' (HtF, 2002: 1). Interestingly, at the time of the study, the Benefits Agency in Manchester suggested that £5.00 per hour is the rate needed to make it economically viable for a person to forgo benefits and take on paid employment.

In six cases, interviewees aimed to pay slightly above the minimum wage so as to attract and retain staff. One of the chain pubs provided an interesting insight into this approach: 'They are based on local competition we try and pay more than the competition and in general we pay the best rates locally. We pay £4.80 per hour starting rate for bar staff.' Interestingly, when asked about staff turnover, this interviewee said: 'we don't have a big problem with staff turnover; the people who leave the company are mainly students at the end of their courses, or people moving to another branch to get a promotion.' The exhibition centre interviewee and some in the retail sector adopted a similar strategy to this firm, preferring to pay above the NMW because it helped them to recruit and retain staff.

In other cases the key consideration was the local 'going rate' and labour market conditions. One of the fast-food restaurant interviewees stated that she paid the London weighting wage rate in the Manchester City Centre stores. She explained:

> We often get compared with Liverpool City Centre but a lot more young people live in the city centre there than in the middle of Manchester. Most of the people who live in the middle of Manchester are professionals because of the property prices.

In some cases, such as with the cinema, a rate was nationally negotiated, and in many cases the jobs were being recruited to these national rates. Only one interviewee, based at a local authority leisure centre, stated that they negotiated with a trade union. In one case the rates were fixed outside the UK, but serve to provide a benchmark for others. One of the interviewees in Manchester claimed to pay well above the NMW because wages were set by the head office staff in Sweden.

Determining wage rates appears to be a by-product of wider employment policies and business strategies. For some employers the basic strategy is to pay the minimum that ensures recruitment. The link to the local labour market, or at least keeping in line with it, was echoed by many of the employers interviewed, particularly those recruiting into jobs where there are low skill barriers to entry. These jobs do not require high levels of prior training and experience, there are potentially large numbers of recruits and wages were generally pitched at the 'going rate'. In other cases, the employers were recruiting staff with highly specialized or professional skills and these pay rates were determined by the labour market for that particular profession. Interestingly, some firms were clearly following a 'more quality' focused strategy and recruitment policies tended to be consistent with recruiting 'good quality staff' even into the operative-level posts. One of the pub companies and one of the retailers at Trafford Centre reported this approach, and both reported having high levels of staff retention and few recruitment problems.

12.2.5 Unreported and latent skill deficiencies

Rowley *et al.* (DfEE, 2000) suggest that these surveys of employer perceptions of skill gaps and shortages can be limited by managers not knowing what it is that they do not know. In the Manchester study, there was a general reluctance to reflect on the interviewee's own skill gaps and development needs. They suggest that there was no evidence of a deliberate reluctance or unwillingness to report skill deficiencies, rather they were a result of managers own limited perceptions. Furthermore, Rowley *et al.* (DfEE, 2000) comment that:

> We found few managers who thought outside the traditional modes of operating, or anticipated how new technology could and would impact on their business in the medium-to-long term. There was a widespread failure to appreciate the importance of foreign language skills in this tourist related industry. All of these deficiencies reflect the most fundamental deficiency of all: managerial skills at all levels.
>
> (DfEE, 2000: 12)

The report suggested that research on skill shortages and skills needed to be aware of the potential for unreported and latent skill deficiencies. That is, managers are often reluctant or unable to identify skill shortages or gaps where these relate to their own development or where these relate to operating strategies outside traditional approaches.

The Manchester survey also found no reason to suggest that the employer interviewees intentionally under-reported or misrepresented skill shortages and gaps. Indeed, many of the perceptions reported here are consistent with a number of national reports (HtF, 2001a,b,c). However, there is a difficulty that stems from research methods involving interviews with subjects who fundamentally report on their perceptions of issues. They may, or may not, perceive themselves as having skill gaps or development needs.

An example identified above relates to labour turnover and staff retention. Many of the interviewees, particularly in the hospitality sectors, just did not recognize the levels of staff turnover in their businesses as a problem. In general, they were able to recruit replacements to unskilled jobs with little difficulty. In the cases of chefs and other skilled jobs, they were finding it difficult to retain staff once they had been recruited. In both cases, labour turnover management is a skill deficiency among some managers, though it is not reported as such. In many cases, the managers reported that the problems were due to the nature of the recruits or the actions of competitors.

In fact, management training and skill development was not identified as a deficiency by any of the interviewees, and yet several of the issues reflect limited human resource management skills. When asked about their own recent education and training, ten interviewees claimed to have done no training or development during the last 2 years. Five of these were in the hospitality sector – four in restaurants. Thirty attended regular training provided or funded by their employer, usually focused on immediate unit management tasks. In some cases, these were certificated, but few were linked to formal qualifications.

The skill development of managers is acknowledged as key to developing international competitiveness in tourism activities. Keep and Mayhew (DfEE 1999: 43) summarize a point made by others:

> Without a more skilled managerial cadre it is hard to envisage how any effort aimed at systemic improvement and upgrading in the strategic managerial capacity of the sector can succeed. The ability of management to analyse, develop coherent long-term plans and offer the practical and strategic leadership needed to promote and manage the transition to a higher quality, higher value added approach to competition is a prerequisite for creating a world class sector.

12.2.6 Skills supply and demand issues

The perception that demand for employees was increasing and that there is generally an under-supply of people to fill the posts available was largely confirmed by interviews with recruitment agents who specialized in filling jobs in the hospitality sectors of tourism within Manchester. Four of the five firms interviewed expressed the view that demand for chefs, kitchen assistants and waiting staff occupations was increasing and the fifth interviewee, who stated that there was a decrease, expressed the view that it was a temporary situation. All five interviewees expressed the view that there was an under-supply of people in these occupations.

These findings are consistent with the North West Tourist Board (2001) skills survey. The report showed that a 6.4% net increase in hotel employment had occurred over the last 12 months. During the same period there had been a 4.5% increase in employment of permanent staff in attractions and a 1.7% increase in restaurant employment of permanent staff. The survey also suggested that employers were predicting large net increases in employment over the 12 months. Though the figures quoted, ranging between 8.7% and 12.0%, are potentially optimistic predictions and will have been affected by the impacts of events in the USA in September 2001, employment is predicted to grow by 5% by 2004 (Questions Answered, 2001: 25). Most recruitment agents specializing in travel and tourism firms indicated that they felt there was a decrease in demand for employees. The only exception was that two of the firms mentioned a shortage of supply of business travel agents, although, again, it has to be remembered that these interviews were conducted in autumn 2001.

Attempts to quantify the number of recruits needed and employment across the various sectors in Manchester are somewhat difficult because data are not always available at the level that can inform flows and policies aimed at specific occupations. The following figures have to be viewed as tentative, using the best regional data extrapolated to Manchester. Apart from the lack of immediate employment data, the nature of tourism employment is fraught with definitional difficulties with which we shall not engage here, although the North West Tourism Skills Study (Questions Answered, 2001) does make an attempt and this Manchester study was guided by their findings.

In addition to staff replacement that represents people 'churning' jobs within the industry, some staff leave the industry permanently. The report (Questions Answered, 2001) suggests that in the serviced accommodation and restaurant sector approximately 32% of staff will permanently leave the industry. This skill leakage adds to the problem for tourism skill shortages in the Greater Manchester area. Finally, the report estimated that over the next 3 years another 4200 jobs will be created in tourism within the region. This represents a further 1260 direct permanent tourism jobs in Greater Manchester, and the bulk of these are likely to be in serviced accommodation and restaurants.

When increased demand and 'leakage' from the sector are taken into account, Greater Manchester needed to produce in the same period something like another 1450 chefs, 2400 waiting staff and 1900 kitchen porters/catering assistants. These are needed just to meet the immediate permanent employees required to cover losses to the industry and new job creation. At the same time, employers will be recruiting somewhere in the region of 9000–10,000 employees per annum to meet the staff turnover in these same posts. Over the next 3 years they could be recruiting 25,000–30,000 merely to support staff turnover.

12.3 Conclusion

The findings from this research exploring tourism skill shortages and skill gaps in Greater Manchester echo many of the findings of research across the UK. Of the broad array of establishments that contribute to tourism activities, skill shortages and recruitment difficulties are most acutely experienced in the 'hospitality sectors'. Both employers and recruitment agencies report particular recruitment difficulties for chefs and kitchen staff in general, as well as restaurant and bar staff.

That said, it is hard to conclude that there is a general skill shortage in the tourism sector. Museums and cultural activities, sports, recreational activities, travel agencies and tour operators did report some difficulties over recruiting into highly specialist jobs, but usually they managed to recruit into these posts eventually, and difficulties were not exacerbated by the high levels of staff turnover found in the hospitality sectors. Like Keep and Mayhew (DfEE, 1999) and Rowley *et al.* (DfEE, 2000: 52), it is hard to reach the conclusion that there is an aggregate skills shortage even in the hospitality sectors. Reported recruitment problems are largely a product of employment policies. The barriers to entry for many of these jobs are low and as a consequence there is potentially large pool of labour available. These 'routine unskilled' jobs attract low wages, and employers frequently reduce pay rates even further by employing young people beneath the NMW protection levels. The key strategy being followed by most of the hospitality firms is one of 'cost leadership', but it is a strategy based on a limited analysis of costs. Few firms used a 'balanced score card' approach to assessing business performance and most had no real awareness of the costs of staff replacement, low productivity or lost customers.

Labour turnover adds particularly to perceptions of skill shortages because at any one time many hospitality employers have vacancies as they are not able to retain the staff they have recruited. As replacement employees were relatively easy to recruit, few employers appreciated that low levels of staff retention presented a problem to their business. None of the firms in this survey had any idea of the real costs of replacing employees. Only a minority recorded even the overall levels of staff turnover. Work by Lashley and Rowson (2000) suggests that conservatively it costs an average of £500–1000 to replace each employee and staff turnover in the City could cost £25 million each year.

Those employers who complain of the lack of social skills and/or customer care skills of their recruits rarely recognize this as a consequence of recruitment policies. Young, low-skilled employees may well originate from a section of the labour market that has few life skills and experiences of being guests in restaurants, hotels or bars frequented by tourists.

Latent and unreported skill deficiencies flow from these observations because they relate to levels of management development and the narrow cost-driven business strategy being followed in some of these firms. The recognition of staff turnover as a key problem that has an impact on recruitment difficulties is one obvious issue. In particular, the loss of former employees to other sectors of employment creates an added need for recruits new to tourism. When the expansion of demand is included, the Greater Manchester area needs a higher number of recruits than are being produced within local colleges and other providers. Although these problems are not shared across all sectors of tourism, they are experienced in key sectors of the tourism industry. While hospitality employment practice continues to be the weakest link, it will hamper the City's attempts to develop a profile as a high-quality tourist venue.

References

Baum, T. (1995) *Managing Human Resources in the European Tourism and Hospitality Industry: a Strategic Approach*. Chapman & Hall, London, 281 pp.

Brander Brown, J. and McDonnell, B. (1995) The balanced score card: short term guest or long term resident. *International Journal of Contemporary Hospitality Management* 7(2/3), 7–11.

DfEE (Department for Education and Employment) (1999) *The Leisure Sector. Skills Task Force Research Paper 6*. DfEE, London.

DfEE (2000) *Employer Skill Survey: Case Study Hospitality Sector*. DfEE, London.

Eaglen, A. and Lashley, C. (2001) *Benefits and Costs Analysis: Exploring the Impact of Training on Hospitality Business Performance*. Leeds Metropolitan University, Leeds, UK.

Eaglen, A., Lashley, C. and Thomas, R. (1999) *Benefits and Costs Analysis: the Impact of Training on Business Performance*. Leeds Metropolitan University, Leeds, UK.

Eccles, R.G. (1991) The Performance Measurement Manifesto. *Harvard Business Review* January–February, 131–137.

Garavan, T.N. (1997) Training, development, education and learning: different or the same? *Journal of European Industrial Training* 21(2), 39–50.

Geanuracos, J. and Meiklejohn, I. (1993) *Performance Measurement: The New Agenda.* Business Intelligence, London, 436 pp.

HCTC (Hotel and Catering Training Company) (1995) *Training, Who Needs it? Research Report.* HCTC, London.

HtF (Hospitality Training Foundation) (1999) *Look Who's Training Now: Perceptions on Training in the Hospitality Industry.* HtF, London.

HtF (2001a) *Labour Market Review 2001 for the Hospitality Industry.* HtF, London.

HtF (2001b) *Skills and Employment Foresight 2001 for the Hospitality Industry.* HtF, London.

HtF (2001c) *Workforce Development Plan: A Strategy for the Hospitality Industry.* HtF, London.

HtF (2002) *Labour Market Review 2002 for the Hospitality Industry.* HtF, London.

Jameson, S. (2000) Recruitment and training in small firms. *Journal of European Industry Training* 24(1), 43–49.

Lashley, C. and Rowson, B. (2000) Wasted millions: staff turnover in licensed retailing. In: *Ninth CHME Research Conference Proceedings.* Huddersfield University, Huddersfield, UK, pp. 121–133.

Lashley, C. Rowson, B. and Thomas, R. (2002) *Employment Practices and Skill Shortages in Greater Manchester's Tourism Sector.* Leeds Metropolitan University, Leeds, UK.

North West Tourism Board Research Services (NWTB) (2001) *Report on Tourism Skills.* North West Tourism Skills and Employment Network, Manchester, UK.

Pizam, A. and Ellis, T. (1999) Absenteeism and turnover in the hospitality industry. In: Lee-Ross, D. (ed.) *HRM in Tourism and Hospitality: International Perspectives.* Cassell, London, pp. 109–131.

Questions Answered Ltd. (2001) *Tourism Workforce Development Plan for the North-West of England.* North West Tourism Skills Network, Manchester, UK.

Stone, C.L. (1996) Analysing business performance: counting the soft issues. *Leadership and Organisation Development Journal* 17(4), 21–28.

Thomas, R. and Long, J. (2001) Tourism and economic regeneration: the role of skills development. *International Journal of Tourism Research* 3(3), 229–240.

Thomas, R., Lashley, C., Rowson, B., Xie, G., Jameson, S., Eaglen, A., Lincoln, G. and Parsons, D. (2000) *The National Survey of Small Tourism and Hospitality Firms 2000: Skills Demand and Training Practices.* Centre for the Study of Small Tourism and Hospitality Firms, Leeds, UK.

Ttento (2001) *Skills Foresight Report – Preparing for the Future.* Ttento, London.

13 A Typology of Approaches towards Training in the South-east Wales Hospitality Industry

STEPHEN MOORE

Welsh School of Hospitality, Tourism and Leisure Management, University of Wales Institute, Cardiff, UK

13.1 Introduction

The UK hospitality industry is a £43 billion industry, employing over 7% of the UK workforce and creating one in every five new jobs. The hospitality industry is a prominent sector of the Welsh economy contributing 13% to the gross domestic product (GDP) of Wales (Welsh Office, 1998). In south-east Wales, the growth of the service sector has countered the decline of traditional industries, such as agriculture, mining and manufacturing. However, despite recognition of the GDP contribution, attitudes to training within this growth sector in the UK are disappointing. In 1994, the Hotel and Catering Training Company (HCTC) revealed that 45% of full-time employees and 74% of part-time employees had not received any job-related training. Similarly, in 1996 the Hospitality Training Foundation (HtF) found that: 40% of hotels consider their employees to be inadequately skilled; only 11% of employees receive training (compared with nearly 15% of employees across all industries); 43% of employers only provide induction training; and most training is linked to statutory requirements rather than staff development, with employers regarding training as a cost, not an investment. Furthermore, HtF found that 50% of all vacancies reported by hospitality organizations in 1997 were hard to fill; 64% of chef/cook vacancies and 56% of waiter/waitress vacancies advertised by the Employment Service were left unfilled; and 43% of bar vacancies were unfilled in Wales (HtF, 1996). These findings are juxtaposed by serious skills shortages in key areas, predominantly chefs, waiting staff, bar staff and porters. Therefore, this situation is of particular concern to small and medium-sized enterprises (SMEs), who cannot offer employees the same benefits afforded by large hospitality organizations.

In south-east Wales, skills shortages are found among skilled crafts and food service, more so than managerial and supervisory grades. The most commonly cited occupations experiencing shortfalls are: qualified chefs; kitchen staff;

©CAB International 2005. *Tourism SMEs, Service Quality and Destination Competitiveness* (eds E. Jones and C. Haven-Tang) 197

bar staff; waiting staff; and counter staff (Stevens and Associates, 1998). Difficulties in recruiting staff are exacerbated by the growth of the local economy in south-east Wales, in particular competition from the retail sector, as it is perceived to offer better working conditions and higher rates of pay. The situation is compounded by changing demographic factors, which have resulted in fewer young people entering the labour market than 10 years ago. Stevens and Associates (2000) state that the current difficulties in recruiting and retaining skilled staff will only worsen if appropriate actions are not taken. Future plans for accommodation, entertainment, restaurant and other tourism developments throughout south-east Wales will exacerbate the current skills shortage problems. Consequently, if staff are not recruited and trained appropriately to resource these new developments, poor service quality across the south-east Wales hospitality industry will be inevitable. The status and reputation of Cardiff as a capital city and an emerging tourist destination demand that issues surrounding the training and development of appropriately skilled staff within its hospitality industry are addressed. However, such action requires employers and employees to perceive training as an investment for the future.

This chapter considers factors that influence attitudes to training in the hospitality industry and highlights differences between SMEs and larger companies. A typology of training models currently used in the different hospitality sectors is developed, resulting in the production of an overall model of factors influencing the success of training within the south-east Wales hospitality industry, which, it is hoped, will raise SME awareness of strategies to enhance staff retention.

13.2 Training and the Hospitality Sector

13.2.1 What is training?

A fundamental requirement for any hospitality business, whether an SME or a larger company, is to assess what training is designed to achieve. The Manpower Services Commission (1981, cited in Reid and Barrington, 1999: 7) states that:

> Training is a planned process to modify attitude, knowledge or skill behaviour through learning experience to achieve effective performance in an activity or range of activities. Its purpose, in the work situation, is to develop the abilities of the individual and to satisfy the current and future needs of the organization.

An alternative definition is offered by Miller *et al.* (1998: 198): 'Training, in a hospitality setting, simply means teaching people how to do their jobs . . . Three kinds of training are needed in food and lodging operations: job instruction, re-training, and orientation.' Job instruction is concerned with what the job entails and how to do it; re-training applies to current employees; and orientation refers to induction programmes for new employees.

From literature reviews it may be assumed that training is relatively simplistic. However, there are other key issues that emerge from the literature which add to the discussion. There exists an argument that, in order for staff to take an interest and participate in training, it is necessary for them to achieve something at an individual level. Rainbird and Maguire (1993) cited in Beardwell and Holden (1994: 336) found that:

> much of the training reported was for organizational rather than individual development. This suggests that many employees would not regard the training they receive as training at all since it neither imparts transferable skills, nor contributes to personal educational development.

As is clearly evident in the hospitality industry, training is not just about achieving a specified standard of staff competence, but also about investing in employees in order to retain them. As East (1993: 14) states: 'Training and education will help employers to retain valuable employees, attract more people to the industry, and encourage those who have left to return.' Boer and Teare (1996) partially agree with this argument, but suggest that hospitality managers should redirect their energies from continually recruiting new staff to developing and training their current staff. They argue that it is the quality of staff employed, not the quantity, that is important.

A clear message, reiterated by several interviewees in this study, is that, in order for training to be effective, the right staff for the job need to be employed in the first place. As Barrows and Powers (1999: 535) state: 'There is no point in spending time, money and effort on somebody who turns out to be unqualified for, or disinterested in the job.' Unfortunately, as is often the case in south-east Wales and other areas, there is a shortage of labour, which restricts the opportunity for employers to choose the 'right staff'.

13.2.2 The need for training in SMEs and other hospitality organizations

Training needs for the hospitality industry, particularly the perceived shortage of formalized training evident within SMEs, have been highlighted:

> Less than 40% of the workforce, including management within the hotel and catering industry, has any appropriate training, and the output of all the college courses would not keep pace with replacement needs, let alone the needs generated by the growth of the industry.
>
> Boella (2000: 114)

One of the reasons for this statement is that many hospitality managers still believe that training is an unnecessary function with a high cost. Linley (2000: 21) comments that: 'The hotel and catering industry generally does not invest properly in training and development, and operates a "take, take, take" rather than a "give-and-take" attitude when it comes to employment.'

However, Jones and Pizam (1995: 61) suggest that there are many additional reasons for the lack of training within the hospitality industry, which apply on a global basis: 'Education and training often suffers from a lack of financial resources, in-house training programs and manpower planning; together with a shortage of training institutions, programs and instructors capable and sufficient enough to satisfy training needs.' Focusing on the situation in the UK, Roberts (1995: 191) adds that: 'While over 350 colleges provide training for students and

employees, the majority of employees remain untrained and without qualifications.' This is the current picture across the UK, and explains the high level of
unqualified and untrained staff employed in the south-east Wales hospitality
industry, especially in SMEs, despite various initiatives in an attempt to improve
the level of training, including national vocational qualifications (NVQs), Scottish
vocational qualifications (SVQs) in Scotland, modern apprenticeships and a
variety of other short-lived training schemes.

Many hospitality managers in all sectors, including SMEs, recognize the need
for training and formal qualifications in order to achieve a workforce that can
operate to the desired standard of product and service delivery. However, funding
and the cost of training are key considerations. East (1993: 12) states: 'When
times are good training budgets get total backing but during more difficult times
. . . training is one of the support functions that invariably gets axed.' However, an
alternative perspective is put forward by Riley (1996: 151), who suggests that
training is a difficult area for management to encourage due to the fact that
'training outputs are often hard to quantify and that costs are difficult to allocate'.

13.2.3 The 'costs' of training

Riley's (1996) perspective on the training debate is an established argument
used by some traditional managers in the industry. However, a significant counter-argument is made by Barrows and Power (1999), who suggest that, while
training is unquestionably costly, especially in relation to the time employees
must be paid while undertaking training and the costs of the trainer, the key issue
is the cost of not training. They believe this to be more costly to a company than
the actual cost of training itself:

> The alternative to training, not training, may be even more expensive. Training
> does cost a lot; but the cost of not training is poor service and lost customers, and
> a lost customer may never return. Thus, the lost revenue from poor service far
> exceeds the cost of training a worker properly.
>
> Barrows and Power (1999: 535)

This key argument is pursued by Miller *et al.* (1998: 200), whose view is that
the cost of inadequate or no training ultimately results in the loss of staff:

> When good training is lacking there is likely to be an atmosphere of tension, crisis and
> conflict all the time, because nobody is quite sure how the various jobs are supposed
> to be done and who is responsible for what. Such operations are nearly always
> short-handed because someone didn't show up and somebody else just quit.

This suggests that, in order for SMEs or larger companies to develop and maximize the staff input, training needs must be recognized. These training needs are
generally identified as a result of organizational problems in production or service. Goldsmith *et al.* (1997: 81) state that the symptoms of ineffective and poor
training are: 'low productivity, high production costs, poor control, excessive
waste, employee dissatisfaction, poor discipline, high labour turnover and high
absenteeism'. This is a comprehensive list of symptoms, but a key symptom
neglected by Goldsmith *et al.* (1997) is recognized by Boella (2000), who points

out that dissatisfied customers are the absolute result of service problems. For many years, the hospitality industry has recognized that customers ultimately choose with their feet and that a loss of custom is a consequence of a poor product and/or service resulting from poor staff training. It is evident, therefore, that recognition of these symptoms and identification of the requisite training needs are a function of any hospitality manager who is serious about their business intent. Goldsmith *et al.* (1997: 81) suggest that training needs arise from the following situations: 'an expansion of the business, bringing new products and/or services on line, new technology, organizational changes, and human resource planning needs, e.g. promotion, transfer, recruitment and retirement'.

Identification of training is therefore revealed as an essential modern-day hospitality management function. Ferdinand (1988, cited in Chiu *et al.*, 1999: 78) describes identification of training needs as: 'A rational process by which an organization determines how to develop or acquire the human skills it needs in order to achieve its business objectives.' Hence, training is a complex, expensive, on-going function which has an impact on the effectiveness and smooth running of SMEs as it does on larger organizations. However, the key message from the literature is that there is a definite need for training in order for any modern-day hospitality business to operate at optimum levels. A positive approach to training is the basis of future business success and survival in today's increasingly competitive, consumer-driven market.

13.3 Methodology

13.3.1 Phase one research

The first piece of research was undertaken during July and August 2000 to support a European Social Fund (ESF) project within the Welsh School of Hospitality, Tourism and Leisure Management at University of Wales Institute, Cardiff (UWIC). This project, entitled Network of Excellence for Action in Tourism (NEAT), is concerned with assisting hospitality and tourism employers in Wales to develop their business potential by meeting as 'cluster groups'. These groups were established in several areas throughout south-east Wales to operate as a support network, meeting to share ideas and develop business practices. NEAT focuses on improving the quality management (operational, human resource development, environmental) of existing SMEs and on facilitating cooperation between micro and medium-sized SMEs. One of the first and most successful cluster groups comprises employers in Rhondda Cynon Taff (RCT), immediately north of Cardiff, operating a range of hospitality outlets, including hotels, restaurants, tourist attractions and public houses. Initial discussions of the RCT cluster included the types of training that participating organizations felt would be beneficial to their individual organizations. To discover the degree of overlap and/or individuality of the perceived training needs of the RCT cluster, a training needs analysis exercise was undertaken. An additional finding of this exercise was the supportive attitudes of employers towards training. This exercise was a catalyst for phase two of the research.

13.3.2 Phase two research

During the late summer and autumn of 2000, 16 in-depth interviews were undertaken with hospitality employers across Cardiff and RCT. The employers contacted represent a diverse cross-section of the hospitality industry operating within these areas including: hotels; restaurants; fast-food outlets; catering services; and motorway service stations. The purpose of the interviews was to develop a typology of vocational training models used in the different sectors of the industry, and to identify how employer attitudes to training vary in these different sectors. Specifically this phase of the research was concerned with:

1. Comprehensively exploring factors that influence attitudes towards training.
2. Identifying the types of training models employed in different sectors of the industry across south-east Wales.
3. Producing an overall training model which consolidates the findings of phase 1 and phase 2.

13.4 Results and Discussion

The types of training undertaken and the approaches to training vary considerably depending on the particular sector of the hospitality industry. The size of the hospitality unit is also a significant factor, as is the type of ownership. There are clear messages for SMEs, in terms of staff recruitment, retention and development in relation to business performance. Table 13.1 provides an overview of the types of training undertaken in the different sectors of the south-east Wales hospitality industry and is followed by an analysis of the findings from each of the individual hospitality sectors included within this research.

13.4.1 Large hotels (more than 20 rooms)

All the managers interviewed indicated that they have formalized induction and staff training programmes. The managers regard staff development as critical to business success and growth. As stated by a personnel and training manager: 'We are very proactive in terms of staff development at all levels. The level of training is increasing all the time. Our model is proactive rather than reactive.'

Operational managers (food and beverage and reservations) also recognized the importance of training, but admitted that they expect a high level of staff turnover, especially within Cardiff. Two operational managers admitted that, because Cardiff is busy between Monday and Thursday nights, there is a certain level of complacency about staff turnover levels and this is reflected in attitudes to training. As a result, training and staff development can take second place when business pressure is high, and this can result in the less than satisfactory service received by guests. This attitude was not evident in RCT. In terms of staff retention and training, at unskilled operative level, money appears to be the key motivator for staff, especially where students working on a part-time basis

Table 13.1. Types of training undertaken in the south-east Wales hospitality industry.

	Hotels < 20 rooms	Hotels > 20 rooms	Restaurants	Fast-food	Catering service	Public houses	Motorway service stations
Formal induction training	✓	✗	✓ ✗	✓	✓	✓ ✗	✓
Ongoing practical skills development	✓	✗	✓✗	✓	✓	✓ ✗	✓
Health and safety	✓	✓	✓	✓	✓	✓	✓
Interpersonal/ customer care skills	✓ ✗	✗	✗	✓	✓	✓ ✗	✓
Selling skills	S M	✗	✗	✓	✓	✓ ✗	✓
Building teams/ leadership skills	S M	✗	✗	S M	✓	✗	S M
Operating IT training	✓	✓	✓	✓	✓	✓	✓
Use of NVQs	✓	✗	✗	✓ ✗	✓	✓ ✗	✓

✓, yes; ✗, no; S, supervisory level only; M, management level only; IT, information technology.

form a large proportion of the workforce. 'Staff retention is difficult . . . because competitor hotels will constantly be trying to poach our best staff. Usually this is done by offering a higher wage rate per hour.'

In order to address this problem, several of the hotels tried to accommodate requests from their staff for specific working hours. They also try to present themselves as 'caring' employers, concerned that full-time staff receive staff development appropriate to their career aspirations and encouraging part-time staff by providing appropriate training and offering working hours around their primary occupation. All the large hotels interviewed offer well-established staff development programmes to their full-time staff. These include in-house courses (health and safety, food hygiene, etc.); NVQs; and more formal management qualifications, including Chartered Institute of Personnel and Development (CIPD) and degree programmes. One manager stated: 'All staff are encouraged to achieve their potential within this company. The training model used depends on the member of staff and their identified training needs.'

13.4.2 Small hotels (fewer than 20 rooms)

There was a marked contrast between the progressive and 'proactive' approaches to training evidenced in the large hotels and the smaller, independent hotels. In such hotels the traditional training model 'sitting next to Nellie' is the most common approach. Smaller hotels argue that they do not have the financial resources, 'financial safety nets' or time available compared with larger hotel organizations. Nevertheless, as a proportion of the total workforce, labour turnover in small hotels is not as significant as in the larger hotels. Although the training provided is very basic in small hotels, one of the key reasons offered as to why staff retention levels are high is that 'there is more of a family atmosphere, therefore people stay'. The research findings indicate that, in this sector, there is little evidence of formal induction, on-going training or career enhancement strategies, such as encouraging staff to study for further qualifications. However, the fact that little, if any, training is carried out is not perceived as an issue in terms of business success within the small hotel sector. One manager revealed that the key issue is: 'bottom-line . . . we don't have time [for training], everything else is a secondary consideration'.

13.4.3 Restaurant sector

This is probably the most diverse sector within the hospitality industry, ranging from branded national restaurants to specialist local restaurants. In the branded restaurants there is a more articulated approach to training, with a good knowledge of the NVQ framework, and yet there is little evidence of formal training beyond induction and adherence to the necessary health and safety legislation. High staff turnover is regarded as inevitable, with young people and students forming a high percentage of the total workforce. In smaller, privately owned, non-branded restaurants, training is regarded as a low priority because 'it doesn't generate revenue'. This attitude is very typical among small employers in the hospitality industry, who provide little training beyond induction. Therefore, non-branded restaurants display similar attitudes to the smaller independent hotels in terms of providing less post-induction training when compared with their larger branded counterparts. Unfortunately, in south-east Wales, it is small and medium-sized businesses which form the basis of the commercial hotel and restaurant sector, hence the significant consequential impact of a lack of training on the end-product.

13.4.4 Fast-food sector

Evidence from this research indicates that training in this sector is 'regimented and structured', with formalized training extending from operative level to senior management. Managers in this sector revealed that, within the fast-food industry, staff are unable to progress in the organization without passing the training appropriate to that level/stage. Although staff turnover levels are high, the fast-food organizations do regard themselves as 'caring' employers, encouraging all employees to 'progress within the company as far as their abilities permit'. The major fast-food operators make significant resources (financial, physical and time) available for staff training and their staff training is extensive, with standards manuals that cover almost every eventuality. However, the biggest problem for this sector is not the lack of formalized training offered to and undertaken by staff, but that the fast-food industry employs a large proportion of young people, who are transient and wage-sensitive, for whom money is the key motivating factor.

13.4.5 Catering services sector

In recent years the catering services within education, hospitals and industry have been provided by contract caterers, and as such the catering provision is no longer an 'in-house concern'. This research found that staff employed by the main contract catering companies all receive induction training, followed immediately by training in basic skills at operative levels: 'The intention is that our staff are immediately made to feel a useful part of the unit in which they are employed. It is important that they believe that they have a valuable role from day one.'

The contract catering companies are very proactive in terms of staff training. The research indicates that all staff from operative to senior management regularly attend refresher and development workshops. The companies are also concerned about their external image, and believe that being regarded as a 'caring employer who invests in its employees' is important for their future business development. Formalized and ongoing training (including the achievement of NVQ qualifications) is therefore a key feature of this growing hospitality sector, where staff retention levels are high.

13.4.6 Public house sector

The public house sector replicates many of the features found in small hotels. One of the managers admitted: 'Our current approach to training is very basic. In terms of induction training staff spend the first couple of shifts working closely with a more established member of staff. It's very much a case of learning by doing.'

As in the small hotel sector, a large proportion of operative staff (bar staff) are employed on a part-time basis. However, more concerning is the poor retention rate for pub managers:

> We lose too many bar staff, restaurant staff, kitchen assistants, and most importantly the pub managers. This is probably linked to poor selection and training at the start. That's why we've got to improve our approach to recruitment and training.

This research found that the problem exists particularly within the small independent chains of public houses. Traditionally, resources for training have been limited within this sector, although the large breweries are now investing heavily in training and are starting to recognize diversity and a need to change the focus in many British pubs, such as the increase of food sales compared with drink sales. It is not only financial implications which impede the development of the training function in this sector. Another key constraint is time: 'We operate long hours seven days a week, finding time for training during the working day is very difficult.'

13.4.7 Motorway service stations

As in other sectors, there is a high turnover of young staff at operative level. However, supervisory and management staff tend to be 'more reliable and stay . . . there is a reward for the training investment'. In this sector formal training is provided for all staff at induction and further specific training is provided throughout their employment. NVQs are used primarily for food production skills and other in-house training courses are provided either on or off site, depending on demand. From the research it was evident that the major employers have a high commitment to training. However, as in other sectors, time is a major constraint on the amount of training completed by operative staff and management.

13.5 Developing the Training Model

In order to develop an overall training model which applies to both SMEs and larger companies, it is necessary to further examine the interview responses and training typology, considering the effectiveness, suitability and acceptability of the different approaches.

13.5.1 Induction training

All the hospitality sectors recognized the benefits of good staff retention, and most acknowledged that a formal induction programme indicated to new employees that the hospitality organization was 'caring' and recognized the importance of staff in the delivery of hospitality products and services to customers. All the organizations which undertake formal induction programmes pay the staff during their training. Some organizations conclude their induction process by awarding formal certificates of achievement to the employees. This was seen by one hotel as a very necessary part of the induction process, as awarding a certificate with the company name and logo embossed upon it made the new employee feel part of that successful organization.

13.5.2 Time and resources for training

Most of the employers interviewed recognized that a formal on-going individual training plan which is regularly discussed and reviewed with each employee indicates a commitment to training. However, the daily operational pressures of the business often mean that training is relegated in terms of importance during busy periods, when the need to make money is the priority. This was particularly evident in the 'traditional' commercial sectors and within SMEs. The time factor is a key influencing factor in determining how and when staff will undergo training and the frequency of training. In theory, larger organizations have more staff and can therefore more easily afford to take staff 'off the front line' for training purposes. However, this research indicates disparities in practice. The catering services and motorway service station sectors ensure that staff have individual training plans which are adhered to, with operative staff attending regular staff development activities despite the operational pressures of the business. Additional staff are used to cover their shifts and where necessary overtime rates are paid. The larger, brand-name hotels also timetable staff training days/events, but admit that sometimes unforeseen operational pressure can cause these events to be postponed. As a result, staff are requested to attend these training events at a later date because, as stated by a hotel restaurant manager: 'the immediate priority is to deal with the current volume of business and make money'.

The resources made available also influence the effectiveness of the training function. These include the financial commitment of an organization to the training function and specialist rooms/areas for such training to be undertaken. The larger organizations, including hotels with over 20 rooms, motorway service stations, fast-food operators and the catering services sector, were found to have the best resource allocations. Training in the fast-food sector, for instance, was found to be well-resourced financially.

Although organizations were not willing to divulge financial information, it was evident that within the above sectors staff undertook training at the unit where they are employed or at designated 'training centres'. The importance of a 'pleasant, comfortable environment, removed from operational pressures' was considered to be a key factor by a training manager from the large hotel sector. The staff running such events are usually employed within the personnel and training function, or include specialist training consultants hired as and when necessary. Specialist videos have also been commissioned by hotel companies, motorway service stations, branded public houses and organizations within the catering services sector. A willingness to pay for staff to attend college courses as part-time students (particularly for accreditation of NVQs) was also evident among the above operators. However, such companies are increasingly recruiting staff who hold requisite training and development lead body (TDLB) units so that formal NVQ accreditation can be undertaken in the workplace. SMEs, by their very nature, struggle to compete in respect of available time and resources for training.

13.5.3 Organization size

The most evident factor that influences a commitment to training is the size of the organization. In the larger organizations in both the commercial and catering services sectors, there are either specialist training departments, or alternatively the responsibility for training is embedded in the work of the personnel department. Training records are kept for individual staff members, and within one large hotel group the full-time operative staff are encouraged to work towards either internal company certificates of achievement or external qualifications such as NVQs. Regular staff appraisals for full-time staff were found to be undertaken in all the sectors included in the research, except for the small independent hotels, restaurants and public houses. Clearly this is an issue which SMEs must tackle if they are to compete effectively against the bigger players. It is interesting to note that branded public houses are increasingly using staff appraisals to 'reward' staff for their loyalty to that particular unit, and there is a growing availability of short, sector-specific courses from the British Institute of Innkeeping. The growing demand for training courses within the licensed trade sector is being mirrored by the increased availability of specialist full-time and part-time courses within colleges and universities.

13.5.4 Company image

It is particularly interesting that the licensed trade sector is now recognizing the benefits of training at a time when there is massive investment in public houses in terms of the 'image' projected to consumers. Many licensed premises are being rebranded and refurbished in order to appeal to more discerning customers. Breweries recognize the contribution a trained workforce can make in selling this professional image to the public and many organizations use their staff to present their 'brand image'. For example, T.G.I. Friday's employ staff who are specifically trained to be gregarious and lively when serving the public. The public expect a certain type of meal experience when visiting a T.G.I. Friday's restaurant and the staff reflect that brand. The company achieve this by using effective recruitment and in-house training techniques.

There are clear messages here for SMEs. While SMEs may not need the powerful brand image of a quality restaurant or hotel chain, the customer's first impression will often seal the fate of that SME. Positive introductions by well-trained staff will help ensure repeat business. A poor initial service image will cloud the customer's perception of that SME throughout their visit, regardless of the quality of the product. For SMEs, therefore, as for larger businesses, image is a key factor in today's competitive environment and well-trained staff can enhance that image.

13.5.5 Formality of the training function

A final factor that is perceived to influence the training function is the formality of the training provided. This 'formality' refers to the importance placed on training by the organization; how this importance is conveyed to staff by the unit management; the regularity of staff appraisals; and the type of training records used. Within some non-branded restaurants and SMEs, the training undertaken is very ad hoc, and therefore its importance as a key organizational function is often lost and staff begin to regard training as an inconvenience rather than a benefit. As stated by one restaurant manager: 'It's something [health and safety including fire training] that we've got to cover, but the staff know that we'd rather not have to do it, its impact therefore is probably lost.'

However, at the other extreme, the fast-food sector records all the training completed by all staff at all levels. The process is very competence-based and progressive, with staff not permitted to move up to the next level until all their training at a particular level has been recorded. Unfortunately, this sector suffers from a very high turnover of staff at operative level. This has probably little to do with the organization's commitment to training but more with the type of people employed at this level within the UK fast-food sector – typically young, transient and wage-sensitive with no long-term commitment to the fast-food sector.

Within motorway service stations and the catering services sector, the importance of training is made clear to all new staff at induction. In the branded larger hotels, there is an increasing recognition that all training undertaken by staff needs to be recorded, and new staff are informed of their individual training file at induction. One personnel and training manager stated: 'It's important for staff to feel that training is their responsibility as well as ours – its function within this organization is given a high profile from day one.' Such positive attitudes are doing much to emphasize the importance of training within identified sectors of the south-east Wales hospitality industry, thus making the formality and focus of the training function clear to all employees.

13.6 Conclusion

These research findings have been developed into a model (see Fig. 13.1) which represents the key features influencing training within hospitality SMEs and larger companies. This model summarizes how labour supply represented by a pool of staff within a hospitality organization can either leak away, resulting in wastage for

Fig. 13.1. Impact of labour supply, training and labour turnover on the pool of staff available to tourism and hospitality businesses.

that hospitality organization, or be retained by adopting a combination of several key factors that have emerged from this research, ensuring that the organization works towards better staff retention by displaying a commitment to training.

The tap indicates the labour source available in south-east Wales. As discussed in the introduction, many vacancies within the hospitality industry remain unfilled. Therefore, the tap therefore drips 'water' rather than supplying a steady stream. Hence, the staff that are employed and create the 'pool of staff' need to be cared for by their employers to ensure that they are retained by the organization. It is well documented (e.g. Boella, 2000) that the hospitality industry has a reputation for offering poor levels of pay, unsociable hours of work and poor working conditions. This combination of factors causes many people to prematurely leave hospitality employment. If the training provided is poor or non-existent, then there may be no motivating factor to remain in that employment in order to become better qualified and progress within that organization. Therefore, as indicated by the model, such demotivated staff leak away from the pool of hospitality staff.

Alternatively, organizations can display a clear commitment to training, which is the result of a combination and sum total of several key factors including:

- Image of the organization.
- Size of the organization.
- Time available for training.
- Resources available.
- Formality of the training function.

Although the model presented is a generalization of the current situation across the different hospitality sectors, it is representative and has significant messages for SMEs in south-east Wales. For SMEs to develop and compete in the ever-changing, dynamic and competitive hospitality marketplace, issues relating to staff training and effective implementation need to be given more of a focus. The research indicates that many of the larger organizations already invest heavily in training, but the training may need to be refined, restructured or given greater importance. Unless SMEs follow the lead of larger organizations, many will fail because they are unable to meet the increased expectations and service quality required by today's customers. The hospitality industry makes a significant contribution to the south-east Wales economy and supports a high proportion of jobs in this emerging tourism destination. The model suggests that, if the hospitality industry is to succeed and provide high-quality products and services to an increasingly discerning public, all sectors must invest in their most important asset – their staff. The way to do this is through a commitment to training.

References

Barrows, C. and Powers, T. (1999) *Introduction to Management in the Hospitality Industry*, 6th edn. Wiley, New York, 626 pp.

Beardwell, I. and Holden, L. (1994) *Human Resource Management: a Contemporary Perspective*. Pitman, London, 694 pp.

Boella, M.J. (2000) *Human Resource Management in the Hospitality Industry*, 7th edn. Stanley Thornes, Cheltenham, UK, 348 pp.

Boer, A. and Teare, R. (1996) *Strategic Hospitality Management: Theory and Practice for the 1990s*. Cassell, London, 225 pp.

Chiu, W., Thomson, D., Mak, W. and Lo, K. (1999) Re-thinking training needs analysis. *Personnel Review* 28, 78.

East, J. (1993) *Managing Quality in the Catering Industry*. Croner Publications, Kingston upon Thames, UK, 283 pp.

Goldsmith, A., Nickson, D., Sloan, D. and Wood, R. (1997) *Human Resource Management for Hospitality Services*. International Thomson Business Press, London, 229 pp.

HCTC (1994) *Employer Attitudes and Career Expectations*. Hotel and Catering Training Company, London.

HtF (1996) *Training: Who Needs It?* Hospitality Training Foundation, London.

Jones, P. and Pizam, A. (1995) *The International Hospitality Industry – Organizational and Operational Issues*. Longman, Harlow, UK, 243 pp.

Linley, I. (2000) Stop moaning and invest in workers. *Caterer and Hotelkeeper* 22 June 2000, 21.

Miller, J., Drummond, K. and Porter, M. (1998) *Supervision in the Hospitality Industry*, 3rd edn. Wiley, New York, 434 pp.

Rainbird, H. and Maguire, M. (1993) When corporate needs supersede employee development. *Personnel Management* February.

Reid, M.A. and Barrington, H. (1999) *Training Interventions. Promoting Learning Opportunities*, 6th edn. Institute of Personnel and Development, London, 395 pp.

Riley, M. (1996) *Human Resource Management in the Hospitality and Tourism Industry*, 2nd edn. Butterworth & Heinemann, Oxford, UK, 219 pp.

Roberts, J. (1995) *Human Resource Practice in the Hospitality Industry*. Hodder & Stoughton, London, 299 pp.

Stevens, T. and Associates (1998) *Tourism Employment Action for the Millennium: a Tourism and Hospitality Training Strategy*. Stevens & Associates, Swansea, UK.

Stevens, T. and Associates (2000) *Tourism Employment Action for the Millennium: a Review of the Tourism and Hospitality Training Strategy*. Stevens & Associates, Swansea, UK.

Welsh Office (1998) *Pathway to Prosperity – a New Economic Agenda for Wales*. Welsh Office, Cardiff, UK.

14 The Utilization of Human Resources in Tourism SMEs: a Comparison between Mexico and Central Florida

ABRAHAM PIZAM AND DANA V. TESONE

Rosen School of Hospitality Management, University of Central Florida, Orlando, Florida, USA

14.1 Introduction

The recruitment and retention of quality human resources are essential to the long-term viability of the tourism industry around the globe (Honeycutt *et al.*, 1999). Some studies suggest that documented perceptions of potential tourism workers have a profound impact on occupational career decisions leading to industry professions (Ross, 1992; Getz, 1994). On the other hand, negative perceptions of industry career opportunities have been shown to prevent talented individuals from entry into the industry's workforce (Dubinsky, 1980). Understanding the variables that contribute to the supply of qualified potential workers is crucial to the success of the hospitality/tourism industry (Lewis and Airey, 2001).

This chapter describes and compares the results of two separate studies that were conducted in Mexico and Central Florida, USA, for the purpose of collecting information on current and future utilization of human resources in tourism small and medium-sized enterprises (SMEs), with special emphasis on training and educational activities. Following this, the authors propose a series of recommendations to the respective private and public sectors of each region, in order to address some of the critical issues identified in each of the studies.

14.2 Study Objectives

The objectives of the Mexican study were to: assess the status of the tourism industry and travel-related education in Mexico; identify the major human resources concerns of Mexican tourism employers; identify the major human resources concerns of Mexican governmental tourism organizations; and formulate recommendations to assist the Mexican hospitality and tourism industry and Mexican educational institutions in developing plans to meet the human resource needs of the country's hospitality and tourism industry.

The objectives of the Central Florida (CF) study were to: analyse the perceptions that managers of hospitality and tourism enterprises in Central Florida have of the quality of secondary and tertiary education in general and its relevance to the hospitality and tourism industry in particular, and to formulate recommendations to assist the CF hospitality and tourism industry and the Florida educational institutions in developing plans to meet the human resource needs of the region's hospitality and tourism industry.

14.3 Methodology

In the Mexican study, two postal questionnaires were designed for the purpose of collecting quantitative information on the characteristics and concerns of human resources in the Mexican tourism industry. The first questionnaire was aimed at tourism employers and the second at government tourism organizations. The employer questionnaire consisted of 144 items of information divided into the following sections:

- Company profile.
- Staff information.
- Organization of the training function.
- Difficulties in recruiting for various job categories.
- Job readiness.
- Types of training programmes sponsored.
- Type of skills that need further training.
- Public-sector assistance.
- Effectiveness, relevance and adequacy of external and in-house tourism education and training.
- Company practices in meeting human resources needs.
- Status of the tourism industry in the Mexican society and its economy.

The government questionnaire consisted of 50 items of information divided into the following sections:

- The status of the tourism industry in the country and state.
- Effectiveness, relevance and adequacy of external and in-house tourism education and training.
- The government's role in tourism education and training.

In the case of CF, the CF tourism employer's questionnaire consisted of 50 items of information divided into the following sections:

- Professional profile.
- Staff profile.
- Perceptions/images of successful entry level employees in the hospitality and tourism industry.

- Perceptions/images of quality of training provided by educational and training institutions.

The State of Florida does not have governmental institutions that control, regulate or market the tourism industry; therefore a comparative survey of the opinions of relevant government officials was not possible.

14.4 Results

This section describes and compares the results of the Mexico and CF tourism employers' surveys, together with a discussion of the results of the Mexican survey of governmental tourism organizations.

14.4.1 Employer surveys

14.4.1.1 Organization of training

An absolute majority of the Mexican tourism SME employers did not have a training department. Of those that had a training department, half employed only one full-time employee or less in their training department. Almost half of the companies had no full-time employees in the training department. Less than one-third of the companies had ever conducted training assessments in the past and just over one-third of them had a formal training plan. The largest proportion of the training budget was allocated to skilled/semi-skilled staff, followed by managerial, unskilled staff and terminating with professional staff.

In the case of CF, though a corresponding question was not asked, anecdotal evidence suggests that, while most CF tourism SMEs had training units, the number of employees per unit was minimal and its budget was rather small. Typical training units consist of single person full-time equivalents (FTE) of regularly employed trainers or outsourced individuals. There is also evidence that suggests training units are commonly the first areas to be reduced or completely eliminated during budgetary downturns.

14.4.1.2 Labour supply and recruitment

A previous phase (focus group study) of the Mexican study found that many tourism SME employers expressed concern about their ability to recruit an adequate number of talented and qualified workers to fill job vacancies in the organization. The survey asked employers to indicate the degree of difficulty they had experienced over the last 12 months in the managerial, professional, skilled/semi-skilled and unskilled categories. Though tourism SME employers had fewer difficulties in filling managerial and professional positions, they reported significant difficulties in recruiting qualified skilled/semi-skilled and unskilled employees.

The corresponding phase of the CF study found similar recruitment concerns expressed by tourism SME employers regarding job vacancies within organizations, to a slightly lesser degree relative to those expressed by Mexico's employers. Florida employers concurred with their Mexican counterparts that fewer difficulties existed in filling management and professional positions, with larger recruitment challenges existing within the attraction of skilled/semi-skilled and unskilled workers to positions within organizations.

14.4.1.3 Preparation for work

The Mexican study identified several skill deficiencies by different categories of employees. Managers had only a mild deficiency in foreign languages, while professional employees had a serious deficiency in foreign languages and mild deficiencies in safety and security, marketing and planning. Skilled/semi-skilled employees had a critical deficiency in foreign languages and serious deficiencies in computer skills, safety and security, marketing and financial/accounting skills. These employees also had mild deficiencies in interpersonal skills, 'cultura turistica' (an understanding, appreciation and pride in the Mexican culture, history and traditions and the ability and desire to show this to tourists), leadership and problem-solving skills. Unskilled employees had critical deficiencies in computer and foreign language skills and serious deficiencies in general literacy, interpersonal skills, 'cultura turistica' and safety and security skills. In addition, unskilled employees had mild deficiencies in customer service and technical, self-reliance and confidence skills.

A combined summary of skill deficiencies shows that:

1. The most deficient category of employees was found to be the unskilled employees, followed by skilled/semi-skilled employees, professionals and culminating with managers.
2. The skills that were found to be the most deficient across all categories of employees were foreign languages, computer and safety and security.

A cross-tabulation of skill deficiencies by industry sector found that skilled/semi-skilled employees in restaurants had the highest level of deficiencies among all sectors of the Mexican tourism industry. These deficiencies were manifested in foreign language skills, computer skills, problem-solving skills, financial/accounting skills, 'cultura turistica' and self-reliance skills.

In comparison with the Mexican study, the CF study identified mild deficiencies in interpersonal and team-building skills among managers, while critical deficiencies were reported in the areas of teamwork, realistic career expectations and self-reliance among skilled workers. Employers noted similar areas and levels of deficiencies among semi-skilled and unskilled workers to those reported in the Mexico study.

14.4.1.4 Training sponsored by the companies

The most frequent methods of training that were sponsored by the Mexican SMEs represented in the study were on-site or off-site training using a contracted trainer for managers, professionals and skilled/semi-skilled employees and on-site or off-site training using a staff trainer for unskilled employees.

In the case of CF, though a corresponding question was not asked, anecdotal evidence suggests that most CF tourism SMEs conducted on-the-job training for skilled/semi-skilled employees, using their own experienced employees, who acted as part-time staff trainers. In most scenarios, these programmes were conducted in the absence of training objectives and planning techniques. The common anecdotal perception among industry managers was that this approach was generally ineffective, but better than no training at all.

14.4.1.5 Skills companies were trying to improve

Mexican companies participating in the survey listed language and customer service skills in their top three training priorities for all employee categories, while computer skills were listed as a high training priority for only managers and professionals, despite the fact that in a previous section survey respondents suggested that both skilled/semi-skilled and unskilled employees had serious deficiencies in computer skills. Improving general literacy was listed as a high training priority for unskilled employees and improving interpersonal skills was listed as a high training priority for the category of skilled/semi-skilled employees.

In comparison, CF employers indicated interpersonal communication, team-building and customer service skills as being within their training priorities for most employee categories. Foreign language and literacy skills were emphasized as training areas of importance for semi-skilled and unskilled employees.

Though all sectors of the Mexican tourism industry tried to improve at least one of the five critical skills identified in the study (general literacy, computer skills, foreign languages, customer service and interpersonal skills), some industry sectors went beyond the above five and tried to improve other skills. For example, hotels and transportation companies tried to improve the leadership skills of their managers, and restaurants tried to improve the financial skills of their managers. Hotels and transportation companies had training programmes aimed at improving the technical skills of their skilled/semi-skilled employees, and transportation companies had similar programmes for their unskilled employees.

But more importantly than which skills Mexican SMEs emphasized in their training programmes is to examine the ones that were not emphasized. The skills of marketing, problem-solving and safety and security were not considered to be important enough to be placed in the top three skills that companies were trying to improve, despite the fact that the survey participants considered marketing skills to be deficient among professionals and skilled/semi-skilled employees, and safety and security skills were listed as deficient among professionals, skilled/semi-skilled and unskilled employees.

Conversely, the CF participants indicated an expectation that most skills sets should be provided by external training and education sources. The nature of the responses indicated that employers perceived their role as providing specific technical skills relative to job performance across most levels (skilled, professional and management) of employment positions and that qualified candidates should possess skills mentioned in the five critical skills categories identified in the Mexican study. CF employers indicated an interest in providing in-house training in these categories to workers at the semi-skilled and unskilled levels of employment.

14.4.1.6 Public-sector assistance in meeting human resource needs

Private-sector employers supported their governments' involvement in training and educational activities, including regulation and certification of training institutions and setting of service delivery standards. Respondents perceived that it was very important to improve the quality of general education, increase the number of programmes that prepare first-line managers, middle managers, executives, and skilled and unskilled employees for the tourism industry, as well as programmes that train people already employed in the industry. They supported the idea of government assistance with the design of in-house training programmes and personnel recruitment, and perceived that it was very important to establish training and educational institutions in the interior of the country. A significant proportion of the respondents even supported the concepts of mandating training activities throughout the industry, regulating and certifying training institutions and subsidizing the cost of training provided by employers. Last, but not least, a significant majority of the respondents supported the development of minimum service delivery standards, an act that might restrict the private sector's freedom of conducting business.

14.4.1.7 Tourism education and training

A large proportion of the respondents thought that the external tourism education and training programmes in both Mexico and CF were moderately to highly effective in preparing managers, professionals and skilled/semi-skilled employees for work within the tourism industry. This, however, was reversed in the case of unskilled employees, where more than half of the respondents evaluated these institutions to be ineffective or very ineffective. The same was true for in-house training and education programmes, where a significant proportion of the respondents evaluated their effectiveness in the moderate to high range. In Mexico, restaurant employers evaluated the effectiveness of the existing in-house training for professionals lower than hoteliers or travel agents/tour operators. As to the motivation of employees to participate in in-house training programmes, the majority of respondents in both Mexico and CF rated it as relatively high for all categories of employees.

The material taught in Mexican and CF tourism educational and training institutions was thought to be moderately relevant to the work in the industry for managers, professionals and skilled/semi-skilled employees. This, however, was not the case for unskilled occupations in Mexico, where half of the respondents thought that the material taught in these programmes was totally irrelevant or of low relevance. Hoteliers rated the relevancy of the material taught in Mexican tourism training and educational institutions higher than both restaurateurs and travel agents/tour operators.

Respondents evaluated the currency of the material taught in Mexican tourism educational and training institutions to be moderately up to date for managers and professionals, but relatively outdated for skilled/semi-skilled occupations. The practical training element in Mexican external education and training institutions was rated as somewhat inadequate. The quality of hospitality and tourism educators in Mexican tourism training and educational institutions was rated at slightly lower than average. Contrary to that, CF employers rated the quality of hospitality and tourism educators in tertiary educational institutions as high.

The survey respondents in Mexico felt that there was very little dialogue between the tourism industry and educational and training institutions, with 60% of respondents rating the frequency of the dialogue as low and infrequent. This, however, was totally different in the case of CF employers, who indicated a collaborative relationship between educational institutions and the hospitality/tourism industry. Mexican respondents overwhelmingly suggested that there were not enough tourism educational and training institutions in outlying rural areas, while those from CF made the same suggestion concerning vocational secondary educational institutions in both populated and rural localities.

Practical training opportunities were thought to be insufficient in Mexico. Almost half of the respondents thought that the internship opportunities provided by the tourism industry for the educational institutions in Mexico were totally insufficient or insufficient. CF participants did not provide any commentaries concerning the sufficiency or quality of internship opportunities. However, there is anecdotal evidence to suggest that new entrants to the industry compete vigorously for certain internship opportunities and that successful completion of certain internship programmes provided opportunities for career development.

14.4.1.8 Company practices

A majority of the companies represented in both studies had instituted one or more of the following programmes intended to address human resources needs and concerns within the past 5 years:

- Improved the general or job-specific skills of workers.
- Reduced staff turnover.
- Facilitated career advancement.
- Identified new sources of labour.
- Increased productivity.

14.4.1.9 The status of the tourism industry in Mexican and Floridian societies

While a significant proportion of the Mexican respondents felt that the tourism industry earned a respected status in their society, they were disappointed with the level of recognition and support that the tourism industry received from governments and political institutions. Approximately one-third of the respondents believed that the industry received little, if any, recognition and support from the federal, state and local governments. The respondents evaluated the attitude of the general public towards service occupations to be in the moderately positive range. Similar opinions were expressed concerning the skills of tourism employees in delivering customer service. Half of the respondents thought that tourism employees possessed a medium level of customer service skills, while one-fifth felt that tourism employees possessed few, if any, skills. Compared with hoteliers, restaurateurs thought that Mexican tourism employees were less skilled.

Though this issue was not directly addressed in the CF study, anecdotal evidence obtained from newspaper commentaries and informal discussions with high school students, counsellors and parents indicate that in CF the tourism industry does not possess a high level of respect from the general public. In fact, industry practitioners have been known to argue against perceptions that industry prominence displaces the population of more 'desirable' industries such as information technology (IT), electronics and biotechnology, a notion that has been publicized by media representatives and government officials.

Industry cohesiveness (defined as 'united and speaking with one voice') at both the national and state level in Mexico was judged to be relatively low. Restaurateurs evaluated the cohesiveness of the Mexican tourism industry much lower than the hoteliers did. While CF employers perceived that sufficient levels of industry cohesiveness existed, the study also determined that members of the society subscribed to misguided conceptions relative to the industry's contributions to the state's economy.

The survey respondents from both studies evaluated the career advancement opportunities in the tourism industry to be relatively low. Almost half of the respondents evaluated the levels of salaries in the tourism industry to be lower than in other industries. Both studies suggested that job turnover rates were higher in tourism than in other industries. No significant differences were found between the various sectors of the tourism industry on these perceived turnover rates. Respondents from both studies rated new employees' expectations about work in the tourism industry as being mostly unrealistic and glamorous.

14.4.2 Mexican government tourism organization surveys

14.4.2.1 The status of the tourism industry in Mexican society

Unlike the employer respondents, a relatively small proportion of the government respondents felt that the tourism industry held a modest status and respect in the Mexican society. One-third of them, the same proportion as the employers, believed that the industry received little, if any, recognition and support from governments and political institutions. Compared with employer respondents, government respondents perceived that Mexican citizens had a less positive and less desirable view of service occupations. The respondents rated the service delivery skills of tourism employees somewhat lower than the employers did.

The tourism industry was rated as moderately effective in presenting its case to the public sector and influencing federal government policies on issues that affect its operations. The tourism industry was rated as somewhat less effective in presenting its case to the public sector and influencing state government policies on issues that affect its operations.

Career and advancement opportunities in the industry were rated as moderate. More than one-third of the government respondents rated career and advancement opportunities as very few or some, while another one-third rated these as above average or many. Salary levels in the tourism industry were perceived to be significantly lower than salary levels in other industries. Turnover rates in the industry were evaluated as high. Almost half of the government respondents rated the turnover rates in the tourism industry as higher or much higher than in other industries. Government respondents disagreed somewhat with the employers on the issue of new employees' expectations. Almost one-third indicated that the expectations of new employees were realistic and unglamorous.

14.4.2.2 Tourism education and training in Mexico

A relatively high proportion of the government respondents agreed with the employer respondents that the external tourism education and training programmes in Mexico were moderately effective in preparing professionals and skilled/semi-skilled employees for work in the tourism industry. However, government respondents considered these institutions to be even less effective for training managers than employers did. The majority of the respondents expressed a concern that the number of external tourism education and training institutions was insufficient to meet the human resources needs of the tourism industry in all employment categories but especially in skilled/semi-skilled and unskilled.

Government respondents evaluated the effectiveness of in-house training programmes for all employment categories as moderately effective, but somewhat lower than the employers' evaluation. As was the case with sufficiency of external tourism education and training programmes, the majority of the respondents expressed a serious concern that the number of in-house training programmes was insufficient to meet the human resources needs of the tourism industry in skilled/semi-skilled and unskilled employees.

Government respondents were more critical than employers about the relevance of the material taught in tourism training and educational institutions to the work in the industry. This was particularly true in the case of managerial and professional training, where government respondents evaluated the relevance to be lower than employers. Government respondents agreed with employers and evaluated the currency of the material taught in Mexican tourism educational and training institutions to be moderately up to date for managers, professionals and skilled/semi-skilled occupations, but relatively outdated for unskilled occupations. The quantity of practical training provided by tourism training and educational institutions was judged to be inadequate. Almost half of the respondents felt that it was not adequate and only one-quarter felt that it was somewhat adequate.

The government respondents fully agreed with the employer respondents that there was very little dialogue between the tourism industry and educational and training institutions. While the dialogue between educational institutions and the tourism industry was judged to be insufficient, the dialogue between educational institutions and the government was judged to be more or less sufficient. Unlike employers, government respondents thought that practical training opportunities were moderately sufficient.

14.4.2.3 The role of the Mexican federal and state governments in meeting human resources needs of the tourism industry

Government respondents supported the involvement of the Mexican federal and state governments in tourism training and educational activities, including regulation and certification of training institutions and setting of service delivery standards. Respondents perceived that it was appropriate for both the federal and the state governments to:

- Assist the industry with the design and implementation of in-house training programmes.
- Mandate training activities throughout the industry.
- Regulate and certify training institutions.
- Establish training and educational institutions in the interior of the country.
- Develop minimum service delivery standards.

However, almost half of the respondents commenting on each of the federal and state levels thought that it would not be appropriate for the federal or state governments to subsidize the cost of training provided by employers.

14.5 Recommendations

Based on the results of the above studies, the following strategies are suggested for addressing the critical issues that were found to affect the utilization of human resources in tourism SMEs in both Mexico and CF.

14.5.1 Government

Government tourism organizations (GTOs) should take a more active role in educating the general population and government officials on the importance and contribution of the tourism industry to the economic well-being of their communities.
      To improve the status of the tourism industry and achieve greater recognition and financial support from all branches of government, GTOs at local, state and national levels in both Mexico and CF are encouraged to regularly conduct, in collaboration with the private sector, a range of activities and events intended to elevate the visibility and importance of the industry. Such activities should begin with the commissioning and publication of studies on the economic impacts of tourism, and culminate with periodical public relations events, such as a national tourism appreciation week; educational seminars for public officials; field trips to tourism enterprises; and school contests on tourism topics.

GTOs should initiate a number of steps intended to increase the public awareness of career opportunities in the tourism industry for properly educated and motivated individuals.
      In both Mexico and CF, tourism occupations are not perceived as having high status, excellent working conditions and high-paying jobs. Evidence from the CF

study suggests that teachers and school officials tend to direct their more talented students to academic institutions and industries that have a 'more respectable image'. This provides frequent reinforcement of this conception. Therefore GTOs at all levels should develop a series of activities aimed at 'educating the educators' on the career opportunities in the tourism industry for educated and talented individuals, and the high rewards associated with successful job performance. Such activities as organizing field trips and educational seminars for teachers and high school career counsellors, introduction of tourism modules in elementary and high school curricula, and essay contests on tourism jobs would assist in gradually changing the erroneous image of tourism careers.

GTOs at both the national and state level should increase the number of external tourism training and educational institutions in order to supply the needs of the Mexican tourism industry in the 21st century. Special emphasis should be placed on the establishment of such institutions in the interior of the country, where such institutions are almost non-existent.

To supply the needs for highly qualified and educated human resources, the fast-expanding Mexican tourism industry would require tens of thousands of well-trained and properly educated new employees. Since most Mexican tourism firms are rather small and cannot afford to undertake the training of such employees by themselves, the public sector would have to take the responsibility of training such employees in all job categories: managerial, professional, skilled/semi-skilled and unskilled.

In Mexican localities where in-house training is not a mandatory activity required by law or regulation, Mexican GTOs should establish joint private–public task forces to discuss various means of encouraging tourism enterprises to initiate and conduct in-house training activities.

The Mexico study found very strong support for increasing the quantity and scope of in-house training activities. The majority of respondents from both private and public sectors even favoured making such training activities mandatory. Because compulsory training may not be appropriate for each locality, it is hereby suggested that each locality should develop and implement methods that will be best suited for encouraging its tourism industry to undertake permanent training activities. Such methods could range from tax incentives, through subsidies, most favoured status and culminate with compulsory training.

GTOs in collaboration with tourism educational institutions should establish a series of no-cost or low-cost training courses for 'training the trainers' and extending inexpensive consulting services for designing and implementing in-house training programmes.

One possible explanation for the scarcity of in-house training programmes and their relatively middle-of-the-road level of effectiveness is lack of expertise in designing and implementing such programmes. As previously indicated, both the Mexican and the CF tourism industries are composed of mainly small to medium sized firms that cannot afford to purchase this expertise from external sources. Therefore, the most viable means of improving the quality of in-house training programmes is through the provision of 'training the trainer' services by the public sector.

Mexican GTOs should embark upon national or state-wide programmes to regulate and/or certify all external tourism training and educational institutions.

In Mexico, tourism educational and training institutions vary in quality and performance. Some are first-rate institutions manned by qualified administrators and experienced instructors, with teaching updated and relevant material in modern facilities. But others are mediocre, if not poor quality, programmes, manned by people who have minimal educational qualifications and little, if any, industry experience. Potential students do not possess the necessary skills to be able to distinguish between the high-quality and low-quality institutions, and it is, therefore, the responsibility of the national or state governments to regulate this sector and protect its consumers. Regulating and/or certifying such institutions will achieve consistency between programmes, and the result will be an overall increase in the quality of incoming human resources.

Mexico's National Tourism Organization, in cooperation with national education authorities and tourism industry representatives, should establish a tripartite council, the purpose of which will be to design competency-based skills standards for most occupations in the tourism industry.

The creation of such standards, which have been highly favoured by employers and GTO representatives alike, will be directly translated into training and educational programmes, and result in more effective and relevant programmes that will ensure a better fit between what is taught in the classroom and what is needed at the workplace. The council will be mandated with the periodical updating of these standards in order to meet the needs of a fast-changing industry in a period of massive technological developments.

14.5.2 The tourism industry

Tourism employers should increase the budgeting and staffing priority that is assigned to human resources development activities.

Though an overwhelming proportion of the employers in both studies recognizes the importance of human resources to the success of their business, this recognition is not reflected in budgeting and staffing allocation for training and educational activities. A significant proportion of the companies in the surveys do not allocate any financial resources to training and education, and many of the ones that do allocate too little.

The Mexican tourism industry through its trade associations should create a strong national industry body that will serve as a unified voice that represents the entire industry.

One of the possible reasons for the lack of influence and recognition from governments and political institutions is the industry's lack of cohesiveness.

To be recognized, appreciated and, most importantly, properly funded, the industry must cease to speak with many voices and unite behind one cause. Mexico would benefit by learning from the US experience in this area. Over time the tourism industry in the USA has developed an array of powerful tourism trade associations, such as the American Hotel and Lodging Association and the National Restaurant Association. Association chapter affiliates exist on state and local levels with the support of the national organization. The industry is collectively represented to the legislature through lobbying efforts in the nation's capital.

The Mexican and the CF tourism industries must strive to restructure themselves from industries that employ people in jobs to industries that offer lifetime career opportunities.

By providing career ladders and increasing the opportunities for personal development for each employee, tourism firms will be able to overcome the stigma that is often attached to this industry, namely low-paying jobs in poor working conditions with high turnover rates. Integrating jobs within the organization and providing the necessary training to be promoted along the career ladder will not only improve the motivation and satisfaction of the employees and reduce labour turnover, but will also attract more talented and educated individuals and thus totally change the industry's image.

The Mexican tourism industry, in cooperation with external tourism training and educational institutions, should endeavour to create more realistic expectations than students have of the industry and its occupations.

One possible reason for the high turnover rates that are common in the tourism industry are the false and unrealistic expectations of new employees and especially those coming out of higher education programmes. Those employees arrive at work with glamorous expectations of fun, plenty of travel, excellent pay and plush managerial jobs. When confronted with reality, they are severely disappointed and quit when a better job becomes available. To prevent this disappointment, educational institutions, with the assistance of the industry, should provide the students with a more realistic and less 'rosy' picture of the industry and thus prepare them for 'real life'. It is plausible to suggest that one of the reasons that the CF employers gave high ratings to the quality of university tourism education in CF is the realistic presentation of career expectations embedded across hospitality and tourism curricula.

The Mexican tourism industry should provide its tourism training and educational institutions with more opportunities for internships and practical training.

A large proportion of the employers in the study admitted that the industry was not providing the education sector with sufficient opportunities for student internships and practical training. If students are to be trained in subjects that are relevant to the workplace, then they have to be given the opportunity to observe and learn how the theoretical material that is presented in class is manifested at work. Increasing the number of internship and practical training opportunities will have a significant effect on the overall quality of incoming employees, even though the benefits may not be immediately apparent to employers. Once again, Mexico can learn from the US experience, where mandatory internship requirements are common among university programmes of hospitality and tourism management. To accomplish that, all industry sectors provide internship opportunities, which often result in job offers for high performers upon graduation.

The Mexican tourism industry must strive to improve the level of its employees' skills in the areas of foreign languages, computers and safety and security skills.

To be able to compete with tourism destinations in other parts of the world, the tourism employees will have to catch up with the 'high-tech/high-touch' skills (employing sophisticated technologies concurrent with providing a high level of personal service) that their colleagues in the USA, Europe and Asia/Pacific already possess.

14.6 Conclusion

Although Mexico's tourism SMEs are at an earlier stage of evolution than those in CF, both locations share a number of symptoms that seem to pose barriers of entry for qualified human resources across the categories of unskilled, skilled, professional and managerial workers. There appears to be a glaring implication that a triad of entities (industry, government and educational institutions) share responsibilities for the tribulations, as well as potential success, of the tourism industry in both destinations. Issues that include industry social status, employee preparation and post-employment training appear to be key drivers that influence tourism recruitment and retention in both regions. It seems logical that collaborative interfaces among education, industry and government should drive future strategies for tourism development and sustainability in Mexico, as well as the USA.

References

Dubinsky, A.J. (1980) Recruiting college students for the sales force. *Industrial Marketing Management* 9, 37–45.

Getz, D. (1994) Student's work experiences, perceptions and attitudes towards careers in hospitality and tourism: a longitudinal case study in Spey Valley, Scotland. *International Journal of Hospitality Management* 13(1), 25–37.

Honeycutt, E.D., Ford, J.B. and Swinyard, W.R. (1999) Student preferences for dales careers around the Pacific Rim. *Industrial Marketing Management* 28(1), 27–36.

Lewis, A. and Airey, D. (2001) Tourism careers in Trinidad and Tobago: perceptions of secondary school students. *Tourism and Hospitality Research* 3(1), 7–20.

Ross, G.F. (1992) Tourism and hospitality industry job-attainment beliefs and work values among Australian school leavers. *International Journal of Hospitality Management* 11(4), 319–330.

15 Investment Support for Tourism SMEs: a Review of Theory and Practice

STEPHEN WANHILL

School of Service Management, Bournemouth University, Poole, Dorset, UK

15.1 Introduction

Around the globe, governments have intervened to assist and regulate the private sector in tourism development because the practicalities of economics dictate that the market system has to operate under certain parameters to have any success. The complex nature of the tourist product makes it unlikely that private markets will satisfy a country's tourism policy objectives, producing a balance of facilities that meet visitor needs, benefit the host community and are compatible with the wishes of that same community. Thus, governance and the market are complementary rather than mutually exclusive activities. As Stiglitz pointed out (2002) the 'Washington Consensus' as applied to less developed countries (LDCs) and the transition economies of Eastern Europe has resulted in several false directions for the market and disillusionment on the part of many in those societies.

The growing interest in community tourism development is paralleled in the developed world, less so in LDCs because of limited capital markets, by a shift from large automatic grants attracting inward investment projects, towards small firms and indigenous development. This is a change in direction from the 'Fordist' production era of economies of scale (Curran and Blackburn, 1991) influential in the development thinking of governments prior to the 1970s, which marked a period of turbulence owing to successive 'hikes' in the price of oil. The proponents of these ideas see such constructs as offering sustainable models for the future development of outlying economic areas, since the emphasis is on the need to build regional autonomy and foster the collaboration of industry, employees and the public sector at that level. Within the European Union (EU), the objectives of the Common Regional Policy (CRP) are to 'create a greater convergence between the economies of the Member States and to ensure a better spread of the economic activities throughout its territory'. A critical aspect

©CAB International 2005. *Tourism SMEs, Service Quality and Destination Competitiveness*
(eds E. Jones and C. Haven-Tang)

of the progress to regional convergence is the position of small and medium-sized enterprises (SMEs). The argument for this is on the basis that small firms provide the community structure for entrepreneurship and job creation and flexibly customize products to customers, adapting production techniques to the specifics of place and in networking.

In a Europe-wide context, SMEs are defined as companies with a workforce fewer than 250 employees, a definition that embraces quite readily the majority of the tourism businesses in Europe, for microbusinesses (fewer than ten employees) form the largest division within the overall category of tourism SMEs (Middleton, 2000; Thomas, 2000). Currently, the most common forms of multinational assistance for SMEs in the EU are the structural funds, specifically the European Regional Development Fund (ERDF). Multinational assistance for SME development in Eastern Europe and the Commonwealth of Independent States (CIS) within the Russian sphere of influence is the province of the European Bank for Reconstruction and Development (EBRD). The ERDF is focused mainly on productive investment, infrastructure and SME development in less favoured regions, and holds the bulk of EU money for regional aid. Disadvantaged regions in Europe usually have a strong representation of micro-tourism firms performing an important role economically and socially in stabilizing fragile areas (Middleton, 2000). In this respect, tourism has received increasing amounts of regional aid under successive EU programmes (Wanhill, 1997): a notable example is Ireland, where a combination of liberalization on the demand side and investment in the product (particularly special activities, cultural heritage and genealogy), supported by grants and a reduced rate of value added tax (VAT), has produced a renaissance in Irish tourism since the mid-1980s (Deegan and Dineen, 2000).

15.2 Governments and Tourism

Since the tourism sector does not control all those factors which make up the attractiveness of a destination and the impact on the host population can be considerable, it is necessary that the options concerning the development of tourism should be considered at the highest level of government and the appropriate public administrative framework put in place to ensure both economically viable and sustainable development. As a rule, the greater the importance of tourism to a country's economy, the greater the involvement of the public sector, to the point of having a government ministry with sole responsibility for tourism. To realize the objectives of a tourism development plan, governments have to develop an investment policy conducive to developers and investors and provide a regulatory framework to ensure that development 'meets the needs of present tourists and host regions, while protecting and enhancing opportunities for the future'. Over-focus on economic effects and ignoring environmental and social impacts led to the World Bank abandoning its tourism projects division in the 1970s and 1980s. These latter values are the missing ingredients that have brought the Bank back into tourism. Only governments can have sustainability as a sole objective, since the travel trade will, in the main, sell destinations according to how profitable they are.

The case for a government investment strategy rests on concepts of market failure: where the social return to tourism projects is greater than the assigned public-sector discount rate, but private profit rates are inadequate, governments will need to give incentives to encourage the desired pattern of tourism development. For example, the stated overall objective of the UK government's support for tourism is to maximize the economic benefit of tourism to the nation, in terms of higher output and employment creation, an objective that can be found in most national tourism strategies.

Section 4 (S4) assistance, under the 1969 Development of Tourism Act (House of Commons, 1969), was intended to help realize this objective by counteracting market failure in an industry characterized by SMEs. It states that:

4. (1)   A Tourist Board shall have power –

(a)   in accordance with arrangements approved by the relevant Minister and the Treasury, to give financial assistance for the carrying out of any project which in the opinion of the Board will provide or improve tourist amenities and facilities in the country for which the Board is responsible:

(b)   with the approval of the relevant Minister and the Treasury, to carry out any such project as aforesaid.

(2)   Financial assistance under subsection (1) (a) of this section may be given by way of grant or loan or, if the project is being or is to be carried out by a company incorporated in Great Britain, by subscribing for or otherwise acquiring shares or stock in the company, or by any combination of those methods.

(3)   In making a grant or loan in accordance with arrangements approved under subsection (1) (a) of this section a Tourist Board may, subject to the arrangements, impose such terms and conditions as it thinks fit, including conditions for the repayment of a grant in specified circumstances; and Schedule 2 to this Act shall have effect for securing compliance with conditions subject to which any such grant is made.

(4)   A Tourist Board shall not dispose of any shares or stock acquired by it by virtue of this section except –

(a)   after consultation with the company in which the shares or stock are held; and

(b)   with the approval of the relevant Minister and the Treasury.

The limiting case is where governments themselves set up a tourism development corporation (TDC) and invest directly, perhaps up to 100% ownership in revenue earning activities such as hotels, which are traditionally regarded as the preserve of the private sector. Instances around the world include Egypt, India, New Zealand, Malaysia, Mexico and many African countries. In Mexico, tourism began as a totally private-sector activity. Its growth was limited in size (largely in the area of Acapulco), the product on offer was generally poor and developments were unplanned. To counteract this, the government of Mexico, in 1974, created Fondo Nacional de Formento al Turismo (FONATUR) for the purpose of developing resorts funded by oil revenues and World Bank loans. Apart from trying to regulate development, the principal reasons for state involvement were:

• Realize potential demand by increasing the number of resorts.

- Generate foreign exchange.
- Create employment.
- Regional development, in particular moving the jobless from Mexico City to the new resorts and raising regional gross domestic product (GDP).

The government gives FONATUR the development land it requires without charge, the resources to develop a master plan and the money to construct the necessary infrastructure, including hotel building. Once complete, the investment is sold to the private sector. The terms for private-sector projects are generous: loans for up to 50% of the capital investment, over a period of 15 years. The 'flagship' resort was Cancun on Mexico's Caribbean coast, but this is now mature and issues have arisen about spillover developments outside the original zone and adverse impacts on the environment.

The general drift in market-oriented economies is that, once the resort has been built, the TDC's function ceases and the assets are transferred to the private sector (at a price) and the local authority. The rising trend towards greater economic freedom, which gathered momentum during the 1980s, has led states increasingly to divest themselves of trading operations that could be undertaken by the commercial sector. On the other hand, the counter to increasing market power has been the growing concern for the environment and sustainable tourism development. Given that tourist movements will increase both nationally and internationally, there will be a need for more regulation and improved management of tourism resources to prevent environmental degradation. For example, some time ago, the European Commission (Commission of the European Communities, 1995) identified three objectives for governing EU involvement in the field of tourism:

- Supporting improvements in the quality of tourism by taking greater account of the trends in tourism demand.
- Encouraging the diversification of tourist activities and products through improving the competitiveness and profitability of the industry.
- Incorporating the concept of sustainable and balanced growth in tourism by giving due regard to the cultural and environmental dimensions of tourism.

These objectives have a wide level of support and it may be thought that the learning process of market interaction might lead to some regulating structure that can overcome identified weaknesses in the industry, thus ensuring that businesses remain economically viable, while environmental and other free goods are conserved and maintained in line with Local Agenda 21, so that the basis of the tourist industry is sustained. In practice, this is seldom the case: evidence suggests that only government intervention will enable this to happen, because of the high degree of fragmentation in the industry and asymmetric information flows.

Thus, market mechanisms will not create socially optimal solutions. Externalities are important in the expansion of tourism but not in individual private businesses; hence a practical approach to development often becomes one of regulatory control and the provision of public money and technical support to channel the energies of the private sector in directions that are both sustainable and profitable. The implementation of policy therefore becomes a process of maintaining the balance between the various objectives as opposed to trying to maximize any single one.

15.3 Implementing Investment Policy

Where there is obvious commercial profit to be gained, the government may only be required to demonstrate a commitment to tourism by, say, marketing and promoting the region, particularly abroad, and giving advice and information to prospective developers. Such circumstances occurred in Bermuda during the early 1970s and so, in order to prevent over-exploitation of the tourism resources, the Bermuda government imposed a moratorium on large hotel building (Archer and Wanhill, 1980).

Following early work by Bodlender (1982) and Jenkins (1982) and again by Bodlender and Ward (1987), it is possible to draw a broad classification of investment incentives along the following lines:

- Financial incentives:
    Reductions in capital costs.
    Reductions in operating costs.
- Investment security.

Illustrative examples of the kinds of incentives that are commonly available in many countries are shown in Table 15.1. The objective of financial incentives is to improve returns to capital so as to ensure that market potential, which is attractive to developers and investors, may be turned into financially sound projects. The purpose of providing investment security is to win investors' confidence in an industry that is very sensitive to the political environment and the

Table 15.1. Classification of investment incentives.

Capital cost reductions	Operating cost reduction	Investment security
Capital grants	Direct and indirect tax exemptions or reductions	Guarantees against nationalization and adverse legislation changes
Soft loans	A labour or training subsidy	Repatriation of invested capital, profits, dividends and interest
Equity participation	Subsidized tariffs on key inputs such as energy	Ensuring the availability of trained staff
Provision of infrastructure	Special depreciation allowances	Loan guarantees
Provision of land on concessional terms	Double taxation or unilateral relief	Provision of work permits for 'key' personnel
Tariff exemption on construction material		Availability of technical advice

economic climate, the former becoming increasingly important in recent years due to acts of terrorism and criminality.

Bloom and Mostert (1995) draw a further distinction between incentives that are financial, which may or may not yield cash flow advantages to the business, and incentives that are purely fiscal measures. The point here is that due to government budget constraints in LDCs, benefits in kind, such as site provision at minimal cost and permissive taxation rules, are more likely to prevail than cash grants or 'soft' (cheap) loans, since they do not exert direct pressure on treasury finances in the short term. In the longer term, the loss to the treasury is not predictable and, as with all legislated incentives, there is no control over the quality of the product.

15.3.1 Financial incentives

The impact of financial incentives on the amount of investment is illustrated in Fig. 15.1. The schedule SS_1 represents the supply of investable funds in the first instance, while D_1D is the schedule of returns to capital employed. D_1D slopes downwards from left to right as more and more investment opportunities are taken up – the declining marginal efficiency of investment. In the initial situation, equilibrium is at A, with the amount of investment being I_1 and the internal rate of return i_1. Conditions of market failure imply that the community benefits from tourism investment are not entirely captured in the demand function D_1D.

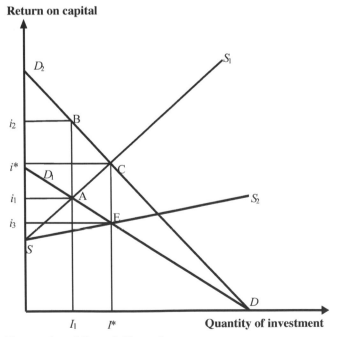

Fig. 15.1. Economics of financial incentives.

Optimal economic efficiency is where the demand function that includes these externalities, D_2D, intersects the supply curve at I^*, yielding a return i^*. To achieve this, the government implements a range of financial incentives which have the effect of raising the private rate of return per unit of capital towards the higher economic rate of return (or social rate, if issues related to the distribution of income are taken into account), by moving the marginal efficiency of investment schedule to D_2D. At i^*, the amount of government subsidy to induce entrepreneurs to invest I^* is the area i^*CEi_3, and the effective rate of subsidy, say s, is $(i^* - i_3)/i_3$, which implies that $i^* = (1 + s)i_3$ and the total subsidy is sI^*. The private opportunity cost of the investment funds is the area under the supply curve, I_1ACI^*, while the public willingness to pay for correcting the externality is the area I_1BCI^*; subtracting the two areas gives a net gain represented by the area ABC.

If the amount of investable funds available for tourism is limited at I_1, then the impact of incentives serves merely to raise the return to investors by raising the equilibrium point to B. The loss to the government treasury is the area i_1ABi_2, which equals the gain to private investors, and there is no net economic gain to the community. There is no doubt that many countries have been forced into situations that are similar to those above by the competitive pressures to obtain foreign investment. Countries can become trapped in a bidding process to secure clients and, as a result, the variety of financial incentives multiplies, together with an escalation of the effective rate of subsidy, without evaluating their necessity or their true cost to the economy.

The alternative to stimulating demand is to increase the supply of investable funds. In Fig. 15.1, this is shown by a shift in the supply function to SS_2, which reduces the cost of capital to the private sector, thus permitting the marginal project to earn an internal rate of return of i_3 and generating the optimal level of investment I^*. Typically, governments attempt to do this by establishing investment banks, arranging special credit facilities or, as noted above, constituting TDCs. The economic rationale for this is that governments are usually able to borrow at lower rates than the private sector, since they have ultimate recourse to taxation to cover their debts. In the case of LDCs, finance may be obtained from international banks and multinational aid agencies on favourable terms. The counter-arguments to adopting supply-side investment strategies are two-fold: first, there is concern that government actions should not displace or 'crowd out' capital funds from other private investments, which could do equally as well, and, secondly, the wider objectives of governments may generate institutional inefficiencies (and in some cases corruption) in the allocation of investment funds, which will frustrate progress towards I^*. These arguments have found expression in macroeconomic policy by imposing restrictions on government borrowing and the privatization of state enterprises, although the argument in the case of small firms is that existing capital market mechanisms may not be suitable for achieving tourism policy objectives due to the level of perceived risk involved in new projects. In such situations, the 'crowding out' thesis ceases to hold and the principal role of government intervention is to act as a catalyst to give confidence to investors, so that public funds are able to lever in private money by the way in which the government expresses its commitment to tourism and enable the market potential of an area to be realized. Thus, in practical terms, the implementation of financial incentives is often a combination of demand and supply initiatives.

15.3.2 Capital cost reductions

With reference to Table 15.1, capital grants are cash payments that have an immediate impact on the funding of a project, as do matching benefits in kind, such as the provision of land or facilities. Under the old planned economies of Eastern Europe, capital grants could cover up to 100% of the investment, but in market economies they rarely exceed 30%. Grants are usually preferred by investors because they are one-off transactions involving no further commitment and are therefore risk-free. From the standpoint of the authorities they are relatively easy to administer.

Soft loans are funds provided on preferential terms: at their most simple they may be the granting of interest rate relief on commercial loans. Beyond this, the government will normally have to put aside loan funds and create a development agency to administer them. Worldwide, the common features of most soft loans relate to generous interest rate terms (commonly about a third lower than the base rate), extended repayment periods (normally 15 years, with 20 as a maximum), creative patterns of repayment and usually some restriction of the debt/equity mix (a minimum requirement for 20–30% equity) so as to ensure that the project is not too highly geared in terms of loan finance. Too much loan capital in relation to owner's funds makes the business vulnerable to downturns in the market. In some instances, loans may be tied to specific sources of supply; this is very common in country-to-country (bilateral) aid programmes. Creative repayment patterns are methods designed to counter the risk profile of the project or the nature of the cash flow over the project's life. Thus a tourist project, such as a tourist attraction that may be particularly vulnerable in its early stages, can be given a moratorium on all capital repayments, and sometimes interest, for several years. Alternatively, a hotel in which the greater part of the cash flow accrues in the second half of the loan term may be granted 'balloon' financing, in which the principal is paid back towards the end of the term so as to ensure greater freedom of operation during the initial years of the investment.

Bodlender and Ward (1987) point out that providing loan funds for tourism is often considered to be more acceptable politically than the provision of grants. The argument in favour of loans rests on the fact that the funds will be recycled and the cost to the government will only be the preference element. This is not a rational argument, as all incentives have a grant component: for example, in the mid-1980s any hotel of international standard in New Zealand, with a minimum of 100 rooms, could apply for a 10.5% grant-in-lieu of a 22% first-year depreciation allowance. Major tourism development projects could get 48% grant-in-lieu of the first-year depreciation allowance on specified items. Thus it is always possible under conditions of reasonable certainty to prepare a loan scheme that will bestow exactly the same present worth as a cash grant, and vice versa.

Consider a soft loan plan whereby a potential investor is offered a loan L for T years on concessionary terms. The latter are a moratorium or 'grace' period for m years, followed by a straightforward mortgage repayment at a preferential interest rate of $p\%$ per annum for the remaining years of the loan. Under this scheme the grant element G is the difference between the initial value of the loan L and the present value of the repayment plan. Mathematically this is:

$$G = L - \left(\frac{L(\text{CRF})}{(1+r)^{m+1}} + \cdots + \frac{L(\text{CRF})}{(1+r)^T} \right)$$

where

CRF = the capital recovery factor at $p\%$ for $T - m$ years
$$= p(1+p)^{T-m} / [(1+p)^{T-m} - 1)]$$
r = the commercial cost of capital

The grant element may be further enhanced if inflation is not adequately accounted for in the repayment plan. G may also be interpreted as a reduction in the cost of capital to the project, which serves to raise the internal rate of return. The true cost of capital may be found by calculating that value of r for which $G = 0$.

In a world of uncertainty the grant is riskless, while the loan plan becomes part of the risk environment of the project. Any risk premium attached to this environment will differ from project to project, so that the equivalence of the preferential element of the loan and the capital grant can no longer be assured. The instance under which the loan is chosen in preference to the grant would correspond to the situation where the investor is unable to raise the capital funds over and above the grant from elsewhere. This raises the question as to the cause of the inability to secure funds; it may be due to the size of the project raising matters connected with the security of the investment and then it is up to the government to give the necessary guarantees.

Equity participation involves the public sector investing in the commercial aspects of tourism development with the private sector. In addition to TDCs, there are also government-sponsored development banks that have the ability to buy equity in a project. As the objective is frequently the encouragement of the private sector, there are usually restrictions on how much of the equity in a single project such banks can hold (varies from minimal to 30%), with arrangements for selling after 8–10 years, once the project has reached financial stability.

Perhaps more than any other industry, the development of tourism involves the exploitation of real estate. In many countries, the state owns considerable tracts of land and by providing sites on concessional terms the government may be able to attract the investors which best match its tourism policy objectives. The worth of such sites to investors is reinforced by the provision of the necessary construction works, such as access roads and utilities (water and energy supplies). The ownership of land for development, particularly by out-siders, is often contentious, but failure to resolve issues to do with title, leasing and planning approval is a major disincentive to investors. If land ownership is only leasehold, then this should be generous, with appropriate development compensation.

15.3.3 Operating cost reductions

To improve operating viability, governments may offer the range of incentives shown in Table 15.1. Indirect tax exemptions and reductions cover such items as waivers on import duties for materials and supplies, exemption or reductions in relation to property taxes, licences and VAT. The latter is a tax on labour and payments for capital in use, whether capital is in the form of debt or equity. As the principal form of indirect taxation around the world, pressure grows to harmonize VAT rates between nations for global industrial sectors such as tourism, on the grounds of international competitiveness (Jensen and Wanhill, 2002); for example, within the EU the standard minimum rate must be 15%. In principle, exports should receive a VAT credit and imports should be charged the same rate as domestically produced goods and services, so there is no interference to relative competitiveness, though in practice this does not apply within the single market of Europe: the range of rates may be observed from Table 15.2, which compares levels across Member States according to the components of the tourist product. Denmark levies the highest rate of VAT on tourism – a matter of continual concern to the Danish tourist industry, due to the belief that this is a key factor in the industry's poor financial performance in a very competitive market. Only three states, Denmark, Germany and the UK, apply the standard rate across the commercial aspects of this sector, which has invoked protests about unfair competition from the industry. It should be noted that those coming from outside the EU can, as a rule, reclaim VAT in relation to shopping purchases, but this is not always arranged in an administratively convenient manner for visitors.

Table 15.2. VAT in the European Union tourism industry (percentages) (from European Commission, 2002).

Country	Standard	Hotels	Restaurants	Passenger transport	Admission: fun park	Admission: museum
Austria	20	10	10	10	10	10
Belgium	21	6	21	6	6	Ex
Denmark	25	25	25	Ex	25	Ex
Finland	22	8	22	8	8	Ex
France	19.6	5.5	19.6	5.5	19.6	5.5
Germany	16	16	16	16	16	Ex
Greece	18	8	8	8	8	8
Ireland	21	12.5	12.5	Ex	12.5	Ex
Italy	20	10	10	10	10	10
Luxemburg	15	3	3	3	3	3
Netherlands	19	6	6	6	6	6
Portugal	17	5	12	5	5	Ex
Spain	16	7	7	7	7	Ex
Sweden	25	12	25	6	6	6
UK	17.5	17.5	17.5	0	17.5	17.5

Ex, exempt.

Exemption from direct (income or profits) taxes through 'tax holidays' and special depreciation allowances only have meaning when the project is profitable and therefore over the hurdle of initial start-up risks, though there is a benefit if net losses can be carried forward after the 'holiday' period. Tax holidays and reduced profit tax rates are some of the most popular forms of incentives given to new tourism projects and, more recently, are especially noticeable in the packages offered to investors by the expanding Eastern European regions and the CIS: their approach has been to offer tax holidays from 2 to 5 years after the first year's profits have been recorded, whereas such holidays have tended to be between 5 and 10 years for developments in LDCs. After the expiration of a tax holiday, governments may offer reduced rates of income or profits tax to firms, for example, in the Krygyz Republic in the CIS, depending on:

- The amount of profits invested locally.
- How much foreign exchange is generated.
- Improved economic linkages through purchases from domestic suppliers.
- Staff training undertaken by the firm.

Depreciation allowances and tax holidays are often used in tandem; thus a 5-year tax holiday may be followed by special depreciation allowances. The latter may vary from permitting the organization to write off its assets to its best advantage over an 8-year period, to providing a substantial initial allowance on the capital cost and a normal 'wear and tear' allowance thereafter. By this means, firms are able to write off more than 100% of their capital against tax, as, for example, in Western Samoa, where it has been possible to recover 120–140% of the initial investment. The effect of special depreciation allowances is to deter tax payments, which amounts to an interest-free tax loan from the government (Bloom and Mostert, 1995). This favours longer-term investments, because, the longer the life of the capital asset, the greater is the present value of the tax loan. Investment allowances favour assets that are replaced frequently, allowing the firm to take advantage of the tax savings.

The matter of labour subsidies is indicative of the employment creation objective in tourism development. Capital subsidies are criticized for promoting a capital-intensive structure, whereas the emphasis is on generating jobs. A labour subsidy will always improve employment opportunities, but the effects of a capital subsidy may actually reduce employment through switching technologies. This is less so in activities such as tourism, where many services are 'embodied' in that there is a direct link between production and consumption. Hence labour subsidies are generally combined with training payments, either at the workplace or through a government-sponsored institution. Tourist authorities can counter the contrasting effects of subsidizing capital by giving priority in funding to employment-creating projects. A ready method of doing this is to tie the amount of support to the number of full-time equivalent (FTE) jobs created (Wanhill, 2000). The latter allows for the fact that a good number of tourism jobs are often part-time or seasonal. This presumes an element of discretion in the awarding of incentives, which is not always possible when they have been laid down by legislation and are therefore automatic.

Tourism projects involving hotel developments are high users of energy, particularly where there are climatic extremes, such as in tropical areas, where there is a need for air-conditioning, or in colder climes, where the requirement is for continual heating. In these circumstances, energy use and management become a key element in the operating budget of the hotel. Large hotel corporations have always been able to negotiate energy prices with suppliers, but, where the energy supplier is a public utility, as is the case in many newly emerging destinations, then the government is able to offer the additional incentive of reduced tariffs to strengthen the profitability of the business.

Double taxation and unilateral relief are country-to-country or single country agreements to ensure that multinational investors are not taxed on the same profits in different locations. Suppose a company controlled in Country A trades in Country B through a permanent establishment in the latter country; it will pay tax on its trading profits both in Country A and Country B, but, if there is a double taxation agreement between these countries, then a tax credit in respect of Country B's tax will be allowed against Country A's tax. If there is only unilateral relief, the company will be entitled to offset its tax liability elsewhere against tax payable in Country B.

15.3.4 Investment security

Investment security is not usually questioned within Western economies, where the most common approach is state loan guarantees, but in other countries political and economic uncertainty and a deficient legal framework, particularly in respect of the protection of private property and ideas, for example, the lack of bankruptcy and patent laws or provisions against expropriation or nationalization, are among the main obstacles perceived by investors. To counter bureaucratic inefficiency, complicated administrative processes and the lack of transparency in the legislation affecting businesses, together with frequent modifications to the legislation, governments, as for example in Eastern Europe and the CIS, have established 'one-stop shop' agencies to ease the path of investors, as well as including 'grandfathering' clauses in the legislation. The latter applies to legislation that exempts new enterprises from unfavourable fiscal changes for up to 10 years.

To enhance the actions shown in Table 15.1, there is the broader issue of the government's support for tourism. National tourism administrations (NTAs) have been forced to prepare crisis management plans to counter the spillover effects of outbreaks of infectious diseases and terrorist acts. Setting the right economic climate includes the promotional activities of the NTA, reducing administrative delays, simplifying the planning process, easing frontier formalities, initiating liberal transport policies and so on. The converse, such as foreign exchange controls and restrictions on market access through protective air policies and visas, will retard tourism development and investment. Without confidence in the government to set the right economic climate for the tourist industry to prosper, investment incentives on their own may be of limited value in attracting outside funds or mobilizing domestic investment in tourism. Tourism is a sector which requires considerable public-sector support to flourish, namely, political stability and security, assurance as to the standards of facilities, and support infrastructure, such as banking services, medical facilities, communications, utilities and general retailing, which are over and above specific tourist infrastructure, such as accommodation, restaurants, attractions, entertainment and souvenir shops.

15.4 Assisting Tourism SMEs

Tourism SMEs are dominated by family businesses and owner-managers, whose motivations have been found to encompass a spectrum that runs from commercial goals and policies to lifestyle intentions (Foley and Green, 1989; Hornaday, 1990). In their classic study of Cornwall, Shaw and Williams (1990) noted that family enterprises are of two kinds: first, the self-employed, who use family labour, have little market stability, low levels of capital investment, weak management skills and are resistant to advice or change; and, second, the small employer, who uses family and non-family labour, has a better business foundation, but can share similar behaviour patterns to the self-employed and is therefore equally vulnerable.

The vulnerability of tourism SMEs is also highlighted in the work of Morrison *et al.* (1998), where they conclude that such businesses are managed essentially by their owners and have negligible market power to influence purchases and sales. The owners are often married couples, which Getz and Carlsen (2000) describe as 'copreneurs'. They are most likely to have a substantial portion of their wealth in the firm and their incomplete management expertise is no help in dealing with a difficult business climate in respect of securing finance and penetrating the market. They have a widespread inability to think more than 1 year ahead and so act as 'price-takers' in the manner of the perfectly competitive economic model, because they are unaware of market trends. It appears that transactions and information costs are taken as major barriers to obtaining knowledge of their demand curves. This forces them to behave in a cost-oriented manner in what is a market-oriented industry (Kotas and Wanhill, 1981). Hence, it is not surprising that local bank managers operate a 'rule of thumb' to the effect that about one-third of SMEs are successful, one-third are surviving in a struggle that could go either way and the remaining third should not be in business in the first place! The goal, therefore, of public intervention should be to help SMEs manage their own future, rather than spend their time 'fire-fighting' in every situation.

In deciding the appropriate intervention policy, there are a couple of significant economic considerations to take into account: namely, the distinction between 'feasibility' and 'viability' of tourism businesses or investments and the dominant cost structure in the industry. From Fig. 15.2, it may be seen that at a level of V_2 visitors the business is feasible, since it produces a surplus BC over C^*C^* (the operating costs schedule), but it is not viable because there is a gap AB in the funds available to service the capital, as the business falls between CC (the total cost schedule) and C^*C^*. To the left of D the business is neither viable nor feasible as it

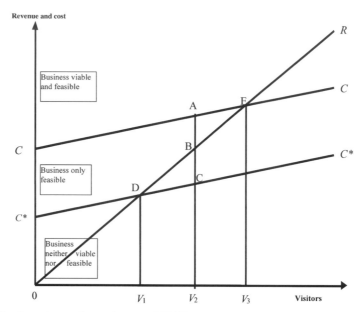

Fig. 15.2.   Investment incentives and SMEs.

falls below C^*C^*, whereas the converse is true at point E, because the revenue line now lies above CC. If intervention policy is discretionary rather than mandatory, then the area of economic interest for tourism policy should normally reside between the two cost lines where the business is feasible but not viable. The rationale for this is that viability depends upon the cost of capital, which has a floor rate that is a macroeconomic variable set by the monetary authorities. To assist a business operating at a level to the left of D would probably involve the public sector in providing continuous support and might just be 'throwing good money after bad'. Beyond point E, the business is viable and has no need of public assistance: this has been termed (Wanhill, 2000) the 'additionality rule', which is practised in the UK, whereby public assistance will only be given if the business or project would not go ahead without it, so as to ensure that firms receive what is sufficient for their needs and no more, thus allowing the government to earn 'best value' for the money that it disperses to private bodies.

Not always apparent is the principal cost structure among tourism organizations: typically, they have a high operating leverage, which means a high level of fixed costs arising out of the initial capital investment, and low operating costs, resulting in organizations that are very sensitive to variations in demand. The problem is illustrated in Fig. 15.3, where it is assumed that there are two firms that have exactly the same revenue line, R, and break-even point (BEP). However, one business has a high operating leverage, as shown by the cost line C_1, and the other a low operating leverage, represented by C_2. The possible outcomes of these two businesses are shown by V_1, V_2 and V_3. Suppose V_3 visitor levels are achieved, then the firm with the high operating leverage makes substantially more profit than the other. This is represented on Fig. 15.3 by the difference between the revenue and cost schedules, where it may be seen that

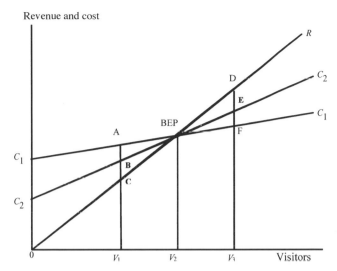

Fig. 15.3. Effects of operating leverage.

DF > DE. On the other hand, if the outcome is V_1, then the business with the cost structure C_1 will make large losses, AC > AB. In addition to the above, it has already been indicated that tourism at the destination end is extensive in its use of land and property. This tends to induce elements of real estate speculation, but the non-transferability of assets such as accommodation or attractions to other uses hinders their worth as a property investment. Add to this the seasonality of demand, which produces irregular cash flows, and it is not surprising that financial institutions view tourism developments as risky investments.

On the assumption of the desirability of the firm in terms of the overall tourism development strategy, the tourism authorities must have as a target the viability of the business after assistance has been given. To ensure viability the tourism authorities have a number of options, presented by Fig. 15.2. They could implement capital incentives, commonly 'substitute' equity in the form of grant aid or soft loans, so as to move CC down in a vertical direction to B, until the enterprise becomes viable at V_2 visitors. From a financial perspective, this is the most satisfactory option as capital incentives act directly on the main source of risk, which is the high operating leverage (Wanhill, 1986). Alternatively, the authorities may reformulate the business plan and provide technical support to facilitate market expansion to raise turnover, so as to drive the business outwards towards the break-even point E on the revenue line R at V_3 visitors. Finally, they could reduce operating costs directly by subsidizing inputs or assist in implementing efficiency/productivity measures, so as to drive down C^*C^* and bring the firm to a break-even at B.

However, in the light of the importance being attached to indigenous development at the community level and given that many small tourism businesses are trading marginally and have great difficulty in planning ahead and investing, then there are a number of activities that authorities may want to implement to 'hedge' their position through an integrated programme to combine the various options arising from Fig. 15.2, namely:

- Ensuring a sound financial structure.
- Increasing market awareness.
- Improving distribution channels.
- Upgrading the customer experience.

15.4.1 Ensuring a sound financial structure

Business finance and the ensuing funding package are in essence the result of a strategy to spread the risk inherent in any scheme in such a way as to reconcile the divergent views of borrowers and lenders. In this respect, investment incentives, besides being used to attract new business ventures, may also have the important catalytic effect of defining an acceptable risk strategy. The most important source of investable funds is domestic capital formation, which implies that effective financial institutions are necessarily a major driving force in a country's development. They are the key channel between savings and investment, and their efficiency is of great significance to economic growth. Foreign capital can also have a critical role to play: in addition to the money flows, it often brings with it higher technical standards in terms of market regulation, disclosure of information and more market services in the shape of financial instruments.

The most common themes to emerge from investigations into small business finance (Stanworth and Gray, 1991) are:

- The establishment of small business loan funds, supported, as necessary, by investment incentives, to bridge the gap in the availability of medium- to long-term finance that exists between the retail and investment banking sector.
- The creation of a small business advice or extension service.

The issue as to whether the public sector should be involved with funding SMEs depends on the effectiveness of existing financial intermediaries. A common argument is that, where there is a sophisticated capital market, the task of the state is merely to set the right economic climate via the appropriate macroeconomic controls. Yet most countries have some form of small business schemes and special consideration may be given to tourism on the basis of the complex nature of the product and the fragmented nature of the industry. An examination of Table 15.3 will show that for most EU Member States the mechanisms for tourism already exist. What is needed is an element of fine tuning to ensure that prospective investors only have to deal with one organization and that the rates of grants and the terms on which loans are made are compatible with the needs of SMEs, whose most common complaints are about access to low-interest, long-term loans and the complexity of grants. An important aspect, of which Austria is an example, is the provision of soft loans not only for new capacity (which is not always needed), but also for improving and modernizing existing facilities.

Small business funds may be channelled through the existing banking system with the appropriate state guarantees and agreements as to terms and conditions, thus reducing government administration. For example, in the UK it is possible to have state surety on 85% of a commercial loan up to £250,000.

Funds may even come from international institutions, thus the EBRD has arrangements for providing loans and making equity investments in approved domestic financial intermediaries (within Eastern Europe and the CIS) for onward lending to SMEs. Alternatively, funds may be made available through a development or investment bank, which is usually a government-financed institution that has the ability to offer loans and/or buy equity in new ventures. For microbusinesses, grant aid is often most appropriate, as they usually have substantial debt already and are in no position to lever in more. In some cases, there are separate funding schemes for particular ethnic groups, for example, the Maori in New Zealand and the Sami in Sweden. Particular sectors may also be targeted with individually tailored loan schemes: craft-workers are important for the provision of souvenirs, so special provision has been made for them in New Zealand through the Arts Council.

It would be difficult to meet the strategic objectives laid out by the EU without the creation of a small business advice or extension service. The fragmented structure of the tourist industry imposes transaction costs that are too high for the normal workings of the market mechanism to bring about the necessary changes, except at the margin. Trade associations are unlikely to have the legitimate authority and support to create such a service on their own. It follows that such a service has to come from a government-created body, usually the NTA, or, at a more local level, a partnership formed between the local authority or municipality, the tourist bureau and the various trade associations. Such actions would be an appropriate step for those regions bidding for European structural funds to develop their tourism. Where the tourist authority facilitates grants or loans in support of SMEs, an audit of the business is usually common practice and support should be conditional on the essential benchmarks and verification systems either being currently in place or in place at the end of any sponsored investment.

A small business agency may also take on a coordinating role for funding sources: SMEs can obtain sponsorship money from outside organizations, particularly when they have charitable objectives. This money can come from commercial organizations, which are looking for public relations benefits, and also other charitable institutions, for example the Heritage Lottery Fund in the UK. However, it is also possible to source equity funds through institutional contacts, lawyers, insurance brokers or business 'angels'. The latter are normally high net worth individuals with substantial business experience participating in informal venture capital networks that make themselves known to most development authorities.

15.4.2 Increasing market awareness

Wood (2001) observes that marketing information systems used within SMEs are largely confined to internal data that are supplemented by customer surveys and informal investigations about local competitors. External data tend to be drawn from personal contacts and episodic monitoring of a miscellany of sources such as trade associations and magazines. Information technology is not greatly

Table 15.3. Investment incentives in European Union tourism (from NTAs and industry departments of Member States).

Country	Special to hotels and tourism	Financial incentives		Investment security
		Capital	Operating	
Austria	Yes, more favourable than manufacturing	Grants and soft loans	Reduced VAT	State loan guarantees
Belgium	Yes	Grants and soft loans	Indirect and direct tax reductions	
Denmark	No, general schemes only			
Finland	No, general schemes only, save for VAT		Reduced VAT	
France	Yes, manufacturing similarly provided for if to do with regional development	Grants and soft loans	Indirect tax exemptions/ reductions, special depreciation allowances	
Germany	No, general schemes only			
Greece	Yes, wide range of incentives for tourism	Grants, soft loans and interest rate subsidies	Indirect and direct tax exemptions/reductions, special depreciation allowances	
Ireland	Yes	Grants	Special depreciation allowances	

Italy	Yes	Grants and soft loans	Indirect and direct tax exemptions/reductions, special depreciation allowances
Luxemburg	Yes	Grants	Indirect and direct tax exemptions/reductions
Netherlands	Yes	Grants and soft loans	
Portugal	Yes, tourism particularly favoured	Soft loans and interest rate subsidies	
Spain	Yes	Soft loans principal form of aid but grants also available	
Sweden	Yes, but only for regional development	Grants and soft loans	
UK	Yes, but only in parts of the UK	Grants principal form of aid; occasionally soft loans	

used to aid information gathering, analysis and management. Yet raising the level of market intelligence is essential if SMEs are to plan their business and target their marketing expenditure more effectively.

In order to move SMEs from a cost-oriented stance to a proactive one in the marketplace, there is a need to create an interactive database, which can be accessed from personal computer (PC) networks, to research and analyse market trends, enabling small businesses to:

- Understand their customers' needs and profile.
- Monitor the effectiveness of their marketing effort.
- Understand customer satisfaction levels.
- Monitor sources and times of bookings to establish patterns.
- Compare their demand position to the wider picture.

15.4.3 Improving distribution channels

Technology is continually making it easier to customize, package, book and price the product for the visitor. Global computer reservation system (CRS) networks have made it easier to book a foreign trip (with unequivocal price transparency) than a domestic holiday and have enabled the large players to switch to highly sophisticated database marketing to communicate their product offers to potential customers. These initially started in the 1960s as closed internal reservation systems for airlines and it was only in the mid-1970s that they were progressively opened up to other airlines and travel agents. Hotel chains and car rental companies were added later as these systems became more interconnected through a series of mergers, acquisitions and alliances.

Global CRSs are targeted at travel intermediaries, who give priority to the security of the booking, instant confirmation and the certainty of receiving commission (Beaver, 1996; Buhalis, 1998); thus the majority of suppliers, unless they are part of a tour operator's itinerary at the destination, are excluded (admittedly in some cases on their own volition by refusal to pay commissions) from selling either at home or abroad through the modern communication and reservation systems of the travel trade. Instead they resort to traditional methods of promoting themselves through marketing consortia, travel guides, tourist board guides and brochures, newspaper supplements and magazines, leaflet distribution, local media and 'word of mouth' to place their product in the market place and take bookings. This situation is not so serious in terms of domestic tourism, where the general pattern is still one of customers using local knowledge to make their own travel arrangements, but it does mean that SMEs are missing out on their share of international visitors (Buhalis, 1999).

On the other hand, the World Wide Web is growing quickly and has the potential for direct holiday information, bookings and consumer feedback, although SMEs are generally poor in e-marketing and e-commerce technologies. In addition, CRS networks are gradually becoming open to the general public through Internet portals, thus giving potential visitors the opportunity to adjust their trip to their specific needs. Internet access to airline reservation systems has also opened new possibilities for discounted last-minute air travel with established carriers and has seen the rise of low-cost airlines, such as Ryanair and EasyJet, who are not on the global networks.

For a number of years there has been government interest in creating computer-based national reservation systems. NTAs in Europe have already been operating 'holiday hotlines' and out-of-hours telephone information. In many areas, local tourist information centres (TICs) offer a booking service to personal callers, though still very much a manual system requiring TIC staff to telephone accommodation establishments to check availability. In Britain, the TIC network was used to develop the 'Book a Bed Ahead' scheme for independent travellers touring different parts of the country. However, as more and more bookings are being made electronically, a fully networked computerized reservation system is required for SMEs to benefit from:

- A database to assist with direct mail campaigns.
- Assistance in monitoring occupancy.
- Information on source markets.
- Evaluation of improvements to packaging and pricing to meet changes in demand.
- Enhancement of sales promotion through recommendations from satisfied visitors.

Beaver (1996) recommends a complete destination management system that acts as a neutral facilitator to the tourism sector. The implementation of such a system via the NTA or regional tourist association is no easy task: in the past, proposals at the local level have foundered on the unwillingness of SMEs to give commission, to make booking allocations available, competitive jealousies concerning the equity of how bookings will be distributed by TIC staff and arguments over classification and grading, an essential ingredient for the inclusion in such a scheme, as in all tourist bureau publications. Such experiences suggest that a computerized destination management system cannot be implemented or sustained without a great deal of public-sector involvement, particularly if the European Commission's ideal of Europe as a single destination is to be realized (Commission of the European Communities, 1995). Examples of such systems can be found in Austria, Denmark and Switzerland, and, although research into common European portals is ongoing, the currently favoured route among Member States is for NTAs to act as facilitators to bookings through provision of information on their websites and links to agencies providing reservation services.

15.4.4 Upgrading the customer experience

There is always the danger that investment support for SMEs is confined largely to physical capital, whereas investment in human capital may be equally, if not more, important. The latter is, for example, a particular aspect of Swedish regional policy, in which a central element is the diffusion and spread of knowledge in order to stimulate innovative development at the local level. Nilsson *et al.* (2005) report on a project in Arjeplog, northern Sweden, where the implementation of policy was through investing in the human competencies of the owners of the businesses and focusing upon motivation and business education for tourism in eight tourism SMEs over a 4-year period. The objectives were to expand the participants' ability to utilize and adjust to the changing business climate, thus raising economic efficiency. It was not simply giving consultancy advice, but was attempting, through long-term involvement, to bridge the divide between commercial and lifestyle goals by demonstrating a substantial degree of complementarity rather than mutual exclusiveness between the two goals, namely, that a better business organization can give rise to a better lifestyle. It is recognized that lifestyle goals are 'a fact of life' in small firms and investment support must accommodate them within commercial objectives.

In general, activities that may be considered to raise standards and improve competitiveness are 'benchmarking', sharing good practice and investing in the skills of both the management and the labour force. Because of generally low skill levels and long hours of work, many owners and managers of small businesses have limited knowledge of industry standards of good practice. They may be unaware of the levels of business being achieved by similar establishments, how much repeat custom is being generated, profitability ratios, and so on. The aim of benchmarking is to help SMEs achieve basic standards of good working practice and be credited for this achievement. Setting minimum standards should not create uniformity, because they should not affect the intrinsic character of the product: it will be up to the service provider to add value in order to differentiate his/her product from competitors. Exemplars can be communicated to others through trade association meetings and journals, and similar activities undertaken by the local tourist bureau. Subject areas that are candidates for benchmarking are:

- Management and financial accounting methods for improving profitability.
- Employment and development of staff, including working conditions and training.
- Quality control systems.
- Environmental management.
- Health and safety procedures.
- Equal opportunities.
- Involving staff directly in the business.
- On-site tourist information.

Benchmarking needs to be accompanied by the assessment of training needs and the development of training programmes, for example, national customer care schemes. In the UK, the government-sponsored national quality standard scheme 'Investors in People' (Investors in People, 1997; Scott, 1999) sets a level of good practice for improving organizational performance through its people. Its aims are to ensure that everyone who works in the organization understands the business objectives, is properly qualified and skilled, is committed to continual improvement and knows that the business is committed to them. This is part of the process of improving standards, thereby increasing 'value for money' and enabling operators to raise prices for a better quality product that is effectively marketed. Quality assurance is developed through classification and grading schemes, which are normally run at the national level via the NTA, and the entry of new operators into the market to displace those who do not have the means or the skills to come up to the required level. While raising the skills base can create barriers to entry, this may be regarded as beneficial if it serves to improve the products of existing firms and reduce the exit rate.

15.5 Administration of Investment Incentives

For an investment policy to be effective, it must be situated within an appropriate administrative framework. Where incentives apply to all sectors of the economy, their administration is commonly placed within the development or investment division of the Ministry of Industry and Commerce (or its equivalent), or in a separate development agency. Specific incentives for tourism are normally to be found within the Ministry of Tourism, a TDC or the NTA.

15.5.1 Organization

A tourism development organization or division can only have truly operational involvement if it is given funding to engage in projects with the private sector and implement training programmes and activities. If this is not the case, then it can only take on a coordinating and strategic role. The former is achieved by acting as a 'one-stop shop' for prospective developers, through intermediation to obtain planning permission, licences and any financial assistance or incentives from the relevant authorities. This may not always be possible, but the lack of coordination between ministries and bureaucratic delays resulting in time and cost overruns are to be avoided. In the event of these things happening, there should be an arbitration procedure where parties may seek redress.

In a strategic role the development division will acquire the planning functions, but it is better to separate these activities. The reason for this rests on the fact that an operational development division is likely to be too heavily involved in day-to-day project management to be able to incorporate long-term development planning. The latter is a research activity and therefore best located in a unit equipped for this task. The ability to offer planning services is an important addendum to the role of an NTA, in that it seeks to capitalize on the expertise of the organization to provide advice and even undertake studies for the private sector and other public bodies, for example, drawing up tourism plans for local communities.

An important aspect of any investment agency or division is the promotion of its product. This may be undertaken through trade missions and exhibitions overseas, as well as seminars and briefings for domestic investors and financiers. Collateral material can be simply an investment prospectus listing the incentives available and contact points or, more extensively, a tourism development manual.

15.5.2 Legislation

In implementing a tourism investment policy, the government has to decide to what extent incentives should be legislated as automatic entitlements, as against being discretionary awards. Automatic incentives may give too much money away, when what is required to ensure that the Treasury receives maximum benefit from its funds is the application of the additionality rule. The implication of this is an ideal situation where all incentives are discretionary and therefore offered selectively, as is generally true of the incentives given by the EU Member States (Table 15.3). The legislation for this would be fairly general, empowering the ministry responsible for tourism to offer loans, grants, tax exemptions and equity investment as it sees fit, as previously noted in the UK's Development of Tourism Act 1969.

With general investment legislation, the granting of incentives to prospective developers becomes subject to ministerial guidelines. The latter should be regularly reviewed in response to the level of tourism activity and changes in policy. These guidelines may include statements giving priority to certain kinds of tourism investments, which, for example, provide specific benefits to local or ethnic communities, extend the tourist season, enhance the range of tourist facilities at the destination, offer full-time employment, give access to disabled visitors, attract both domestic and foreign visitors and preserve the landscape. In sum, discretionary incentives allow tourist agencies to:

- Switch sector priorities with the object of encouraging new developments, modernization and achieving a balanced development of tourist facilities in specific locations.
- Support investments which have high income- and employment-creating potential.
- Select investments which have most chance of success, and are socially and environmentally sustainable.
- Adjust the money awarded to oblige the applicant to meet any investment specifications in respect of type, quality and quantity.

To have only discretionary incentives, however, is a counsel of perfection. Competition for tourism investment frequently requires countries to legislate for automatic financial help in order to attract investors in the first instance. Some countries may legislate for all the incentives discussed here, others for a subset of them. Many countries have been guilty of copying the incentive legislation of their neighbours without any real grasp of the meaning of this legislation. For example, members of the eastern Caribbean common market in the mid-1970s had totally different measures of local value added for tax purposes caused by a drafting error reversing the sign in the calculating formula.

As a rule, to control costs, government treasuries are against giving blanket reductions in general taxation, since it is difficult to prevent them applying to 'old' capital as well as new investment. The emphasis on incentives is due to their ephemeral nature for the purposes of providing the foundation for new investments to establish themselves, but equally what is to be avoided are confiscatory tax policies at a later stage to try and recover what has been given through incentives. Essentially, the tax system should be seen by investors to be simple to apply, easy to administer, transparent (therefore leaving little to discretion in tax collection), stable and robust to inflation. Businesses should be able to make project decisions with a proper understanding of the likely cash flow that will service the investment in terms of the post-tax returns to equity and loan interest plus repayments.

15.6 Conclusions

In many parts of the world, governments have intervened in tourism because the complexity of the product makes it unlikely that private markets will meet national tourism policy objectives. Investment incentives are policy instruments that can be used to correct for market failure and ensure a development partnership between the public and private sectors. The partnership approach has particular significance for regional development, particularly in peripheral areas, due to the existence of many small communities, lack of resources, areas in decline and the fragmented nature of the supply by a range of small and micro-tourist establishments. The disparate character of the industry at this level requires a proactive role from public bodies in the form of a coordinated tourism strategy and business support, in order to give a sense of direction and engender confidence through local community involvement. With tourist movements set to increase both nationally and internationally, there will be a need for more regulation, direction and improved management of tourism resources to prevent environmental degradation and implement tourism development plans in a sustainable manner.

The spillover benefits of tourism in terms of income and employment creation are well known, and, more than any other industry, tourism deals with the use of natural and cultural resources, which in outlying regions are often their major asset. The lessons of the past indicate that it is unwise for the state to abandon its ability to influence the direction of tourism development either through the provision of finance and technical assistance or through legislation. The short-term gains sought by capital markets are often at odds with the long-term sustainability of tourist environments. The appropriateness of the various financial incentives depends on understanding the nature of the business risk and the likely returns of the tourist industry, as well as the ability of the country to afford them. Thus developing countries may find themselves in no position to offer grants or cheap loans. It is evident that part of the business risk in tourist projects lies in the fact that services are perishable (a hotel bed unsold is lost for ever) and that demand is generally seasonal. This implies that peak demand determines capacity (unless capacity is regulated by planning legislation in order to preserve amenity value), so that the industry is always facing excess capacity at other times. This inculcates a certain reluctance among banks and other financial institutions to lend to the tourism industry, particularly as they often experience difficulty in appraising the financial viability of both tourism products and the managers of the enterprises. But small and medium tourism businesses, which dominate the operational aspects of the industry, are of critical importance to the progress of tourism. Apart from a range of investment incentives, what is outlined here is an action programme to create the right business environment for SMEs in order to improve their quality, diversity, competitiveness and profitability.

References

Archer, B. and Wanhill, S. (1980) *Tourism in Bermuda: an Economic Evaluation*. Bermuda Department of Tourism, Hamilton.

Beaver, A. (1996) Lack of CRS accessibility may be strangling small hoteliers, the lifeblood of European tourism. *Tourism Economics* 1(4), 341–355.

Bloom, J. and Mostert, F. (1995) Incentive guidelines for South African tourism: implications and challenges in the context of developing socio-political trends. *Tourism Economics* 1(1), 17–31.

Bodlender, J. (1982) The financing of tourism projects. *Tourism Management* 3(4), 277–284.

Bodlender, J. and Ward, T. (1987) *An Examination of Tourism Incentives*. Howarth & Howarth, London.

Buhalis, D. (1998) Strategic use of information technology in the tourist industry. *Tourism Management* 19(5), 409–421.

Buhalis, D. (1999) Tourism on the Greek Islands: issues of peripherality, competitiveness and development. *International Journal of Tourism Research* 1(5), 341–358.

Commission of the European Communities (1995) *The Role of the Union in the Field of Tourism*. COM (95), 97 final, European Commission, Brussels.

Curran, J. and Blackburn, R. (1991) *Paths of Enterprise: the Future of Small Businesses*. Routledge, London, 198 pp.

Deegan, J. and Dineen, D. (2000) Developments in Irish Tourism, 1980–96. *International Journal of Tourism Research* 2(3), 163–170.

Foley, P. and Green, H. (1989) *Small Business Success*. Paul Chapman Publishing, London, 115 pp.

Getz, D. and Carlsen, J. (2000) Characteristics and goals of family and owner-operated businesses in the rural tourism and hospitality sectors. *Tourism Management* 21(6), 547–560.

Hornaday, R. (1990) Dropping the E-words from small business research. *Journal of Small Business Management* 28(4), 22–33.

House of Commons (1969) *Development of Tourism Act 1969*. HMSO, London.

Investors in People (1997) *Better People, Better Business*. Investors in People UK, London.

Jenkins, C. (1982) The use of investment incentives for tourism in developing countries. *Tourism Management* 3(2), 91–97.

Jensen, T. and Wanhill, S. (2002) Tourism's taxing times: VAT in Europe and Denmark. *Tourism Management* 23(1), 67–79.

Kotas, R. and Wanhill, S. (1981) PSA: its nature, significance and applications. *International Journal of Tourism Management* 2(3), 176–188.

Middleton, V. (2000) The importance of micro-businesses in European tourism. In: *Proceedings of the 34th TRC Meeting*. Bologna, Italy.

Morrison, A., Rimmington, M. and Williams, C. (1998) *Entrepreneurship in the Hospitality, Tourism and Leisure Industries*. Butterworth Heinemann, Oxford, UK, 250 pp.

Nilsson, P., Petersen, T. and Wanhill, S. (2005) Public support for tourism SMEs in peripheral areas: the Arjeplog project, northern Sweden. *Service Industries Journal* (in press).

Scott, A. (1999) Investing in people? *Hospitality Review* 1(1), 26–30.

Shaw, G. and Williams, A. (1990) Tourism, economic development and the role of entrepreneurial activity. In: Cooper, C. and Lockwood, A. (eds) *Progress in Tourism, Recreation and Hospitality Management*. Belhaven Press, London, pp. 67–81.

Stanworth, J. and Gray, C. (1991) *Bolton 20 Years on: the Small Firm in the 1990s*. Paul Chapman Publishing, London, 292 pp.

Stiglitz, J. (2002) *Globalization and its Discontents*. W.W. Norton, New York, 282 pp.

Thomas, R. (2000) Small firms in the tourism industry: some conceptual issues. *International Journal of Tourism Research* 2(5), 345–353.

Wanhill, S. (1986) Which investment incentives for tourism? *Tourism Management* 7(1), 2–7.

Wanhill, S. (1997) Peripheral area tourism: a European perspective. *Progress in Tourism and Hospitality Research* 3(1), 47–70.

Wanhill, S. (2000) Small and medium tourism enterprises. *Annals of Tourism Research* 27(1), 148–163.

Wood, E. (2001) Internet use for market intelligence. *International Journal of Tourism Research* 3(4), 283–300.

16 Business Confidence in Wales: the *Wales Tourism Business Monitor*

HUGH SMITH

*Moffat Centre for Travel and Tourism Business Development,
Glasgow Caledonian University, Glasgow, UK*

16.1 Introduction

The challenges of developing tourism small and medium sized enterprises (SMEs) continue throughout the UK. Critical to any development and support mechanism offered by the public sector to the tourism sector is the availability of robust data to inform and advise tourism operators. This chapter is based on the experiences of the author in the production and delivery of a monthly business confidence survey carried out on behalf of the Wales Tourist Board (WTB) during 2001 and 2002 and published as the *Wales Tourism Business Monitor* (WTBM).

The WTBM was developed as a means of collating and utilizing industry data to aid understanding of performance in the tourism sector and to help to explore any perceived barriers to growth. The WTBM is an example of a public intervention by the WTB to supply pertinent and current management information through the production and distribution of the WTBM to tourism accommodation and visitor attractions operating within Wales.

The chapter commences with consideration of the politics of government involvement in tourism before considering the importance of SMEs to the sector. The objectives of the WTBM are then considered prior to presenting the results from the collected data. The results are further considered within the context of wider economic factors, with conclusions offered on the benefits such a study offers.

16.2 The Public Sector and Business Confidence Surveys

It is essential that the government works in partnership with the tourism sector to ensure that public-sector intervention is both necessary and appropriate. Hall (2000: 134) identified eight main types of public-sector involvement as follows:

- Coordination.
- Planning.
- Legislation and regulation.
- Government as entrepreneur.
- Stimulation.
- Social tourism.
- Tourism promotion.
- Public interest protection.

Clearly the role of government plays an important part in the success of the tourism sector, as acknowledged by authors such as Elliott (1997) and Hall (1994), who have explored such intervention to varying extents. In relation to rural tourism, Wilson *et al.*(2001) noted that the importance of local government was enhanced in areas such as: funding; promotion; infrastructure; zoning; maintenance of the community; education; and occupational support. It has also been noted that participation and collaboration with the local community, including the private and voluntary sectors, were paramount to success (Fayos-Sola, 1996; Wilson *et al.*, 2001).

Business confidence surveys are used in many sectors of the economy. For example, the Bank of England Agents' 'Summary of Business Conditions' provides a detailed analysis of information compiled from discussions held with some 2000 businesses. Other surveys, such as the quarterly Confederation of British Industry (CBI) Industrial Trends Survey, the CBI/PriceWaterhouseCoopers Financial Services Survey, the Institute of Directors Business Opinion Survey and the Chartered Institute of Marketing's Marketing Trends Survey, provide examples of those regarded as a thermometer of industry opinion, reaction and assessment of current and future markets (BDO Stoy Hayward, 2002). While the Fraser of Allander Institute conducts a Scottish Tourism Business Survey on a quarterly basis, it has been acknowledged that generally there has been a lack of research into the role of small tourism organizations in the economy of destination areas (Page *et al.*, 1999).

Academics have acknowledged that the factors influencing the growth of small firms in general can be 'many, complex and inter-related' (Barkham *et al.*, 1996: 126), and, due to each firm being unique, there is no guaranteed success formula that can produce growth (Burns and Dewhurst, 1996; Burns, 2001). However, some recommendations include networking, strengthening the community bond within the sector and using available sectoral information (Deakins and Freel, 1999).

16.3 Tourism in Wales

The tourism sector represents some 8% of the gross domestic product of Wales and accounts for 10% of all employment (Wales Tourist Board, 2000a). In Wales, 99.8% of all businesses fall into the category of SMEs, defined as those with fewer than 250 employees. This percentage is the same for the UK overall; however, when considering private enterprises, the SMEs in Wales amount to 71% of all private-sector enterprises and 63% of business turnover, compared with 57% and 54%, respectively, for the UK (Federation of Small Businesses in Wales, 2003). On a wider European scale, such businesses represent over 94% of the tourism sector (European Union, 2002). It is in the service sector, within which tourism is included, that growth has been greater in volume and rate than in any other business sector (Bryson *et al.*, 1997). Despite this perceived importance, it is 'surprising how little attention has been paid to small tourism businesses' (Shaw and Williams, 2002: 159), notwithstanding their substantial representation in many countries. Wales also has a high percentage of operators based in rural locations, with 28% of holiday trips by UK visitors taking place in a countryside/village location (Wales Tourist Board, 2000b). Richardson (2001) contends that the tourism sector relies on infrastructure provided for other purposes and that a lack of statistics that demonstrate economic significance may hinder public-sector planning for such tourism. The provision and collation of statistics on economic performance could improve the situation and contribute to enhanced investment potential as a result of 'well-informed business plans and feasibility studies'(Richardson, 2001: 57) developed from the statistical information supplied.

16.4 Towards an Understanding of Business Confidence in Wales

The First Secretary of the National Assembly for Wales stated in 2000 that the greatest challenge was to 'realise the full potential of our unique tourism assets in a sustainable way' (Wales Tourist Board, 2000a: 1). The WTBM was developed to collect and collate industry data to aid understanding of performance in the tourism sector and to help to explore any perceived barriers to growth. The WTBM was to be distributed to key public-sector tourism agencies and to tourism accommodation and visitor attractions operating within Wales. The WTB had collated business performance information on a monthly basis from specific sectors of tourism during the year 2000 and sought to develop this reportage into a more structured and continuous survey. During the period from July 2001 to December 2002 inclusive, the WTBM was produced on a monthly basis by the Moffat Centre for Travel and Tourism Business Development (the Moffat Centre), on behalf of the WTB. A total of 18 monthly newsletters were produced and distributed to the participants from the accommodation and visitor attraction tourism sectors in Wales and representatives of the WTB, VisitScotland, Northern Ireland Tourist Board and VisitBritain (formerly the English Tourism Council and British Tourist Authority).

Initially, a sample size of 60 tourism operators were identified as willing participants. The operators were selected from differing sectors, such as serviced accommodation, self-catering accommodation and visitor attractions. It was also an aim to encompass a mixture of small, medium and large businesses and also focus on regional variations between North, Mid and South Wales. However, by the end of the project there were only 40 operators that were willing to continue participation in the survey. The response rate differed on a monthly basis;

however, overall the visitor attraction sector responded more positively, with an average response rate of approximately 70%. The accommodation sector did not appear as enthusiastic in participation and accordingly the average response rate was around 50%. Some reasons for this discrepancy are highlighted in the conclusions at the end of this chapter.

The WTBM provided a detailed monthly analysis of valuable data on business confidence in the Welsh tourism sector. It supported WTB's intention to provide market intelligence, set standards and develop a proactive partnership with the tourism sector, providing tourism specific data with analysis and interpretation. The research also complemented other wider research that was being produced, including the Wales Serviced Accommodation Occupancy Survey, the Wales Self Catering Occupancy Survey and the Wales Visitor Attractions Survey.

The main purpose of the WTBM was to track the Welsh tourism sector's 'main pulse' and 'business confidence'. The development of an innovative and dynamic serviced accommodation sector, together with a revitalized visitor attractions sector, was considered essential by WTB for the future success of tourism in Wales. The main users of the WTBM reports were initially considered likely to be the WTB and tourism operators to assist in improved planning at both operational and strategic level. It was considered important that the information was provided as close to 'real time' as possible. It was anticipated that the WTBM would also be used by trade and national press and national, financial and property communities, suppliers of goods and services, consultants and industry stakeholders/opinion formers in general. The Visitor Attraction Barometer produced by the Moffat Centre on behalf of VisitScotland had already achieved the aim of valuable reporting to the sector on a monthly basis, with a rapport built up with the participants ensuring a high participation rate in excess of 90%.

The WTBM explored trends in visitor numbers and general business performance, including fluctuations in sales, pricing, salaries, employment costs, expenditure and profit and loss performance. In addition, the participants were asked to provide additional information on their levels of confidence in the operation of their business for the following year. Reportage also focused on qualitative feedback from the participants on the prospects for the sector for the year ahead. It included references to the involvement of the National Assembly for Wales in tourism and also considered operational issues for tourism businesses in rural locations.

The value of the WTBM was, however, predicated upon the information provided by the businesses involved. Separate questionnaires were developed for the visitor attractions sector and the accommodation sector. The questionnaires were posted to participating businesses for return normally by the end of the second week of the month following the month under analysis. Many of the businesses included in the survey were microbusinesses with fewer than ten employees and there were occasions where a reminder contact had to be made to obtain the completed survey. Issues such as staff shortages, meetings and the time pressures of day-to-day operations with participating businesses resulted in limited or no time being available to complete a questionnaire. In such cases, where no survey had been received by the required date, a number of methods were used to elicit a response from the participant, including telephoning the contact for the business (normally the owner or manager of the business), sending a short reminder message by e-mail or sending a facsimile message.

The information obtained from the completed surveys was input to a Microsoft Access database that had been created specifically for the project. The information received was checked to ensure as high a level of accuracy as possible. In addition to the quantitative data that were received from the participants, more qualitative data were included in the reports, including a review of recent news events that were relevant to tourism in Wales. The completed report was normally sent to each participant, together with representatives of the various tourist boards at the end of the month following the month under analysis.

16.5 2001/2002: Unusual Years for Comparison

Prior to considering the findings from the WTBM participants' feedback, it is necessary to give consideration to several factors that have been identified as having a substantial effect on the trading performance of the tourism operators. The period under analysis covered from July 2001 to December 2002. The questionnaire required that comparison was made with the previous year's performance statistics. However, for a variety of reasons 2001 and 2002 were unusual years for comparison, which should be taken into account when considering the findings of the WTBM. The specific factors which need to be taken into account include the outbreak of foot-and-mouth disease in 2001, the terrorist attack of 11 September 2001, the Queen's Golden Jubilee in 2002 and the strength of sterling.

16.5.1 The outbreak of foot-and-mouth disease, 2001

During 2001, the tourism sector was heavily affected by the foot-and-mouth outbreak that commenced in February. The damaging effects were visible in many parts of rural Wales. Information provided by Department for the Environment, Food and Rural Affairs (DEFRA) indicates that a total of 113 premises in Wales were affected by the outbreak (see Table 16.1).

Table 16.1. Number of infected premises in Wales (from Department for the Environment, Food and Rural Affairs, 2002).

	Number of infected premises
Caerphilly	2
Newport	3
Neath Port Talbot	1
Powys	70
Rhondda Cynon Taff	1
Monmouthshire	23
Isle of Anglesey	13
Total	113

Statistics provided by DEFRA and the Department of Culture, Media and Sport indicate that the outbreak led to a potential loss of business to all industries linked to tourism in the UK amounting to between £2.7 billion and £3.2 billion. Within this potential loss there were, of course, differing circumstances, where some businesses were not affected and, indeed, others may have experienced increased business due to displacement from affected areas. Losses were incurred in both rural and urban areas, although it is acknowledged that rural areas were generally more adversely affected (DEFRA, 2002). In January 2002, the National Assembly for Wales estimated the economic costs of the foot-and-mouth outbreak in relation to tourist spending at a sum of around £140 million (National Assembly for Wales, 2002). As a result of the outbreak many of the WTBM participants remained closed over the winter period of 2001/2002 and did not reopen until spring 2002. In August 2001, the most affected area was reported as the Brecon Beacons, with an estimated £50 million loss to local tourism, but some positive signs were emerging as footpaths reopened. Indeed, by the end of October 2001, 95% of paths had reopened and Wales was finally declared free of foot-and-mouth in December 2002 (National Assembly for Wales, 2002).

16.5.2 11 September 2001

The second factor to be considered concerns the terrorist attacks which took place in the USA on 11 September 2001. Various estimates of reduced visitation to the UK had been produced. In September 2001, the British Tourist Authority (now VisitBritain) estimated that there would be a downturn in overseas tourism of some 20% as a result. The following month, the Office for National Statistics anticipated a 17% reduction and the British Incoming Tour Operators Association reported a potential reduction in overseas visitors of some 26%. For Wales, the WTB estimated in December 2001 that there would be a potential decline of 15% in international tourism during 2002, equating to a potential loss of £40 million. Overseas visitation accounted for some 7% of all trips/visits to Wales during the years from 2000 to 2002 (StarUK, 2003). In June 2002, the British Tourist Authority considered that a slow recovery for overseas visitation was evident for the period between January and April 2002. This was reflected in the feedback obtained from the selected operators. Although over half of those responding indicated that the number of overseas visitors had reduced over the same period in comparison with 2001, this is an improvement on the comparative results received during the period from July to November 2001. During that period, around two-thirds of operators experienced a reduction in the number of overseas visitors in comparison with the same period in the year 2000. However, from the responses it was apparent that by the end of 2002 more static visitation was evident in comparison with 2001. In June 2002, the World Tourism Organization (WTO) reported that the decrease in world tourism arrivals during 2001 had actually been in the region of only 0.6%. Although there are, of course, varying levels of performance throughout the world, the WTO reported that Europe, in general, recorded a small decrease in arrivals.

16.5.3 The Queen's Golden Jubilee, 2002

The Queen's Golden Jubilee in 2002 also caused comparison difficulties between 2002 and 2001 due to the additional official holidays granted during June 2002. It was reported that the celebrations produced an average increase in revenue of 49% on the same period in the previous year (Wales Tourist Board, 2003b).

16.5.4 The strength of sterling

In addition, the strength of sterling was an important factor for the participating businesses. This factor had been mentioned consistently throughout the year by more than half of operators as having a detrimental impact on business performance. Figure 16.1 indicates the strength of sterling against the US dollar and the Euro over the period from July 2001 to December 2002.

16.5.5 Other factors

The cost of fuel in the UK was another factor that had been a major issue for operators and had been mentioned by a significant percentage of operators every month. The final factor for consideration was the weather, which had evoked a mixed response from operators as it was regarded as positive or negative depending on the type of operation and location. Seasonality was related to this factor and many of the operators did in fact close for a time over the winter period, reopening in time for Easter, which fell in March 2002 as opposed to April 2001. WTB statistics confirmed that some 38% of all UK visits to Wales take place during the period from July to September. In addition, some 60% of all holiday spend occurs within those 3 months (Wales Tourist Board, 2000b).

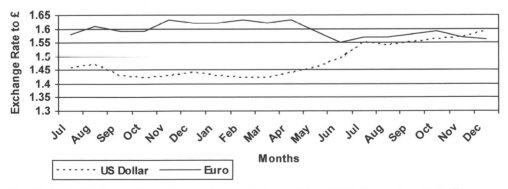

Fig. 16.1. US dollar and the Euro: value in sterling – July 2001 to December 2002 (from Bank of England, 2002).

16.6 Business Confidence Issues in Wales: Results from the WTBM (2001/2002)

Consideration will now be given to the findings and analysis of the results from the WTBM. In the wake of the foot-and-mouth outbreak, the 11 September terrorist attacks and uncertainty over conflict in the Middle East, trading had been difficult.

16.6.1 Sales and pricing

An average of some 56% of respondents identified an increase in food sales over the period, with a further 23% having suffered a decrease and the remaining 21% experienced static sales in comparison with the previous year (Fig. 16.2). However, the main positive year-on-year comparison emanated from feedback received during the latter half of 2002, with no respondents indicating a decrease in sales since May that year. This was not surprising, however, due to the comparison with 2001 data, which were affected to an extent by the foot-and-mouth outbreak.

Some 50% of respondents benefited from an increase in beverage sales, although an additional 27% experienced a decrease in comparison with the previous year's trading. The best trade performance months over the year were from March to December 2002. Accommodation sales figures demonstrated that the second half of 2001 was a particularly difficult trading period. In certain months, some two-thirds of respondents suffered a reduction in sales. However, again, since March 2002, results had been mainly positive, with the exception of the 'Easter in March' factor, as mentioned previously, which resulted in low comparisons between April 2002 and April 2001.

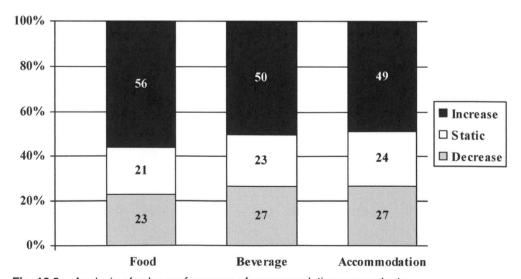

Fig. 16.2. Analysis of sales performance of accommodation respondents.

By analysing further by sector, the most positive results were relating to retail sales by visitor attractions, where some 67% of operators reported higher sales than the previous year (Fig. 16.3). When considering the visitor attraction sector, on average half of the respondents reported an increase over year 2001 figures. For the retail and catering sales statistics, a picture had emerged dividing the comparative statistics into two periods. Larger increases were evident in the comparison period from March to June 2002 than with the comparison period of July to December 2001. However, the sales from admissions were mixed, with increases and decreases being evident throughout the whole 18 months.

The reportage on all pricing indicates that prices were mainly static throughout the year until April 2002, when more operators reported an increase in food and beverage prices averaging 3.5%. However, by the end of 2002, prices were again mainly static. There is also evidence that some 15% of the accommodation operators introduced a reduced pricing policy and discount-based marketing approach for accommodation sales. Increased pricing in this sector was also evidenced by around 60% of operators from the period from April to September 2002 in response to a more positive trading environment, but again static pricing was highlighted thereafter.

16.6.2 Wages and salaries

Respondents highlighted increases in the costs of wages and salaries of operational and supervisory staff throughout the research period (Fig. 16.4). In addition, the costs of part-time workers had increased more than the other categories

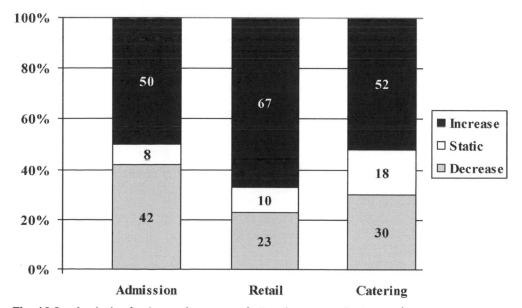

Fig. 16.3. Analysis of sales performance of attraction respondents.

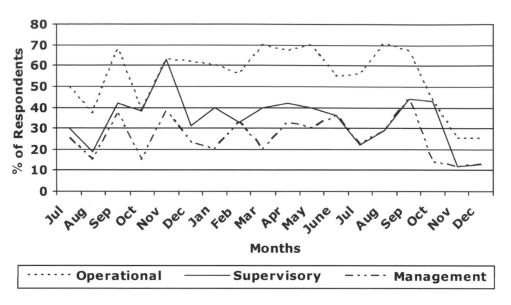

Fig. 16.4. Wages and salaries: respondents identifying an increase.

during the period. Management costs were mostly static. Some evidence of reduced costs in all categories was reported in the second half of 2001 as a result of the external pressures on businesses.

The operational staff category was also perceived as one of the most problematic to recruit alongside part-time staff. There were also difficulties in recruiting seasonal staff, particularly in the latter half of 2002, and temporary staff from spring 2002.

16.6.3 Expenditure and business performance

Although, overall, there was limited evidence of a significant change in expenditure levels by the respondents, certain categories did experience some increases. For example, electronic media, in particular, were highlighted throughout the year by an average of 60% of respondents. Investment in marketing was also a very positive factor affecting business performance, as identified by around 60% of respondents consistently throughout the year. Other positive influences were special offer promotions, bargain breaks and incentives. Summer and winter festivals also played a positive role in attracting visitors to destinations.

The negative factors affecting performance included the strength of sterling, the cost of fuel and the previously discussed impacts of the foot-and-mouth outbreak. Other negative factors included increased competition and the effects of seasonality.

16.6.4 Business confidence levels

From an analysis of the business confidence level information provided by participants over the year there is evidence of a degree of confidence in the future.

Over the period, some 31% of visitor attractions operators and 53% of accommodation respondents stated that they felt confident about the future of their business for the year ahead (Figs. 16.5 and 16.6). It was evident, however, that the confidence levels of the attractions operators reduced from August 2002, becoming more static. The accommodation operators were more confident, particularly regarding future profits, over the summer 2002 period; however, confidence in future sales diminished towards the end of 2002. Confidence was demonstrated by continued investment in information technology at an organizational level. This was further supported by some with the view that good returns were available. Mixed views were held concerning the availability of internal and external finance. At a wider level, there was participation in new promotional campaigns led by WTB and British Tourist Authority/VisitBritain such as 'Wales – The Big Country', 'Wales – Land of Myths and Legends' and 'Only in Britain – Only in 2002'. However, negative views continued on the uncertainty of future demand. Concern was expressed about the increase in the number of free attractions, notably those forming part of the National Museums and Galleries of Wales, which introduced free admission at their sites in April 2001. Some private attractions which required paid admission acknowledged that they experienced some difficulty competing against the free attractions.

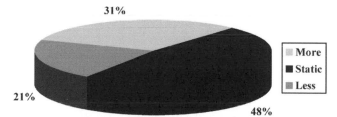

Fig. 16.5. Business confidence: attractions by confidence levels.

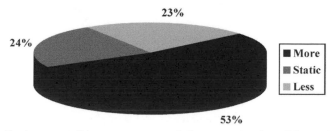

Fig. 16.6. Business confidence: accommodation operators' confidence levels.

16.7 Conclusions

In addition to the findings of the WTBM, during July and August 2002 a sample of 30 participants was asked to provide feedback on the WTBM layout and content and also highlight any issues they experienced while completing the questionnaire over its duration. Over half of the respondents provided positive comments on being able to benchmark the performance of their own business against the information provided in the WTBM, including trends analysis. In view of the extent of the information requested, a third of respondents felt that the information assisted them in the preparation of business plans and marketing strategies. All respondents provided positive feedback on the fact that the report was tourism focused, produced on a regular monthly basis and that the information was robust. Finally, some 80% of those interviewed felt that the WTBM benefited from being succinct, easy to read and in a user-friendly format.

However, there were some negative comments mentioned by the interviewees. Time is an extremely scarce resource for many small businesses. The time taken to control the operational side of the business, including employment issues where appropriate, impinged on the time available for the strategic side of operations. The completion of business surveys can at times seem the last task that an operator would wish to undertake. Several interviewees therefore mentioned that, due to this lack of available time and the quick turnaround time, the information provided may not have been as accurate as they would have liked it to be. Some respondents also mentioned that the completion of other surveys may have affected their willingness to complete the WTBM and that such surveys tend to request similar information. A small number of respondents considered the WTBM to be too detailed and that it was 'too ambitious' in its aims. They felt that the questionnaire form and the report could be further simplified. From analysis of the findings of the WTBM over the year of operation and the additional feedback received from the telephone interviews, the results were positive. The WTBM was considered a valuable report that was welcomed by the sector and encouraged a regular contribution from the participants. There were, however, some useful suggestions on improving the quality of the reportage to further enhance its usefulness to the participants and the industry in general. Suggestions that were considered include:

- Producing two separate surveys for attractions and accommodation operators.
- Obtaining a larger sample size to improve the quality of reporting.
- Analysis of regional variations and by locations such as coastal, urban and rural.
- Simplifying the questionnaire and reducing the number of questions where possible.
- Providing incentives for participation in the business monitor, for example, such incentives could have included the introduction of best practice seminars and 'master classes' for which there would have been no fee for participating operators.

- Introducing an on-line version of the questionnaire to improve the number of actual participants.
- Investigating the possibility of amalgamating the monitor with other surveys that were undertaken in Wales.

The WTBM provided a foundation upon which the opportunity exists to build a more valuable and accurate monitor. It enjoyed industry usage and merited further development, but such development, has to be undertaken with cognizance of other ongoing data capture. In this respect, WTB is considering joining the quarterly UK Business Barometer Survey conducted by VisitBritain. This survey and other surveys, such as the *WTB Easter Survey* (Wales Tourist Board, 2003a) produced in April 2003 and the *Tourism Trends Digest* (Wales Tourist Board, 2003b), will continue to provide the linkage between public-sector organizations with a remit to develop tourism and private- and public-sector operators within Wales. Its existence will also contribute towards ensuring there is an ongoing supply of relevant sectoral information for tourism in Wales.

References

Barkham, R., Fagg, J. and Stone, I. (1996) *The Determinants of Small Firm Growth: an Inter-regional Study in the United Kingdom 1986–1990*. Jessica Kingsley, London, 167 pp.

Bank of England (2002) www.bankofengland.co.uk/mfsd

BDO Stoy Hayward (2002) *The BDO Business Trends Report – August 2002*. BDO Stoy Hayward, London.

Bryson, J.R., Keeble, D.E. and Wood, P. (1997) The creation and growth of small business service firms in post-industrial Britain. *Small Business Economics* 19(4), 345–360.

Burns, P. (2001) *Entrepreneurship and Small Business*. Palgrave, Basingstoke, UK, 418 pp.

Burns, P. and Dewhurst, J. (eds) (1996) *Small Business and Entrepreneurship*, 2nd Edn. Macmillan, London, 352 pp.

Deakins, D. and Freel, M.S. (1999) *Entrepreneurship and Small Firms*, 2nd Edn. McGraw Hill, London, 278 pp.

DEFRA (Department for the Environment, Food and Rural Affairs) (2002) *Foot and Mouth Disease 2001: Lessons to be Learned Inquiry*, www.defra.gov.uk/footandmouth

Elliott, J. (1997) *Tourism, Politics and Public Sector Management*. Routledge, London, 279 pp.

European Union (2002) *Enterprise and Tourism*, http://europa.eu.int/comm/enterprise/services/tourism/index_en.htm

Fayos-Sola, E. (1996) Tourism policy: a midsummer night's dream? *Tourism Management* 17(6), 405-412.

Federation of Small Businesses in Wales (2003) www.fsb.org.uk/policy

Hall, C.M. (1994) *Tourism and Politics, Policy, Power and Place*. John Wiley & Sons, Chichester, UK, 238 pp.

Hall, C.M. (2000) *Tourism Planning: Policies, Processes and Relationships*. Prentice Hall, Harlow, UK, 236 pp.

National Assembly for Wales (2002) www.wales.gov.uk

Page, S.J., Forer, P. and Lawton, G.R. (1999) Small business development and tourism: terra incognita? *Tourism Management* 20(4), 435–459.

Richardson, P. (2001) Rural tourism micro-enterprises (RTME) sector statistics: the need for and current lack of statistics in RTME. In: Lennon, J.J. (ed.) *Tourism Statistics: International Perspectives and Current Issues*. Continuum, London, pp. 52–58.

Shaw, G. and Williams, A.M. (2002) *Critical Issues in Tourism – A Geographical Perspective*, 2nd edn. Blackwell, Oxford, UK, 371 pp.

StarUK (2003) www.staruk.org

Wales Tourist Board (2000a) *Achieving Our Potential. A Tourism Strategy for Wales*. Wales Tourist Board, Cardiff, UK.

Wales Tourist Board (2000b) *Tourism in Wales, 1999*. Wales Tourist Board, Cardiff, UK.

Wales Tourist Board (2003a) *WTB Easter Survey – April 2003*. Beaufort Research, Cardiff, UK.

Wales Tourist Board (2003b) *Tourism Trends Digest*. Wales Tourist Board, Cardiff, UK.

Wilson, S., Fesenmaier, D.R., Fesenmaier, J. and van Es, J.C. (2001) Factors for success in rural tourism development. *Journal of Travel Research* 40(2), 132–137.

World Tourism Organization (2002) *Tourism Proves as a Resilient and Stable Economic Sector*, http://www.worldtourism.org/newsroom/Releases/morereleases/june2002/data.htm

17 The Role of a National Tourism Organization in Developing a National Tourism Quality Scheme: the Case of Hungary

ZSUZSANNA BEHRINGER AND TÜNDE MESTER

Directorate for Marketing Research, Hungarian National Tourist Office, Budapest, Hungary

17.1 Introduction

Tourism has a key role in the Hungarian economy, currently generating 5 8% of Hungarian gross domestic product (GDP) and with a good potential for growth. After the breakup of the Soviet Union in the early 1990s, while the Hungarian tourism industry has had the opportunity to develop new markets in response to the growing interest in Hungary as a tourism destination, it has also had to address new challenges – not least consumer demands for a higher quality product. Privatization has led to a significant increase in the number of tourism small and medium-sized enterprises (SMEs), although their economic contribution has remained low. However, both the public and private sectors agree about the importance of tourism and the emerging need for standardization and quality control. In response to this, the Hungarian National Tourist Office (HNTO), which coordinates the various sectors of the Hungarian tourism industry, has launched its new project: the Hungarian Tourism Quality Award (HTQA), which is based on total quality management (TQM) and the European model for business excellence developed by the European Foundation for Quality Management (EFQM). The aim of HTQA is to improve the quality and competitiveness of the Hungarian tourism product.

This chapter describes the development of HTQA. As HTQA is a new initiative, the HNTO has to: prepare criteria for the tourism sector; assess the use of quality management methods by service providers; and research their willingness to participate in HTQA. Additionally, the HNTO has surveyed the needs and expectations of tourists in order to establish quality criteria and to persuade service providers to participate in HTQA. The research is framed within the context of the current operating situation for the Hungarian tourism industry, in particular, the different conditions experienced by tourism SMEs.

©CAB International 2005. *Tourism SMEs, Service Quality and Destination Competitiveness* (eds E. Jones and C. Haven-Tang)

17.2 The Hungarian Context for Tourism Development

17.2.1 Social and economic context

The transition period from communism to a market economy in Hungary started in the late 1980s and continued into the early 1990s and was precipitated by the drawing back and falling apart of the Soviet Union, which resulted in the transformation of the economies of all the countries of the region, accelerated by globalization (Csáki *et al.*, 2001). The most significant change was probably the privatization and disintegration of state property. By 1994, 82% of companies were in private ownership and 15% were foreign-owned, with only 3% of companies remaining in public ownership. The concept of private property had been practically non-existent in Hungary before this period (Németh, 2001).

The transition to a market economy required the establishment of appropriate legal and monetary systems. The Hungarian National Bank (HNB) was made (relatively) independent from the government and, by the end of the 1990s, a 'Western style' banking system was established. New foreign exchange laws were passed and the Hungarian forint (HUF) became convertible. One of the most important changes was the liberalization of foreign trade and, as a result, Hungarian foreign trade relations changed completely, so, while in 1985 70–80% of the trade was with the Council for Mutual Economic Assistance (COMECON), by 1995 the proportion of trade with the European Union (EU) was 70% and a significant volume increase was reached (Magyar Nemzeti Bank, 1990–2002). Today, Hungarian company law is practically in accordance with the European norms. Some implications of transition were less favourable to the Hungarian economy – the rate of inflation and unemployment increased significantly. By the end of the 1990s, inflation had been reduced to some extent, but unemployment remained high. In 2002 the rate of unemployment was 5.8% and the rate of inflation was 5.3% (Központi Statisztikai Hivatal, 2003a).

17.2.2 Development of the Hungarian tourism industry: 1990–2002

After 1990, Hungary's most important tourism indicators, i.e. visitor numbers and income from tourism, started to increase (see Fig. 17.1). In parallel to this, the number of Hungarians travelling abroad remained constant during this period (Központi Statisztikai Hivatal, 1990–2001, 2003b; Magyar Nemzeti Bank, 1990–2002).

Hungarian tourism was unfavourably influenced by a series of crises that took place on the Balkan Peninsula, predominantly the war in Sarajevo in 1994, conflict between Bosnia and Croatia in 1995 and the war in Kosovo and the North Atlantic Treaty Organization (NATO) bombing of Belgrade and other places in Yugoslavia in 1999 (Infoplease.com, 2002). Although 1996 saw a downturn in the number of visitors to Hungary, tourism receipts increased dramatically as visitors arriving by plane and staying in better hotels have a higher per capita spend. Hungary's traditional tourism-generating markets are

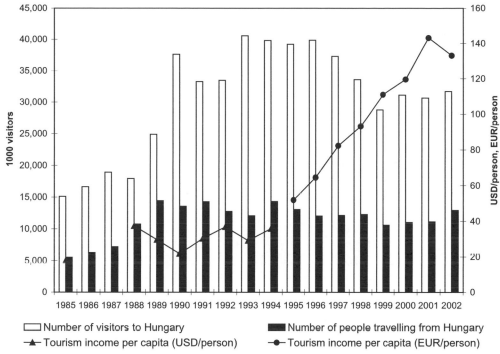

Fig. 17.1. The development of Hungary's most important tourism indicators, 1990–2001. USD, US dollars; EUR, Euros. (From Központi Statisztikai Hivatal 1990–2001, 2003b; Magyar Nemzeti Bank 1990–2002.)

Germany, Switzerland, Italy, the Benelux countries, the USA and Poland. New markets include Russia, the Czech Republic, France, Spain, Portugal, Scandinavia, the UK, Greece, Israel, Japan, China, South America and Canada. Currently the major tourism-generating countries are: Austria, Romania, Slovakia, Croatia, Germany, Yugoslavia, Slovenia, Poland, Italy, the USA, the Czech Republic, Greece, The Netherlands, the UK, Turkey, France, Switzerland and Scandinavia. Global issues, *e.g.* economic recession, climate changes, health and security problems, terrorism and wars, have had a negative impact on Hungarian tourism – in the first 6 months of 2003, the number of visitors increased by only 2.2% and tourism receipts decreased by 14.1% compared with the same period in 2002 (Központi Statisztikai Hivatal, 2003c).

17.2.3 Tourism SMEs in Hungary

17.2.3.1 Defining SMEs in Hungary

Micro-enterprises employ fewer than ten people. Small enterprises have fewer than 50 employees and net sales of either less than 700 million HUF or a balance sheet total of less than 500 million HUF. Medium-sized enterprises have fewer than 250 employees and net sales of less than 4 billion HUF or a balance sheet total of less than 2.7 billion HUF.

17.2.3.2 Characteristics of the Hungarian SME sector

In the 1970s, and 1980s, the Hungarian economy was like an 'upside-down pyramid' and alongside giant (but not strong) state-owned companies were a small number of weak privately owned SMEs. By the mid-1990s, this upside-down pyramid had been transformed into an 'hourglass' rather than a normal pyramid (Árva et al., 2001). This model shows that the significance of large enterprises in the Hungarian economy was maintained and, although a wide range of SMEs were established, these enterprises are not organically connected to the sphere of large enterprises. Table 17.1 shows the relative numbers of micro-, small, medium and large enterprises. Micro-enterprises, despite their outstandingly high number, account for only a small contribution to the gross value added (GVA) (which, together with the balance on product taxes and subsidies, estimates their contribution to the GDP, although there are no data available on this) as opposed to the small number of large companies, which make a large contribution to GVA (Kállay et al., 2002).

17.2.3.3 Tourism SMEs in Hungary

The HNTO has published detailed information on tourism enterprises for the period 1996–1999 (Behringer, 2001). Of all existing enterprises, 4% operate in the field of tourism (including accommodation establishments and catering facilities) and employ 3% of the Hungarian workforce. Between 1996 and 1999, the number of tourism enterprises grew by 28%, the number of employees by 12% and the proportion of equity capital in tourism SMEs increased from 2% to 3%. The number of large enterprises declined by 8%, while the number of medium-sized, small and micro-enterprises increased by 13%, 16% and 30%, respectively.

Table 17.1. The economic significance of enterprises, 2001 (from Kállay et al., 2002).

	Micro-enterprises[a] (%)	Small enterprises (%)	Medium enterprises (%)	Large enterprises (%)
Number	96.3	3.0	0.6	0.1
Employees	38.5	13.8	15.1	32.6
Net sales	13.3	7.9	17.8	61.0
Contribution to gross value added	10.5	8.7	16.5	64.3

[a]Enterprises without employees included.

17.2.3.4 SWOT analysis of Hungarian tourism SMEs

Table 17.2 summarizes a SWOT analysis of Hungarian tourism SMEs developed from an analysis of secondary data (Árva *et al.*, 2001; Behringer, 2001). Strengths include: strong domestic and inbound tourism markets; stable economic, political and social conditions; early presence of large foreign companies brings international quality standards; traditional family ventures and brands; tourism service prices which represent good value for money. The major weaknesses are: lack of marketing orientation and consumer-friendly attitude;

Table 17.2. SWOT analysis of Hungarian tourism SMEs (from Behringer, 2001).

Strengths	Weaknesses
• Traditional family ventures and brands meant good starting point at the beginning of transition	• Credit problems
	• World crises have an unfavourable effect on inbound tourism
• Attractive living conditions	• Part of the population has been elbowed out from domestic (and also outbound tourism) by income restructuring
• Hungary was a relatively popular tourist destination before the transition	
• Stable economic, political and social conditions in the country	• Inappropriate management skills
• A stable domestic consumer segment with travel behaviour by the end of transition	• Lack of proper professional training
	• Lack of competent knowledge of languages
• Large foreign companies were present quite early in Hungary, countless techniques and procedures have been adopted	• Market- and consumer-oriented attitude has not yet spread sufficiently
	• Quality problems
• Favourable price level of tourism services	• Negative impacts of complicated administration, especially on small ventures
• Strong domestic and inbound tourism	• Insufficient growth of interest protection and professional organizations
• Tourist attractions	
• Hospitality	
• Security	
Opportunities	**Threats**
• Progressing EU integration	• World economic recession
• Rapid development of e-commerce	• Global climate changes
• Increasing Foreign Direct Investment inflow	• Health problems, Severe Acute Respiratory Syndrome (SARS)
• Growing interest in Central and Eastern Europe as a tourist destination	• General fear of terrorist attacks
	• War in Afghanistan and Iraq
• Growing interest of European tourists for close and safe destinations	• No sign of a solution for credit problems
• Due to the economic recession, price/value ratio becomes more and more important	• No sign of simplification of administration obligations
• National development plan	• Disappointed tourists can 'promote' Hungary as a 'not expensive, but not very good either' destination
• Széchenyi plan	

over-bureaucratic administrative and financial systems; environmental difficulties; and under-exploitation of SME advantages.

Opportunities include the recent growth of interest in Europe, particularly Central and Eastern Europe, and the rapid uptake of e-commerce. Hungary joined the EU on 1 May 2004 and subsequently became eligible for support from EU structural funds and cohesion fund, most notably Objective 1 funding for underdeveloped regions (i.e. regions where the per capita GDP is below 75% of the EU average). To secure this funding, the Hungarian government must prepare a national development plan and will continue the work of the Széchenyi Plan – a medium-term economic development programme launched at the end of 2000, in which tourism is one of seven main programme areas, seeking to improve the efficiency of inbound tourism, strengthen domestic tourism and improve service quality.

Although ongoing bureaucracy and issues for credit provision create serious threats to tourism SME development, the most overwhelming problem for the Hungarian tourism industry is visitor perceptions of Hungary as a cheap but poor-quality destination. It is this specific problem that the HTQA is designed to address.

17.3 The Hungarian Tourism Quality Award

The HTQA, planned to be launched in 2005, is designed to orientate the tourism industry to improve the quality of its services. The HNTO – a marketing organization that networks with the whole Hungarian tourism industry – is developing the HTQA. However, the management of HTQA is likely to be coordinated by the Ministry of Economy and Transport. The HTQA is based on TQM and EFQM and aims to improve the quality and competitiveness of the Hungarian tourism product and the quality consciousness of suppliers. The HTQA will be a marketing tool in domestic and international markets. While ultimately criteria will be developed for all products in the tourism service chain, there is an initial focus on the development of criteria for tour operators and travel agencies, accommodation establishments, tourist guides and pubs and restaurants.

The Award will be the sign of trust for both consumers and suppliers. Service providers will be able to apply for HTQA voluntarily, evaluating themselves after a training course and achieving the Award for 2 years. During this period they can be checked at any time by mystery shoppers. HNTO will prepare a special brochure to promote the enterprises that have achieved the Award. The Award will benefit enterprises bidding for financial support from the Ministry of Economy and Transport.

17.4 Methodology

From exploratory research undertaken by college students and our other sources of secondary information, the following hypotheses were formulated:

- There are gaps between supply and demand perceptions of the importance of quality – consumers consider quality important and feel that suppliers do not properly understand their needs and expectations.
- Managers of hotels and restaurants with loyal customer bases understand their guests' expectations.
- Word of mouth is an important quality indicator.
- HTQA will promote consumer confidence, especially for SMEs.
- HTQA may not add value to larger and chain businesses, which are strong, established brands, although this may change once HTQA is well established.
- Big service providers may benefit from being founding partners in HTQA.

Primary research carried out in June 2002 involved a quantitative survey of 784 domestic tourists and 508 service providers. The opinions and attitudes of domestic tourists were gathered using face-to-face interviews in the home of interviewees. Random stratified sampling was used so that the sample was geographically representative and appropriately weighted for gender and age. The survey of service providers included tour operators, travel agents, accommodation establishments, restaurants, pubs and tourist guides and was designed to be representative of a type of activity and geographical location. All Hungarian five-star hotels were interviewed and the surveys were prepared by HNTO's contractual partner, MÁST Market and Public Opinion Research Company (MT RT, MÁST, 2002).

17.5 Results and Discussion

17.5.1 Consumer behaviour

Table 17.3 summarizes the most important factors in tourism service provider selection by consumers. For travel agents, accommodation establishments and restaurants/pubs, the price/value ratio and quality were rated as the most important factors when selecting tourism service providers. For travel agents, the

Table 17.3. Hungarian consumer ratings of the importance of different factors when selecting tourism service providers (from MT RT, MÁST, 2002).

Factor	Travel agent	Accommodation establishments	Restaurants and pubs	Tourist guides
1	Price/value ratio	Price/value ratio	Price/value ratio	Expertise and professional knowledge
2	Quality	Quality	Quality	Helpfulness
3	Good previous experience	Hygiene	Hygiene	Friendliness
4	Expertise of employees	Security	Nice atmosphere	–

expertise of the employees and good previous experiences were influential in their selection behaviour. For both accommodation establishments and restaurants/pubs, hygiene was the next most important factor, with security being the next most important for accommodation establishments and nice atmosphere being the next most important for restaurants/pubs. For tourist guides, the most important factors relate to the quality of the interaction between the guide and the customer with expertise and professional knowledge being followed by helpfulness and friendliness.

17.5.2 Attitudes towards quality

We asked the entrepreneurs in the study to evaluate the importance of quality at their company. They had to use a seven-point Likert scale to evaluate, where 7 equals absolutely important and 1 equals not important at all (see Fig. 17.2). Generally the supply side understands the importance of quality for customers. However, it is disappointing that quality is not an absolute priority for all sizes of businesses. The average mean rating was 7.0 in the case of large companies, but it was only 6.88 in the case of medium and small enterprises and the average mean rating was only 6.77 in the case of micro-enterprises. When we examined micro-sized companies according to their activities, we found that micro-sized pubs and restaurants rated quality least important (mean rating 6.5) and tourist guides the highest mean rating, which presumably reflects the way they interact with consumers and the continuous requirement for high performance.

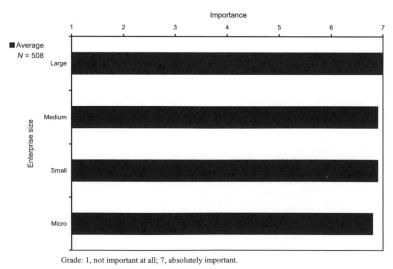

Grade: 1, not important at all; 7, absolutely important.

Fig. 17.2. Importance of quality at the interviewed enterprises (from MT RT, MÁST, 2002).

17.5.3 Awareness of consumer expectations

Both the demand and the supply side were evaluated to ascertain service provider awareness of consumer expectations (see Table 17.4). Suppliers rated their awareness of consumer expectations much higher than the consumers rated their supplier awareness, emphasizing a gap in understanding consumer expectations.

17.5.4 Understanding of consumer satisfaction

This gap in understanding of customer expectations leads to disgruntled and misunderstood consumers. According to our survey (see Table 17.5), tourists feel that service providers are even less aware of their satisfaction than they are of their expectations. Proper management of customer complaints would give service providers an insight into areas of underperformance.

Table 17.4. Knowledge of consumer expectations evaluated by consumers (demand) and service providers (supply). Mean response to attitudes towards quality on a Likert Scale with 1 = not important and 7 = very important (from MT RT, MÁST, 2002).

	Demand	Supply		
		Micro	Small	Medium
Tour operators and travel agents	3.9	6.4	6.3	6.6
Accommodation	4.3	6.4	6.7	6.6
Restaurants and pubs	4.5	6.3	6.3	6.7
Tourist guide	4.0	6.6	–	–

Table 17.5. Knowledge of consumer satisfaction evaluated by consumers (demand) and service providers (supply). Mean response to attitudes towards quality on a Likert Scale with 1 = not important and 7 = very important (from: MT RT, MÁST, 2002).

	Demand	Supply		
		Micro	Small	Medium
Tour operators and travel agents	3.6	6.3	6.4	6.3
Accommodation	4.1	6.2	6.7	6.6
Restaurants and pubs	4.3	6.2	6.3	6.2
Tourist guide	3.8	7.0	–	–

17.5.5 Assuring quality in Hungarian tourism SMEs

Most micro- and small-sized service providers did not have any quality systems in place. Among medium-sized enterprises, 60% of tour operators and travel agents, 72% of accommodation establishments and 67% of restaurants and pubs already have some kind of quality system. The International Organization for Standardization (ISO) and Hazard Analysis and Critical Control Points (HACCP) were mentioned most frequently, but internal quality control systems (e.g. at a hotel chain) were mentioned as well. Only 28% of service providers plan to introduce quality systems. However, for restaurants and pubs HACCP was compulsory from 2003.

17.5.6 The need for HTQA

Although this may lead to some improvements, our research (MT RT, MÁST, 2002) shows that these quality control systems are not sufficient. Tourism as a service is characterized by heterogeneity, intangibility, perishability and inseparability (HIPI). Since tourism products are delivered outside a consumer's normal environment, tourists need to be confident that service quality is appropriate. This is likely to be even more important for inbound tourists. HTQA has the potential to enhance consumer confidence in service providers.

Nearly three-quarters of consumers think that there is a need for the HTQA for tour operators and travel agents, accommodation establishments and restaurants and pubs (see Table 17.6). On the supplier side, small-sized enterprises are more enthusiastic than micro- and medium-sized ones (see Fig. 17.3). Generally, accommodation establishments are very committed to the concept of HTQA, while restaurants and pubs are more reserved. Consumers are less concerned about HTQA in relation to tourist guides, which may reflect the fact that travel agents act as intermediaries in the selection of tourist guides and that quality issues in relation to tourist guides will be dealt with by travel agents. Some tourist guides expressed a desire for independent evaluation, which would open up the market.

Table 17.6. Percentage of consumers and service providers who considered there is a need for the Hungarian Tourism Quality Award (HTQA) (from MT RT, MÁST, 2002).

	Demand	Supply		
		Micro	Small	Medium
Tour operators and travel agents	73%	67.8%	78.6%	73.3%
Accommodation	73%	77.6%	91.7%	87.9%
Restaurants and pubs	71%	65.4%	92.3%	66.7%
Tourist guide	55%	74%	–	–

17.5.7 The HTQA advantage

Consumers think that companies with HTQA will derive benefits and be more competitive (see Table 17.7). Presumably this implies that HTQA will promote consumer confidence and that consumers are more likely to select an HTQA-accredited service provider.

Some 92% of consumers reported that they would prefer to choose an HTQA-accredited tour operator or a travel agency, 91% reported that they would prefer to choose an HTQA-accredited accommodation establishment, 93% would prefer an HTQA-accredited restaurant or pub and 88% would rather choose an HTQA-accredited tourist guide instead of an operator without HTQA. Nevertheless, an interesting finding is that in spite of this fact, a smaller proportion of micro-, small- and medium-sized companies expect HTQA to provide them with advantages, with the lowest percentages registered among pub and restaurant managers.

Furthermore, consumers reported (MT RT, MÁST, 2002) that their confidence will be stronger, the quality of services will be improved and hygiene will

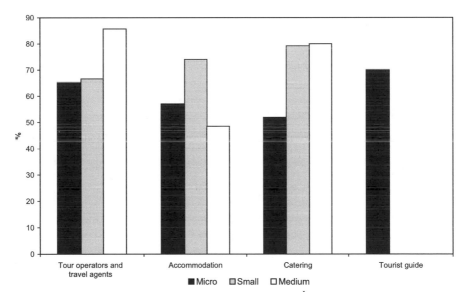

Fig. 17.3. SMEs willing to join HTQA (from MT RT, MÁST, 2002).

Table 17.7. Advantage provided by HTQA according to consumers (demand) and service providers (supply) (from MT RT, MÁST, 2002).

	Demand	Supply		
		Micro	Small	Medium
Tour operators and travel agents	92%	74%	7%	10%
Accommodation	91%	42%	36%	10%
Restaurants and pubs	93%	17%	22%	2%
Tourist guide	88%	68%	–	–

be better. Those with negative feelings towards HTQA mentioned that HTQA could be devalued by corrupt practices and it is important that the HNTO therefore addresses this issue during the introduction of HTQA.

In addition to information shown in Table 17.7, we found (MT RT, MÁST, 2002) that larger service providers express less enthusiasm for participation in HTQA. Those providers against HTQA argue that they are only interested in the opinion of their guests, or they do not need this qualification because they have regular guests. Some service providers expressed a fear of HTQA resulting in higher additional costs. Providers who welcome HTQA expect stronger consumer confidence and that it will enable the benchmarking of the performance of different service providers. Furthermore they recognize that HTQA could be a powerful marketing tool for them.

The HNTO must take all issues into consideration when introducing HTQA. However, it is clear that, with proper marketing, this Award could be widely adopted and much coveted. Consumer demand might be the most powerful instrument in encouraging participation among even the largest providers. As more service providers join HTQA, it will become an imperative to maintaining market position and competitiveness.

17.5.8 HTQA evaluation criteria

Last, but not least, the demand and the supply sides were invited to identify criteria for HTQA. Appropriate criteria must match customer expectations. However, differences were observed between the suppliers and the customers (see Table 17.8).

Generally, consumers consider price very important. Although price cannot be a criterion for HTQA, having a clear pricing policy can be a criterion. Consumers are more interested in overall quality than in the qualifications of staff.

Table 17.8. Evaluation criteria of tourism sectors suggested by consumers (demand) and service providers (supply) (from MT RT, MÁST, 2002).

	Demand side	Supply side
Tour operators and travel agents	Price Reliability Quality	Quality of services Reliability Qualification of staff
Accommodation establishments	Hygiene Price Behaviour of staff	Quality of services Expertise Hygiene
Restaurants and pubs	Price Hygiene Attentive service	Quality of services Hygiene Expertise
Tourist guides	Expertise Friendliness Helpfulness	Professional knowledge Knowledge of foreign language Personal suitability

Reliability is considered very important for both supply and demand. In the case of tour operators and travel agents, consumers and managers agree that quality and reliability are important, although their order of importance is different. In the case of accommodation establishments and pubs and restaurants, hygiene and the human factor are considered important by demand and supply sides, but their importance ranking of these factors differs. In the case of tourist guides, expertise is of equal importance to consumers and guides, but consumers placed more emphasis on the personal elements.

We noted an interesting difference between the demand and the supply side in the case of human factors: behaviour and attitude. The 'emotional aspects' (behaviour, attentive service, friendliness, helpfulness) are more important for consumers than for managers. Managers tend to think of objective criteria which can be standardized and which are not based on individual personalities, such as qualifications of staff, expertise and professional knowledge.

When we examined this topic from the perspective of company size using more in-depth information from our research (MT RT, MÁST, 2002), we found that there are some differences between the criteria set by different-sized companies. Micro-sized enterprises agreed with the above criteria, but small-sized enterprises consider qualifications of staff, consumer-friendly attitudes of their employees and consumer satisfaction the three most important factors. Medium-sized companies evaluate reliability, overall quality of service, qualifications of staff and stable financial background as equally important. Quality, followed by expertise and then hygiene, is considered most important by accommodation providers. Small-sized enterprises consider the behaviour of staff more important than hygiene, and medium-sized enterprises rate the range of services more important than hygiene; therefore, there is a wide gap, which can lead to consumer dissatisfaction.

There are differences between the criteria system of consumers and service providers for restaurants and pubs. Consumers consider the services of pubs and restaurants to be more personal, similar to accommodation-related services and therefore they mentioned attentive service, while service providers considered expertise more important. Small-sized enterprises consider the design of their restaurant or pub more important than hygiene, and medium-sized companies evaluate expertise and attentive service as the most important.

We also observed some different priorities in the evaluation of consumers and tourist guides. Tourist guides feel that professional skills and knowledge are more important, while consumers attribute greater importance to the personal friendliness and helpfulness of the tourist guide.

17.6 Conclusions and Recommendations

Our research demonstrates strong consumer demand in the Hungarian tourism industry for a quality assurance accreditation system such as the HTQA. Consumer pressure is likely to sway the attitude of even the most resistant service providers. Therefore HTQA has great potential for success if introduced with effective marketing. Small and medium-sized businesses see lots of advantage for HTQA, particularly if appropriate quality criteria meeting consumer expectations are developed. Enhanced quality will have an impact on customer perceptions of the ratio of quality to price, which is considered very important by consumers. Participation in HTQA will enable them to exploit a wider range of marketing opportunities.

From this research we make the following recommendations:

- SMEs must enhance the quality of the services they provide by learning more about their customers, either through market research or at least through the implementation of effective approaches to customer feedback and complaints.
- The HNTO must develop appropriate criteria for HTQA that matches customer expectations for each industry sector.
- HTQA must be strongly promoted by the HNTO in domestic and international markets.
- The HNTO must ensure that it addresses appropriately any concerns that stakeholders have about HTQA.
- SME participation in HTQA should be facilitated by subsidizing training costs.
- The benefits of HTQA for customer perceptions of price/quality ratios must be emphasized through marketing.
- The HNTO should collate and disseminate appropriate market research and market intelligence to service providers.

References

Árva, L., Behringer, Zs. and Mester, T. (2001) A kis- és középvállalkozások helyzete, jövobeni kilátásai az átalakuló gazdaságokban, kiemelve a magyar turisztikai szektort. *Turizmus Bulletin* 2001, 4, 40–46.

Behringer, Zs. (2001) The role of tourism SMEs in European economies in transition: the case of Hungary. In: World Tourism Organization (ed.) *Seminar Proceedings: the Future of Small and Medium-sized Enterprises in European Tourism Faced with Globalization*. World Tourism Organization, Madrid, pp. 31–44.

Csáki, G., Papanek, G. and Viszt, E. (2001) A muködotoke import és a közép-európai országok EU-csatlakozása, *Közgazdasági szemle* 48, 25–32.

Infoplease.com (2002) *World Events 1990–2000*, http://www.infoplease.com

Kállay, L., Kőhegyi, K., Kiss Kovács E. and Maszlag, L. (2002) *State of Small and Medium Sized Business in Hungary*. Hungarian Institute for Economic Analysis, Budapest, pp. 76–97.

Központi Statisztikai Hivatal (1990–2001) *Idegenforgalmi Statisztikai Évkönyv*. Központi Statisztikai Hivatal, Budapest.

Központi Statisztikai Hivatal (2003a) http://www.ksh.hu

Központi Statisztikai Hivatal (2003b) *Turizmus 2002*. Központi Statisztikai Hivatal, Budapest.

Központi Statisztikai Hivatal (2003c) *Gyorstájékoztató a Központi Statisztikai Hivatal legfrissebb adataiból, Turizmus, 2003, január–június*. Központi Statisztikai Hivatal, Budapest.

Magyar Nemzeti Bank (1990–2002) http://www.mnb.hu

MT RT Magyar Turizmus Rt., MÁST Piac és Közvéleménykutató Társaság (2002) *A Magyar Turizmus Minoségi Védjegy bevezetésével kapcsolatos vélemények 2002 nyarán.* Magyar Turizmus Rt., Budapest.

Németh, K. (2001) The role of small and medium sized enterprises in Hungarian economy – the past, the present and prospect for the near future, http://www.gki.hu

18 Leadership and Coordination: a Strategy to Achieve Professionalism in the Welsh Tourism Industry

DIANA JAMES

Tourism Training Forum for Wales, Cardiff, UK

18.1 Introduction

Tourism is a particularly important contributor to the economy of Wales, but the quality of the Welsh tourism product is threatened by problems in recruiting and retaining staff and by skill gaps. This chapter describes Wales's strategic approach to addressing this issue through the creation of the Tourism Training Forum for Wales (TTFW), set up to provide leadership and to coordinate stakeholders in achieving professionalism in the Welsh tourism industry. It provides the context in which the Forum was created, describing how the tourism industry was being handicapped by an insufficient supply of skilled staff. It then illustrates how Wales decided upon a model that would meet the needs of Wales, explaining the changing political scene that was unfolding as the result of devolution. The chapter goes on to describe how TTFW was set up as a voluntary partnership, the achievements between 1998 and 2001 and the Forum's evolution into an independent body with new challenges and new objectives to meet these. It concludes by considering the future, particularly the potential benefits accruing from partnership with the emerging sector skills councils (SSCs).

18.2 The Context

Tourism is one of the key industry sectors in Wales, benefiting from £2 billion in direct visitor spending and contributing 7% to the gross domestic product (GDP) in Wales (Wales Tourist Board, 2000: 6). The competitiveness of the Welsh tourism industry relies on the know-how of those running tourism businesses, and equally on their ability to attract, retain and develop employees in order to deliver high-quality service to their customers. However, available evidence (Future Skills Wales, 2000) points to an industry in crisis, where the investment of money, time and energy into marketing and capital development is not matched by a parallel investment in people. This situation is not a new one, and is the result of a combination of factors within both the industry and the education and training structure.

There are few barriers to entering the industry, and many set up business without the necessary skills. The microbusinesses that are predominant in Welsh tourism may lack the time and disposable income needed to improve their skills levels, but additionally some are still failing to appreciate that the continuous professional development of everyone working in a business is a prerequisite for its success (Hospitality Training Foundation, 2003). The Hospitality Training Foundation (2003) reports that the industry is a strong job creator, but wage levels in the hospitality industry are among the lowest, and career development and training opportunities are the exception rather than the rule. The results of this can be seen in the high number of 'hard to fill' vacancies, the high staff turnover and the poor image of the careers opportunities offered by tourism and hospitality (Hospitality Training Foundation, 2003). Tourism has failed to attract skilled staff, and has failed to develop skills in existing employees (Hospitality Training Foundation, 2003).

Despite a wide range of available training some employers have found the provision on offer to be irrelevant to their needs (ELWa, 2002). A culture of competition, reinforced by past funding regimes, has led to duplication of provision and a lack of coordination and partnership among providers. In some cases, it appears that providers have little understanding of the needs of the industry they are seeking to serve. This is exacerbated by the difficulties training providers face in communicating effectively with a fragmented tourism industry.

18.3 A Change of Approach

It became essential to move towards a strategic and coordinated approach that would effectively address these issues. Evidence pointed to the need for leadership and guidance to raise the profile of human resources for tourism among politicians and other decision makers, to bring the demand for and the supply of tourism training closer together, to ensure comprehensive, relevant and high-quality education and training and to achieve higher levels of participation by tourism businesses in skills development. To achieve these objectives the TTFW was created in February 1998. TTFW was a voluntary partnership of representatives drawn, on the one hand, from tourism business interests and, on the other, from the post-16 education and training sector. All were motivated by the desire to improve the professionalism of the industry.

At the outset, TTFW looked to models adopted by other countries, such as CERT in Ireland and the Tourism Training Trust in Northern Ireland. In particular, the TTFW partnership learned a great deal from Tourism Training Scotland and its successor body Tourism People. Those closely involved in these organizations were generous in sharing with TTFW their experience of implementing a strategy to raise skill levels in the tourism industry.

Tourism Training Scotland's primary focus was developing a number of new national training programmes to complement existing initiatives, such as Scottish vocational qualifications; the British Hospitality Association's 'Excellence through People' programme; and Investors in People. The new programmes were Scotland's Best (quality service seminars for managers and staff), the natural cooking initiative and developments of Welcome Host to meet the needs of the conference and golf markets. In 2000 there were major changes to the structure of Scottish tourism. The Scottish Tourist Board was replaced by VisitScotland, and in place of Tourism Training Scotland came a new tourism skill group, Tourism People. In lieu of developing further new training courses, the new organization concentrated on increasing awareness among businesses of the benefits of training and driving a continual increase in the demand for training (Tourism People, 2000). A similar focus on stimulating interest in training among small tourism businesses was needed in Wales. However, rather than adopting a model from another country, which had been developed in response to its own unique set of circumstances, it was agreed that what was required was an approach developed in Wales and for Wales.

18.4 The Political Scene

TTFW came into being at a time of important political change when Wales was heading towards devolution. The National Assembly for Wales's structure was such that economic development, and education and training were the remit of separate committees headed up by different ministers. At agency level, the development of tourism was the responsibility of one Assembly-sponsored public body, the Wales Tourist Board (WTB), while post-16 education and training became the remit of Education and Learning Wales (ELWa). ELWa was created to combine the work that had previously been carried out by the four training and enterprise councils with that of the Further Education Funding Council Wales, as part of the National Council for Education and Training for Wales, the biggest public body in the country. This presented a challenge to TTFW, whose success depended on bridging the gap that existed between the economic development of tourism and the provision of vocational education and training for the sector. It was important to ensure that people issues remained a priority for the WTB, and to show ELWa that investing resources in tourism education and training was worthwhile.

TTFW sought political support from ministers and Assembly. Tourism People Scotland was directly responsible to a minister that had responsibility both for economic development and for lifelong learning. It was unlikely that this could be replicated in Wales but engaging with and informing Assembly members was to be a key activity for TTFW, as without political support it would not have a future. A period of change offers opportunities as well as challenges. TTFW understood that Wales's new structures would be seeking to work more effectively than their predecessors, and that this presented an opening for convincing the new decision makers that a strategic and coordinated approach to tourism education and training in Wales would be successful.

18.5 Evolution of the Tourism Training Forum for Wales

18.5.1 A voluntary partnership 1998–2001

TTFW's initial lifespan was 3 years. A private-sector chairman was appointed and WTB provided the secretariat and project funding to support the activities of TTFW. It was agreed by the partners that at the end of that period there would be an objective evaluation of what had been achieved, and this would provide a basis for deciding about any future developments.

A 3-year strategy and action plan was prepared. Objectives were agreed, and these were to:

- Develop a culture of education and training to provide a higher-value tourism product and enhance visitor experience.
- Lobby for the interests of tourism education and training in Wales.
- Form strategic alliances between public and private training and funding sectors to maximize resources.
- Ensure faster response to the creation of new training developments and initiatives.
- Develop and improve training programmes to meet the specific requirements of the tourism sector.
- Encourage operators to plan and undertake education and training.
- Provide a specialist advisory source for career development with good-practice business support.
- Provide a forum to plan for the education and training needs of the future.

18.5.2 Priorities

As a starting point four priorities for action were identified:

- Communications and public affairs.
- Identifying best practice in training.
- Information on training provision.
- Information and communications technology.

Working groups were set up to drive the work forward. The chairs of each working group, with the TTFW chairman and WTB's training and business support manager, came together to form a steering group that coordinated activity.

18.5.2.1 Communications and public affairs

The first priority was to develop a communications strategy that would reach all TTFW stakeholders. At a political level, it was essential to engage the support of the new National Assembly for Wales. The First Minister gave the keynote speech at the launch of TTFW, an important step in establishing our credentials with the devolved government. The launch was followed up by a strategic public affairs and public relations campaign, designed to raise awareness about TTFW and its work, and to engage a wide range of stakeholders.

18.5.2.2 Identifying best practice in training

TTFW was aware that businesses enjoy the opportunity to network with their peers. Similar businesses are often regarded by small and medium-sized enterprises (SMEs) as a credible source of information and advice, and TTFW wanted to capitalize on this to aid business development. A competition was launched, 'Stars in their Field', inviting businesses that were making significant investments in training to apply. Attractive financial prizes acted as an inducement to entry. The most interesting applications were developed into case studies, which were published and disseminated to businesses through every available channel.

18.5.2.3 Information on training provision

Tourism businesses were finding it difficult to access the information about training that they needed. They receive many promotional leaflets from different training providers, but for many it was proving impossible to differentiate between the courses and services on offer. Too often the result was that the businesses' learning and development needs remained unmet. TTFW's answer was to produce 'The Essential Guide to Tourism Training', which gave details of all the key contacts for information about tourism education and training in Wales.

18.5.2.4 Information and communications technology

Using appropriate information and communications technology can bring great benefits to small tourism businesses, but in 1998 there was no information about the incidence and purpose of the use of computers in the tourism sector in Wales. TTFW carried out an evaluation of the situation as a precursor of work to encourage businesses to extend both their use of technology in their businesses and their exploitation of its potential as a learning medium.

18.5.3 Evaluation

As planned, an independent evaluation of TTFW was commissioned and reported in June 2000. The report identified that substantial and significant progress had been made in raising awareness of TTFW and completing the initial action points. As expected, it also identified that there was still much work to be done, particularly in engaging the industry in training and helping to shape a clearer understanding of the tourism industry in Wales. It identified that TTFW was in a unique position to influence, guide and provide the leadership required to develop the training, education and business development needed for the tourism industry in Wales over the next 5 years. However, in order to fulfil this potential, TTFW required its own executive and a dedicated budget to implement a new strategy, which built on achievements to date and expanded to encompass a greater range of activities.

18.5.4 Independence from the Wales Tourist Board

If the ambitious plan for the future of TTFW was to be realized, it was essential to secure the approval of the Welsh Assembly government, and commitment from both WTB and the developing National Council for Education and Training that they would work with and through TTFW on all matters relating to skills for the tourism sector and provide the funding necessary to meet the costs of the proposed new organization. Therefore, following receipt of the report, TTFW spent several months meeting with Assembly members and senior officers from WTB and the National Council, informing them about the recommendations and seeking their support in implementing them. By July 2001 TTFW was confident enough to move towards independent status.

TTFW was incorporated as a company limited by guarantee in November 2001, and a small executive team of four was appointed. TTFW aims to engage with everyone with an interest in skills development in and for the tourism industry, and actively encourages stakeholders to become members of the company. To ensure continuity, the steering group of the voluntary partnership formed a transitional Board of Directors. The intention was that the Board membership would change in stages over a 3-year period until all Directors were drawn from the tourism industry. A consultative committee of experts drawn from trade bodies, universities, colleges and private training providers, the careers and employment services, and the government agencies with responsibility for the tourism and the education and training sectors was convened to support the Board and the executive team.

18.5.5 Revised objectives

The new company reaffirmed its mission – to provide leadership, guidance and coordination for tourism training and education in Wales, for the benefit of all individuals, businesses, communities and education and training providers that have a stake in the tourism industry in Wales. Its objectives were few and clear:

- To encourage education and training providers to ensure they offer relevant, accessible and high-quality services to the whole breadth of the tourism industry in Wales.
- To encourage tourism businesses to take advantage of relevant training and business development, and facilitate their access to beneficial provision and services.
- To promote effective partnerships to encourage the development of human resources for the tourism industry in Wales.
- To ensure that the economic benefits of tourism education and training are given due priority within all the National Assembly for Wales's committees that have an impact on tourism.
- To achieve this through an independent Tourism Training Forum for Wales.

Partnership would be the key to achieving these objectives, and TTFW ensured that it took every opportunity to make friends and worked to influence the agendas of all organizations whose work affected and could benefit tourism in Wales. The new independence of TTFW meant that it could be objective, and this was to prove invaluable in developing its relationships with other stakeholders. For its partnership working to be successful, TTFW needed to:

- Achieve consensus on the big goals.
- Be transparent in its dealings with all partners.
- Gain the trust of all its partners.
- Agree clear roles and agendas with its partners.
- Be neutral.
- Ensure that all partners benefited from the partnership.
- Recognize that partners had to operate within their own organizational constraints.
- Persuade partners to play to their strengths and positively exploit their differences.
- Acknowledge and build on past experience.

18.5.6 Challenges

The major and ongoing challenges for TTFW were to understand its key audiences:

- To understand the priorities of tourism businesses and influence them to invest in learning and skills development.
- To understand what drives tourism education and training and influence that agenda.

In the first 4 months of operation, TTFW's coordinator for businesses met face to face with 500 tourism operators from across the country, representing about 10% of the companies that work with public-sector agencies. This provided a good insight of the challenges facing tourism businesses, their staff and skills needs and their priorities for action. Many businesses reported difficulties in attracting staff, and staff turnover was also a problem. Most tourism operations in Wales are microbusinesses that find it difficult to find the time or money to take part in external training courses; it is estimated that 80% of all training undertaken by small businesses is in-house (Future Skills Wales, 2003) but few owner-managers have undertaken any preparation for this role. Even where external training provision is an option, businesses said that they were often overwhelmed by promotional material from various training providers, but lacked objective information that would allow them to make a rational choice. Some businesses felt that much of the training on offer was not relevant to their needs so chose not to participate even when it was affordable. There was also a degree of criticism about the level and relevance skills of those leaving school or college and entering the industry.

At the same time, the coordinator for education and training was meeting tourism academics from higher and further education institutions and private training providers. A wide range of courses was on offer, but usually these had been developed in response to direction from government or funding agencies, and there were limited opportunities for employers to influence the development of qualifications or the curriculum. It became apparent that there was no common approach to the management of tourism provision. Tourism provision in colleges is often spread across a number of departments, and frequently no adequate mechanism is in place to facilitate integration. This communications gap between staff and departments needed to be addressed if colleges were to ensure that the advice given to individuals and businesses seeking help is accurate and comprehensive.

This grass-roots research fed into the development of TTFW's 5-year action plan. One key action was to identify and disseminate best practice in tourism training provision, and similarly to discover businesses that could act as exemplars of good employment and training practice to their peers. TTFW was committed to supporting the continuous professional development of those delivering tourism education and training, and events for lecturers, trainers and students were built into the action plan. A bold plan to develop an interactive website to be a 'one-stop shop' for small tourism businesses seeking information and advice on skills and learning was at the centre of the plan, as it would provide the avenue for disseminating the outcomes of all TTFW's research and activities. A comprehensive mapping exercise of all tourism-related provision and projects would be undertaken, and the results fed into an interactive database, so that businesses could easily access the right training. Innovative work would include: developing a model for businesses to use the 'low' season as an opportunity for training; exploring the potential for combining Hospitality Assured and Investors in People into a single quality mark for the industry; and training key staff from exemplar businesses to mentor new businesses or those seeking to improve their human resource management.

18.6 Conclusions

To date, TTFW can claim to have made strides in realizing its objectives. Its task is formidable, but it has become clear that its approach is paying off and needs to be pursued. It has established its reputation as a central informed source of information on tourism education and training matters in Wales; it has forged valuable working partnerships with tourism trade bodies, education and training networks, the careers and employment services, and the WTB and the National Council for Education and Training at both national and regional levels; tangible outcomes from its early projects, as previously described, are coming on stream. For example, in 2003, TTFW launched *Success through your People*, a human resource management toolkit aimed at all tourism businesses who either employ staff (from one part-timer to hundreds of full-timers) or who are considering employing staff in the future. The toolkit provides comprehensive support on employment issues for tourism employers and, through an auditing flow chart, enables managers to pinpoint key areas of underperformance in relation to their employment practices. It showcases examples of good employment practice and provides templates of documents, e.g. contracts of employment, induction programmes and appraisal forms, which can be customized for individual business needs. TTFW is also exploring various mechanisms to deliver innovative training to tourism businesses. One recent project, involving TTFW, WTB, the BBC and the University of Wales Institute, Cardiff (UWIC), delivered 'Overnight Success' – a series of three programmes and a website designed to enhance quality standards in bed and breakfast operations through learning journeys (http://www.bbc.co.uk/overnightsuccess). Overnight Success attempted to undermine perceptions of ease of entry to the tourism industry. Whodoiask.com is an example of another recent collaborative project (http://www.whodoiask.com) and serves as an information resource for the tourism industry in Wales. The site has been designed for tourism providers and offers relevant information on business start-ups, customer care, marketing, training and financial and legal requirements.

Currently, the UK government is replacing 70 national training organizations with 20 Sector Skills Councils (SSCs). These are employer bodies that will take the lead in identifying and meeting the skills needs of the industry sectors within their footprint. SSCs have appreciated the need to work with and through existing national mechanisms, and TTFW has been approached by the emerging Sector Skills Council for Hospitality, Leisure, Travel and Tourism (People 1st) to be its Welsh arm. This will be a mutually beneficial partnership that will allow People 1st to effectively access the regions of Wales and, through TTFW, ensure that Wales can influence and benefit from UK-wide research and initiatives. In addition, TTFW continues to work with Lantra (the SSC for the land-based industries) and SkillsActive (the SSC for the sports and recreation industries), as well as the developing SSC that has responsibility for the creative and cultural industries.

TTFW is working to effect a transformation at a deep level, and that cannot be achieved overnight. Continuous development of the organization and its activities, working in collaboration with its sponsors and partners, will ensure that it fully realizes its potential as an agent of change that will make Wales a world-class tourist destination.

References

ELWa (2002) *Learner Satisfaction Survey*. Education and Learning Wales, Cardiff, UK.

Future Skills Wales (2000) *Future Skills Issues Affecting Industry Sectors in Wales: Tourism, Hospitality and Leisure Sector*. Future Skills Wales, Cardiff, UK.

Future Skills Wales (2003) *Future Skills Wales Generic Skills Survey*. Future Skills Wales, Cardiff, UK.

Hospitality Training Foundation (2003) *Market Assessment for the Hospitality, Leisure, Travel and Tourism Sector*. Hospitality Training Foundation, London.

Tourism People (2000) *Tourism People Action Plan*. Scottish Enterprise and Highlands and Islands Enterprise, UK.

Tourism Training Forum for Wales (2003) *Success Through Your People: A Human Resource Management Toolkit*. TTFW/WTB. Available from http://www.whodoiask.com

Wales Tourist Board (2000) *Achieving our Potential – A Tourism Strategy for Wales*. Wales Tourist Board, Cardiff, UK.

19 Identifying and Exploiting Potentially Lucrative Niche Markets: the Case of Planned Impulse Travellers in Hong Kong

ERIC CHAN AND SIMON WONG

School of Hotel and Tourism Management, The Hong Kong Polytechnic University, Hung Hom, Hong Kong

19.1 Introduction

Tourist behaviour has been a major topic for decades in tourism research. In the process of purchasing products in a market, consumers have to decide what to buy and where to buy in order to maximize the effective use of their time and to achieve value for money. One of the most constructive ways to think about the consumer-buying process is as a problem-solving behaviour described in five different stages: (i) problem awareness; (ii) information search; (iii) alternative evaluation; (iv) decision; and (v) post-purchase concern (Powers, 1997). Before travelling abroad, many travellers conduct their 'information search' by contacting their travel agent, accessing the web pages of different hotels or seeking advice from friends, relatives or business colleagues to determine which hotel to stay in. They will then go through a decision making process to evaluate alternative options, normally based on their perceptions of the importance of the different attributes of hotels, before making a final decision. These attributes may include good hotel service, a convenient location, attractive prices, the cleanliness of rooms and safety. Their overall attitudes towards different hotels will determine their final choice. It is also likely that a traveller's favourable post-purchase experience may lead to repeat business if his/her expectations of the hotel service are satisfied. Hotel marketers can utilize decision making models such as the multi-attribute attitude model to predict a consumer's choice of hotel if they are able to accurately identify the key attributes that consumers will use to evaluate their products and services, as well as other external factors such as discounted rates offered by competitors.

However, not all travellers plan in advance and arrange hotel accommodation before arriving at a destination. What happens with unplanned buying? What factors affect or stimulate the 'walk-ins' or the travellers calling from the airport who have not prearranged their hotel accommodation? To the authors' knowledge, there are few studies that have investigated this subject. Although many hotels strive to increase the sales effectiveness of their reservation staff, many still overlook the numerous sales opportunities that front-desk staff encounter every day. One such opportunity is the walk-in enquiry or the enquiry from the airport. The sales from this market, termed 'planned impulse travellers' (PITs) in this study, can represent a significant source of additional revenue. Anecdotal evidence from a front-office manager of a four-star hotel with more than 1000 rooms in Hong Kong suggests that on-day pick-up bookings, including walk-ins and pick-ups from the airport and other channels, can average over 10% of the total number of daily reservations and thus potentially represent a significant source of additional revenue. In fact, the yield generated from this business is normally higher, as hotel tariff rates rather than contract rates are likely to be confirmed to guests during the enquiry. Unfortunately, it seems that the hotel industry overall does a less than adequate job of selling to this category of customers.

This chapter introduces the reader to the study of the hotel booking behaviour of PITs. It starts with a discussion of unplanned buying and why the term PITs is used in this study to describe 'walk-in' customers and all those who book a hotel room after they have arrived at the airport of destination. It also provides an overview of different types of travellers' perceptions of hotel attributes when selecting a hotel in which to stay. The chapter concludes with a detailed discussion of how the buying behaviour of PITs could affect the marketing strategies of small or medium-sized hotels that aim at exploiting niche markets left by larger firms.

19.2 Unplanned Buying

Despite a paucity of studies investigating the hotel booking behaviour of PITs, there is a wealth of research about impulse buying in the plethora of marketing journals. To a certain extent, walk-ins or last-minute bookings from the airport can be viewed as impulse buying but in a non-store format. In the following section, a review of the literature on impulse buying may provide some insight into the behaviour of PITs in selecting hotels.

In fact, impulse buying is an enigma in the marketing world, although it accounts for a substantial volume of the goods sold every year across a broad range of product categories, with few products being unaffected by impulse buying (Kollat and Willett, 1967; Bellenger et al., 1978; Weinberg and Gottwald, 1982; Cobb and Hoyer, 1986; Han et al., 1991; Rook and Fisher, 1995). Welles (1986) in his study indicated that most people – almost 90% – make purchases on impulse occasionally, while between 30% and 50% of all purchases can be classified by the buyers themselves as impulse purchases (Kollat and Willett, 1967; Bellenger et al., 1978; Cobb and Hoyer, 1986; Han et al., 1991). These studies show that there is an underlying upward trend in impulse buying.

What, then, is impulse buying? Stern (1962) provided the foundation for defining the behaviour described as impulse buying. According to Stern, buying behaviour can be classified as planned, unplanned or impulse. Planned buying behaviour involves a time-consuming process of searching for information, followed by rational decision making (Stern, 1962; Piron, 1991). Unplanned buying refers to all purchases made without such advance planning and includes impulse buying, which is distinguished by the relative speed with which a buying 'decision' occurs. Similarly, Cobb and Hoyer (1986) conducted a study identifying three types of purchasers – planners, partial planners and impulse buyers. Planners are those who intend to purchase both the category and the brand, partial planners intend to purchase the product category but not the brand and impulse purchasers have no intention of purchasing the category or the brand. In their study, Engel and Blackwell (1982: 552) also defined an impulse purchase as 'a buying action undertaken without a problem previously having been consciously recognized or a buying intention formed prior to entering the store'. Conversely, Phillips and Bradshaw (1993) do not distinguish between unplanned and impulse purchases, but make the important point that consumer research also needs to focus on the point-of-sale interaction with the shopper – an often neglected area.

Impulse buying is also closely tied to reflexes or responses stemming from external or environmental stimuli, as well as from internal stimuli (Youn and Faber, 2000). The action or reaction to stimuli is processed affectively, cognitively or by a combination of the two. The four different types of impulse buying classified by Stern (1962) can be categorized according to the amount of affect versus cognition present in the decision process. Pure impulse buying, where an emotional appeal triggers the impulse to buy, represents the least amount of cognitive involvement. The remaining three types involve a combination of cognitive and affective influence, with cognition increasing respectively. A suggested impulse buy occurs when a shopper sees an item for the first time and the desire to buy is formed without a prior knowledge of the product. Planned impulse buying occurs when a shopper has some specific purchase in mind; however, the actual purchase depends upon price specials, coupon offers and the like. Reminder impulse buying results from a predetermined need that is prompted upon encountering the item while shopping (Stern 1962).

Stern (1962) has identified nine product-related factors that may be influential in the purchase of consumer products: low prices; a marginal need for the product/brand; mass distribution; self-service; mass advertising; a prominent store display; a short product life; a small size; and ease of storage. Although these factors do not directly relate to the hotel product – rooms – they can give some idea of the influences on PITs when they make an impulsive purchase. For instance, more expensive products requiring more time and effort to use are less likely to be bought on impulse.

19.3 Planned Impulse Travellers (PITs)

In general, hotel guests can be classified according to: (i) their purpose for visiting (i.e. leisure or business travellers); (ii) numbers (i.e. independent or group travellers); and (iii) their origin (i.e. local or travellers from overseas). Frequent independent travellers (FITs) refer to all international tourists who make their own travel arrangements and purchase accommodation independently (Baker *et al.*, 1994). These travellers, who are not travelling together with a tour group, are usually looking just for accommodation. Some FITs pre-book accommodation, others – PITs – do not for a variety of reasons, including failing to secure a room before leaving; their belief in the possibility of bargaining for a better room rate because of the 6 p.m. claim policy; or a sudden change in their travel itinerary. Although Stern (1962) has classified impulse buying into different categories, the walk-in enquiry and enquiry from the airport can be viewed as planned impulse buying since the traveller has a specific purchase in mind – a hotel room; however, the actual purchase depends upon attributes such as an attractive price or a convenient location rather than on pure impulse. It is unclear whether there has been an increase in such business, and what factors may affect unplanned and impulse bookings that will allow hoteliers to grasp the golden opportunity to optimize their room rates.

19.4 Traveller Perceptions of Hotel Attributes

Although no study has focused on investigating what attributes will affect PITs in their selection of a hotel, a number of studies have previously been conducted on travellers' preferences when selecting a hotel in which to stay. In studying the hotel attributes desired by travellers, some intangible attributes – e.g. security, dependability, service quality, reputation and staff behaviour – have been identified by various researchers (Lewis, 1985; Knutson, 1988; Ananth *et al.*, 1992; Banerjee, 1994). Tangible attributes include price, the appearance of facilities, location, the presence of alternatives, word of mouth communication, advertising, a familiar name and past experience. Most researchers also think that these are the most important attributes, and that all travellers would consider them when booking a hotel. In addition, a convenient hotel location and overall service are the most determinate factors (Rivers *et al.*, 1991).

19.4.1 Business versus leisure travellers

Notwithstanding, some researchers have argued that different travellers emphasize other attributes. Business and leisure travellers may have different perceptions of hotel attributes in their hotel selection criteria. Barsky and Labagh (1992) found that employee attitude, location and rooms are the most important attributes desired by both business and leisure travellers. However, they agreed that these two segments of travellers hold a different viewpoint on employee attitude, location and room. Lewis (1985) also echoed the view that the needs of business and leisure travellers are not the same. Business guests are more concerned about service quality, security and image, while leisure guests place more emphasis on quietness, service quality and location. Weaver and Heung (1993) found that the convenience to businesses, the good reputation of the hotel and friendly staff are the important attributes for business travellers in selecting a hotel. On the other hand, other researchers (Ananth *et al.*, 1992) have suggested that leisure travellers will also consider price first because they have to pay for the accommodation themselves, while business travellers will be reimbursed by their company. Furthermore, Banerjee (1994) also mentions that leisure travellers are gradually paying more attention to the factor of security. Other studies support the importance of security and room rates for leisure travellers (Marshall, 1993; Clow *et al.*, 1994).

While most researchers have concentrated on tangible attributes, another group of researchers, including Parasuraman *et al.* (1985) and Knutson (1988), have pointed out that intangible attributes such as quality of service (SERVQUAL) and past experience are factors that are as important in determining the choice of hotels by leisure travellers.

19.4.2 Travellers of different genders and ages

Customers of different genders and ages may also hold different perceptions of the importance of the attributes when choosing a hotel. McCleary and Weaver (1991) found that female business travellers consider security, personal services and low price to be the more important factors when selecting a hotel. Lewis (1984) also stated that cleanliness and good housing are factors more likely to satisfy women than men. On the other hand, service, convenience, security and price are considered important attributes by both mature and young travellers (Ananth *et al.*, 1992).

Although some studies indicate that price is one of the attributes that may influence travellers in selecting a hotel, McCarthy (2001) argued that room rate is not a problem for people who are truly committed to the belief that their selected hotel's prices represent the best dollar-for-dollar value. This means that the customers do not really expect the hotels to meet or beat the price of an inferior product. Feiertag (2001) also argues that cutting room rates may not be the answer to building additional room occupancy, and questioned how much additional room occupancy is needed to justify the rate cuts.

19.5 Methodology

The above information gave the authors some insights when they developed the questionnaire. After a pilot test on some tourists and colleagues of the authors in the School of Hotel and Tourism Management at the Hong Kong Polytechnic University, 11 attributes were developed into 11 statements to investigate the booking behaviour of the PITs through a qualitative interview with ten tourists, who were asked what factors influenced their selection of hotel when they arrived in Hong Kong without prior arrangements. The 11 statements are: (i) 'Good hotel service'; (ii) 'Good hotel reputation'; (iii) 'Great varieties of facilities such as a swimming-pool, non-smoking floors, restaurants with different cuisine';

(iv) 'Convenient hotel location'; (v) 'The attitude of the hotel employee who answers reservation enquiries'; (vi) 'Information from the Hong Kong International Airport's Information Desk/Hotel Reservation Centre'; (vii) 'Availability of hotel's airport representatives'; (viii) 'Incentives – being a member of hotels/airlines' frequent travel package'; (ix) 'Had stayed at this hotel before'; (x) 'The lowest room rate you can get during the reservation enquiry'; and (xi) 'Advertisement in airline's in-flight entertainment, or in-flight magazines or hotel promotional materials'. Respondents were asked to indicate their feelings using a Likert scale of 1 to 5, where '1' indicates the 'lowest degree of influence' and '5' the 'highest degree of influence'.

A descriptive cross-sectional research design was used to survey tourists departing from Hong Kong International Airport. Out of a non-random sample of 1120 people interviewed, 631 were identified as independent travellers. Of these 631 individuals, 80 PITs (12.7%) had no prior hotel booking before their arrival in Hong Kong. The data were analysed using the Statistical Package for the Social Sciences (SPSS) program. Descriptive statistics were used to rank the degree of influence of different attributes. An independent t-test and analysis of variance (ANOVA) were performed to see if there were any significant differences between various demographic groups. Factor analysis was also utilized to identify the main constructs that are likely to influence a customer's choice.

19.6 Results and Discussion

19.6.1 Respondent profiles

Table 19.1 indicates that the PITs with no prior hotel booking were mainly from Taiwan (36.3%), mainland China (16.3%) and the USA (16.3%). Among the respondents, 70.9% were repeat customers to Hong Kong, 65.8% were male, and 48.8% had completed a college/university degree. From the trip profile (Table 19.2), it was found that 83.3% had stayed for 4 nights or more, and 37.5% of them came to Hong Kong for a vacation while 32.5% did so for business reasons. Surprisingly, 32.5% of business travellers coming to Hong Kong had not secured a hotel booking before they arrived. It is also reasonable to note that 58.8% travelled alone and 98.7% came without children and, therefore, may not have been too concerned about making a hotel booking in advance.

19.6.2 Key factors influencing purchasing decisions of PITs

As shown in Table 19.3, the overall mean value of the 11 statements was 2.48, indicating a neutral to lower degree of influence on the intentions of the PITs. This is quite understandable, as this particular category of FIT does not pay attention to these factors before they arrive at their destination. Still, 'Convenient hotel location' scored the highest mean value (3.91), followed by 'Good hotel service' (3.31) and 'Good hotel reputation' (3.04). The least influential factor was

Table 19.1. Demographic profiles of visitors.[a]

Composition	No. of respondents	Percentage
Country of residence (*n* = 80)[b]		
Mainland China	13	16.3
Taiwan	29	36.3
Singapore	4	5.0
USA	13	16.3
Canada	7	8.8
Australia	2	2.5
Malaysia	12	15.0
Age group (*n* = 77)[b]		
25 or less	6	7.8
26–35	32	41.6
36–45	19	24.7
46–55	11	14.3
56–65	5	6.5
66 or above	4	5.2
Gender (*n* = 79)		
Male	52	65.8
Female	27	34.2
Highest educational level achieved (*n* = 80)		
Less than secondary/high school	2	2.5
Completed secondary/high school	17	21.3
Some college or university	11	13.8
Completed college/university diploma degree	39	48.8
Completed postgraduate degree	11	13.8
Total expenses in HK (HK$) (*n* = 80)		
Less than 1,000	15	18.8
1,000–2,499	16	20.0
2,500–4,999	17	21.3
5,000–9,999	13	16.3
10,000 or more	19	23.8
Annual household income (US$[c]) (*n* = 72)		
Less than 10,000	9	12.5
10,000–29,999	15	20.8
30,000–49,999	14	19.4
50,000–69,999	9	12.5
70,000–99,999	9	12.5
100,000 or more	13	18.1
No income/retired	3	4.2

[a]1120 individuals were interviewed for the international visitor survey (IVS 2000); however, only 631 were independent travellers and stayed overnight in commercial accommodation (i.e. hotels); and, of 631 individuals, only 80 PITs arrived in Hong Kong without a hotel booking.
[b]Different total no. of visitors in different categories due to missing data in each category (*n* = 80).
[c]US$1 = HK$7.8.

Table 19.2. Trip profiles of visitors.[a]

Composition	No. of respondents	Percentage
Length of the whole trip (n = 78)[b]		
3 nights or less	13	16.7
4 nights or more	65	83.3
Length of stay in HK (n = 80)[b]		
3 nights or less	46	57.5
4 nights or more	34	42.5
Purpose of visit (n = 80)[b]		
Vacation/leisure	30	37.5
Business/meeting	26	32.5
Visiting friends	8	10.0
Visiting relatives	4	5.0
Other	12	15.0
No. of visits to HK (n = 79)		
First time	23	29.1
Repeat visit	56	70.9
HK as the only destination of this trip (n = 79)		
Yes	23	29.1
No	56	70.9
HK as the main destination of this trip[c] (n = 58)		
Yes	12	20.7
No	46	79.3
Main destination[d] (n = 46)		
Mainland China	25	54.3
Europe, Africa and Middle East	1	2.2
South and South-east Asia	10	21.7
The Americas	1	2.2
Taiwan	5	10.9
Australia, New Zealand and South Pacific	2	4.3
Multiple destinations	2	4.3
Size of travel group (n = 80)		
One	47	58.8
Two	21	26.3
Three or more	12	14.9
No. of adult males in the group (n = 79)		
None	16	20.3
One	53	67.1
Two	5	6.3
Three or more	5	6.3
No. of adult females in the group (n = 79)		
None	39	49.4
One	30	38.0
Two	5	6.3
Three or more	5	6.3

Composition	No. of respondents	Percentage
No. of children under 18 in the group ($n = 79$)		
None	78	98.7
One	1	1.3

[a]1120 individuals were interviewed for the international visitor survey (IVS 2000); however, only 631 were independent travellers and stayed overnight in commercial accommodation (i.e. hotels); and, of 631 individuals, only 80 PITs arrived in Hong Kong without a hotel booking.
[b]A different sample size for each category is due to missing data ($n = 80$).
[c]Applies to respondents who answered 'No' to Hong Kong as the only destination.
[d]Applies to respondents who answered 'No' to Hong Kong as the main destination.

'Availability of hotel's airport representatives' (1.64). Thus, 'Convenient hotel location' and Good hotel service' are still the key factors influencing PITs with no prior hotel booking in selecting hotels. This further confirms the study by Rivers *et al.* (1991) indicating that the 'Convenience of a hotel's location' and 'Overall services' are the most important factors to travellers when they book hotels. Although the location of a hotel, the 'Place' in the marketing mix, can hardly be changed, hoteliers should consider offering a discounted or free limousine service to/from the airport and nearby shopping/commercial areas to enhance 'Accessibility' 'Good hotel service', having a mean value of 3.31, shows the importance of hotel service in the eyes of customers when they have to make a choice from a list of hotels. Therefore, constant attention should be paid to ensuring good hotel services such as efficient check-in/out, guest-room cleanliness and friendly staff. For capturing walk-ins, fundamental guest-service principles will help a hotel gain a competitive edge. For instance, greeting the guest before s/he greets you, establishing eye contact, smiling and using positive body language will set you apart from competitors. When quoting the room rate to guests, different room types should be offered when possible, so that the guest is encouraged to think of the available options. Additionally, a full description of the room furnishings and views should be given to the guests to help them take psychological possession. Following this, 'Good hotel reputation' scored a mean value of 3.04. This shows a similar notion – that reputation, though intangible – is one of the external cues vital to attracting potential customers. Hotel marketers should also put more effort into building a good image in the minds of customers. This may include advertising awards that they may have gained, such as International Organization of Standardization standards ISO 9000 and ISO 14001, in promotional materials that serve to influence the consumer's perception of the quality of the hotel's products. Noticing that a hotel has been recognized with different prestigious awards, a consumer's confidence in the quality of the hotel's services will increase, and this is likely to lead to the hotel finally being chosen.

Table 19.3. Factor analysis with varimax rotation and a reliability analysis of the underlying factors affecting PITs in Hong Kong (n = 80).

Attributes	Mean	Factor loading	Communality	Factor and overall mean	Eigen value	% of variance	Cumulative variance	Cronbach alpha
● Good hotel service	3.31	0.91	0.86	Factor 1 Hotel product attribute: 3.09	4.07	37.01	37.01	0.85
● Good hotel reputation	3.04	0.87	0.78					
● Great variety of facilities such as a swimming-pool, non-smoking floors, restaurants with different cuisines	2.58	0.74	0.65					
● Convenient hotel location	3.91	0.70	0.56					
● The attitude of the hotel employee who answers reservation enquiries	2.60	0.60	0.73					
● Information from Hong Kong International Airport's Information Desk/Hotel Reservation Centre	2.08	0.89	0.80	Factor 2 Airport information: 1.86	1.64	14.93	51.94	0.66
● Availability of hotel's airport representatives	1.64	0.82	0.74					

Remarks:

1. The overall mean value of all 11 statements was 2.48, with a standard deviation of 0.88.
2. Statement Incentives – being a member of hotels/airlines' Frequent Traveller Programme was loaded into Factor 4 alone. Although its factor loading was 0.86 with an eigenvalue of 1.02 and a 9.27% variance, with only a single item it was not selected as an independent factor.
3. Statement 'Had stayed at this hotel before' was originally loaded into Factor 1. Although its factor loading was 0.53, which was higher than 0.50, it was not selected for Factor 1 because if this statement was deleted, the Cronbach alpha would change from 0.8497 to 0.8727.
4. The statements 'The lowest room rate you can get during the reservation enquiry' and 'Advertisement in airline's in-flight entertainment, or in-flight magazines or hotel promotional materials' were loaded into Factor 3. Although their factor loadings were 0.79 and 0.56, respectively, with an eigen value of 1.05 and a 9.56% variance, with a Cronbach alpha of 0.36, which was lower than 0.50, Factor 3 was not selected as a factor.

19.6.3 The effectiveness of airport representatives

The statement with the lowest mean value of 1.64 was 'Availability of hotel's airport representatives'. This shows that the presence of airport representatives will not persuade walk-in customers to book into a certain hotel. In fact, the job of airport representatives is solely to pick up guests arriving with advanced booking. Although travellers with no advance bookings are unlikely to need the assistance of the hotel airport representatives who often greet guests with reservations, hoteliers would be well advised to establish good relationships with airport customer service staff, who can help promote a hotel on the spot. For instance, some tourists without room reservations will normally contact the Hotel Reservation Centre (HRC) located in the area in Hong Kong International Airport reserved for hotel information and reservations. Some hotels will have regular meetings, either formal or informal, with the HRC staff to maintain good and professional relationships and at the same time update them with new products or services of their hotel so that the HRC staff can help promote these to the tourists. In fact, factor analysis revealed that airport information in addition to hotel product attribute dominated the selection criteria of this group – both factors scored an eigen value of higher than 1: hotel product attribute (eigen value = 4.07) and airport information (eigen value = 1.67). The cumulative variance of these two factors was found to be 51.94%. An internal reliability test was conducted, which revealed that both factors were internally consistent, with an alpha value of 0.85 for hotel attribute and 0.66 for airport information.

19.6.4 The use of a loyalty programme

Additionally, it is important to introduce/maintain a hotel loyalty programme to encourage repeat patronage among business travellers, as a high percentage of this sector is unlikely to secure a booking in advance, as indicated in our findings. PITs who are members of a hotel loyalty programme may fully trust 'his/her' hotel's ability to secure them a room whenever they need it and this benefit should be emphasized by a hotel when introducing the programme to potential members, in particular, to business travellers.

19.6.5 Differences between demographic groups

An independent t-test and ANOVA were performed to see whether there were any significant differences between various demographic groups. No significant differences were found, except for the length of stay, as shown in Table 19.4. PITs that stayed in Hong Kong for 3 nights or less scored significantly higher (i.e. felt a bigger impact) than visitors who stayed for 4 or more nights in terms of Factor 1: Hotel product attribute. In other words, PITs staying for a shorter period of time demand better hotel products, including location, good hotel service and hotel reputation. The finding is logical, as travellers who are planning to stay in a hotel for a longer period of time will normally have their

Table 19.4. Summary of the impact of the demographic characteristics of PITs on two factors identified by an independent t-test and ANOVA ($n = 80$).

Demographic variables	Valid n	Factor 1 (mean)	F value	Significance	Valid n	Factor 2 (mean)	F value	Significance
Gender			0.01	0.25			3.76	0.19
Male	50	3.18			50	2.00		
Female	25	2.82			25	1.62		
Age			0.66	0.66			2.14	0.07
25 or less	6	2.87			6	2.42		
26–35	32	3.22			32	2.22		
36–45	18	3.18			18	1.47		
46–55	9	2.78			9	1.56		
56–65	5	2.56			5	1.40		
66 or above	4	2.30			4	1.00		
Country of residence			2.16	0.06			0.97	0.45
Mainland China	13	2.72			13	1.88		
Taiwan	27	3.39			27	1.76		
Singapore	4	2.65			4	2.50		
USA	12	3.18			12	2.21		
Canada	7	1.80			7	2.21		
Australia	2	4.20			2	1.00		
Malaysia	11	3.29			11	1.41		
Length of stay in HK			0.88	0.03*			0.85	0.99
3 nights or less	44	3.33			43	1.86		
4 nights or more	32	2.70			33	1.86		

	N			N		
Annual household income		1.70	0.14		1.51	0.19
Less than US$10,000	9	3.76		9	1.72	
US$10,000–29,999	14	2.54		14	1.68	
US$30,000–49,999	13	2.80		13	1.67	
US$50,000–69,999	9	3.42		9	1.78	
US$70,000–99,999	7	2.80		7	2.57	
US$100,000 or more	13	3.52		13	2.54	
Don't know/unsure	3	2.33		3	1.00	
Highest education attained		1.10	0.36		0.97	0.43
Less than secondary/ high school	2	3.90		2	1.00	
Completed secondary/ high school	17	3.13		17	1.59	
Some college or university	10	2.62		10	1.60	
Completed college/university	37	3.25		36	2.08	
Completed postgraduate degree	10	2.56		11	1.95	
Main purpose of visit		0.91	0.46		0.48	0.75
Vacation/leisure	30	3.10		30	1.98	
Business/meeting	23	3.26		22	1.66	
Visiting friends	7	2.26		8	1.94	
Visiting relatives	4	2.75		4	1.38	
Others	12	3.18		12	2.04	

accommodation prearranged. It also implies that the hotel may be able to persuade PITs to stay a bit longer by providing well-designed and maintained facilities as well as quality service to them.

19.6.6 Implications for small and medium-sized enterprises

Although small and medium-sized enterprises (SMEs) play an increasingly important role in many economies, it seems that it is not easy to define what an SME is; as stated by Gore *et al.* (1992), a small firm is one of those things that is recognized when seen but difficult to define. Storey (1994) also echoed the view that there is no single, uniformly acceptable definition of a small firm in an industry. In general, the most widely accepted definition is based on the ideas of the Bolton Committee (1971). According to the committee, a small firm should meet the following criteria:

- They should have a relatively small share of their marketplace.
- They should be managed by owners or part-owners in a personalized way, and not through the medium of a formalized management structure.
- They should be independent, in the sense of not forming part of a larger enterprise.

No matter what definition we use to define what a small firm is, there is no doubt that limited resources characterize smaller enterprises. In the hotel industry, where customers use different internal or external cues to evaluate a hotel, many hoteliers may use many different external cues, such as the hotel brand, room rate, hotel facilities, hotel grading and the awards the hotel has received to influence the consumer's perceptions of their product. Notwithstanding, small hoteliers may not be able to spare the additional resources to invest in those attributes, however much they may wish to further develop the PIT market. For instance, most hotels of this type may not have their own fleet of limousines to provide free/discounted airport round-trip services. They also may not want to pay for accreditation to have their hotels accredited with some internationally recognized awards, such as ISO 9000. In addition, they are usually the weaker partners in marketing-channel relationships and their wider influence in the marketplace is generally quite restricted. As a result of these constraints, partnership with both private- and public-sector firms could represent a potential marketing strategy for small hoteliers. For instance, small hotels may consider establishing alliances to promote their brand names together and to share the same airport transportation facilities for guests, in order to enhance a guest's confidence in their services and, at the same time, to save on operational costs. In fact, there are many potential strategic partners a small or medium-sized hotel firm could consider. These include reservation services, marketing consortia, airlines, car rental agencies, credit card companies, tour operators, etc. The partnership could create benefits from a mix of resources, the meshing of firms, culture and functions, thus offering a strong synergistic opportunity. Despite the possibility of losing a certain degree of autonomy in operations in addition to the joining fee, group solidarity can be achieved, which can secure a small hotel firm a better position to compete with the larger chains.

Rhys (1989) has suggested that a small firm should pursue its marketing function in a way that aims at insulating it as much as possible from direct competition with more efficient producers. That is, small firms should exploit niches left by larger firms. As larger hotels do not pay much attention to 'walk-ins and tourists calling from the airport', small and medium-sized hotels could change their business strategies slightly to focus on this relatively high-yield market. They may use a more personal selling technique to communicate with their target audiences, such as hotel booking counter staff and other customer service staff at the airport. Establishing networks of personal contacts and making good use of such contacts are an important aspect of the way SMEs do business.

19.7 Conclusions

Although many studies have been conducted in the past to investigate the preferences of travellers in selecting a hotel, little research has been conducted into the buying behaviour of PITs who have not secured a hotel booking before they arriving at their destination. This study has shown the importance of understanding how PITs will select a hotel after they have arrived at their destination. It also examines the attributes that this market may perceive as important in determining their final selection. Convenient hotel location, good hotel service and good hotel reputation are the top three factors influencing their decision. Based on the findings from the study, it is suggested that hoteliers adopt strategies such as offering complimentary/discounted round-trip airport transportation to enhance accessibility, maintaining good hotel services and cultivating a good image of the hotel in the minds of customers. Small and medium-sized hotels are advised to pursue other strategies in developing this niche market, which is often neglected by larger hotel firms. With limited resources, these hotels could consider establishing partnerships with other service suppliers to enhance the confidence of customers. Additionally, they should devote more resources to building up personal networks with their target business audiences through activities such as personal selling techniques in order to trade first-hand information, understanding customer needs and wants and providing business opportunities.

Acknowledgements

This research project was funded from the President's Reserve, the Hong Kong Polytechnic University. The authors would also like to acknowledge the cooperation of the Hong Kong Tourism Board and the Airport Authority of Hong Kong.

References

Ananth, M., DeMicco, J., Moreo, J. and Howey M. (1992) Marketplace lodging needs of mature travellers. *Cornell Hotel Restaurant Administration Quarterly* 33(4), 12–24.

Baker S., Bradley P. and Huyton J. (1994) *Principles of Hotel Front Office Operations.* Cassell, London, 36 pp.

Banerjee, N. (1994) A safe traveller is a happy traveller. *Wall Street Journal* 223(2), B1.

Barsky, Jonathan, D. and Labagh, R. (1992) A strategy for customer satisfaction. *Cornell Hotel Restaurant Administration Quarterly* 33(5), 32–40.

Bellenger, D.N., Robertson, D.H. and Hirschman, E.C. (1978) Impulse buying varies by product. *Journal of Advertising Research* 18(6), 15–18.

Bolton Committee (1971) Report of the Committee of Inquiry on Small Firms, November 1971 (The Bolton Report).

Clow, K.E., Garretson, J.A. and Kurtz, D.L. (1994) An exploratory study into the purchase decision process used by leisure travellers in hotel selection. *Journal of Hospitality and Leisure Marketing* 2(4), 53–72.

Cobb, C.J. and Hoyer, W.D. (1986) Planned versus impulse purchase behaviour. *Journal of Retailing* 62(4), 384–409.

Engel, J.F. and Blackwell, R.D. (1982) *Consumer Behaviour*, 4th edn. Dryden Press, Chicago, Illinois, 552 pp.

Feiertag, H. (2001) Don't jump the gun on lowering room rates: sell more actively. *Hotel and Motel Management* 216(16), 26.

Gore, C., Murray, K. and Richardson, B. (1992) *Strategic Decision Making*, Cassell, London, 115 pp.

Han, Y.K., Morgan, G.A., Kotsiopulos, A. and Kang-Park, J. (1991) Impulse buying behaviour of apparel purchasers. *Clothing and Textile Research Journal* 9(3), 15–21.

Knutson, B.J. (1988) Hotel services and room amenities in the economy, mid-price and luxury market segments: what do frequent travellers expect? *Hospitality Education and Research Journal* 12(2), 259–264.

Kollat, D.T. and Willett, R.P. (1967) Customer impulse purchasing behaviour. *Journal of Marketing Research* 4(1), 21–31.

Lewis, R.C. (1984) Getting the most from marketing research (part III): the basis of hotel selection. *Cornell Hotel and Restaurant Administration Quarterly* 25(3), 54–69.

Lewis, R.C. (1985) Predicting hotel choice: the factor underlying perception. *Cornell Hotel Restaurant Administration Quarterly* 26(3), 82–96.

McCarthy, T. (2001) Commitment to rates is crucial. *Lodging Hospitality* 57(5), 11.

McCleary, K.W. and Weaver, P.A. (1991) Are frequent-guest programs effective? *Cornell Hotel Restaurant Administration Quarterly* 32(2), 38–45.

Marshall, A. (1993) Safety top guest's priority list; sell security as no. 1 amenity. *Hotel and Motel Management* 208(11), 21.

Parasuraman, A., Zeithaml, A. and Berry, L. (1985) A conceptual model of service quality and its implication for future research. *Journal of Marketing* 49(4), 41–50.

Phillips, H. and Bradshaw, R. (1993) How customers actually shop: customer interaction with the point of sales. *Journal of the Market Research Society* 35(1), 51–62.

Piron, F. (1991) Defining impulse purchasing, *Advances in Consumer Research* 18(1), 509–514.

Powers, T.F. (1997) *Marketing Hospitality,* 2nd edn. Wiley, New York, 440 pp.

Rhys, G. (1989) Smaller car firms – will they survive? *Long Range Planning* 22(5), 22–29.

Rivers, M.J., Toh, R.S. and Alaoui, M. (1991) Frequent-stayer programs: the demographic, behavioral, and attitudinal characteristics of hotel steady sleepers. *Journal of Travel Research* 30(2), 41–45.

Rook, D.W. and Fisher, R.J. (1995) Trait and normative aspects of impulsive buying behaviour. *Journal of Consumer Research* 22(3), 305 313.

Stern, H. (1962) The significance of impulse buying today. *Journal of Marketing* 26(2), 59–62.

Storey, D.J. (1994) *Understanding the Small Business Sector.* Routledge, London, 355 pp.

Weaver, P.A. and Heung, C.O. (1993) Do American business travellers have different hotel service requirements? *International Journal of Contemporary Hospitality Management* 5(3), 16–21.

Weinberg, P. and Gottwald, W. (1982) Impulsive consumer buying as a result of emotions. *Journal of Business Research* 10(1), 43–57.

Welles, G. (1986) We're in the habit of impulsive buying. *USA Today* 1, 21.

Youn, S.H. and Faber, R.J. (2000) Impulse buying: its relation to personality traits and cues. *Advances in Consumer Research* 27(1), 179–185.

20 Small and Medium-sized Libyan Tourism Enterprises and the National Tourism Development Plan for Libya

Mokhtar Jwaili,[1] Brychan Thomas[1] and Eleri Jones[2]

[1]Welsh Enterprise Institute, University of Glamorgan Business School, University of Glamorgan, Treforest, UK; [2]Welsh School of Hospitality, Tourism and Leisure Management, University of Wales Institute, Cardiff, UK

20.1 Introduction

Libya (see Fig. 20.1) is heavily dependent upon the oil industry, which generates almost all its foreign currency earnings and contributes about 25% of Libya's gross domestic product (GDP) (Central Intelligence Agency, 2004). Libya has a small population (5.6 million) and one of the highest per capita GDPs in Africa and is moving towards a more market-based economy by introducing plans for privatizing industry, removing subsidies and applying for membership of the World Trade Organization (Central Intelligence Agency, 2004). The tourism industry is becoming increasingly important in Libya in terms of investment, job creation, competitiveness and quality and is perceived to be the best long-term alternative to the oil industry. With 1820 km of coastline, five United Nations Educational, Scientific and Cultural Organization (UNESCO) World Heritage sites and spectacular mountain and desert landscapes, Libya has outstanding natural resources for tourism which are unrivalled in the Mediterranean region (Abboud, 2004). Tourism planning focuses on adventure travel in the desert and cultural tourism and entertainment in coastal resorts, where there are plans to build marinas to attract yachts sailing in the Mediterranean (Abboud, 2004). Libya has a target of 1.2 million visitors for 2006, having experienced 800,000 visitors in 2003 – a substantial increase over the 1993 figure of 15,000 visitors (Stalker, 2004).

The nature and activities of small and medium-sized enterprises (SMEs) are an important consideration for the development of the tourism industry in Libya. SMEs are of strategic importance to economies like Libya as they: contribute to growth in employment at a higher rate than larger firms and they may well, in the long term, provide a significant share of overall employment; help in the restructuring and streamlining of large state-owned enterprises by enabling them to abandon and/or sell off non-core production activities and by absorbing redundant employees; provide the economy with greater flexibility in the provision of

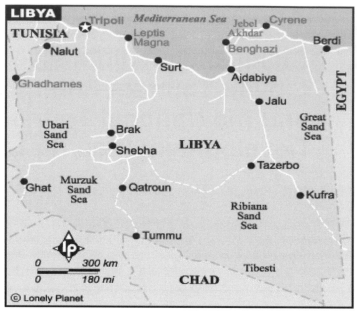

Fig. 20.1.   Libya (from Lonely Planet, 2004).

services and the manufacture of a variety of consumer goods; act as a seed-bed for the development of entrepreneurial skills and innovation; play an important role in the provision of services in the community; and can make an important contribution to regional development programmes.

Libya's National Tourism Development Plan (NTDP) identifies a number of initiatives to develop the Libyan tourism industry and emphasizes the role of the public sector in destination development through short- and long-term planning, marketing, infrastructure and human resource development. However, it recognizes neither the role of SMEs in tourism development nor the role of the public sector in supporting SMEs. This chapter considers the role of SMEs in destination development in Libya. SME reaction to the NTDP is investigated through a series of semi-structured interviews with SME owner-managers. The chapter concludes with a series of recommendations for public-sector interventions appropriate to SME development within the Libyan tourism sector.

20.2 The Development of the National Tourism Development Plan

The organizational framework of the Libyan tourism industry was initially developed in the late 1960s. In 1968, the first Tourism Ministry was established through Royal Act Number 44, setting out its organizational structure and activities, which included: welcoming and facilitating incoming tourists; classifying hotels, guesthouses, restaurants and other tourist establishments; granting exemptions to foreign investors to allow ownership of capital assets in the country; managing security and safety in tourism areas; setting out licensing laws for all tourist activities; controlling employment procedures within the tourism industry; and approving price lists in tourism establishments.

The Libyan General Board for Tourism (LGBT) was the main body for all tourism-related activity and was established in 1989. Since 2003, the General People's Committee for Tourism (GPCT) has continued the work of the LGBT. A major contribution of the LGBT was to complete the development of the NTDP, which was commissioned in February 1997 by the World Tourism Organization acting as the executing agency of the United Nations Development Programme for the GPCT. The NTDP was published in December 1998 – its aim was to provide Libya with:

> a realistic and implementable base for the development of the sector through the establishment and promulgation of a policy framework, short and long term objectives, supporting strategic guidelines and a five year action programme for the period 1999 to 2003.

> (NTDP, 1998: i)

One recommendation of the NTDP was to establish the Tourism Investment and Promotion Board (TIPB). The mission of the TIPB was to promote and invest in various aspects of tourism, and to introduce the richness of Libya's unique history, culture and people to international tourists.

20.3 The Structure of the Libyan Tourism Sector

The tourism industry in Libya comprises eight types of business. Five of the eight types comprising 3935 businesses (99%) are SME-based (see Table 20.1). The

Table 20.1. Type and number of enterprises forming the Libyan tourism industry (from Abuzed, 2001).

Type	Number	Public/Private	SME based	%
Local tourist authority	4	Public	No	0.1
Hotels and guesthouses	195	Private	Yes	4.9
Museums	18	Public	No	0.4
Historical sites and buildings	19	Public	No	0.5
Nature reserve services	6	Public	Yes	0.1
Sports and sport recreation services	12	Public/Private	Yes	0.3
Tourism education and training institutions	6	Public	No	0.2
Tour operators	15	Private	Yes	0.4
Travel agents	225	Private	Yes	5.6
Restaurants and cafés	3500	Private	Yes	87.5
Total	4000			100

largest category are restaurants and cafés, with 3500 (87.5%) of the enterprises, followed by travel agents, with 225 (5.6%), hotels and guesthouses, with 195 (4.9%), and tour operators, with 15 (0.4%). All of these enterprises fall under either direct or indirect control of the GPCT.

20.4 Challenges to the Development of Libyan SMEs

The problems facing SMEs and public-sector policy measures in Libya can be considered in two categories. The first category is comprised of the general problems which face many tourism industries in developing countries (SESRTCIC, 2001) and which include:

- Lack of knowledge and awareness: there is a lack of awareness of the economic importance of tourism as an industry. This is true for both its positive impact as a potential source of foreign exchange and employment and its negative impact as a leakage of the country's own resources.
- Lack of tourism-related infrastructure: the country lacks sufficient infrastructure requisite for the development of a successful tourism sector. Most important among these are hotels and lodging services, transportation, communication and tourism information services.
- Lack of tourism investment: investment in services-oriented projects is considered high risk, and foreign investors, especially private companies, are still demanding more assurances from the government to encourage their inward investment.

The second category is the more specific problems faced by SMEs in Libya, many of which result from public-sector agendas (see Table 20.2). If these problems are addressed and the role of SMEs in the problem-solving process is recognized, this will have positive benefits for the development of the Libyan tourism industry.

20.5 Methodology

The study adopted both secondary and primary data collection. Secondary data were used to identify the existing environment for the tourism industry in Libya. Semi-structured interviews were designed to examine, in detail, the reflections of SME owner-managers on the NTDP and its importance to the SME sector. Interviews were conducted with the six SME owner-managers who have the highest participation rate in promotional programmes run jointly with GPCT and TIPB, which include international tourism shows and fairs. One interview was undertaken with a senior policy maker in the TIPB. All interviews were conducted during visits by the interviewees to the World Travel Market in London in November 2003.

Table 20.2. Problems affecting Libyan SMEs (from Abuzed, 2002).

Lack of coordination between LGBT/GPCT and tourism companies about tourism marketing and the organization of tourism shows and festivals inside and outside the country

The capacity of the transport system is insufficient to cope with the increasing demand in all the various types of tourism activities offered by the industry, e.g. desert tourism

Accommodation outlets do not meet international standards and prices are higher in relation to the services provided. This is disadvantageous in international markets especially when compared with other regional competitors

Lack of foreign language capability in places of interest to tourists and in ports across the country

Cleanliness of all cities, towns, roads and places of interest is not high on the agenda

There is a lack of facilities in almost all places of interest to the tourist

There is a lack of preparation and training of all personnel in the tourism guidance sector

There is a lack of coordination to develop a competitive pricing policy

Visa procedures for tourists are still complicated

There is a lack of regulations to encourage local investors

The LGBT/GPCT have delayed the establishment of regional tourism offices

There is no comprehensive regulation for the tourism industry that allows it to benefit from developments in the international tourism market or from international tourism research

20.6 Results and Discussion

20.6.1 SME reaction to the NTDP

The people interviewed represent some of the most active SMEs in Libya. However, not all the interviewees had participated in the development of the NTDP, even though they were in business at the time. All participants emphasized their high expectations of the NTDP as a master plan – a professional and comprehensive blueprint for the development of the requisite infrastructure on which to grow the Libyan tourism industry – identifying key projects necessary for the development of tourism in Libya and proposing an organizational structure for the Ministry of Tourism and the organizations and institutions needed to deliver the change. The SMEs stressed the importance of the marketing aspects of the NTDP and particularly of recognizing that, before the development of the NTDP, there had been no coordinated approach to promoting the country as a tourist destination and putting Libya on the international tourism map. The SME owner-managers commented that the NTDP provided a foundation for the marketing efforts of individual companies. The NTDP as the cornerstone for the tourism industry was seen as critically important for the coordinated development of the industry by all interviewees.

Participants reported that the NTDP had given them an extra incentive to start their business with more trust in what for Libya must be regarded as a new industry. However, these high expectations soon evaporated as problems arose early in the process. The objectives identified within the plan were not seen to have been achieved by the SME owner-managers. Both SME owner-managers and the representative of the TIPB agreed that, to date, the government has not done what should have been done to implement the plan. Ongoing changes in the organizational structure and arrangements for tourism in Libya were perceived to be major issues in this respect. A key issue associated with the plan was that it was drawn up during the time of the sanctions on Libya and according to the prevailing conditions. The scenario is completely different in post-sanctions Libya. Another issue identified was that the plan had taken only 2 months to be developed, which was considered by the SME owner-managers to be too short a time-scale for such a major plan. The lack of participation of local experts and interest groups has resulted in poor location of the projects identified for support of the industry. The government was seen as being responsible for the non-implementation of the plan. The SME owner-managers perceived that the government had never made any real efforts to implement the plan and accomplish its objectives. In fact, the only NTDP objective that was seen to have been achieved was the establishment of the TIPB.

Not all of the interviewees were familiar with the objectives of the NTDP. However, all agreed that it was critically important to have objectives for the industry as a whole. There was a strong feeling that, for example, the marketing objectives should be monitored annually to determine the performance that had been achieved and revised in the light of the findings, with any problems being addressed. However, this has not happened.

The SMEs were trying to do their best to benefit from the objectives laid out in the NTDP but emphasized the key role of the public sector in helping them to do that. SME planning had taken place before the development of the NTDP and SMEs have had, of necessity, to have very clear objectives. However, SME plans by their very nature take a fairly short-term view. SMEs tend to work independently and there is little or no coordination between them – a situation which can often lead to conflict between SMEs. SMEs perceived that they are the only stakeholders trying seriously to develop the industry, as they are the direct beneficiaries (or otherwise) of the industry's prosperity. The SMEs stressed the importance of development and competitiveness in both domestic and international markets and the key role of participation in international events, brochure updating and the use of the Internet in product marketing.

None of the SME owner-managers interviewed could understand why the government had spent so much money on a plan it was ignoring. There were strong feelings that the NTDP was not delivering its objectives. The Ministry of Tourism was seen as key to the industry's future, with an urgent need to monitor the performance of the sector and to revise the NTDP appropriately in the light of the monitoring exercise, addressing any issues of underperformance, and to ensure its ongoing fitness for its purpose.

20.6.2 What would SMEs like the Ministry of Tourism to do?

SME owner-managers emphasized the World Tourism Organization's assertions that in the 21st century tourism will be the number one economic activity globally and will exceed industrial and agricultural returns. They stressed the high priority for tourism planning and investment effort in order for the country to become a successful tourist destination and were very aware of the magnitude of the tourism agenda for the country, in terms of creating an appropriate environment for tourism, marketing, infrastructure development and education and training. The agenda that the SMEs would set for the Ministry of Tourism would include: gathering market intelligence; coordinating marketing activity and promoting Libya on the international travel market; unpacking the NTDP into smaller time periods; development of the tourism infrastructure; resolution of financial issues; development of an appropriate legislative and regulatory framework to support tourism activity; coordination of new product development and differentiation of the Libyan tourism product; development of education and training capacity; and recognition of the need for research.

20.6.2.1 Gathering market intelligence

Ongoing environmental scanning and the gathering of market intelligence is a function that could usefully be coordinated by the Ministry of Tourism. Market intelligence and particularly trend data are essential to an understanding of consumer behaviour and making the Libyan tourism product responsive to consumer needs.

20.6.2.2 Coordinating marketing activity and promoting Libya on the international travel market

There was a strong feeling that more attention should be paid to international fairs and markets to promote Libya's rich heritage and that there should be better coordination between the public and private sectors in promoting the country in international events. The SMEs felt that tourism offices should be established in key markets, notably Europe, Japan and China. SMEs also expressed a perception that membership of international organizations would be of major benefit to developments related to international tourism markets. SMEs wanted to be involved with the public sector in arranging familiarization visits for media and tour operators.

20.6.2.3 Unpacking the NTDP into smaller time periods

With regard to the NTDP, it was felt that the 20-year time frame for the plan was too large and that the plan should be broken down into smaller and more digestible time periods (6 months to 1 year). The SMEs would like to see a reassessment of the NTDP's objectives to ensure that they are realistic and appropriate for the needs of the industry.

20.6.2.4 Development of the tourism infrastructure

The Libyan tourism infrastructure – airports, hotels, camps, restaurants, road signs, transportation and telecommunication systems – is in urgent need of attention. One way that the SMEs felt that this could be addressed was through the government providing more incentives for foreign direct investment in tourism. Libya's international image may deter foreign investment and, as Morgan and Pritchard (2004: 62) comment: 'investors may take longer to return to what they perceive as unreliable business climates'.

20.6.2.5 Resolution of financial issues

SMEs are experiencing a number of problems associated with financial issues, either directly or indirectly via the impact on tourists. There is an urgent need to improve the financial system to simplify financial transactions and enable the use of credit cards. SMEs would also like to see better financial support for SMEs through better coordination with financial institutions and the provision of enhanced services for SMEs. They want the government to find a way of financially assisting SMEs through grants, low-interest loans and longer periods of repayment.

20.6.2.6 Development of an appropriate legislative and regulatory framework to support tourism activity

The tourism law, which is based on the first tourism law passed in 1968, is in urgent need of updating. SMEs reported that a proposal has been forwarded to the General Board for Tourism and Antiquities in relation to this issue. Alongside developments of the legislative framework, the SMEs would like to see developments in the regulatory framework for tourism activity. Specifically the SMEs pointed to the need for a unified licensing system – the SMEs would like to see a review and updating of the quality grading classification system for all tourism products (hotels, guest-houses, restaurants, travel agents, etc.).

20.6.2.7 New product development and differentiation of the Libyan tourism product

In commenting about what the SMEs should do in relation to development of the Libyan product, SMEs felt that there needs to be a focus on creatively developing a distinctive Libyan tourism product which is well differentiated from its competitors – brand Libya! However, the challenges of marketing brand Libya in the global marketplace must not be underestimated and, alongside product differentiation, issues of product pricing to ensure destination competitiveness must be addressed. Current pricing of Libyan tourism products makes them expensive and lower value for money in comparison to neighbouring competitors with similar products, notably Tunisia. SMEs feel that there should be more concentration on independent, up-market tourism rather than mass tourism and recognition of the strengths of Libya as a tourist destination, e.g. historical and archaeological sites, virgin beaches and security. In terms of product development, the SMEs want to see a larger and more diverse range of tourism products.

They would like to see more attention paid to the potential of ecotourism, especially in beach areas.

20.6.2.8 Development of education and training capacity

The SMEs want to see the development of better education and training facilities for the industry through the establishment of new institutions/centres and better support for established tourism training institutions and centres. They feel that more concentration should be directed towards training the manpower for the industry to ensure high-quality service provision.

20.6.2.9 Recognition of the need for research

The SMEs want to see Libya becoming a member of international organizations to share benefits from research related to the environment and sustainable tourism development. SMEs perceive that successful research needs to involve both national and international institutions and centres working in partnership, so that the Libyan tourism industry can benefit through participation from both the wider experience of international research institutions and in-depth knowledge of the local environment held by national research institutions and ensure that proposed developments meet local needs. It was felt that there is particular merit in collaboration with neighbouring countries with a longer experience in the tourism industry, notably Egypt and Tunisia, particularly in relation to marketing and workforce development.

20.6.3 Establishment of a single voice for the Libyan tourism industry

The SMEs felt that there was plenty of opportunity for SMEs to develop a clear coordinated plan of action and that enhanced coordination would help the promotion of Libya as a tourism destination. SMEs perceive a need for the creation of an institution to be a link between SMEs and the government. One suggestion from the SMEs was the establishment of a tourism council to represent the private sector as a single voice for the tourism industry, facilitating interaction with related sectors and lobbying the government. Such a body could work collectively to arrange charter flights from destinations unable at the moment to offer cheap flights to Libya with the objective of facilitating tourism arrivals in Libya.

20.6.4 Consensus on the essential nature of the public sector in tourism development and optimism for the future of the Libyan tourism industry

There was overwhelming consensus among the SMEs about the critical importance of the help provided by the public sector (including the Ministry of Tourism, other governmental organizations, non-governmental organizations and financial institutions) to SMEs and, particularly, the importance of it being available at the right time and in the right place. The SMEs felt that the help provided by the public sector is vital for the growth and development of the Libyan tourism industry as it provides the guidelines for personnel and companies engaged in activities related to tourism in the country, as well as providing the support SMEs need to manage their businesses and overcome obstacles.

All of the SMEs were optimistic about the future of the tourism industry in Libya, some cautiously optimistic, and others extremely optimistic and felt that there is no doubt that Libya possesses what it takes to be an internationally competitive tourist destination. All the SMEs saw the role of the Ministry of Tourism as key to the successful development of the Libyan tourism industry. The SMEs stressed the importance of recognizing that tourism interests cross the public and private sectors and involve a range of diverse interests: transportation; catering; administration; telecommunications; security; general services; and banking. To enhance the competitiveness of Libya as a tourist destination will require coordination of and improvement in all these sectors.

20.7 Conclusions

SMEs represent 99% of the enterprises involved in the industry and are important stakeholders in the development of the Libyan tourism industry. There are a number of factors in Libya that make it difficult for tourism to flourish. The SME owner-managers interviewed identified a number of interventions which they would like the Libyan government to make to enable them to achieve their full potential. These interventions fall into seven key areas relating to: the legislative framework; the economic environment; investment in infrastructure development; public-sector support for the tourism private sector; development of world-class quality standards for Libyan tourism products; coordination of marketing initiatives; and enhanced education and training for human resource development.

Key priorities for the Libyan government as identified by Libyan SMEs would be:

- Raising public awareness of the opportunities and challenges facing the country's tourism industry.
- Introducing regulations to control tourism service quality.
- Development of more facilitative support for tourists through the provision of better tourist information, immigration and visa systems and police services.
- Encouraging investment (domestic and foreign) in infrastructure development.
- Encouraging and coordinating private-sector initiatives and promoting public–private partnerships for tourism development.
- Raising the standards of personnel in the sector through improving education and training institutions involved in tourism-related qualifications and education programmes.
- Improving banking and financial services, particularly those facilitating the transfer of money.
- Enhancing cooperation and benefiting from the opportunities available to neighbouring countries, especially Tunisia and Egypt.

It is clear that there are major opportunities for the Libyan government, through the Ministry of Tourism, to enhance the operating environment for SMEs and to implement specific initiatives that will support the development and marketing of the Libyan tourism industry and enhance the competitiveness of Libya in domestic and international markets, thus enabling the industry to achieve its full potential, to the ultimate benefit of the Libyan economy.

References

Abboud, N. (2004) Libya: a non-Western style tourism. *Islamic Tourism* 10, 70–74.

Abuzed, Z. (2001) Data taken from an interview on Libyan SMEs with Z. Abuzed, Head of Licensing and Classification Department, General Board for Tourism and Antiquities, Tripoli, Libya.

Abuzed, Z. (2002) Report on tourism problems presented to the Secretary of General Board for Tourism and Antiquities, General Board for Tourism and Antiquities, Tripoli, Libya.

Central Intelligence Agency (2004) Libya. In: *The World Factbook* [on-line]. Available from: http://www.cia.gov/cia/publications/factbook/geos/ly.html Accessed on 30 April 2004.

Lonely Planet (2004) Libya [on-line]. Available from: http://www.lonelyplanet.com/mapshells/africa/libya/libya.htm Accessed on 30 April 2004.

Morgan, N. and Pritchard, A. (2004) Meeting the destination branding challenge. In: Morgan, N., Pritchard, A. and Pride, R. (eds) *Destination Branding: Creating the Unique Destination Proposition,* 2nd edn. Elsevier Butterworth-Heinemann, Oxford, UK, pp. 59–78.

NTDP (National Tourism Development Plan) (1998) *Tourism Planning and Development,* Vol. 1. World Tourism Organization, United Nations Development Programme and the General People's Committee for Tourism, Tripoli, Libya.

SESRTCIC (2001) Tourism development in the OIC countries: further steps towards promotion of cooperation. In: *Second Islamic Conference of Ministers of Tourism.* Kuala Lumpur, Malaysia. Statistical, economic and social research and training centre for Islamic countries, Ankara, Turkey, pp. 360–362.

Stalker, I. (2004) Libya: optimism about the future of tourism. *Islamic Tourism* 11, 58.

21

'A Virtual Huanying, Selamat Datang and Herzlich Willkommen!' The Internet as a Cross-cultural Promotional Tool for Tourism

WOLFGANG GEORG ARLT

Leisure and Tourism Management, University of Applied Sciences, Stralsund, Germany

21.1 Introduction

The Internet is an important cross-cultural promotional tool for tourism that can be used to weave together text and graphics to globally market individual tourism businesses and destinations. The Internet is an *extremely cost-effective* marketing medium, which has the potential to level the playing field for small tourism businesses. However, in order to stand out from the Internet crowd, it is important that small and medium-sized tourism enterprises (tourism SMEs) can demonstrate an appreciation of cross-cultural issues, e.g. language, colour and the significance of images, in the development of their websites. Visitor images of destinations are important drivers of consumer choice and, therefore, how destinations integrate text and images to communicate information to potential visitors is critically important to image formation.

This chapter discusses the role of tourism in inventing the world and the growing importance of tourists from non-Western cultures, together with the relationship between tourism and the Internet. It then considers the Internet as a cross-cultural communication tool in tourism and reports the results of two studies conducted in 2002. The chapter concludes by providing practical recommendations for destination management organizations (DMOs) and tourism SMEs.

21.2 The Role of Tourism in Inventing the World

Tourism is one of the strongest narrative forces in the world, 'without doubt, one of the major social and economic phenomena of modern times' (Sharpley 2002: 11), and has shaped the world as we know it today. How we see 'Elsewhereland' –

the part of the world where we are strangers – is increasingly determined by touristic experiences which are not naïve first-hand experiences but are informed in advance by diverse media, especially 'cultural mediators' (Ooi, 2002) that shape our expectations and our 'gaze' (Urry, 2001) and which are beyond the control of the tourism industry, as images are not simply the result of official promotions (Goodall and Ashworth, 1988). Destination images are informed by non-tourist information, such as history, architecture, art, film, literature, religion, news coverage and, last but by no means least, by friends and colleagues who have actually been there.

Notwithstanding this, some parts of image formation are controllable and the responsibility of tourism marketing departments all over the world. DMOs have more opportunities to influence image formation through marketing for less familiar and accessible 'other' destinations (Bieger, 2002). 'Otherness' is perceived in the same way distances are perceived in tourism – not in kilometres, but in accessibility, including cultural and linguistic accessibility. Marketing activities are more effective for places regarded as more exotic, e.g. China for Europeans or Europe for Chinese.

21.3 The Growing Importance of Non-Western Tourists

There is almost no country in the world where the government does not see tourism as an important business sector and where the people do not see travelling for pleasure as a desirable, even if not yet affordable, pastime. Tourism is 'one of the most obvious forms of globalisation' (Meethan, 2001: 34).

In 2002, international, i.e. cross-border, tourism generated 702 million departures and US$472 billion tourism receipts (WTO, 2003). Despite slow growth in 2001/2002, the World Tourism Organization (WTO) is still maintaining its prediction of 1 billion international departures in 2010 and 1.6 billion departures in 2020 (WTO, 2003). Most of these 1 billion 'new' tourists will originate from East, South-east and South Asia. In 2002, the combined spending of Japanese and Chinese international tourists (including tourists from Hong Kong) accounted for 11.4% of total tourist spending, which is second only to the USA (WTO, 2003).

Different estimates place the number of citizens of the People's Republic of China with the economic means to travel abroad at 50 million (Arlt, 2002), 65 million (Chon, cited in Smith, 2003) or even 80 million (Xu, 2002). From almost 17 million international tourists from China in 2002 (China National Tourist Office, 2003), the WTO predicts 100 million Chinese international travellers by 2020.

Hence, for the first time, tourism will become a two-way highway between the Occidental and the Oriental world. According to WTO predictions, not only will China become the number one tourist destination worldwide, but it will also become the fourth biggest source market for tourists. For European cities, regions and companies, it will be the decisive factor in their quest for growth if Asian travellers perceive them as coveted tourist destinations.

21.4 Tourism and the Internet

It seems difficult to believe that the Internet has been in existence for less than a decade, having become an indispensable daily tool for about 12% of the world population (Globalreach, 2004), which is well above the approximate 4% of all global citizens who engage in international travelling (WTO, 1997). Roughly one-third each of the approximate 700 million users are located in the USA, Asia and rest of the world, respectively. Likewise in three almost equal parts, the user community is divided into having English, another European or an Asian language as their mother tongue. Chinese, Japanese and Korean speakers comprise more than one-quarter of all Internet users. As far as the Internet is concerned, Africa is a non-entity (Globalreach, 2004).

While the English-speaking world has more or less reached saturation point in Internet access, Internet usage is still increasing rapidly in countries like China and the relative importance of English has dwindled from more than 50% in 2000 to 35% in September 2003. Non-English content is, however, still found on only about one-third of the approximately 3 billion online web pages (Arlt, 2003).

Travel and tourism are a major field of Internet usage. In terms of sales, tourism products, such as air tickets, hotel rooms and last-minute holiday packages, are the most common products sold via the Internet, apart from books. This demonstrates that the Internet is functioning as a booking machine. In 2002 online travel sales reached US$27 billion in the North American market and 7.6

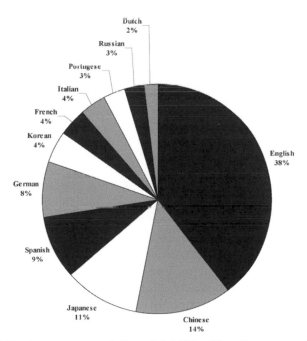

Fig. 21.1. Online language populations: total 680 million (from www.glreach.com September 2003).

billion Euro in the European market, capturing 14% and 5% of the total market, respectively (Marcussen, 2003).

The situation is different for incoming tourism, as travel decision making requires qualified information and confidence. In this situation, the Internet is primarily an image-building tool, important to the decision of going (or not) to a specific destination or to use the services of a company at the destination. Incoming tourists are less spontaneous. Asian travellers tend to travel in groups and are less likely to determine the details of their itinerary themselves. There-fore, perceived images will play an important role in their decision to join a tour group which offers certain destinations or services.

Whereas established markets can be reached by active communication via direct marketing, trade exhibitions, traditional public relations (PR) and adver-tisements, new incoming tourists are not easy to target. In using the Internet as a marketing channel, it is important to understand that customers find the business more than the business finds the customer – potential new visitors use the Internet to independently locate a website. Despite this, the Internet is undoubt-edly the cheapest, most convenient and efficient way to address these potential new customers in distant countries.

21.5 Cross-cultural Internet Marketing

Herbig opens his classic *Handbook of Cross-cultural Marketing* with the statement that: 'Over 450 definitions of the word culture exist' (Herbig, 1998: 11). No attempt will be made here to add to the debate, as the statement that there are cultural differences between European destinations and Asian source markets will probably not be disputed. It is useful to introduce the concept of four different tourism cultures as a thinking tool (Thiem, 1994). Thiem (1994) distinguishes between the daily-life cultures of both the source and the target region plus the specific culture of travellers away from home, which differs from their daily-life culture. The fourth culture is the one on show to the tourists, as a 'genuine fake' (Brown, 1996) or a 'mediated authenticity' (Ooi, 2002). For cross-cultural marketing this communicated culture can be adapted to each source market culture, stressing common points or explaining local culture in terms of relating to the source culture and therefore making it easier for the source market to understand. Gesteland (2002: 15) states that the 'Iron Rule No. 1' for cross-cultural marketing is that 'in international business, the seller is expected to adapt to the buyer'. For cross-cultural Internet marketing this can be expanded to three rules. The potential customer has to be able to:

• Find the information.
• Understand the information.
• Feel comfortable about the way it is presented.

The technical problem of finding the information has been reduced with the operation of better global search engines; however, domain addresses which are neither dot.com addresses nor top-level domains of the targeted market will impair the ability of users to find specific websites. Keywords in the language of the target markets and links from local websites will enhance the visibility of the website to potential customers.

Understanding starts with language. Only one-third of all Internet users have English as their mother tongue. To argue that many non-Western travellers affluent enough to be tourists understand English ignores the fact that, to make these travellers feel welcome, information in their mother tongue will make all the difference. Also, information which might be considered irrelevant for local users will in many cases be essential for potential international visitors. Few Scottish or Danish people will need to be informed about the fact that they can enjoy 16 hours of daylight in midsummer; yet for a Singaporean this might be informative in helping to shape travel plans. Maps and illustrations will also help to engage international Internet users.

To make potential visitors feel comfortable and welcome is the most complicated but also the most rewarding part of cross-cultural Internet marketing. The mayor of a city singing a welcoming song in Japanese in a video clip is, perhaps, an extreme example, but a photograph showing Asian visitors in front of the city's cathedral will have a more positive effect than a lengthy translation of an art historian's text about the cathedral. In addition, colours and symbols have different meanings in different cultures. The expected carriers of trustworthy information will vary – they will be the 'authorities' for some and peer group members for others. The provision of pages for international tourists will be perceived as welcoming to those tourists and a message that their needs are being taken into consideration.

21.6 Study Results

If non-Western tourists are the biggest growth market for European destinations and the Internet is the most efficient mode of communication with them, how do European destinations respond to this opportunity? In 2002, the author conducted two studies. The larger, a European study of websites in Gemany, Austria and Switzerland, was conducted in February 2002. In association with a consulting company, it studied the internationality of the websites of 60 tourism destinations in Germany, Austria and the German-speaking part of Switzerland. In September 2002, a smaller study was conducted for the Wales Tourism Alliance Conference in Cardiff, which analysed the multilingual and multicultural content of the regional British Tourist Authority (BTA) visitor websites.

21.6.1 European study

In the European study, the 30 cities and communities with the highest number of international overnight visitors and a tourism website with non-German language content were selected for the German sample. As 12 of these destinations did not provide any information in a foreign language, including three of the top 12 destinations for international visitors to Germany, the sample included destinations as far down as 43rd in the overall ranking.

For the Austrian sample, the 15 cities and communities were selected in the same manner according to the figures provided in the Statistical Yearbook of Austria. Only one community had no non-German website and had to be substituted by the 16th community in ranking.

For German-speaking Switzerland no ranking was available, so all communities with more than 20,000 inhabitants were selected, plus the destinations characterized as important destinations on the national tourism promotion website www.myswitzerland.com. Many communities were found to have no foreign-language content, even though Switzerland is a multilingual country and the majority of visitors in most destinations are non-German speaking.

By drawing on the experiences of the author with a similar study outside tourism, analysing other Internet research projects from other industries and through discussion with experts, a list of 65 weighted criteria was developed under the headings of 'accessibility', 'languages', 'technical quality', 'design quality', 'international content', 'target group specific content', 'up-to-dateness' and 'interactivity'. Altogether 1000 points could be achieved by each website. The websites were analysed in February 2002.

The final ranking was as shown in Table 21.1. The clear winner of the study was the Austrian capital Vienna, the only destination which achieved more than three-quarters of possible points by providing up-to-date information in many languages, including two different newsletters in English; current pages in Japanese and Chinese; and information adapted to the requirements of international short-stay visitors. Zurich scored high, less for its creativity or warm-heartedness, but for a website which at the time of the survey was state-of-the-art on its international pages. The skiing resort of Saalbach-Hinterglemm took the bronze medal over Berlin for innovative, interactive features in several languages, such as giving visitors the opportunity to upload their *après-ski* snapshots on to the website and multilingual chat-rooms.

Five out of the ten top places went to Austrian destinations, whereas the large German cities, apart from Berlin, but including Munich, all finished in the bottom quarter of the table. A surprising result was the final results of the Swiss destinations, with the exception of Zurich. Whereas the national website www.myswitzerland.com has been setting an example in the industry for years, local websites often consisted of little more than an English-language homepage. French- and Italian-speaking Swiss, as well as the many international visitors, were obviously expected to understand German – or stay away! This was the (surely unintended) message of more than 60% of the surveyed destinations, which could not reach half of the possible points.

Typical examples of bad practice included: abandoned English-language parts of the websites, like press releases translated for 1 week after the launching of the website and then never repeated; open refusal to send out information material to addresses outside Germany; sentences like 'For more information please consult the German pages' or very bad translations by a non-native

Table 21.1. Ranking of all 60 destinations in Germany, Austria and German-speaking Switzerland (February 2002). Maximum points achievable: 1000.

Rank	Destination	Points	Rank	Destination	Points
1	Vienna	890	31	Mainz	425
2	Zurich	745	32	St. Anton	420
3	Saalbach-Hinterglemm	710	33	Würzburg	420
4	Berlin	695	34	Bad Ragaz	415
5	Innsbruck	675	35	Karlsruhe	395
6	Sölden	670	36	Eben/Maurach	390
7	Baden-Baden	645	37	Seefeld	385
8	Bremen	640	38	Lübeck	375
8	Lech	640	39	Gersau	370
10	Trier	615	40	Kirchberg	360
11	Leipzig	610	41	Zug	355
12	Gstaad	600	42	Boppard	350
13	Regensburg	585	43	Basel	340
14	Rothenburg	580	44	Braunwald	330
15	Salzburg	565	45	Mannheim	325
16	Zell am See	560	46	Augsburg	315
17	Scuol	555	46	München	315
18	Hamburg	550	48	Hannover	305
19	Heidelberg	545	49	Winterberg	295
19	Nuremberg	545	50	Dresden	280
21	Essen	540	51	Brunnen	265
22	Engelberg	535	52	Köln	260
23	Ischgl	525	53	St. Gallen	255
24	Stuttgart	500	54	Schaffhausen	250
24	Tux	500	55	Solothurn	240
26	Lucerne	465	56	Frankfurt	235
27	Wiesbaden	460	57	Andermatt	220
28	Garmisch-P.kirchen	445	57	Neustift	220
29	Aachen	435	59	Rüdesheim	215
30	Mayrhofen	430	60	Bonn	200
				Average points per website	450

speaker. Detailed explanations of how to reach the next highway exit were translated into English but no information about the nearest airport was included. There was a high incidence of broken links, missing graphs or links labelled in English but leading to German-language pages. Dedicated information about places of non-Christian worship or addresses of foreign-community associations were always missing. Pictorial current information by using web cams, an easy way to transmit all kinds of information about the daily life in a destination, were seldom used. Asian languages or information targeted towards Asian visitors in English were only provided by a few destinations, including some cities in the Rhine valley.

21.6.2 British study

In September 2002 a smaller study was conducted for the Wales Tourism Alliance Conference Cardiff 2002, which analysed the regional BTA visitor websites for their multilingual and multicultural content. Britain is blessed with being the home of the major international language, yet figures from the BTA show that only 32% of all international visitors to Britain speak English as their native language (Arlt, 2003). The results of this second study are shown in Table 21.2, which shows that more than half of all British tourist board websites were completely monolingual. This is not a question of money, as the national website www.visitbritain.com contains readily available pages with basic information about all areas in languages such as German, French, Portuguese and Japanese. Specifically customized pages that offered more than a simple translation, however, could only be found in Scotland and Jersey.

21.6.3 Revisiting the studies

Both studies were revisited in early 2004 and some improvements were found:

- Düsseldorf, which did not have a single non-German page in 2002, now sports some information in English and a Russian, Japanese and Chinese homepage.
- Bonn (60th in the European study) now provides current information about exhibitions in English.
- Wales and London have introduced completely new multilingual websites.

However, these improvements can be seen as following the general improvement of Internet usage of DMOs. Very few websites provide as much functionality for other languages as they provide for their own language. Additionally, customized information beyond a one-to-one translation is still almost non-existent. Some progress has been achieved in the usage of other languages, but not in cross-cultural marketing.

21.7 Practical Consequences for SMEs and DMOs

Most European tourist destinations and companies, including SMEs, have a potentially rosy future, considering the fact that almost 1 billion newcomers, mainly Asians, will enter the international travel market in the next two decades. Adequate usage of new media, especially the Internet, is presenting a new, fast and economic channel of communication with potential customers around the world, with many more opportunities for up-to-date and one-to-one cross-cultural marketing than any printed brochure sent out by 'snail-mail' can provide. The Internet is first and foremost a communication tool, not an online booking machine.

Effective Internet communication across cultures is about much more than having a static website with maybe just a few pages translated word by word into another language. Money is not the key resource: the customers are, and interactivity is the key tool. By actively communicating with visitors, their special

Table 21.2. Multilingual and multicultural content of main British Tourist Authority visitor websites (September 2002).

The top three websites	
Scotland	Very detailed and customized information in French, German, Dutch, Flemish and for US visitors, links to multi-language websites of Glasgow and Perthshire
South-east England	Detailed and up-to-date information in French, German, Dutch
Jersey	Entry pages in more than a dozen languages, including Japanese, Finnish, Norwegian, etc., mainly giving links to airlines and travel companies in the relevant country

Websites that are 'trying'	
East of England	Short greeting pop-ups in French, Dutch, German
Guernsey	German version of some pages, newsletter abandoned after first issue in 2001, usability's crumbling
London	No foreign-language content, links to private sites in French, German, Italian are hidden inside the English website as links to 'non-English websites'
Wales	Country of origin is asked for on the homepage but results in no changes to the English content provided. No link to existing French/German content of www.southernwales.com

English-only websites	
Cumbria	No foreign-language content or link to foreign-language content
Heart of England	No foreign-language content or link to foreign-language content
Northumbria	No foreign-language content or link to foreign-language content
North-west	No foreign-language content or link to foreign-language content
Northern Ireland	No foreign-language content or link to foreign-language content
Southern England	No foreign-language content or link to foreign-language content
South-west England	No foreign-language content or link to foreign-language content
Yorkshire	No foreign-language content or link to foreign-language content

requirements for information and different forms of communication will be considered and provided and destinations will demonstrate to potential visitors that others from their home country have enjoyed visits to that destination.

DMOs, as well as tourism SMEs, can:

- Give the visitor the opportunity to access downloads, e-postcards, newsletters and images from web cams.
- Use the website as an opportunity to ask visitors about their wishes and ideas and to provide the information requested.
- Invite visitors to comment on the information provided or experiences of their visit in their own language.
- Let visitors communicate among themselves by (monitored) guest-books, testimonials and tips.
- Allow visitors to put their own snapshots of their visit online.
- Identify and use existing information which has been translated into other languages.
- Provide up-to-date information about events and exhibitions which cannot be found in guidebooks.

21.8 Conclusions

Interactivity is not online hotel room booking. Interactivity is about succeeding in conveying that a destination or a service is interesting and offers something for visitors from the relevant source market, and tells the potential customer that their comments and experiences are welcome. Good usage of the Internet as a cross-cultural incoming tourism communication tool can provide active tourism companies and destinations with a clear advantage, especially in the new Asian market. Considering the customers' needs and wants can be more difficult when the customers come from different cultural backgrounds, but establishing lines of communication with them through the Internet can bring significant business and image formation advantages.

References

Arlt, W. (2002) Die Eingeborenen sind wir – Ostasiaten als Inbound-Touristen. In: *VOYAGE. Jahrbuch für Reise und Tourismusforschung*, DuMont Publishers, Cologne, pp. 144–153.

Arlt, W. (2003) Connecting with Cultures. *Locum Destination Review* 11, 43–46.

Bieger, T. (2002) *Management von Destinationen*. Oldenbourg, Munich, 365 pp.

Brown, D. (1996) Genuine fakes. In: Selwyn, T. (ed.) *The Tourism Image: Myths and Myth Making in Tourism*. John Wiley & Sons, Chichester, UK, pp. 33–48.

China National Tourist Office Toronto (2003) *Statistics on China's Tourism 2002*. Accessed at: www.tourismchina-ca.com

Gesteland, R.R. (2002) *Cross-Cultural Business Behavior: Marketing, Negotiating and Managing Across Cultures*, 3rd edn. Copenhagen Business School Press, Copenhagen, 282 pp.

Globalreach (2004) *Online Language Populations*. Accessed at: www.glreach.com

Goodall, B. and Ashworth G. (1988) *Marketing in the Tourism Industry: The Promotion of Destination Regions*. Croom Helm, London, 244 pp.

Herbig, P.A. (1998) *Handbook of Cross-Cultural Marketing*. International Business Press, New York, 375 pp.

Marcussen, C.H. (2003) *Trends in European Internet Distribution/Trends in the US Online Travel Market 2000–2002*. Centre for Regional and Tourism Research, Denmark. Accessed at: www.crt.dk/uk/staff/chm/trends.htm

Meethan, K. (2001) *Tourism in Global Society. Place, Culture, Consumption*. Palgrave, Basingstoke, UK, 214 pp.

Ooi, C.S. (2002) *Cultural Tourism and Tourism Cultures: the Business of Mediating Experiences in Copenhagen and Singapore*. Copenhagen Business School Press, Copenhagen, 277 pp.

Sharpley, R. (2002) Tourism: a vehicle for development? In: Sharpley, R. and Telfer, D.J. (eds) *Tourism and Development: Concepts and Issues*. Channel View, Clevedon, pp. 11–34.

Smith, V.L. (2003) *East to West: The New Wave of Tourism*. Global Frameworks and Local Realities Conference, University of Brighton, Brighton, UK.

Thiem, M. (1994) Tourismus und kulturelle Identität. *Aus Politik und Zeitgeschichte B* 47 (2001), 27–31.

Urry, J. (2001) *The Tourist Gaze*, 2nd edn. Sage, London, 224 pp.

WTO (1997) *Tourism 2020 Vision: A New Forecast*. World Tourism Organization, Madrid.

WTO (2003) *Tourism Highlights, Edition 2003*. World Tourism Organization, Madrid.

Xu, S. (2002) DZT *Marketinformation China*. German National Tourist Office, Beijing.

22 The Heterodoxy of Tourism SMEs

CLAIRE HAVEN-TANG AND ELERI JONES

Welsh School of Hospitality, Tourism and Leisure Management, University of Wales Institute, Cardiff, UK

22.1 Introduction

The book has explored some of the special characteristics of tourism small and medium-sized enterprises (SMEs) and the challenges they pose for top-down, government-driven, destination management organization (DMO)-mediated interventions to enhance service quality, promote business growth and enhance regional integration and destination competitiveness. The various chapters contribute to an enriched picture of SMEs. The aim of this chapter is to draw the contributions together under three headings – public-sector interventions (section 22.2), tourism SME approaches (section 22.3) and destination coherence (section 22.4) – before developing some overall conclusions (section 22.5).

22.2 Public-sector Interventions

The various case studies identify a number of different public-sector interventions to promote the development of a competitive destination, which can be organized under four subheadings: funding; developing destination quality standards; marketing and market intelligence; and training and human resource development. These will each be considered in turn.

22.2.1 Funding

Wanhill (Chapter 15) emphasizes the use of financial incentives in attracting, coordinating and controlling tourism development in line with government tourism policy and defining a framework for economically viable and sustainable development, emphasizing that investment policies must be favourable for both developers and investors. Indeed, limited access to financial resources and government regulations are among the key factors affecting the growth of tourism businesses (Augustyn and Pheby (Chapter 6)). Wanhill advocates that the aim of public-sector interventions should be to help SMEs proactively manage their future, rather than to react to situations, and that the disparate nature of regional level tourism requires a hands-on approach from public-sector bodies, particularly as the short-term objectives of capital markets often conflict with long-term tourist environment sustainability. Indeed, Manyara and Jones (Chapter 4) observe that the lack of tourism policy in Kenya has resulted in unsystematic tourism developments and a reliance on foreign investment. Wanhill asserts that investment incentives can be seen as policy instruments to facilitate public- and private-sector partnerships and to correct market failure, as governance and the market should complement rather than compete.

Apart from various investment incentives, Wanhill promotes the creation of an appropriate business environment to enable tourism SMEs to improve their competitiveness, diversity, quality and profitability and advocates the partnership approach as being significant for regional development, especially in peripheral tourism destinations. Furthermore, he reports that, while most European Union (EU) Member States have tourism funding mechanisms, streamlining is required to ensure that investors only need to communicate with one organization and that grants and loan terms are compatible with the needs of tourism SMEs. Murphy (Chapter 8) notes that increased interest in community tourism development was paralleled in the EU by a shift away from large grants to attract inward investment to small firms and indigenous development. Jwaili *et al.* (Chapter 20) report that Libyan tourism SMEs are seeking better financial support through improved coordination with financial institutions and services such as grants, low-interest loans and longer repayment periods. In contrast, Hall and Rusher (Chapter 9) found little support for the suggestion that government assistance was essential for business growth, illustrating that bed and breakfast (B&B) operators in New Zealand may not have a funding-dependent culture – unlike some countries that seek government or other public-sector financial assistance for training, quality enhancements and product/service development.

However, Wanhill cautions that investment incentives and appropriate business environments will vary depending on the destination, for example, local community access to financial resources is a key issue that needs to be addressed by tourism destinations such as Kenya, so Manyara and Jones propose different taxation systems for Kenyan-owned establishments to promote indigenous SME development, rather than foreign ownership. Wanhill also gives examples of separate funding initiatives for ethnic groups and particular tourism sectors. Manyara and Jones suggest that the implications of improved access to financial resources, tourism training, favourable taxation and employment legislation would be increased numbers of indigenous tourism SMEs and an improved tourism multiplier effect for Kenya, ultimately benefiting the local communities and enhancing destination competitiveness. They outline the 'ideal scenario' for Kenya, with tourism developments owned and controlled by Kenyans, and emphasize the role of indigenous tourism SMEs as a tool for poverty alleviation. This challenges the traditional Kenyan approach of encouraging foreign ownership of tourism resources, which has resulted in leakage and minimal com-munity benefits. Their view is in stark contrast to that of Libyan SMEs, which want the Libyan government to provide more incentives for direct foreign invest-ment in tourism infrastructure development. This seemingly contradicts their ambition to develop niche, up-market tourism rather than mass tourism, as well as affecting the development of indigenous tourism SMEs that would generate socio-economic benefits for the local community.

However, Manyara and Jones's 'ideal' scenario requires more than simply funding indigenous business start-ups. Strategies and financial resources need to be in place to ensure that indigenous communities have basic literacy and numeracy skills, together with industry-specific skills and managerial and entre-preneurial abilities. Furthermore, Manyara and Jones advocate an equal partnership approach, whereby indigenous tourism SMEs and existing tourism enterprises complement and cooperate to empower local communities. In support of this, Wanhill warns of the danger of confining investment support for SMEs to physical capital and underestimating the significance of human capital investment.

22.2.2 Developing destination quality standards

Behringer and Mester (Chapter 17) outline the development of a national tour-ism quality scheme in Hungary, where privatization has been a catalyst for the increased number of tourism SMEs. In a survey of providers, they found that quality was not an absolute priority for all sizes of tourism providers, there were gaps in tourism providers' understanding of consumer expectations and few small and micro-sized businesses had any quality systems in place. The Hungar-ian Tourism Quality Award (HTQA) has been designed by the Hungarian National Tourist Office (HNTO) to orient the tourism industry to improve the quality and competitiveness of its services, with the intention that it can be used as a marketing tool in domestic and international tourism markets. Improving service quality is an inherent component of other Hungarian public-sector poli-cies, such as the Széchenyi Plan, thus demonstrating public-sector recognition of the significance of service quality in relation to the tourism product and a com-mitment to improve the quality of the Hungarian tourism product, thereby strengthening domestic and inbound tourism.

Behringer and Mester report that the larger tourism providers in Hungary are less enthusiastic about the HTQA compared with SMEs. This challenges the top-down approach, whereby quality standards in large tourism organizations can influence quality standards within smaller businesses in the destination – in the case of Hungary the opposite may occur, in that, if tourism SMEs adopt HTQA, the larger organizations may be forced to engage and collaborate, as consumer confidence and buying behaviour are likely to be influenced by the HTQA. This demonstrates the influence of consumer pressure and the pivotal role of the national tourism organization in the coordination, development and implementation of HTQA. Chan and Wong (Chapter 19) also note that quality awards serve to influence consumer perceptions and confidence in tourism products. Manyara and Jones highlight the importance of quality in destination competitiveness and the need for clear guidelines for quality standards in the Kenyan tourism industry and endorse the Hungarian approach of establishing a national standards organization to improve quality, increase consumer confidence and enhance destination competitiveness. Similarly, Jwaili *et al.* identified that tourism SMEs want the Libyan government to introduce regulations to control tourism service quality so that quality, up-market tourism products can be developed to attract niche markets.

Pizam and Tesone (Chapter 14) found that a significant majority of private-sector employers in Mexico and Central Florida supported government involvement in setting minimum service delivery quality standards, even though this might restrict business operations. Wanhill argues that quality developments achieved through national classification and grading schemes create new tourism operators, who displace those lacking the skills to ensure quality; hence, although raising the skills base is likely to create barriers to entry, there may be benefits if it improves existing tourism products and slows the exit rate of tourism SMEs. Furthermore, Behringer and Mester report the association between HTQA and SME funding, in that tourism SMEs who have achieved HTQA will be in a more advantageous position when bidding for financial support from Hungarian government departments. The findings of Pizam and Tesone demonstrate a commitment from industry to work with the public sector to address quality standards and issues of professionalism. Additionally, they recommend that Mexican government tourism organizations should regulate and/or certify all external tourism training and educational institutions to achieve consistency of training programmes and increase the quality of human resources. However, the findings of Hjalager (Chapter 11) should be considered, in that industry-specific training and good employee qualification attainment rates will not guarantee employee retention in the tourism sector.

22.2.3 Marketing and market intelligence

Smith (Chapter 16) stresses the need for robust data to inform public-sector interventions designed to assist tourism operators, which supports the views of others (e.g. Behringer and Mester; James (Chapter 18); Wanhill) that government bodies need to work in partnership with the tourism sector to ensure that public-sector interventions are necessary and appropriate. Poor market research and knowledge management means that tourism SMEs often fail to take full advantage of their potential and may misunderstand their customers – as reported by Behringer and Mester. Hall and Rusher also note that B&B operators in New Zealand have weak connections with the formal business and tourism sectors, reinforcing negative images of the informal nature of the B&B sector among organizations that influence national and regional tourism policies. Smith demonstrates how the *Wales Tourism Business Monitor* (WTBM) developed and was used by the Wales Tourist Board (WTB) to collect industry information to determine performance and barriers to growth. Hence, the WTBM provides a monthly analysis of business confidence, enabling the WTB to provide market intelligence, set standards and develop a proactive partnership with the tourism sector, while allowing operational and strategic planning to be improved and quality to be enhanced, ultimately improving destination competitiveness. Additionally, the provision of trend analysis information allows operators to benchmark their tourism business. Di Domenico (Chapter 7) reports that to ensure the most appropriate form of tourism development, emphasis is often placed on local initiatives, values and key community stakeholders. As such, small-scale guesthouses are key players in some localities, responsible for shaping tourist views and experiences. She also asserts that these operators are encouraged to represent images of their society and culture to tourists by national and regional tourist boards. Hence, the influence wielded by such tourism SMEs can be immense.

Murphy asserts that the key to successful and efficient organizational management is the utilization of information and the ability to access and manipulate that information to the advantage of the business. For a hotel, this may cover existing and potential customers, as well as the business environment. For example, Smith reports that investment in marketing was a very positive factor affecting business performance among tourism SMEs in Wales. Murphy is also critical of the role of tourist boards during the first phase of diffusion of information and communication technology (ICT) in hospitality SMEs, as she notes a lack of direction, guidance and infrastructure in relation to the development of integrated systems at a time when hospitality SMEs needed regional integrated computer information reservation management systems to support the consumer. Furthermore, the shift in the EU, as noted by Murphy, away from large grants to attract inward investment to small indigenous developments aligned to community tourism development created a need for collaboration in destinations to produce meaningful information.

Gathering market intelligence can assist the establishment and growth of tourism SMEs and help to identify alternative tourist markets. Manyara and Jones discuss the pitfalls of relying on a single tourist market, such as vulnerability to external conditions. They also comment on a lack of tourism awareness at all levels in Kenya and emphasize the importance of public campaigns to raise tourism awareness. Similarly, Jwaili et al. comment on a lack of tourism awareness and the need for market intelligence to inform new product development for niche markets.

The media can have positive and negative impacts on tourism destinations in terms of marketing the destination to tourists. For example, Kenya has suffered from negative media images, which have been detrimental to the Kenyan tourism industry. Countering negative publicity requires media management strategies for coordinated, cohesive public-sector interventions best implemented at a destination level. Conversely, Getz et al. (Chapter 5) note that successful tourism SMEs offering high-quality products which exploit the family name and engage in 'family branding' can benefit the destination by communicating quality and value, tradition, personality and culture or tradition. Arlt (Chapter 21) states that travel decision making requires qualified information and confidence; while destination images can be informed by non-tourist information, many aspects of destination image formation are controllable and

DMOs can influence image formation. He discusses the significance of the Internet as an image-building tool at the destination and business level.

Jwaili *et al.* report that the National Tourism Development Plan provides a sound foundation for the coordinated marketing efforts of Libyan tourism SMEs. Additionally, Libyan tourism SMEs are seeking improved coordination between the public and private sectors, especially at international marketing events, e.g. tourism SMEs want more involvement in familiarization visits for tour operators and the media, demonstrating that they understand the need for cooperation and collaboration with the public sector.

22.2.4 Training and human resource development

James outlines the national strategic approach adopted by Wales to address the issues of staff recruitment and retention. In a destination where the industry is characterized by SMEs, which by their very nature are diverse and fragmented, one of the major threats to destination competitiveness is the inability to ensure that a coherent image is projected to potential visitors through service quality, as the human element of the service is crucial. A strategic approach is essential to provide leadership and to raise the profile of tourism human resources among key stakeholders, as well as to coordinate tourism training demand and supply. For example, Murphy reports that hospitality SMEs had no evident source of independent information technology (IT) advice, an issue which should be addressed through education and training initiatives. The dilemma at a national strategic level is how to ensure destination competitiveness through training and development. In cases where training and development opportunities are not available to employees of SMEs or microbusinesses, it is about identifying how the intimacy and quality of the tourism product and people can contribute to overall destination competitiveness through professionalism within the industry. James emphasizes the long-term implications of transforming the tourism industry from a human resource (HR) perspective to ensure a world-class destination. Part of this process is the cultivation of young people to ensure the long-term sustainability of tourism, particularly in rural areas, and to guard against in-migration and transient workers. The latter is a trend which is becomingly increasingly evident in tourism destinations such as Wales. A shortage of local recruits has forced some employers to actively source recruits from overseas. While this solves an immediate recruitment problem and may allow for the transfer of particular skills, it is not a long-term solution, particularly in the light of public-sector interventions which seek to promote the national language and culture of a destination, such as the 'Sense of Place' initiative introduced by the WTB. The recently launched 'Success through your People' HR toolkit is an example of a national public-sector intervention which can be customized at an individual business level.

Pizam and Tesone support the approach discussed by James, as they emphasize that the tourism industry, government and educational establishments share responsibility for the success of tourism within any destination, and that collaboration should drive future strategies for tourism development and sustainability in Mexico and Central Florida. Indeed, they found that private-sector tourism employers supported government involvement in training and education, including the regulation and certification of training institutions, as well as government assistance with the design of in-house training programmes. Moreover, Mexican government tourism organizations are advised to increase the number of external tourism training and educational institutions, especially in areas where such institutions are currently non-existent, in addition to establishing public–private task forces to initiate and deliver in-house training activities and designing competency-based occupational standards. Libyan tourism SMEs hold similar views to those in Mexico and Central Florida, as Jwaili *et al.* point out, they want improved education and training facilities for the tourism industry through enhanced support for existing institutions, supplemented by the establishment of new training institutions. Manyara and Jones also highlight the need for collaboration between the Kenyan tourism industry and educational (particularly higher educational) establishments and discuss how this would benefit the sector through knowledge exploitation and technology transfer – as evidenced in the Kenyan agricultural sector. James, Pizam and Tezone, Haven-Tang and Botterill (Chapter 10), Lashley (Chapter 12) and Moore (Chapter 13) all concur that HR development for the tourism industry is essential for high-quality service provision.

Haven-Tang and Botterill assert that the future of a skilled and quality tourism workforce begins at home with the attitudes of parents towards the industry as a career, hence tourism SMEs need to target information accordingly and collaborate with strategic public-sector interventions. This approach is also advocated by Pizam and Tesone, who state that government tourism organizations should develop a series of activities to educate people about career opportunities within the tourism industry for educated and talented individuals. However, this approach is complicated by the fragmented nature of the industry, particularly in destinations dominated by small and microbusinesses, and the unrealistic assumption that young people are free agents in the career decision making process – with little regard given to the formal and informal social contexts that influence the career decision making process. Educational institutions should be concerned with Hjalager's finding that tourism may be regarded as a platform for a more salaried and secure career in other sectors, as those with tourism training backgrounds also contribute to labour turnover in Denmark. Thus a proliferation of tourism training alone does not improve service quality, as, although training may ensure quality among human resources, career paths need visibility together with improved remuneration for retention in tourism employment, which supports the findings of others (e.g. Haven-Tang and Botterill, Lashley, Pizam and Tesone). Essentially, Hjalager asserts that a specialized tourism education does not 'pay' and a generalized education may bring more benefits in terms of future career and salary.

Hjalager illustrates the major influence of employment legislation, not just in protecting the rights of workers and ensuring good working conditions, but also in relation to the image of the industry as an employer, labour turnover and whether tourism offers long-term career opportunities. She asserts that, in Denmark, social legislation combined with unemployment legislation provides support for businesses seeking numerical flexibility. Although Hjalager reports that the Danish system has few restrictions on hiring and firing, others (Lashley, Pizam and Tesone,

Moore) note that recruiting unskilled employees is often a challenge in destinations such as Manchester, Mexico, Central Florida and south-east Wales, which may reflect different labour market conditions and employment legislation. In addition, Manyara and Jones call for Kenyan employment legislation to be redefined to give preference to local communities in tourism development.

Of huge significance to any public-sector intervention is Lashley's conclusion that reported recruitment problems in Manchester are largely a product of employment policies – specifically the inability of management to control labour turnover and undertake effective recruitment and selection – rather than an aggregate skills shortage; a similar situation exists in Denmark, whereby the legislative system facilitates hiring and firing. Lashley found that employers complaining of a lack of social and customer care skills among recruits did not recognize this as a consequence of their recruitment policies, nor did they recognize these as being skill gaps within their workforce. Tourism SMEs operate in a very different manner from larger organizations and generally lack specialist managers to oversee their various activities. For example, a lack of people management skills means that SMEs may not exploit the potential of their human resources to the benefit of the business and the individual employee. Additionally, Lashley reports that employers misunderstand the significance of pay levels in relation to staff turnover and consequent recruitment difficulties, while Moore also notes a need for management development and a commitment to staff training. Augustyn and Pheby argue that, for tourism SMEs to be successful and maintain growth, they need to achieve a capabilities-based competitive advantage. However, the challenge for operators is understanding how to achieve this and how to convert their internal resource base into capability platforms to give them a competitive advantage and enable growth, whereby the focus is on developing capabilities rather than products. Thus, public-sector interventions may be necessary to help operators identify and convert their resource base.

This demonstrates the need for public-sector interventions to disseminate examples of best practice in human resource management (HRM) policies and procedures and to emphasize the need for management development, as businesses need to be able to manage people, recognize skill gaps within their business and identify factors which influence their workforce.

22.3 Tourism SME Approaches

22.3.1 Attitudes

Tourism SME operator motivations are often different from those of large organizations, as profit and business expansion are not necessarily business objectives. Hence, the failure rates of SMEs are a frequently debated issue, particularly as the industry is characterized by ease of entry. Getz et al. emphasize that high business turnover rates can damage tourism destinations, particularly if new owners fail to address existing business problems, and many tourism SME operators are 'debt-averse' and reluctant to take business risks, thus often sacrificing growth potential. Ensuring the growth and development of SMEs can benefit destinations, as family business stability and commitment facilitate capital and knowledge accumulation. In New Zealand, Hall and Rusher found that respondents from the B&B sector saw profit as extremely significant and had a strong desire for business growth, balanced alongside lifestyle gains and job satisfaction.

Di Domenico found that lifestyle entrepreneurs in Scotland do not measure business success in terms of growth criteria, strengthening the belief that the personal motivations of lifestyle entrepreneurs are not necessarily aligned with rational economic decision making. However, they were found to have a desire for profit and financial success – which was viewed independently of growth. Entrepreneurs had a need for a specific 'way of life' influenced by their particular circumstances and, while the needs of the business were found to be important, this was only where they did not significantly impede the entrepreneur's quality of life, hence supporting Hall and Rusher's finding that fulfilling the lifestyle goals of the owner-manager is almost equal to meeting business goals: 'lifestyle is a strategic business objective'. Di Domenico cites examples of 'downsizing', which supports the argument that lifestyle entrepreneurs lack a true commitment to business growth.

The entrepreneurs studied by Di Domenico fall into one of two categories in terms of their decision to run a guesthouse. Lifestyle preferences, such as the desire to be one's own boss, indicate a voluntary need for increased flexibility and personal control. Conversely, lifestyle circumstances, such as family commitments, signify an imposed need for flexibility and personal control. Similarly, Hall and Rusher identified two significant clusters of business types in relation to income dependence on accommodation. They established that, for the majority of B&B operators, accommodation accounts for a very small proportion of their income (less than 30%), while 21% of their B&B survey respondents depended on accommodation for over 80% of their income. Linked to this is Lashley's finding that those who run tourism SMEs for motives other than commercial success are less likely to engage in management development. Di Domenico also observed that business growth was defined as an increase in the size of the operation, the range of services offered and staffing levels – all of which were deemed to be undesirable by her study sample, often because of a decline in their quality of life and the difficulty of maintaining personalized levels of service, which were seen to give tourism SMEs a competitive advantage over larger establishments.

Smith reports that many tourism SMEs found engagement with the WTBM difficult due to time constraints and lack of incentives, even though the information generated might aid their business. This may demonstrate the insular attitudes of tourism operators towards individual business success, rather than considering how their business contributes to the bigger picture, i.e. destination competitiveness. Similarly, Jwaili *et al.* note that Libyan tourism SMEs work independently, which can lead to conflict. In addition, attitudes can impede the adoption of tools which benefit the business, such as IT. Murphy asserts that, if the hospitality SME operator has an aversion to technology, then adoption is unlikely, which can have implications for marketing and gathering intelligence on the business and customers. Quality is dependent upon the motivations of owner-managers, as well as tourist facilities, and Hall and Rusher raise an important point about small and microbusinesses. They found that small businesses, such as B&B operations in New Zealand, are often viewed as an 'informal' tourism sector, which can damage a tourism destination because such businesses may be unable to provide services upon tourist demand. Getz *et al.* support this by their observation that tourism SMEs are often regarded as 'amateurs', providing variable standards of tourism product and service quality.

Developing a competitive tourism product and a coherent tourism destination is highly dependent on employees. Haven-Tang and Botterill identify the wider implications of attracting a skilled and quality workforce. Many employers are facing shortfalls in recruitment, which are often deemed to be the result of the negative image of the industry. They assert that school students gain much of their careers information and guidance from non-specialist sources, such as parents, who shape attitudes towards careers by conveying beliefs and values. While family members can be credible sources of information, they are not always best equipped to give advice, as their occupational experience and attitudes towards work may be biased, outdated or ill-informed. This illustrates the importance of providing non-specialist deliverers of careers guidance with accurate and up-to-date information about careers in the tourism industry, as well as ensuring the visibility of career paths. The latter is supported by Pizam and Tesone, who recommend that the tourism industry restructures itself to ensure that it is seen to offer lifetime career opportunities, rather than 'jobs'. However, delivering such messages can be undermined by the different structure and motivations of tourism SMEs. Di Domenico found that lifestyle entrepreneurs consciously avoided certain activities, such as formally employing staff, regardless of the potential for increased revenue, in order to avoid staffing problems that would impede their quality of life. Equally, Hall and Rusher report that the majority of B&Bs in New Zealand are self-managed, with few employing staff and those who do are unlikely to offer formal training. Lashley suggests that employers' attitudes to skills development and utilization tend to be indicative of other aspects of business management. For example, those who promote employee development are likely to be concerned with quality systems, marketing and cost control. Of significant concern is Hjalager's finding that, from the Danish employee's perspective, tourism is not the most obvious sector for a dedicated and consistent career.

Evidence from Moore underpins the strategic national training approach discussed by James, as he found that larger organizations in south-east Wales were more coordinated in their approach to training than their independent counterparts and that consideration needs to be given to attitudes towards training, as well as the external factors that affect the training model. Interestingly, Moore highlights that staff turnover in smaller hotels may not be as significant as that experienced by larger hotels. This demonstrates the influence of developing a cohesive 'family atmosphere' within the business operation. While in the case of SMEs this approach may not provide employees with training and development, the atmosphere created may add value to the visitor experience and their perception of service quality levels. This may enhance the destination's competitiveness in the eyes of the visitor. Indeed, Hall and Rusher note that the social motivations of running a B&B indicate the potential for stronger customer orientations than businesses where staff are not interested in making social connections with customers, and Di Domenico reports that lifestyle entrepreneurs often exhibit a desire for social relationships. Similarly, Getz *et al*. assert that the family is often part of the tourism product and, where staff are employed in a family business, their activities and attitudes will be shaped by the owner-manager, resulting in a very different service from that of a larger establishment. However, the attitude and approach of the operator is fundamental to business success, as Getz *et al*. report that a paternalistic or autocratic form of control does not necessarily generate high levels of morale or service quality; indeed, this type of approach can have a detrimental effect on communication within the business. Quite simply, a genuine desire to 'be the best' or to be unique compared with the rest should bring benefits for the business, visitor and destination.

22.3.2 Knowledge and skills

Manyara and Jones assert that the Kenyan tourism industry is vulnerable to conditions determined by the West because of the country's dependence on Western markets. In order to ensure destination competitiveness and the economic sustainability of the tourism industry, Manyara and Jones recommend that the Kenyan government redefine its tourism markets and give greater consideration to domestic and regional tourism. However, this necessitates the acquisition of market intelligence on potential tourism markets. The need for market intelligence is also raised by Williams and MacLeod (Chapter 3). They conclude that perceptions of peripherality differ between markets. Examining consumer interpretations of peripherality and identifying the gap between reality and perceptions would inform destination managers in the achievement of competitive advantage.

Augustyn and Pheby list a number of internal factors that are responsible for diverse performance levels among tourism SMEs operating within similar external environments, including: inability to attract and retain quality staff; inability to attract and retain customers; inability to manage supply chains and develop effective distribution channels. They purport that these internal barriers are related either to a lack of adequate resources or to the inability of the business to convert their resource base into distinct organizational capability platforms. Among the tourism SMEs studied, Augustyn and Pheby found that experience and professionalism, employee and management commitment, management continuity and knowledge were important human resources, as well as networking and IT skills. Intangible resources included high-quality service, membership of professional bodies, organizational culture, customer base and external recognition. Foundation capabilities encompassed infrastructure or service flexibility, reputation and customer loyalty. They identified that the development of appropriate capabilities enabled the tourism SMEs studied to grow incrementally.

Tourism SMEs need to have a greater awareness and understanding of their customers and should integrate this knowledge into organizational goals. For example, Chan and Wong state that customers of different age and gender will have different perceptions of the importance of different attributes when selecting a hotel. Obtaining such information is essential in terms of developing the tourism product and targeting specific markets. In gaining market intelligence, tourism SMEs should also develop a greater appreciation of cross-cultural issues, such as those highlighted by Arlt, including the use of language, colour and image. Arlt argues that understanding begins with language and to ignore the fact that only one-third of all Internet users have English as a first language is to overlook the welcome which could be extended to non-English-speaking tourists. He also notes that colours and symbols have different meanings in different cultures, asserting that a carefully considered image may have a more positive impact on image formation than literal text translations. While he concedes that meeting customer needs and wants can be difficult when customers are from different cultural backgrounds, he maintains that establishing communication channels with them through the Internet can bring business and destination image benefits.

Manyara and Jones suggest that the development of new culturally based products unique to Kenya can be used to make the destination distinctive and to ensure destination competitiveness, and a similar approach to product development is recommended for Libya by Jwaili *et al*. Oliver and Jenkins (Chapter 2) assert that quality products have the potential to contribute to place distinctiveness in terms of their specific place-related characteristics, while Williams and MacLeod note the emergence of new ways of differentiating tourism products and services in an increasingly competitive rural tourism marketplace, such as the utilization of local identity. Their peripheral study region findings indicate that local identity is used to add value to the tourism product and is a function of the area's peripherality. However, unique cultural tourism experiences generally demand skills and knowledge from local employees – if employers cannot recruit from within a destination, they are forced to source non-local and transient labour. This can seriously hamper the distinctiveness of a tourism destination, the quality of the tourism experience and ultimately destination competitiveness.

Hall and Rusher note the lack of incentives for small tourism firms to join formal tourism networks, especially when many undertake independent rather than collective marketing activities. Similarly, Smith reported the difficulties of getting tourism SMEs to engage with the WTBM, even though their business might have benefited from the process. Getz *et al*. assert that it is only a small minority of tourism SMEs that will actively pursue innovation and alliances to promote the destination – those who are 'exceptional', whose key business objectives include profit and expansion and who appreciate the contribution their business makes to the development of destination competitiveness. Hall and Rusher also argue that the ease of developing an Internet presence for tourism SMEs may work against collaborative developments. However, Arlt emphasizes the importance of the Internet in destination image formation, especially for emerging tourist markets. He asserts that consideration of cross-cultural issues, such as language, colour and the significance of images in developing visitor perceptions of destinations, should not be underestimated by tourism SMEs. Hence, it is important for the different elements of the tourism product in the destination to work together to attract and meet the needs of 'new' tourist markets. Murphy also stresses the importance of acknowledging the characteristics of tourism SMEs when destination websites are being developed. Furthermore, she notes the need for SMEs to operate and communicate with their customers in the digital economy.

While tourism SMEs generally lack the resources to invest in market research, their small size provides the flexibility required to respond to niche markets, which may also help them develop a capabilities-based advantage. The approach suggested by Chan and Wong challenges the perception of SMEs as an 'informal' tourism sector, by proposing that SMEs can exploit niche markets by gathering market intelligence, developing marketing strategies to attract these niche markets and collaborating with other similar businesses to service these niche markets. This approach should provide SMEs with the incentive to join more formal tourism networks – reputed to be lacking by Hall and Rusher – as well as placing them in a better market position and ultimately enhancing destination competitiveness and visitor experiences. In addition, Oliver and Jenkins assert that it is cooperation, rather than competition, between stakeholders that facilitates the attainment of wider development goals. Jwaili *et al.* identified an awareness of this approach among Libyan tourism SMEs, who want a tourism council to be established to collectively represent the private sector, lobby government and facilitate interaction with other sectors.

22.3.3 Behaviour

The nature of the tourism product often results in a lack of consistency among tourism SMEs with regard to product, service and quality management processes. SMEs have typically lagged behind larger tourism businesses, particularly in their adoption of ICT and the integration of business websites into business strategies. Murphy asserts that hospitality SMEs experience distinct drivers in relation to technology, including the destination management system, market pull by Internet customers, peripherality and lifestyle characteristics of hospitality SME operators. Furthermore, ICT is increasingly a major prerequisite in forming strategic alliances, developing innovative distribution, communicating and meeting customer needs – particularly as consumer confidence in Internet transactions has increased. Nevertheless, Murphy questions whether SMEs are too small to benefit from technology, as some SME hotels have few rooms and cannot guarantee the release of inventories to web-based retailers, thus affecting the supply chain, which has serious implications for destinations that are dominated by small, micro- and lifestyle businesses, as it suggests that the needs of tourists will not necessarily be matched by supply. In addition, it reduces the potential to create a 'joined-up' destination with a coherent marketing image. Obviously this will have a detrimental effect on the visitor experience and development of destination competitiveness.

Getz *et al.* cite numerous examples of family businesses in Australia, Canada and New Zealand that stress the quality of their business, product and service and yet rarely had a specific focus on customer service – personal service was simply a unique selling point of the family business. Fundamentally, Getz *et al.* state that, while there are inherent factors that hamper quality in family businesses and impede destination competitiveness and quality, there are also inherent factors that can generate excellent visitor experiences and successful family businesses – which, coupled with owner-managers who pursue profit and growth, can positively contribute to destination development and competitiveness. Furthermore, Getz *et al.* note that, where there is unanimity, the family can effectively deliver quality experiences; however, where decision making is impaired by family dynamics, product and service quality might suffer.

While many tourism SMEs, particularly family businesses, may succeed in establishing a high-quality product and excellent visitor experience, there are concerns over whether this can be sustained within a destination, especially when operators wish to sever their ties with the business. Getz *et al.* report that children in family businesses often reject taking over the family business because of the perception of hard work for little profit. They also identify a low rate of inheritance and succession planning by tourism SME operators, with few businesses surviving the founders – interestingly, large organizations are often heavily criticized for failing to undertake adequate succession planning in the form of HR planning. In a similar vein to Getz *et al.*, Di Domenico states that the lifestyle entrepreneurs in her study had not considered how the business might be continued when they reached the end of their business life, as the business was regarded as a home as well as a business. A lack of inheritance and succession planning among tourism SMEs means that, while a destination may have excellent tourism SME products at any one time, when the SME operators reach the end of their business life cycle, the products and ultimately destination competitiveness will suffer. Conversely, tourism SMEs which are passed to the next generation have, to a certain degree, demonstrated their business success in terms of financial sustainability; therefore, as noted by Getz *et al.*, succession within the family should be advantageous for the destination. Correspondingly, Hall and Rusher assert that the retention of individuals for lifestyle reasons may have additional benefits for tourism destinations which far exceed the provision of tourism services.

Many small, micro- and lifestyle businesses struggle to maintain economic viability; hence quality may not be a primary concern. Therefore, these businesses need continuous and progressive support from economic development agencies to develop robust business management practices, enhance quality and add value to their product. The need for continuous and progressive support is underpinned by Augustyn and Pheby's assertion that the sustained growth of tourism SMEs depends on the firm's ability to build incremental growth staircases founded on the development of appropriate capabilities that are specific to the circumstances of individual tourism SMEs at any one time. The incremental process of building capability platforms enabled the tourism SMEs studied to acquire new skills and extend their portfolio of capabilities, which should allow them to grow and gain a capabilities-based competitive advantage. Furthermore, the matrix model proposed by Murphy allows for expansion and provides an incremental approach to measuring, mapping and predicting diffusion –

presenting an opportunity for SMEs to identify their current operational and strategic position.

Chan and Wong discuss the benefits of exploiting the potentially lucrative market of planned impulse travellers (PITs) and how this might affect the marketing strategies of SME hotels. Key factors found to be influential in the purchasing decisions of PITs include convenient hotel location, good hotel service and good hotel reputation, which illustrate the need for SME hotel operators to ensure accessibility and service quality and to promote positive product images. However, they acknowledge that SMEs may be unable to invest resources in ensuring these influential factors in order to exploit the PITs market. Therefore, Chan and Wong advocate small hotel alliances for market promotion and transportation purposes, as well as public-sector partnerships. Although this may result in a loss of complete independence, Chan and Wong suggest that small hotels will secure a better market position to compete with larger hotel chains for PITs. To exploit this market, which is often neglected by the larger hotels, they also recommend developing personal networks and utilizing more personal selling techniques.

With reference to the Danish labour market, Hjalager demonstrates that value added in the tourism sector does not necessarily coincide with mainstream HRM, i.e. that well-managed tourism businesses with low employee turnover and high qualification attainments do not necessarily perform better. The findings show that the more proactive firms are better able to retain staff than those with low value added per employee and that the use of numerical flexibility to compensate for performance deficits is more prevalent in tourism than in other sectors. Her results also challenge the assumption that employee qualification attainment levels are positively associated with economic performance. Hjalager asserts that those enterprises that create the most added value do not have a high proportion of staff with formal qualifications, and the competitive strength of these enterprises is their ability to efficiently organize and manage the work of large numbers of unskilled employees. Nevertheless, employers often place importance on qualifications, as Pizam and Tesone report that employers in Central Florida and Mexico experienced difficulties in recruiting qualified skilled/semi-skilled employees. Hjalager also notes that retention rates and salary levels were significantly higher in larger tourism enterprises and that careers are best pursued in larger organizations, with a clear hierarchy. In a similar vein, Moore states that larger hospitality organizations are more likely to have formalized training programmes, indicating a more progressive and proactive approach to training than small independent hospitality organizations. However, in contrast to Hjalager, Moore found that labour turnover in small organizations was not as significant as in large organizations, even though there was little evidence of formal induction, training or career progression. Nevertheless, in many destinations it is the smaller organizations that form the basis of the tourism sector: hence the significant impact of a lack of training on the tourism product, visitor experience and destination competitiveness.

Whereas Lashley exposes a fatalistic acceptance of high labour turnover among employers, Hjalager reports that, because the transaction costs associated with high turnover are tolerable, enterprises are organizing work to compensate for these costs. Furthermore, she suggests that the labour market system in Denmark helps to reduce transaction costs, which perpetuates labour turn-over. Additionally, Lashley reports that employers' perceptions of skill gaps are often reduced by job redesign and the use of technology to reduce skills needs. Despite the fact that this approach may solve immediate staffing and skills issues, in the long term the tourism product, visitor experience and destination will suffer. While recognizing that the skill levels of employees and a commitment to training do not guarantee business success, they do bring business benefits and influence competitiveness. Lashley highlights how skill shortages and gaps create barriers to tourism development within destinations. Additionally, he suggests that there are fundamental deficits in management skills and training, thus emphasizing the role of skills development for managers in the development of destination competitiveness. Interestingly, Hall and Rusher found that 'informal' B&B operations in New Zealand are not necessarily less well managed or customer-oriented than formal tourism operations, which implies that B&Bs in New Zealand are either well managed or that formal tourism operations are poorly managed – or both. Pizam and Tesone found that the majority of Mexican tourism SME operators did not have a training department and they also demonstrate that even well-established tourism destinations, such as Central Florida, may have barriers to entry for qualified human resources, which are also evident in tourism destinations that are at an earlier stage of their development, such as Mexico.

22.4 Destination Coherence

Arlt asserts that many European tourist destinations are likely to benefit from the estimated 1 billion 'new' tourists over the next two decades and that the Internet is a cost-effective and efficient way of communicating with them in terms of creating destination images. However, if destinations are to take advantage of these new tourist markets, DMOs and SMEs need to pay attention to cross-cultural marketing issues, particularly with respect to the Internet as a promotional tool. Arlt emphasizes the role of the Internet as primarily a communication tool, rather than an online booking facility, and that actively communicating with visitors enables their special requirements to be considered, which will ultimately place the destination in a positive light from a visitor perspective. Arlt also stresses the importance of interactivity with visitors, such as encouraging them to share their comments and experiences. He goes as far as to suggest that a destination not providing web pages for international visitors may be considered 'unwelcoming'. Jwaili et al.'s Libyan SMEs also emphasized the significance of the Internet in product marketing.

Some tourism SMEs find it difficult to define service quality and understand the link between service quality and destination competitiveness, hence failing to recognize the role they play in the bigger picture of destination development. This situation needs to be rectified and DMOs need to secure the participation and collaboration of tourism SME operators. Murphy also suggests that tourist boards and governments should consult and acknowledge the characteristics of

SMEs when developing destination management systems, encouraging a strategy of 'co-opetition'. While Behringer and Mester highlight the role of the HNTO in the development of the HTQA and the benefits of such an award for tourism SMEs and Hungary as a tourism destination, they also remark on the need to address negative feelings towards HTQA, such as the possibility of the award being devalued by corrupt practices. They believe that, if the HNTO addresses such issues, the award will be widely adopted and coveted by tourism providers as a tool to maintain market position and competitiveness.

The approaches described by James and Wanhill demonstrate the importance of streamlining training and funding initiatives for tourism SMEs, establishing partnerships and developing a central informed source on tourism education, training and funding. As documented by Wanhill, the private tourism sector does not have control over all the elements that make a destination attractive. This, together with the potential impacts upon the host population, demands a high level of government involvement and appropriate public administration frameworks. Indeed, Wanhill argues that, without small business advice networks, it would be difficult to meet strategic objectives laid down by the EU. However, governments or public-sector tourism agencies must be seen to be actively involved in tourism development; for example, Jwaili *et al.*'s Libyan SMEs believe that their government is responsible for the non-implementation of the National Tourism Development Plan. Wanhill asserts that a tourism development organization can only have true operational involvement if it receives funding to engage in private-sector projects and implement training initiatives; otherwise, it will only assume a strategic coordinating role.

While Oliver and Jenkins comment on the benefits of sustainability, they also note that integrated tourism is a less passive concept than sustainability and is concerned with motivating local development through the creation of new partnerships and networks. Furthermore, they note that tourism needs to be both embedded and disembedded for future sustainability and viability. If tourism is too embedded in a destination, it can limit the market appeal of the product, such as Kenya's reliance on the 'big five'. Williams and MacLeod also argue that embedded resources can add value to the tourism product and that distinctive images can be created visually which are indicative of peripherality but appeal to intrinsic tourist motivations. DMOs and those involved in public-sector interventions also need to consider and manage the effects of seasonality in destinations dominated by tourism SMEs, as highlighted by Wanhill, Smith and Oliver and Jenkins. Where tourism is highly seasonal, activities are concentrated in the high season, creating negative environmental and cultural impacts; meanwhile, during the low season in such destinations, tourism SMEs struggle to maintain their economic viability. As such, many tourism SME operators may not consider their business to be permanent – affecting investment in the business, quality, training and management development, as well as affecting messages about first-choice careers, rather than seasonal jobs. Haven-Tang and Botterill assert that seasonality, together with a geographically dispersed small-scale tourism sector, can obscure career opportunities and restrict career progression.

In destinations where the national tourism organization does not intervene in the development of destination quality strategies, quality standards will remain

disparate, affecting visitor experiences. Oliver and Jenkins assert that quality products have the potential to contribute to place distinctiveness and that bottom-up
approaches are often the result of strong local participation, which may in turn
increase awareness of local cultural identity – ultimately, this is the approach suggested for Kenya by Manyara and Jones – but which requires appropriate funding
and facilitation. Oliver and Jenkins also refer to how tourism provider and producer structures emerge in order to enhance local products and develop strategies
for their management and delivery. They emphasize the implementation of
endogenous (bottom-up) strategies that focus on specific aspects of a destination
and which usually signify a strong local participation, asserting that this type of
approach is fundamental to ensuring integrated tourism, but that other external
organizations may also be critical in terms of acquiring funding or training that
contributes to tourism development, such as coordinating local producers and
tourism service providers. Moreover, Oliver and Jenkins found that a successful
integrated tourism trajectory moves towards dedicated and specialized production, characterized by niche markets, local embeddedness, personal service, local
technology and knowledge, uniqueness and quality. To achieve a coherent destination, clarity and cooperation are essential as without these there is a potential for
conflict, as evidenced in Kenya by Manyara and Jones, who report a lack of clarity
regarding how tourism development should be integrated with wider development
strategies.

The implications of a lack of commitment to business growth by lifestyle
entrepreneurs are greater than simply a lack of individual business growth. Peak
demand determines capacity; therefore, reducing the range of services and number of facilities means that destinations may not adequately meet the needs of
tourists, enhancing concerns raised by Hall and Rusher about 'informal' tourism
sectors. Di Domenico asserts that those involved with destination development
must consider and understand the motivations of lifestyle businesses, as not all
wish to expand their businesses and lifestyle needs may be given priority over
business needs. Likewise, Wanhill states that lifestyle goals are a 'fact of life' in
SMEs and investment support must accommodate them within commercial
objectives. Getz *et al.* also note that understanding the human and family elements in SMEs is essential if quality is to be improved, but that there are profit-
and growth-oriented tourism SME operators who can assist in the growth and
positioning of their community as an appealing tourism destination and in the
achievement of economic development and destination competitiveness objectives. However, in order to encourage this, the recommendation of Hall and
Rusher should be considered – specifically, that lifestyle goals need to be
incorporated into models of tourism entrepreneurship.

22.5 Conclusions

Based on the preceding chapters, it would seem that the development of
coherence in destinations dominated by SMEs is achievable providing stakeholders involved in destination development learn from successful case studies.

Many of the chapters advocate the benefits of SMEs to the destination, e.g. exploitation of niche markets, lower staff turnover and the potential for collaboration. Furthermore, some claim that particular types of tourism, notably rural tourism, go beyond complementing traditional activities and can catalyse a range of new entrepreneurial activities, partnerships and networks. Indeed, there are examples of successful integrated tourism in some European rural destinations, which illustrate that cooperation between stakeholders enables wider development goals to be achieved. However, if cooperation and collaboration between the public and private sectors are to be successfully pursued, partners must share a consensus on their key goals and must have clear roles, enabling them to play to their strengths and exploit their differences. Partnerships must derive mutual benefits for all participants and each member of the partnership must appreciate the organizational constraints of other partners, ensuring that those involved in the partnership do not work outside their comfort zone. Ultimately, there must be transparency, trust and a clear agenda for action.

Public-sector interventions need to ensure the professionalism of the industry within the context of the tourism destination, highlighting how training and development could enhance the tourism SME product by building on the current skill levels of staff. However, diversity and fragmentation in the sector mean that structured orthodox approaches to business management, training and enhancing professionalism are often difficult for SMEs to adopt. Therefore, intervention strategies need to reflect the local industry, labour market and external factors within each destination. Public-sector interventions focusing on management development are also of strategic importance. Many tourism SME operators lack basic management skills and expertise; hence their business, through poor recruitment and retention, may not fulfil its potential or achieve a capabilities-based competitive advantage through incremental growth. Appreciating the influence of the macro-environment is also important. For example, the determination of salary levels is related to wider employment policies and business strategies, and the use of the Internet as a promotional tool must consider cross-cultural marketing issues. Public–private-sector collaborations also need to focus on interventions to deliver accurate and effective career messages that appreciate the complexity of the career decision making process, to ensure that the benefits of tourism employment are emphasized to those providing career education and guidance, as well as potential employees.

One of the main obstacles for public-sector interventions is establishing cohesion within the industry, particularly in destinations dominated by SMEs. Indeed, a lack of cohesion is detrimental to the tourism industry, as it often lacks a unified body to represent the broader interests of the industry, which can impede recognition, funding, marketing, quality and training initiatives; hence it is important to establish national industry bodies. Fundamentally, DMOs need to develop an enhanced understanding of the heterogeneity among tourism SMEs and the heterodoxy (not unorthodoxy) in comparison with 'big business', particularly the inappropriateness of many orthodox business management strategies which are designed for big business. Parallel to this is an acceptance that, while industry commitment and collaboration in relation to the development of destination competitiveness is to be encouraged, in reality only a minority of tourism SMEs will actively participate – those whose business objectives are aligned to the development objectives of the destination.

Index

cabi-publishing.org/bookshop

Browse Read and Buy

ANIMAL & VETERINARY SCIENCES
BIODIVERSITY CROP PROTECTION
HUMAN HEALTH NATURAL RESOURCES
ENVIRONMENT PLANT SCIENCES
SOCIAL SCIENCES

CABI *Publishing*
A division of CAB International

Online BOOK SHOP

- Search
- Reading Room
- Bargains
- New Titles
- Forthcoming

Order & Pay Online!

MasterCard

VISA

AMERICAN EXPRESS

Crop Pollination by Bees
Keith S. Delaplane and Daniel F. Mayer
CABI Publishing

A DICTIONARY OF Entomology
G Gordh and D H Headrick

Principles of CATTLE PRODUCTION
C.J.C. Phillips

Seeds
THE ECOLOGY OF REGENERATION IN PLANT COMMUNITIES
2nd EDITION
Edited by Michael Fenner

FULL DESCRIPTION   BUY THIS BOOK   BOOK OF THE MONTH

Tel: +44 (0)1491 832111 Fax: +44 (0)1491 829292